The Fantasy Football Guide 1995

The Fantasy Football Guide 1995

JODY KORCH

CONTEMPORARY
BOOKS

CHICAGO

Published by Contemporary Books, Inc.
Two Prudential Plaza, Chicago, Illinois 60601-6790
Manufactured in the United States of America
International Standard Book Number: 0-8092-3425-4
10   9   8   7   6   5   4   3   2   1

CONTENTS

ACKNOWLEDGMENTS

Me? Write a book? I definitely had a few doubts when the whole idea first crossed my mind. This is, after all, something I never, ever thought I would do.

Newspaper writers grow accustomed to the never-ending short-term projects ... write a couple of quick stories for today's paper, then start all over again tomorrow. The closest I ever came to a long-term project was a few three-part series. Nothing like this.

Not to worry, though. My brother, Rick, the author of *The Fantasy Football Guide* the past four years, has a huge amount of confidence in me. For that, I owe him a lifetime of gratitude.

By the way, Rick now works for the Jacksonville Jaguars, so he can't write this book any longer. But he does say that Steve Beuerlein and Desmond Howard and James Stewart (and so on) are all going to be great fantasy football players this year. You see, that's why he can't write this book any longer: He can't be objective anymore. He just wanted to write two words in this year's book, so we'll let him ... "Go Jaguars!"

Once Rick turned this book over to me and I got started, there was no looking back. Full speed ahead. Yes, I *can* do this, and yes, this *is* fun.

Roger Harring, the head football coach at the University of Wisconsin-La Crosse, said it best: If you like your job, you'll never have to work another day in your life.

To the Porterfield School fifth-grade class, who gave me confidence back when I was first getting started and still had some doubts: Thanks, I needed that.

To Wendy, who patiently stood by while I spent every conceivable free minute on the book: Thanks for giving me an education on the world of Macintosh computers.

Thanks to Craig Bolt at Contemporary Books, who also showed confidence in me during the critical early stages. And to Peter Grennen, who again did a great job of copy editing.

Rick also said we have to thank a few other people who have helped with this book over the years: Gene Brissie, who came up with the idea five years ago; Angela Miller, Rick's agent and now mine, too; and Erik

Anderson, Rick's stepson, who input many of the statistics.

But the biggest thanks of all goes to you, the readers. Without you, this book would have been impossible. Please, send for my free Draft Day Update so that you're completely prepared for your draft.

Also, I encourage you to send me suggestions, comments, great thoughts, etc., to help with next year's book. Now, go out and win your league.

INTRODUCTION

It was a Monday night a couple of years ago, and I should have been sound asleep. After all, I start work at 5:45 a.m., and in the newspaper business you cannot afford to slack off for a minute, even first thing in the morning. But the guy I was playing against in fantasy football had one final chance to overcome my seemingly insurmountable 14-point lead.

His starting quarterback that week was Mark Rypien.

No problem, I thought. Rypien will never throw five touchdown passes in this game. I'm home free. Our fantasy football league, which used the Basic Scoring System, made a change before that season to reduce the score on a touchdown pass from six points to three for the quarterback.

But something really strange and improbable happened that night.

Rypien *ran* for two touchdowns and threw for a couple more — and I lost! That was one scenario which hadn't even crossed my mind. Rypien probably hadn't rushed for two touchdowns in a game in his entire life ... at least until I played the guy who started him in a fantasy football game. I nearly smashed my bed and a pillow apart in anger. It just wasn't fair.

But fantasy football isn't fair; it's pure insanity. Why else would you be passionately interested in a meaningless late-season game between the Rams and the Oilers? But, since you're starting Jerome Bettis that week and your opponent is playing Haywood Jeffires, the game suddenly is immensely important.

What else could add a sideshow to a game involving your favorite team? You obviously want your team to win, but its opponent for that week has a wide receiver in your starting fantasy lineup. So you hope your favorite NFL team builds a big lead but still allows your fantasy player to score a touchdown or two. It's not much fun if you're a big 49ers fan and your fantasy opponent has Steve Young on his team. You'll yell, "Go, go. Drive the ball down the field. But let William Floyd run for the touchdown. Don't throw a touchdown pass, and whatever you do, Young, *don't* run it in." Because that would be six points against your fantasy team.

An onlooker who knew nothing about fantasy football might think you're crazy as a loon for your behavior.

"Fantasy insanity" is the best way to explain it.

Everybody who plays this crazy game has stories to tell about improbabilities, strange quirks and other bizarre happenings. When you watch a pass sailing into an end zone, you might be holding your breath, praying that Irving Fryar — the guy in your starting lineup — catches it instead of Eric Green — the starting tight end for your opponent.

This book attempts to sort out the insanity: Everything you'd ever want to know about the NFL's points makers. Their statistics from the past five years, so you can judge how they have played over the long run. An explanation of the many variations on how to play. The player rankings, so you have a guide to go by on Draft Day. The rookie report, so you can pick a player or two to take a chance on in the later rounds. An offseason update — especially important because even diehard fans need a game program to follow their team these days. The incredible scramble for free agents results in a few NFL roster changes every day.

For me, work is pure panic five days a week for the first six hours. Then the newspaper rolls off the press, and I can catch my breath and wind down. And for more than four months a year, I then start thinking about which NFL players I want to start that week.

Be sure to send in for my free Draft Day Update, which will be mailed to you just before the start of the NFL season (see the last page of this book). Whereas other books charge for this type of offer, it's free from us.

Good luck this year.

Jody Korch
May 17, 1995

Chapter 1
HOW TO PLAY

Are you ready for some football? How about some fantasy football? It's your chance to act as your own coach, general manager and owner.

First, you have to decide who will be in your league and how you will run it. One of the best aspects of fantasy football is that you can make the rules any way you want them. There are thousands of fantasy leagues around the country and hundreds of variations on the scoring methods alone.

This book will tell you how to play fantasy football and detail many of the other variations, such as scoring, player transactions and playoffs. But this book is flexible. It's your league, so set it up the way you want to.

You will want anywhere from four to 16 people to form a fantasy football league, with each player getting his own franchise. Each player will stock his team with players, play games, and hopefully win the championship.

First, you will have to decide on a commissioner and a deputy commissioner (who will decide on any possible disputes that may involve the commissioner, if he has a team in the league).

Your league may want to set a franchise fee, just as the NFL does when it expands. All of the money goes into a pot, which will include money that can be charged for player transactions. At the end of the season, the money is awarded to the top teams.

You will decide on a length for your league's season and then make up a schedule so the teams can play head-to-head during the season.

Team owners will gather before the start of the NFL season for the annual fantasy draft. There, they will select players from actual NFL rosters in the following positions: quarterbacks, running backs, wide receivers, tight ends and kickers.

In other variations, you may want to choose a team defense, a coach, sackers, interceptors or other variations for your league (but remember, the more complicated your scoring method, the more time-consuming it will be to tabulate scoring). Every team will have the same roster size, usually two quarterbacks, four running backs, four wide receivers, two tight ends and two kickers.

Teams will be allowed to pick up, drop and trade players after the draft, although your league will have to set rules beforehand so that nobody gains an unfair advantage.

Each team will submit a weekly lineup to the commissioner before a set deadline. The lineup usually consists of one quarterback, two running backs, two wide receivers, one tight end and one kicker, although there are many variations.

Teams will meet in head-to-head competition and score points according to a predetermined scoring method. Results and standings will be posted (or mailed to all teams) by the commissioner.

The season ends with playoffs and the championship game.

So there you have it — the basics of fantasy football. Now it's time to get a little more complicated and go a little deeper into how to play fantasy football.

JOINING A LEAGUE

There are a lot of established leagues that you can join for a fee that award large prizes. *USA Today* has a large league in which, for $99, people can draft, play and trade players by calling a toll-free 800 number. Other leagues are held by *The Sporting News*, Sportsmark, The Sportsbuff Network and many metropolitan newspapers. Check *Pro Football Weekly*, *USA Today*, *The Sporting News*, *Fantasy Football* magazine or any of the many other pro football preview magazines for advertisements of fantasy football leagues.

These are called "play-by-mail" leagues. They usually cost between $39 and $100 per year for each team, and they often have complex scoring methods that they manage with the help of computers, so you don't have to tabulate your team's scoring. The level of competition is also noticeably higher than that in most friendly leagues.

Most play-by-mail leagues conduct their fantasy football drafts through the mail or by entering numbers that correspond to players on a touch-tone telephone. Team owners rank the players in the order they want to draft them. Each service has its own method of making sure each team gets the players it values most.

Some leagues offer phone drafts, in which every team owner gets on a conference phone call with the other members. But this method is more expensive, because drafts usually take two hours or more.

Most of these leagues stipulate that you must have your starting lineup postmarked or entered via touch-tone telephone by a certain date.

Since it might be difficult to get the players you want in the preseason draft, or if a player you drafted gets injured, benched or is playing poorly, you will want to play the free-agent wire often. However, it usually costs several dollars per roster move. You might even receive a few phone calls from other team owners in the league suggesting possible trades.

The best way to decide if you want to join one of these leagues is to write for information, read it and then talk on the telephone to the people who run the games to see if you can trust them.

These leagues usually mail out scores, standings, up-to-date statistics, trade updates, lists of available free agents and injury reports. Many of them also offer stat services to handle your league's weekly scoring and eliminate the hassle that many league commissioners go through. Again, that costs money.

Compared to friendly leagues, weekly and year-end prizes (such as a car or $10,000) are the main reason for fantasy football players to join these leagues. Obviously, they can be quite profitable to the winners (who also get to brag that they are a "national champion").

STARTING A LEAGUE

Number of Teams

The best way to get involved in fantasy football is to start your own league with a group of your friends. The number of players in your league is open, but it should range from four to 16. Eight is the most common number of teams.

Remember, there are only 30 starting quarterbacks in the NFL. Since every fantasy team has two quarterbacks on its roster, if your league has more than 14 teams, some teams will have a real backup quarterback as their backup quarterback (and the same for kickers).

You will also want to have an even number of teams, because it makes scheduling easier with everybody playing head-to-head every weekend, eliminating the need for byes in your league's schedule.

The most important thing to remember in starting a league is to decide the rules first. You don't want to get into the middle of the season and have teams disputing the rules. Obviously, the rules can get complicated, so you might want to decide on the many options in this book before a situation arises in which it's too late to choose one.

Make your league's rules definitive. If there are any gray areas, there will be trouble. The best rules are the simplest ones, but you have to cover all the possible areas that can fall open to debate.

But be willing to change your rules from year to year, such as adding a new scoring variation. Too many leagues resist change over a period of years — the old "why change it if it works?" line. But change for the better should always be welcome and makes each year a little bit more fun. Remember, the NFL made quite a few rules changes in 1994, such as adding a two-point conversion. Your league should consider changing some of its rules every year, too. Rules variations are discussed near the end of this chapter.

Commissioner and His Duties

The commissioner is the Paul Tagliabue of your league. He manages the league, although he does not set the rules. Every team owner should have equal say in the rules.

The commissioner should have the time and organizational skills to do the job. The duties of the league commissioner are to coordinate Draft Day, record rosters, keep track of roster changes, handle fees paid by teams (entry fees, player transaction fees), record the starting lineups, tabulate the scoring, distribute weekly results to the team owners and serve as the league treasurer.

In some leagues, playing rosters are distributed so that every team owner knows what players every team has activated for that game. Thus, each weekend you can keep track not only of how your players are doing but also of how your opponents' players are doing.

After compiling the weekly scores, the commissioner should revise the weekly standings, add up the total points (offensive and defensive) for every team, list all player transactions made the previous week and distribute them to every owner.

Your league should select a responsible person, perhaps somebody who does not have a team in the league. If the commissioner also has a team in the league, you should have a deputy commissioner to help settle disputes that involve the commissioner.

The fantasy league commissioner should be paid at least enough to cover league expenses. If he has a team in your league, the other owners might want to waive his franchise entry fee to compensate him for his services. Either one is a good method.

Size of Rosters

Most rosters consist of approximately 14 players: two quarterbacks, four running backs, four wide receivers, two tight ends and two placekickers.

One of the most common variations is for a roster to include one defensive team.

There are a lot of other variations, however, which are open to a league's preference. They are listed elsewhere in this chapter. Other books tell you to draft a number of players ranging anywhere from 12 to 26. But pick the number you feel is right. It's your league, and you get to set the rules.

In most leagues, half of the players on a roster "play" during any particular week. That is, in the aforementioned 14-player roster, the active or "starting" lineup consists of one quarterback, two running backs, two wide receivers, one tight end and one kicker.

Putting Together a Roster

Your responsibilities as a fantasy team owner are much like those of the general manager and head coach of an NFL team. The general manager assembles the team, and the coach is the on-field leader. But first you have to put your coaching duties aside while the general manager's aspect comes to life.

There are two ways to form your roster: through a draft right before the beginning of the season and, during the season, through a supplemental draft and/or by picking up free agents (and dropping one of your players to keep your roster the same size).

Franchise Entry Fee

Just like in the NFL, most leagues have a franchise entry fee (which ranges from $10 to $1,000). The fees are collected, held and paid out at the end of the season to the best teams in the league. If a franchise entry fee is charged, leagues should also charge a fee for all roster transactions made during the course of the season. These entry fees usually cost more than other types of sports pools, but the entire fantasy football season lasts longer, too.

In most states, however, fee-based fantasy sports leagues that pay prize money are illegal. In Texas, players in a fantasy football league were actually charged with felony gambling. And in 1991, the state of Florida (which, by the way, operates the nation's largest lottery) ruled against fantasy sports leagues, saying they involve a form of gambling. Florida attorney general Bob Butterworth, in a nonbinding opinion requested by the state attorney, said fantasy leagues involve more chance than skill, violating state statute. Nothing has happened in other states in the last few years.

The NFL frowns upon fantasy football because of its so-called "association" with gambling, but the league is probably a bit paranoid. In fact, NFL Properties has licensed a board game called "Fantasy Football," which makes the NFL somewhat hypocritical. Most fantasy players play for fun, not for money. It has been said many times that fantasy football players are the only people in the world who would spend $100 (for newsletters, books, etc.) to make $10.

So it is not necessary to charge an entry fee if team owners want to play just for fun. That's the idea.

Scheduling

Fantasy football seasons — the regular season and playoffs — begin at the start of the NFL's regular season and end on the final week of the regular season. This year, the NFL season kicks off the week of September 3–4.

Some leagues also have a special fantasy playoff league that runs through the Super Bowl. This is for those fantasy leaguers who can't get enough.

Since there are 17 weeks in the NFL season (16 games and one open date per team), you will want to shorten your regular season to 14 or 15 weeks, and then use the remaining two or three weeks for the playoffs, provided that your league intends to have playoffs.

The schedule is determined by the same order of your player draft. Team 1 plays Team 2, Team 3 plays Team 4, and so on. The order changes every week until each team has played the others once, and then the schedule is repeated.

In leagues with 12 or more teams, you may wish to split the teams into divisions of equal size, with teams playing those in their own division twice and the teams in the other division once. Or, if your league has 16 teams, you may wish to split into four four-team divisions. The disadvantage of splitting into divisions is that one division might have most of the good teams, which could result in teams with better records than those in the other division missing the playoffs.

Here is a typical schedule for a 10-team league in which each team plays every other twice:

Team #	1	2	3	4	5	6	7	8	9	10
Week #										
1	2	1	4	3	10	7	6	9	8	5
2	4	5	8	1	2	9	10	3	6	7
3	6	3	2	5	4	1	8	7	10	9
4	9	10	6	7	8	3	4	5	1	2
5	2	1	5	9	3	7	6	10	4	8
6	5	7	4	3	1	10	2	9	8	6
7	10	6	7	8	9	2	3	4	5	1
8	4	3	2	1	10	9	8	7	6	5
9	3	5	1	9	2	8	10	6	4	7
10	5	4	8	2	1	10	9	3	7	6
11	8	9	10	6	7	4	5	1	2	3
12	7	8	9	10	6	5	1	2	3	4
13	3	7	1	5	4	8	2	6	10	9
14	6	4	5	2	3	1	9	10	7	8
15	10	6	7	8	9	2	3	4	5	1
16	Playoffs									
17	Championship Game									

For schedules of leagues of different sizes, see the Appendix.

Not every league will last the entire season. For example, an eight-team league that plays 14 weeks (with each team playing each other twice) and then has two weeks of playoffs will end with one week remaining in the NFL's regular season. If your league is set up that way, I suggest you start your league the first week of the NFL season and end it before the final week of regular-season play. It's likely that not every NFL team will have every player signed by the season opener (because of holdouts), but too many playoff-bound teams rest their top players in the final week of the regular season (do you remember what the 49ers did on the final Monday night game of the 1994 season?) so they don't get injured before the playoffs start. Even the weaker teams sometimes start rookie quarterbacks in the last game to see what they can do.

Thus, there are always a lot of fantasy players in the final week or two who either had to play backups rather than their starters or who got no points from their starters because they didn't play at all.

In Week 1, all games count. In Week 17, you could be in your league championship but your key players might be sitting out in order to rest up for the real playoffs. Be careful.

The NFL will again use a schedule of 16 games in 17 weeks (one open date) for every team (in 1993, every team had two byes in 18 weeks). In an eight-team league with each team playing each other twice and two weeks of playoffs, you may wish to fill the remaining week by reverting back to the schedule for Week 1 before starting the playoffs. That would eliminate the round-robin competition, but it would lengthen the season to run the same as the NFL regular season. This method may, however, give unfair advantages to some teams who might play weaker teams for the added week or two. That's why luck is such a big part of fantasy football.

Playoffs

In some leagues, the traditional head-to-head style of play, with opposing teams facing off week-to-week, determines the league champion by the best won-lost record. Or, in the traditional format for fantasy baseball, cumulative season statistics (most points scored) are used to determine the winner. But fantasy leagues can — and should — use a playoff system, with the four best teams advancing to the playoffs in a single-elimination format. The team with the best record plays the fourth-best team, and the second- and third-best teams play each other. The two winners then face off in the fantasy championship. (The two losers can play to determine third place.)

Tiebreaker — If two or more teams are tied with the same record at the end of the regular season, use a tiebreaker to determine which team goes to the playoffs. There are several methods you could choose (but the method should be decided upon before the start of the season).

Option 1 — Head-to-head competition. If both teams are tied in head-to-head competition (usually one victory each), the next tiebreaker is point differential in head-to-head competition. This system is closest to the one the NFL uses. If teams are still tied, go to Option 2.

Option 2 — Most points scored during the regular season. This system better reflects how a team fared during the entire regular season and lessens the possibility that a team that got lucky in head-to-head games will advance.

Payoffs

Your league should decide before the start of the season how it will split the money paid for the franchise entry fee.

Payment is usually made to the league champion and the runner-up. Your league may wish to split some of the money among the third- and fourth-place teams that also made the playoffs. A typical breakdown might be 50 percent of the pot to the league champion, 25 percent to the second-place finisher, 15 percent to the third-place team and 10 percent to the fourth-place owner. Some leagues also give a "booby prize" to the worst team.

It's best to spread the money around as much as possible. Players usually are not in it for the money so much as to have fun and enjoy camaraderie with other football fans. More payouts keep interest going through the entire season — even for the last-place team.

A payoff to the team that scored the most points during the regular season is also wise, as that is most often the best team in the league regardless of the luck factor that goes into any one game.

Some leagues also hold back a portion of the entry fees to throw a year-end party to formally recognize the league champion and distribute the money. That's easy if your league is a close-knit group of players.

SCORING

Nowhere else in fantasy football are there more variations from league to league as there are in the scoring systems. There are as many different possibilities as one can think of.

Three systems are most commonly used (each with its own variations). Remember that the more complicated the system, the harder it is to determine scores each week.

You can get the official NFL scoring results out of most daily newspapers, but there will occasionally be discrepancies or missing statistics from paper to paper. The best daily sources are *USA Today* and major metropolitan newspapers, and the best weekly source is *Pro Football Weekly* (*The Sporting News* and *Football News* do not list box scores from NFL games).

Some NFL players line up at more than one position, so your league will need to clarify the position at which he will be played. For example, in 1992 the Eagles played Keith Byars at tight end for most of the season, although they continued to list him as a running back on the roster. Select one publication to act as your league's official source, and use its designation for players' positions. *Pro Football Weekly* is the best source for this, because it lists depth charts each week.

Selecting a Scoring System

The best way to decide which scoring system your league should use is to poll the team owners and determine which one is most popular. The basic system is used by most fantasy leagues, but, because luck is such a big factor in it, two other systems have become popular in which performance more than luck determines the league winner.

A. The Basic System

The most widely used scoring method is the basic one — teams receive points only when one of their activated players for that week scores points in an NFL game. When a player scores a touchdown, you get six points. When a kicker converts a field goal it's worth three points, and an extra point is worth one point.

For example, if San Francisco's William Floyd dives over the goal line from the one-yard line, you get six points. Or if Detroit's Barry Sanders runs 80 yards for a touchdown, you also get six points. It's the same way with placekickers — a 20-yard field goal is worth the same as a 55-yarder.

Scoring by Position

Quarterbacks
1. Three points for each touchdown pass thrown.
2. Six points for each touchdown scored rushing.
3. Six points for each touchdown scored receiving.

Running Backs, Wide Receivers and Tight Ends
1. Six points for each touchdown scored rushing.
2. Six points for each touchdown scored receiving.
3. Three points for each touchdown pass thrown.

Kickers
1. Three points for each field goal.
2. One point for each extra point.

Miscellaneous Scores
1. Running backs and wide receivers get six points for a touchdown on a punt or kickoff return.
2. Any player receives six points for recovering a fumble in the end zone for a touchdown.
3. Any player receives two points for an extra point scored running or receiving.

Variations to the Basic Scoring System — One of the biggest faults

HOW TO PLAY

with the basic scoring method in fantasy football is that it rewards those players who pound the ball over from the goal line while ignoring those players who got the ball to the goal line.

For example, in 1991, the Redskins' Gerald Riggs scored 11 touchdowns, most of them from only a yard or two out after teammates Earnest Byner and Ricky Ervins had carried the ball 70 or 80 yards down the field. Byner had two 100-yard games in which he didn't score a touchdown, but Riggs had two games in which he scored two touchdowns although he had fewer than 10 yards rushing. Late in the 1994 season, the Seahawks were letting Chris Warren run the ball up and down the field before giving it to the fullback at the goal line.

My personal favorite was a game a few years ago in which Chiefs running back Barry Word rushed 19 times for 112 yards but didn't score, while his teammate Christian Okoye carried the ball 11 times for only five yards — but he scored two TDs.

That is why so many leagues use variations in their scoring systems. Your league can change the scoring method any way it wants. Here are some of the most popular variations to the basic scoring system.

Passing touchdowns — Most leagues give six points to the receiver (he got the ball in the end zone) and three to the quarterback (after all, he got the ball to the receiver). But some leagues divide the points equally, with three points given to both the quarterback and the receiver (or running back) who scores. The thinking here is that the NFL gives only six points for a touchdown, so the credit should be divided equally between the two players involved. Leagues that give six points for a rushing touchdown and then split the points for a passing touchdown do so for another reason — it's harder to score on the ground. I don't necessarily believe that, however. A lot of running backs have broken free without being touched, whereas a receiver going across the middle of the end zone often gets clobbered while coming down with the ball. And some leagues give six points to quarterbacks for TD passes, though I think that is too much.

Varied-point systems — Some leagues award 10 points for scoring a touchdown (rushing or receiving), five for passing touchdowns and field goals, two points for extra points and 10 points for all defensive scores, regardless of their nature. The only difference is higher points per game, so why not just go with one, three and six points? If you use a varied-point system, do not devalue the kicking game. Points scored on field goals should be half of those scored on touchdowns. For example, don't award 10 points for a touchdown and only three for a field goal.

Yardage — Bonus points can be awarded for yards gained by running backs and receivers, passing yards or even for long plays (for example, double points for scoring plays of over 50 yards). In my league at *Pro Football Weekly*, we award three bonus points to a running back with a 100-yard rushing game, a receiver (wide receiver, tight end or running back) with a 100-yard receiving game and a quarterback with a 300-yard passing game. We also give three bonus points to scoring plays of 40 yards or more (rushing or receiving), two points for a passing touchdown of 40 yards or more and two bonus points for field goals of 50 yards or more.

Defensive scores — In many leagues, teams draft entire defensive units from NFL teams and then award six points for every score made by that defense in a game on a touchdown return of a fumble, interception or a blocked kick. Two points are awarded for a safety.

Sacks — Leagues that draft defensive players usually award one or two points for a sack.

Interceptions — Teams can subtract one point for each interception thrown by a quarterback or add one point for interceptions made by a team defense.

Remember, the more complicated the scoring, the harder it will be to tabulate your league's scores.

B. The Distance System

Some leagues award points according to the length of the scoring plays. This system favors the gamebreakers — players who score on long plays, rather than those who score from a yard out. In doing so, it eliminates much of the luck factor.

There are a variety of ways to give points for long-distance scoring. The following is one of the most common methods:

Passing for a Touchdown

Length of Touchdown	Points
1 – 9 yards	1
10 – 19 yards	2
20 – 29 yards	3
30 – 39 yards	4
40 – 49 yards	5
50 – 59 yards	6
60 – 69 yards	7
70 – 79 yards	8
80 – 89 yards	9
90 – 99 yards	10

Rushing and Receiving for a Touchdown

Length of Touchdown	Points
1 – 9 yards	2
10 – 19 yards	4
20 – 29 yards	6
30 – 39 yards	8
40 – 49 yards	10
50 – 59 yards	12
60 – 69 yards	14
70 – 79 yards	16
80 – 89 yards	18
90 – 99 yards	20

Field Goals

Length of Field Goal	Points
1 – 9 yards	1
10 – 19 yards	2
20 – 29 yards	3
30 – 39 yards	4
40 – 49 yards	5
50 – 59 yards	6
60 and over	7

Extra points are worth one point each.

Here is a different Distance Scoring System used by the Franchise Football League:

Yardage of play	0–9 Points	10–39 Points	40-plus Points
QB pass for TD	6	9	12
RB run for TD	6	9	12
WR/TE catch for TD	6	9	12
QB run/catch for TD	12	18	24
RB catch/pass for TD	12	18	24
WR/TE run/pass for TD	12	18	24
K run/catch/pass for TD	12	18	24
ST/Defense return for TD	12	18	24
Fake field goal for TD	12	18	24

Yardage of Play	17–39	40–49	50-plus
Field Goal	3	5	10

Safety = 12 points
Point after touchdown = 1 point

C. The Performance System

Scoring under this method is based on yards gained, not points scored. The major advantage is that less luck is involved (remember the Chris Warren situation late in the 1994 season?) and the true stars will stand out over the course of the season.

Here is the most common scoring method for the Performance System (although leagues can make their own variations).

Scoring by Position
Quarterbacks, Running Backs and Wide Receivers
1. One point for every 20 yards passing.
2. One point for every 10 yards rushing.
3. One point for every 10 yards receiving.

Kickers
1. Three points for each field goal.
2. One point for each extra point.
3. If a kicker passes, runs or receives for yardage, he is awarded the points that any other position players would receive for the same play.

Points are not deducted for negative yardage. The following is a detailed chart for the Performance Scoring System just described.

Passing Yardage	Points
0 – 19 yards	0
20 – 39 yards	1
40 – 59 yards	2
60 – 79 yards	3
80 – 99 yards	4
100 – 119 yards	5
120 – 139 yards	6
140 – 159 yards	7
160 – 179 yards	8
180 – 199 yards	9
200 – 219 yards	10

220 – 239 yards	11
240 – 259 yards	12
260 – 279 yards	13
280 – 299 yards	14
300 – 319 yards	15

and so on.

Rushing Yardage	Points
0 – 9 yards	0
10 – 19 yards	1
20 – 29 yards	2
30 – 39 yards	3
40 – 49 yards	4
50 – 59 yards	5
60 – 69 yards	6
70 – 79 yards	7
80 – 89 yards	8
90 – 99 yards	9
100 – 109 yards	10
110 – 119 yards	11
120 – 129 yards	12

and so on.

Pass Receiving Yardage	Points
0 – 9 yards	0
10 – 19 yards	1
20 – 29 yards	2
30 – 39 yards	3
40 – 49 yards	4
50 – 59 yards	5
60 – 69 yards	6
70 – 79 yards	7
80 – 89 yards	8
90 – 99 yards	9
100 – 109 yards	10
110 – 119 yards	11
120 – 129 yards	12

and so on.

Another favorite performance method to award points is to develop a scoring system that includes statistics for the following: quarterback — pass-completion percentage, passing yards, passing touchdowns and negative points for interceptions; running backs — rushing yards, rushing average and touchdowns; wide receivers and tight ends — receptions, receiving yards, yards per reception and touchdowns; and kicking — field goals and points subtracted for missed field goals. For defense, a system of 1–10 points is awarded for points allowed (example: 10 points for a shutout), or 1–5 points for rushing or passing yards allowed (5 points for less than 100 yards rushing or 200 yards passing allowed). Defenses are also awarded points for sacks and interceptions. Leagues that use this type of scoring system usually devise it themselves.

Whatever scoring system you use, don't go with one that awards so many points that your game scores are 110–96. Use one with realistic scores somewhere in the range of real NFL scores.

D. The Combined System

This is the scoring system that is now the most fair, and it is getting more popular every year. It is a combination of the basic scoring system and the performance scoring system. Players receive points when they score, as well as for yardage gained and/or the length of scoring plays.

This system negates some of the luck factor that is so prevalent in the basic scoring system, and it is not so heavily determined by yardage, either. In other words, whereas superstars are often no better than goal-line scorers in the basic method or than players who gain a lot of yards but rarely score in the performance system, the value of players is weighted more evenly in this system.

Points are tabulated according to whatever parts of the basic, performance and distance scoring methods are used. For example, a player can be awarded six points for a touchdown scored, three more points if it came on a play of 40 or more yards (some leagues use 50 yards as the barrier), and three more points if he gained 100 yards in the game. Or a quarterback can get three points for a touchdown pass, two or three more for a scoring pass over 40 (or 50) yards and two or three more for 300-yard games.

In fact, the analyses of players in this book are based on the combined scoring system more than any of the others.

E. The Rotisserie System

As in fantasy baseball, some league champions are the teams with the most points scored during the season. This method certainly rewards the best team overall, but it eliminates the week-to-week competition, which is the most exciting aspect of fantasy football once the season gets under way.

The team that scores the most points is justifiably the best team in a league, but it is very possible (and even likely) that it won't win the league championship based on weekly play.

What makes the fantasy-football-to-the-NFL correlation closer than the rotisserie-baseball-to-the-major-leagues correlation is that the highest-scoring team is not always the Super Bowl champion or the winner of a fantasy league.

THE DRAFT

The draft is the most exciting event of fantasy football and, more than anything else, it is what determines how well your team will fare.

Now it's time to stock your team. Your league will conduct a draft that is very much like the NFL draft, except that, instead of drafting college players, you are actually picking players from current NFL teams.

Some leagues, called keeper leagues, continue from year to year with basically the same teams, which allows owners to keep a few of the players from the previous year's roster. It's an interesting option that a lot of leagues use, but the drawback is that everybody should have a chance to draft Jerry Rice and Emmitt Smith. Keep that in mind.

Preparing for Draft Day

Study, study, study. This book will help you immensely as you prepare for your fantasy football draft, because its emphasis is on player evaluation. But you also need to study NFL rosters and have some knowledge of each team's depth charts — who starts and who doesn't. The majority of owners in every league do their homework and prepare for Draft Day. But there are always one or two owners in every league who do not, and they are usually the ones at the bottom of the standings.

Remember, a league of eight teams will include only about 120 out of the approximately 500 skill-position players on NFL rosters. That leaves you with a lot of players from which to choose, making your draft picks the most crucial aspect of putting together your team.

You need to know more than just the players on your favorite team. You need more than last year's NFL statistics or a list of the All-Pro and Pro Bowl teams. You really need to know something about every team in the league — and not just who's good but rather who scores the points. You also need to know your league's rules and draft accordingly (see Draft Strategy).

But do not go strictly on last year's statistics, because many players are inconsistent, and their numbers will go up and down from year to year. Be sure to know whether or not a player's 1994 statistics were truly indicative of his abilities. Last year's statistics are useful only to the extent that they indicate what to expect this season. For example, Jerry Rice's numbers vary somewhat from year to year, but he always ranks at the top of the list of wide receivers. But, while Terance Mathis had a great season last year, that doesn't mean he'll do it again this year. The same holds true for Leonard Russell, Craig Heyward, Brent Jones, Fuad Reveiz and a lot of other players.

And it's just the same for players coming off bad seasons. Mike Pritchard (injury), Kerry Cash (holdout) and Steve Beuerlein (replaced) all had subpar seasons in 1994 for different reasons. But all three of them are very capable of having good or great seasons again in 1995, just as they did in 1993.

Injuries have a lot to do with a player's performance, and injuries to other players often determine whether or not some players will get a chance to perform or not.

Remember, the success of your entire season largely depends on how you do in the draft. Don't take your draft lightly.

When to Hold Your Draft

It is necessary to hold your draft on a day in which every team can be represented. Do not allow an owner of one team to draft players for the owner of another team who cannot attend the draft. If a team is not represented at the draft, it must make its selections from the pool of players that remains after the draft.

You will want to hold your draft as close to the start of the NFL season as possible. The best day is anytime from Tuesday through Saturday during the week before the NFL season starts (September 3), which is after the date that NFL teams make their final cutdown to 45 players.

A quiet environment might be the best spot to hold your draft, since you will want to be able to think. But, for some reason, bars and restaurants seem to be the most-used locations.

If your league's commissioner owns a team, you might want to have an outside friend act as the recording secretary for your draft, since the commissioner will be drafting. You need somebody to keep track of the draft order, record everyone's picks as they are made, maintain time limits between picks and leave the commissioner free to concentrate on his draft.

You might also want to have large boards made up to record the picks so everyone can see them during the draft and will know what players are no longer available.

Some leagues (especially those that have 14-week regular seasons and two weeks of playoffs) hold their drafts one week into the NFL season and then start their leagues at the same time NFL teams are playing their second game so they can run their leagues the remainder of the NFL season, rather than end a week before the NFL playoffs start. This gives them the advantage of seeing how certain players (especially rookies) are doing and helps when it comes to the still-occasional holdouts that prevent veterans and rookies from playing the first few games of some seasons.

Draft Order

The draft begins with each team owner drawing a number. Teams then draft players in order. In succeeding rounds, teams draft players in the reverse order. Therefore, the person with the last pick in the first round gets the first pick in the second round, giving him two picks in a row.

That's why the owner with the last pick shouldn't panic, because it all evens out in the long run. The person with the first pick in the first round does not choose again until the last pick in the second round. Then he gets two picks in a row, because, as the third round begins, he gets the first pick again. At that point, the draft returns to the original first-through-last order.

The third and fourth rounds (and all pairs of succeeding rounds) work just like the first two rounds until every owner has filled his team roster at every position up to your league's roster limit.

Here's how it works:

Team 1 — 1st pick
Team 2 — 2nd pick
Team 3 — 3rd pick
Team 4 — 4th pick
Team 5 — 5th pick
Team 6 — 6th pick
Team 7 — 7th pick
Team 8 — 8th pick
Team 8 — 9th pick
Team 7 — 10th pick
Team 6 — 11th pick
Team 5 — 12th pick

Team 4 — 13th pick
Team 3 — 14th pick
Team 2 — 15th pick
Team 1 — 16th pick
Team 1 — 17th pick
and so on.

You may want to set a time limit on each team when selecting a player, which will keep the draft moving. A one-minute limit should be sufficient if team owners have done their homework and are prepared for the draft. In contrast to the NFL draft, when teams get 15 minutes to make their first-round pick and less in succeeding rounds, it seems like the late picks in fantasy football are the hardest to make. That's when you are trying to fill out a position, where you are looking for sleepers and players with potential and don't want to make a mistake. The early-round picks usually go quickly, because that's when the better, well-known players are selected.

Some leagues like to have their draft order set well in advance of the draft so players can conduct mock drafts beforehand. At the least, it will give you the opportunity to assess who will be available for your first few picks.

An eight-team league will need at least two hours to complete a draft, but the time goes by quickly. And it's a lot of fun.

Drafting Players

The most important factor in fantasy football that determines who wins and who loses — other than luck — is the draft. The team with the best players scores the most points. The team with the most points wins games. So you want to put together the best (meaning highest-scoring) team possible.

You can draft players from any position in any order, but I suggest that you take a quarterback, a running back and a wide receiver with your first three picks. Forget about the tight ends and placekickers until the middle rounds — you want to get as many of the high-scoring players as possible early on.

There is a big disparity between the best players and the very good players at the three aforementioned positions (quarterback, running back and wide receiver), and not as much difference between the best kickers and tight ends.

That's my suggestion, but two years ago I took a running back and two wide receivers in the first two rounds and waited until Round Four to grab a quarterback. That's because I felt there were nine good quarterbacks available that year (it was an eight-team league) and that I would get one of them if I waited another round. So be willing to change your strategy.

In fact, in 1995 you might want to pick a running back and a wide receiver with your first two picks, because quality players at those positions are hardest to find. The pool of good quarterbacks is a bit deeper than those for running backs and wide receivers. Don't be fooled when other team owners are drafting quarterbacks. Unless you can get Steve Young or Dan Marino, you might be better off taking a running back and a wide receiver first. But don't wait too long to draft a quarterback.

For example, Emmitt Smith, Barry Sanders, Natrone Means, Marshall Faulk, Chris Warren and Ricky Watters are the six best running backs to have in fantasy football. If you don't take one of them when you have the chance, there's quite a difference between them and Lewis Tillman, Herschel Walker, Marion Butts and Terry Kirby, four running backs who would likely be available in the fourth round. On the other hand, there is not a lot of difference between the best placekickers, many of whom are capable of scoring 100 or more points. Every team in your league will end up with a decent kicker, so the difference is not very much between them. At tight end, Ben Coates, Shannon Sharpe, Eric Green, Keith Jackson and Brent Jones are easily the best players, and they're worth an early pick, but I would always draft my second running back, wide receiver and quarterback (and perhaps my third running back and wide receiver) before picking any tight end who most likely isn't going to score a lot of points during the season.

Don't draft your second quarterback too early, even if a good one is available; instead, take a running back or wide receiver you will use a lot during the season. A few years ago, one player in my league drafted Jim Kelly in the third round after already having chosen Joe Montana in the first round. The only time he played Kelly all season was the one week when Montana's team had a bye. Of course, any quarterback's susceptibility to injuries warrants having a good backup quarterback on a fantasy football team — much like the Dolphins have a good backup to Dan Marino in Bernie Kosar — but you are better off drafting players who will play and score points for you than having a good player on your team whom you do not play much.

And, if your league uses defenses, don't draft your defensive team until the last round or two, because picking a defense is basically a crapshoot anyway. If you get three touchdowns all season by your team defense, you have done well. I wouldn't even draft the Minnesota defense very high, because there's no way to predict if it will score seven touchdowns again this year as it did in 1994.

After the draft, the commissioner should give every team owner a copy of each team's roster.

Player Auctioning

As they say, *real* fantasy football players stock their fantasy football teams the old-fashioned way — they *buy* them. Established leagues often like to use this method, in which players are bid for in an auction rather than drafted, because it adds another dimension to the draft.

Every team spends the same amount of money to make up, or buy, their teams. This is true free agency in fantasy football, because you do actually own the player. Also, in an auction, every team has equal opportunity to get every player.

Once an order is determined for choosing the players to be bid on, owners bid until one owner has outbid the others for a particular player. There is no ceiling on the player bids, and the best players obviously go for the most money (perhaps as much as 40 or 50 percent of a team's limit). Since only a few players in the league are worth that percentage of a team's "salary cap," you have to be sure you make that choice wisely. Choosing players with good potential for a smaller cost will enable you to outbid other teams for the most-sought-after players.

The auction continues until each team owner fills out his roster, and the cost of those players must not exceed the league's salary cap.

For example, one of the longest-running fantasy football leagues in the country has a $100 limit per team. Players such as Emmitt Smith and Steve Young cost over $40 each, whereas players like Leonard Russell and Jeff George can be had for $2–$5. The objective is to fill out an entire roster with $100 (this league has 12 players per team). Most of the teams try to buy one or two superstars and then fill out their rosters with cheaper players with good potential. But, since every team starts with the same bankroll, the most important thing is to budget carefully.

A regular draft is much shorter than an auction, but an auction is certainly more exciting. But it's not recommended for beginning fantasy players; wait a year or two before taking the plunge into an auction.

Draft Strategy

■ The rules that your league uses concerning its scoring method dictate largely the players you want to draft. If your scoring reflects only those scores made by NFL players every week, you will want to draft players who score the most points. For example, Edgar Bennett can be more valuable than Barry Sanders. But if your fantasy league rewards teams with running backs who rush for 100 yards in a game or quarterbacks who throw long touchdown passes, you will want to take other factors into consideration.

If your league's scoring system gives quarterbacks six points for each touchdown pass thrown, by all means try to draft a quarterback first. And if your league gives bonus points for distance scoring, you will want to go with the gamebreakers — Barry Sanders rather than Ricky Watters, Carl Pickens rather than Terance Mathis, and Steve Christie rather than Matt Bahr.

■ The most important factor in drafting is projecting a player's performance for the upcoming year. So don't place too much emphasis on last year's statistics. On the average, only about 3 of the top 10 scorers among running backs and wide receivers finish in the top 10 the following year. Quarterbacks are easier to judge, with about 70 percent finishing in the top 10 in successive years.

That is why this book lists statistics for up to the last five years of every player's career. If you study players' entire careers, you will see that a lot of players who were injured or had subpar seasons last year will be much better draft picks than you might have thought on first glance. Also, try not to pick based strictly on 1994 statistics; a lot of players who had career years will never reach those marks again.

You also will want to know which of the 1994 rookies who didn't see a lot of playing time last year are ready to break out in 1995, such as Heath Shuler, or Errict Rhett, who didn't play much until the final month of the season.

■ Do not draft too many players from one division. During the weeks that teams have a bye (see the 1995 NFL schedule in the Appendix), you will not be able to play these players, and if too many of your best players are from the same division, you will have to play too many backups on those weekends, almost guaranteeing that you will lose a game or two. So spread your picks around. Also, for the same reason, be sure to pick your two quarterbacks and two kickers from different divisions. A good suggestion is to draft your top three players (quarterback, running back and wide receiver) from three different divisions so you'll always have two of them on the bye weeks.

■ Don't draft too many players from your favorite team. If they have an off year, they will very quickly become your least-favorite players. Be objective, and even take players from a team you do not like, because they will help you win in fantasy football. And don't pass over players like Andre Rison or Thurman Thomas just because they have past reputations as troublemakers. If you have a chance to "steal" either of these players in a lower round, by all means do so.

■ Don't draft too many players from bad teams. Most owners want the bulk of their players from good teams, because they'll have more scoring opportunities. Lawrence Dawsey is a perfect example of a player who would probably accumulate some excellent statistics on a good team, but he can't do that on the Buccaneers.

■ Know which players are holding out, both veterans and rookies. Because of the advent of a salary cap for both rookies and veterans, there are fewer holdouts than in past years. But some players will invariably try to get bigger salaries, so be aware of them.

■ Consider a player's age. Last year, several players seemed to grow old quickly, such as Boomer Esiason and Gary Clark. Players who could slide this year include Warren Moon, Henry Ellard and Herschel Walker.

■ Be aware of which players might lose their starting jobs in 1995. Some of these players are quarterbacks Chris Miller and Jim Harbaugh, running backs Rodney Hampton and Johnny Johnson, wide receivers John Taylor and Michael Jackson and kicker Kevin Butler.

■ Because of free agency, know the players that switched teams who could be due for outstanding years. Some of these players include quarterback Dave Krieg (if he starts for Arizona), running back Ricky Watters and wide receivers Andre Rison. On the other hand, wide receiver Alvin Harper is an example of a player whose statistics might not be as good as they were in 1994 because he went to a weaker team.

■ Know the injury status of players you are thinking about drafting. Among the best players coming off 1994 injuries are running backs Rod Bernstine and Terry Kirby and wide receivers Mike Pritchard and Anthony Carter (see the Injury Report in Chapter 11).

■ Don't put too much emphasis on preseason statistics, because they can be very misleading.

■ Know which teams have changed their offenses. For example, if a team goes to a one-back offense, the backups will not see much action. And Seattle's increased use of multiple wide receivers might mean Chris Warren will get fewer carries. And the Oilers are still trying to add a tight end to their offense, which would mean fewer receptions for some of the receivers. And be aware of possible changes on the nine teams that have new head coaches in 1995 — Houston (where Jeff Fisher had the interim removed from his title), Denver, Philadelphia, Seattle, St. Louis and the Jets and Raiders, as well as the two new expansion teams, Carolina and Jacksonville.

■ Know which rookies have the best chance of contributing right away. A few rookies to keep an eye on are quarterbacks Kerry Collins (Carolina) and Steve McNair (Houston); running backs Ki-Jana Carter (Cincinnati), James Stewart (Jacksonville) and Napoleon Kaufman (L.A. Raiders); wide receivers J.J. Stokes (San Francisco), Michael Westbrook (Washington) and Joey Galloway (Seattle); tight ends Kyle Brady (N.Y. Jets) and Mark Bruener (Pittsburgh); and kicker Steve McLaughlin (St. Louis).

■ When drafting, no matter what round it is, have two or three players in mind. That way, if somebody else picks the player you wanted, you will be able to make a comparable choice. In the middle rounds, many players should be even; what you are looking for is the so-called "sleeper" in every round. There's always one.

■ If you don't think the player you want will be available in the next round, now's the time to draft him.

Here's what a typical roster might look like for the 1995 season:
Round 1 — Emmitt Smith, RB, Dallas Cowboys
Round 2 — Tim Brown, WR, Los Angeles Raiders
Round 3 — Jim Kelly, QB, Buffalo Bills
Round 4 — Jerome Bettis, RB, St. Louis Rams
Round 5 — Irving Fryar, WR, Miami Dolphins
Round 6 — Brent Jones, TE, San Francisco 49ers
Round 7 — Edgar Bennett, RB, Green Bay Packers
Round 8 — Rob Moore, WR, Arizona Cardinals
Round 9 — Jeff Hostetler, QB, Los Angeles Raiders
Round 10 — Jason Elam, K, Denver Broncos
Round 11 — Garrison Hearst, RB, Arizona Cardinals
Round 12 — Mark Ingram, WR, Green Bay Packers
Round 13 — Gary Anderson, K, Pittsburgh Steelers
Round 14 — Chicago Bears defense
Round 15 — Kerry Cash, TE, L.A. Raiders

In this typical roster, players were chosen from all six divisions, which is the ideal spread. And, even though some of the players play for losing teams, they'll still put up some pretty good numbers. But note that most of the players play for winning teams.

ROSTER CHANGES AND TRANSACTIONS

As in the NFL, you are able to make changes in your roster during the season. Just because you didn't have a good draft doesn't mean you have to suffer through the season with a bad team. And when one of your players is lost to his NFL team because of an injury, you also can replace him on your roster with another player. Fine-tuning your roster is a must after the season begins.

The winner of most fantasy football leagues is not the owner who drafted the best team, but the one who did the best job working the waiver wires. In fact, the first roster changes you make after the draft might be the most critical to your team's success. That's when you will be able to answer most of the questions you had on Draft Day — who will be the featured running back on a particular team, for example — or when you will be able to identify emerging players.

There are always talented players — primarily rookies and second-year pros who didn't play much the previous year, as well as players who come out of nowhere to have good seasons — who will be overlooked in your league's initial draft and who would be a valuable addition to a fantasy team. This is how teams catch up to the preseason favorite. In other words, don't just draft a team and sit back to see how you will do. Be active.

Some leagues do not allow roster transactions of any kind after the draft. That's wrong. A fantasy league is supposed to be fun, and flexible roster changes allow every team the opportunity to improve during the season.

There are three commonly used methods to make roster changes: trades, holding a league-wide supplemental draft and the open-waiver system in which every team is allowed to pick up and drop players at any time.

Many leagues charge a small transaction fee for any personnel move. This usually lowers the incentive to make wholesale roster changes and helps to increase the pot for the payoff.

Your roster size may never exceed the limit; for every player you add, you must drop a player. Once you drop a player, he is eligible to be picked up by any team.

Too many fantasy leagues set too many restrictive deadlines and rules for transactions (as well as drafting, weekly lineups and many other aspects of fantasy football). Be flexible. The idea is to have fun and allow every team an equal opportunity to win. You need to be sure the rules are not stretched or broken, but they should not hinder the idea of fantasy football, which is to provide enjoyment to football fans.

Remember, NFL teams change their rosters and lineups constantly throughout the season. So should you. But don't "overmanage." You want to be continuously looking for players to add to your roster, but be careful not to give up on your players too soon. Some players need time to develop, just as you knew when you drafted them.

Trades

Trading players is one of the most fascinating aspects of pro football. Fans spend weeks, if not years, trying to determine which team got the best of a trade. Remember the big trades involving Eric Dickerson and Herschel Walker?

In fantasy football, however, trades are usually a rare occurrence. In fact, some leagues do not allow them at all because of the possibility that two team owners would get together and make a trade that helps one team at the expense of another (especially at the end of the season).

If your league allows trades, you will want to set some safeguards. For example, set a deadline like the NFL does. The NFL does not allow trades after the sixth week of the season, but you will want to set your fantasy league's deadline a little later. Do not allow one team to trade a player or players for "future considerations," for obvious reasons. You can also make trades contingent on the approval of the commissioner or the other team owners to guard against hanky-panky.

Two-for-one trades (in which one team offers two players for one very good player) are allowed, as long as each team obeys the league's roster limit. The team receiving two players must drop another player on its roster, while the team receiving one player must pick up another player.

Just like in professional sports, where the commissioners have the power to veto trades that are not "in the best interests of the league," your commissioner and team owners should have the same power. If the commissioner has a team in the league, a simple majority of owners can veto a trade.

Waivers

In the NFL, teams are free to drop or waive players at any time and pick up or sign players at any time, and this is my suggestion. Teams should be able to improve their roster at any time. In a league of eight teams with 14 players per roster, only 112 players out of approximately 500 skill-position players (quarterbacks, running backs, wide receivers, tight ends and kickers) will be on a fantasy roster. That leaves a lot of good players undrafted; thus there should be no limit on the number of roster changes per team.

Under this method, the first team to pick up a player from the unclaimed pool of NFL players gets him. All he has to do is notify the league commissioner (and pay the appropriate fee, if there is one). For each player obtained via waivers, a player must be released.

Every year there are several players whose midseason addition helps fantasy teams. In 1994, Jeff Blake, Craig Heyward and Terance Mathis came out of nowhere to star for their teams, and it's likely that they weren't even drafted before the start of the season. A few players returned from the injured reserve list a month into the season and were a nice addition for some fantasy teams. And, on September 1, how many people would have expected Brent Jones to score nine touchdowns or Leonard Russell to get eight? Work the waiver wires carefully and you could come up a winner.

The first two weeks of the season are an important time in the success of your team. Keep an eye on players who come out of nowhere, surprise starters and even rookies who were not expected to start or play much.

Supplemental Drafts

A league can also decide to hold a draft after four weeks (or eight weeks) to supplement rosters with players not chosen in the preseason draft (those on current rosters during the season). Team owners are able to drop as many players on their rosters as they want and replace them with new players.

The supplemental draft is conducted just like the preseason draft except that the order changes. Just like in the NFL, teams draft in reverse order of their won-lost records (that is, the team with the worst record drafts first and so on, to the team with the best record). Ties are broken by total points scored (with the team with the fewest points scored considered the weaker team). The draft then reverses order in the second round and continues back and forth until every owner has made the changes he wants to make.

Any player not on a fantasy team is available to be picked up from the supplemental pool. This is especially effective in allowing every team an almost equal opportunity to grab the latest hotshot player in the NFL, as compared to total free agency, in which the first team owner to contact the commissioner gets the player.

Not every team may wish to take part in the supplemental draft, especially if an owner is happy with his team.

If the teams in your league originally acquired players through an auction, you should hold a supplemental draft/auction at some point during the season to allow all teams to bid for new players.

No Transactions

If a league does not allow teams to make transactions, or if a deadline is put on all transactions, you still should allow teams to replace players who are injured.

The simplest way to do this is to allow teams to replace only those players who are actually placed on injured reserve by their NFL teams. No team should be forced to play without a player at a position or be without a capable backup. Players lost to a fantasy team because of trades or waivers would not qualify to be replaced unless your league's rules specify so.

Leagues that do not allow transactions often have larger roster sizes, which gives each team the chance to stock enough players in the draft to get through the entire season.

Injured Reserve

What do you do when one of your top players is injured and placed on injured reserve? In most leagues, you would either keep him on the bench until he is healthy again (thus taking up space that could be occupied by a healthy player), or you could drop the injured player and add another one at the same position. However, if you drop the player, he would be free to be picked up by any team when he is reactivated.

Thus, your league might want to allow teams to have an injured reserve list, so any player who is placed on injured reserve by his NFL team would be retained by the fantasy team and temporarily replaced by a pickup. Then, when the injured player is playing again in the NFL, the fantasy team would either have to activate him and drop the substitute player (or another player) or drop the player on injured reserve (for example, if the substitute player is doing better).

In the NFL, when a player is put on injured reserve, he is not permitted to play for the rest of the season. Many teams leave injured players on their rosters (inactive week after week) in hopes they will return later in the season. It's the same in fantasy football — if you have a deep-enough roster, that is.

LINEUPS

The most enjoyable week-to-week aspect of fantasy football is setting your lineup in advance of each weekend's action.

Now it's time to play coach. You are George Seifert or Don Shula. You don't decide what plays to use, but rather what players to use, and that's how you score points. If drafting is the most important part of fantasy football, then "starting" the right players is the most important decision you make once the season starts. One of the most frustrating moments of fantasy football is knowing that a player you didn't start for a particular week scored a touchdown — or even two! And it's equally frustrating to start a player who doesn't even suit up because of an injury.

Whom to Play

The starting lineup usually consists of:

    1 Quarterback
    2 Running Backs
    2 Wide Receivers
    1 Tight End
    1 Kicker
    1 Team Defense (optional)

Lineup variations: There are a number of variations that your league will have to decide upon before the start of the season. For example, the Franchise Football League recommends 1 quarterback, 2 running backs, 3 wide receivers, 1 tight end, 1 kicker, 1 special-teams player (kick returner), 1 linebacker and 1 defensive back (or one team defense in place of the special-teams player and two defensive players). But, since NFL teams have only six skill-position players on offense, your league should, too.

Those on your team who do not "play" sit on the bench for a week (or, in some cases, all season).

Because of the advent of H-backs, run-and-shoot offenses and three- and four-wide-receiver formations, some NFL teams do not use tight ends and others use them basically for blocking. You may want to allow teams in your league the option of drafting one extra wide receiver in place of a tight end and/or playing one extra wide receiver rather than a tight end any particular week.

That's what we do in my league. Instead of drafting four wide receivers and two tight ends, we allow teams to pick five wide receivers and only one tight end and have the option of playing either three wide receivers *or* two wideouts and one tight end each week. In 1990, some teams didn't play a tight end all season, always starting three wide receivers. So in 1991 we passed a rule in which every team had to play its tight end for at least half of the games. That added an element of strategy to making our lineups and is more fair to tight ends, because it doesn't totally dismiss them. And it is certainly more exciting to start players who have a better chance of scoring than a tight end who might see the end zone only three or four times all season. After all, after Ben Coates, Shannon Sharpe, Keith Jackson, Eric Green and a few others, there's not much left in the NFL in the way of tight ends, and there are a lot of fine wide receivers.

Setting a Deadline

Be sure to set a deadline for teams to submit their starting lineups for each week, but set it as late as possible. You might want to have a deadline set for 7:00 p.m. Friday or 6:00 p.m. Saturday so that your phone is not ringing off the hook Sunday as you are sitting down to watch the NFL pregame shows on television. In the event of Thursday or Saturday games, you will need to adjust your deadlines — even if some teams don't have players involved in those games. All rosters should be turned in before the first game played each week.

Your league might want to allow teams the option to call in a lineup change anytime before 1:00 p.m. EST Sunday, when games begin, if the commissioner can be reached (or if he has a phone-answering machine). This allows teams to make last-minute changes in the event of player injury. It's not as complicated at it might seem, as it might be used only a few times in the course of the season by all of the teams.

Once the deadline has passed, changes cannot be made — even in the event of injuries to a player before a game. If the commissioner has a team in the league, he must turn in his lineup to another league member to guard against cheating.

If a team does not turn in a lineup, its lineup from the previous week will be automatically used.

For leagues that have an early lineup deadline, one option is to allow teams to make one lineup change anytime until the kickoff of Sunday's first game. That allows players to get late-breaking news and injury updates from the Sunday morning pregame shows and adjust their lineups accordingly.

Before choosing your lineup, you should consider several factors, such as injuries, opposing defenses, whether your players are playing at home or on the road and weather. The final factor to consider is which of your players are hot and which ones are cold. But the most important factor is not to put a player in your starting lineup after he has had a big game. You want to put him in at the right time.

Quite often, players who are not listed on the official NFL injury list on Friday afternoon do not play in that weekend's games; thus they can't score any points for their teams. But every team is under the same disadvantage — whether it be fantasy football or real football.

Problem No. 1: One question I am often asked is whether you should play your best players against a strong defense or if you should play weaker players who are going up against easier defenses. For example, do you start Barry Sanders against the Vikings, who have a strong run defense, or do you go with Lewis Tillman against the Buccaneers, who have a weak run defense?

I prefer to start the better players, because the best players tend to play better against good teams. I offer no basis for this, other than that it works for me. Besides, take a look at the Super Bowl. That's when the best players play against the best the NFL has to offer — and the truly great players always shine in the end.

However, my rule does not hold hard and fast. I might go with Rick Mirer against the Broncos rather than Jim Everett against the 49ers, for example. In other words, when dealing with the tier of players just below the stars, it might be better to go with the player facing the weaker competition.

Also, you might want to take into consideration if a player is at home or on the road. In 1991, the Cowboys' Emmitt Smith scored 10 of his 13 touchdowns in the friendly confines of Texas Stadium and only three of them on the road. Then, in 1993, Smith had both of his three-touchdown games on the road. Most teams perform better at home, and so do their players, but it's not a sure thing. So go with your hunch (and hope it pays off).

Problem No. 2: Should you start a player who is listed as probable, questionable or doubtful on the official NFL injury report (which is released every Wednesday night and updated Friday night)? There's nothing more frustrating during a fantasy football season than activating a player for a game and then seeing him standing on the sidelines in street clothes — or not starting him and watching him score three touchdowns! Both of those instances have occurred to every fantasy football player.

Injuries are constant in the NFL; thus depth is very important for a fantasy football team. You will be playing a guessing game, however, just as NFL head coaches have to guess whether or not their opponent is going to start a player who is listed as injured.

In the NFL, teams are supposed to list players with a 75 percent chance of playing as probable, 50 percent chance of playing as questionable and 25 percent chance of playing as doubtful. But not every team follows that guideline. Some list too many players (Dallas listed more than 20 injured players every week late last season after not listing an injured Troy Aikman for one game), some don't list enough players and some don't list an injured player in an attempt to throw off their opponents.

Here's a comparison of the weekly injury reports with how they usually turn out:

Category	Chances of Playing	Reality
Probable	75%	90%
Questionable	50%	60%
Doubtful	25%	10%

So, if a player is listed as probable, in all likelihood he'll play. And you should play him unless you have an equally talented, healthy reserve. If he's questionable and you have a pretty good backup, consider playing the backup. And if the player is doubtful, go with your best backup, even if he has little chance of scoring. Then sit back and watch your "benched" star score two touchdowns!

How to Get Around the Byes
in the NFL Schedule

As you know, NFL teams no longer play every week during the season. In 1995, every NFL team will again have one bye, or one week off, during the course of the season — a 16-game schedule in 17 weeks for every team. Thus you will have to work around these byes when you draft your players and make up your weekly lineups.

The byes mean that every player on your fantasy team will have one week off in which you will not be able to play him. All 30 teams will play on only about half of the weeks during the 1995 season.

The byes don't present much of a problem, as was originally anticipated when they started in 1990, because leagues that provide for good depth are able to deal with them.

Still, don't ignore the byes. Don't just say, "Well, it's only one week." In most leagues, most teams will have about a .500 record, and the difference between making and not making the playoffs could be that one week in which your best players couldn't play.

The byes affect every team the same and balance out over the entire season. So, while you will have to bench Emmitt Smith one game this season and play somebody like Ronald Moore, remember that your opponents have the same predicament. It's really no worse than having one of your players injured for a week when he will have to sit out a game anyway. You just have to live with it — just as the real team's coach does when one of his players is injured and out for one game.

After all, you have as many players on the bench as you normally play, so you still should be able to play a good player, especially if you drafted well before the season started (or made good roster moves).

Be sure to select a method of dealing with the byes before the start of your season. Here are the most commonly used options:

Option 1: When players on your team have a bye, you simply start other players, just as if the players whose teams do not play that week are injured.

The most important thing is not to draft too many players from the same division, because four of the teams in a division usually have an open date at the same time. Ideally, you should select your top three players (usually a quarterback, running back and wide receiver) from three different divisions.

Option 2: Expand each team's roster. Instead of a 14-man roster, you can go to a 19-man roster, adding one player at each position — quarterback, running back, wide receiver, tight end and kicker — during the draft. The bigger roster allows for more flexibility and substitution in all weeks. But, since you will find that even on a 14-man roster some players will never "play," an expanded roster is not really necessary to handle the byes. And larger rosters mean fewer players will be available for all teams to pick up during the season.

Option 3: Allow coaches to place idle players on an "Inactive List" and pick up a replacement player for one week. But chances are that you already will have a better player sitting on your bench than you can pick up (or you had better make a roster transaction right away and pick up that player for good).

Option 4: Players receive the same points during the week their teams have a bye as they will score the following week. That way your best players could play in every game. The biggest disadvantage with this method is that it delays the fantasy results for a week. Also, if the player does not score the second week, the "goose egg" goes down on the scorecard twice.

What is the effect of the byes on fantasy league scoring? In my league one year, the average number of points for both teams in the seven weeks without byes was 56.5 points. During the seven weeks when four NFL teams did not play, the average score was 55.8. In fact, the three highest-scoring weeks in my league that year came during weeks with the byes (although the two lowest-scoring weeks also came on bye weeks). So the byes proved to be negligible, because the backup players were just as capable of scoring as those players who normally would have started. The next year, it was the opposite — 57.8 points per game during the seven non-bye weeks and only 47.9 points during the seven bye weeks. In other words, it has been my experience that open dates have a minimal effect over the course of a year.

TABULATING THE SCORES

Since the team with the highest score in head-to-head competition each week wins, a fun part of fantasy football is tabulating the scoring. This can be a real task, however, if your league has a complicated scoring method. The league commissioner usually has the headache of putting together the stats every week, and he needs a reliable source every Monday and Tuesday to get NFL box scores from every game.

Here's my method for tabulating the scores for a game (the sample is from my league's championship game). We used a basic scoring method of six points for touchdowns rushing, receiving and defensive scores, three points for a touchdown pass thrown and field goals, two points for a safety or a two-point conversion, one point for extra points, a bonus of three points for 100-yard games rushing or receiving or 300-yard games passing. There are also bonus points for scoring plays of 40 yards or longer and field goals of 50 yards or longer.

Grayslake Goonsquad	**The Chimps**
QB — Everett: 33323	QB — Humphries: 3
RB — Watters: 0	RB — B. Sanders: 0
RB — B. Morris: 0	RB — Hampton: 0
WR — T. Brown: 0	WR — Birden: 0
WR — Proehl: 0	WR — Ingram: 0
TE — B. Jones: 0	WR — R. Moore: 0
K — Bahr: 331	K — Reveiz: 313
D — Chiefs: 632	D — Raiders: 0
TOTAL: 32	TOTAL: 10

Some leagues prefer to use the following designations for scores: T for touchdowns scored, P for touchdowns thrown (worth three points), F for field goals, X for extra points and S for safeties. That's simple enough, but I just write down the actual point value for each player.

What's Going On?

One of the most frustrating times for a fantasy football player is not knowing how you and your opponent are doing on Sunday afternoon. Unless your league is set up in such a way that you know what players your opponent has started, you might not even be able to tabulate his scoring.

The hardest part is trying to find out who is doing the scoring on Sunday afternoon. The halftime and postgame highlight shows and evening sports programs don't tell you who made every score in every game — or how long the scores were or how many yards everybody gained. So you will have to wait until Monday morning when your newspaper hits your doorstep.

For most fantasy players, it's always "Was the San Francisco–New Orleans score announced yet?" Or "How'd Emmitt Smith do? Did he score two touchdowns again? Did he get 100 yards?" A few years ago, I heard, "How can Warren Moon throw for 527 yards and Drew Hill not catch a touchdown pass?" That's the fun — and frustration! — of fantasy football.

ESPN's excellent "Prime Time" show on Sunday evenings shows every significant scoring play and is eagerly watched by fantasy football players. But, far too often, by late Sunday night, football fans have watched the same touchdown runs over and over without knowing who made the other scores. It's time for television to take fantasy football seriously!

Computer Software Packages

Many services advertised in daily newspapers and other sports publications supposedly offer easy-to-use computer software packages to manage fantasy football leagues and tabulate scoring. Some of these allow leagues many different options to customize your own rules, rather than restricting you to one set of rules. Most packages are compatible with IBM computers, although a few work on Macintosh computers. The cost for these packages ranges from $40 to $125. Look in *Pro Football Weekly*, *The Sporting News* and NFL preview magazines for these kinds of ads.

Breaking Ties

Occasionally, the score of a game between two fantasy football teams will end in a tie. Unless your league decides that ties are OK, there are two commonly used methods of breaking ties.

Option 1: Add the scores of the players on each team's reserve list (those players not activated that week). This will usually break the ties (if a tie remains, revert to Option 2). This is the best method, as the team's backups should determine a winner and a loser. When a winner is determined, the winning team receives the victory and the loser gets a loss in the standings. But only the points that led to the tie should be added to the cumulative points in the standings (in other words, the points scored by the backups are not added to the team's points in the standings).

Option 2: Teams can list their reserves in the order they would want them used in a tiebreaker. For example, teams would probably list their backup kicker first, and the team with the kicker with the most points would be a winner. If this method is used, you might want only field goals to count for kickers, as it better reflects NFL overtimes (in which there are no extra points).

In some leagues, every game has a home team and an away team. In a tiebreaker, using this method, if the home team's first reserve scores, the home team wins the game. If he fails to score, the visiting team's first player has the opportunity to break the tie. If neither player scores, the tiebreaker goes to the second players on the reserve lists (home team, then visiting team).

This method is more luck than anything, whereas Option 1 truly awards the team with the best backups (for that week, anyway). Besides, in an average season, there won't be more than two or three ties, anyway, and owners shouldn't have to spend all that time determining the order of their reserves, when they probably won't be used.

WHAT DO YOU NEED TO WIN?

In a combined scoring system (a combination of the basic, distance and performance scoring methods) an average score of 30 points per game will usually win most games and make you your league's champion for the regular season. With a poor game in the playoffs, however, all could be for naught.

Thirty points is not a lot. It could break down this way:

QB — 33	WR — 6
RB — 6	TE — 0
RB — 0	K — 3111
WR — 6	Defense — 0

That's all it takes — a good game by just a few of your players. Your quarterback throws two touchdown passes; one running back scores a touchdown while the other doesn't score at all; both of your wide receivers score a touchdown; your kicker hits one field goal and three extra points (not much at all); and your tight end and defense don't get any scores. That's it.

Some weeks, most of your players will be hot, and you will score upward of 50 or 60 points. Some other weeks, you might score only in the teens — and still win. It's also very possible that you can score a lot of points but your opponent's players will be even hotter and score more points — and thus beat you.

VARIATIONS

Every league has its own special rules that make it unique from others. Here are some of the most common variations for fantasy football.

Drafting a Defense

Remember, football isn't just offense. The most common variation is to draft a team defense to be used as an eighth player. Unlike the skill-position players, a fantasy team drafts an entire NFL team's defense. When any member of the team's defense scores a touchdown, whether on an interception, a fumble recovery or a blocked kick, six points are awarded to the fantasy team. And when a defense scores a safety, two points are awarded.

Other scoring methods include rewarding defenses for holding opposing offenses under 300 total yards, under 100 yards rushing or under 200 yards passing. Different point totals are assigned to each category.

See Chapter 8 on Defenses.

Drafting Individual Defensive Players

Some leagues, those with the most complicated rules and scoring methods, actually draft an entire defense — three linemen, four linebackers, two cornerbacks and two safeties. Points are awarded for tackles, assists, sacks and interceptions.

An option here is to subtract defensive points from your opponent's score rather than adding the defensive points to your team's score.

Remember, though, this method gets very complicated — and very few newspapers list statistics for tackles and assists. And, since statistics for tackles are unofficial anyway, they are not really an accurate measure of players' abilities. For example, the leading tacklers for the Falcons and Buccaneers usually have about 200 tackles a season, while teams like the Steelers, Dolphins and Bengals, which decide tackles much more conservatively, have a leading tackler with only about 100 tackles every year.

Drafting a Special Team

Another variation is to draft kick returners or a team's entire special-teams unit (punt and kickoff returners). Six points are awarded whenever a player returns a kickoff or a punt for a touchdown or scores off a fake punt or a fake field goal. (In some leagues, when you draft a team, you get all of its scores, whether scored by its defense or its special teams.)

Drafting a Coach

Each team can draft an NFL coach as an extra player and be awarded three points every time his team wins a game in the NFL.

Re-Drafting for Playoffs

OK, so the regular season is over and you haven't had enough. Fantasy football is in your blood and you want more. So go ahead and do it all over again during the NFL playoffs.

In the week immediately following the end of the regular season, hold a draft just as you did before the start of the season. Some leagues hold their draft the week between the four wild-card games and the first round of the divisional playoffs, because the wild-card teams will all play an extra game if they advance to the Super Bowl. I don't particularly buy this reasoning; drafting players from a wild-card team is taking a chance, since it's rare that one of those teams makes it to the Super Bowl. Most are out of the playoffs after another week.

By the end of the regular season, every fantasy owner should have a good feel for what players are scoring well, but the most important aspect is knowing which teams will go the furthest in the playoffs, because players can produce points only as long as their teams advance in the playoffs. That's why shrewd drafting is essential.

Unlike the regular season in fantasy football, a fantasy league held during the NFL playoffs does not feature head-to-head competition. Rather, the champion is determined by the team that scores the most points overall through the Super Bowl.

Some leagues hold their fantasy league playoffs this way but allow teams to "protect" one or two players from their rosters before beginning a new draft. Other leagues allow players to be drafted by more than one team. Scoring is the same as the method used during the fantasy season, unless you want to make alterations.

Keeper Leagues

In rotisserie baseball, owners retain the rights to players on their fantasy teams from the previous year. You can do that in fantasy football, too, by allowing each team to keep a specified number of players from the previous season's roster.

The best part about keeper leagues is that they are more like the NFL, where teams basically stay the same except for some changes (even teams with a new head coach don't turn over half of the previous year's roster). Keeper leagues provide a sense of continuity from year to year. They allow fantasy owners to form a team identity, and they probably foster more trades throughout the season.

But remember, if you have a keeper league, you are eliminating the single most exciting part of fantasy football — the draft — because every team no longer has the opportunity to draft players like Jerry Rice, Steve Young and Emmitt Smith; they will already be on another owner's team. In effect, you are eliminating the first two or three rounds of your draft, because the top players won't be available.

SOURCES

There are several good sources for fantasy football league players to get in-depth game scores and summaries, weekly statistics, depth charts, rosters and injury updates. Here are the best:

Game Summaries and Box Scores

Good sources for game statistics are daily newspapers, with *USA Today* being the best. *Pro Football Weekly* runs game stories and box scores, but you won't receive it until late in the week.

Statistics

Most daily newspapers print individual statistics by conference, usually in the Thursday sports sections. *USA Today* runs stats by conference for each team on Wednesday and Thursday (one conference each day). *Pro Football Weekly* runs the longest lists of individual statistics, as well as the most complete team statistics and rankings.

Depth Charts

Pro Football Weekly is the only national publication that lists depth charts weekly. Its depth charts come from each NFL team's press releases and are updated weekly.

Rosters

The best place to find rosters for use in the draft is any one of the reputable NFL preview magazines on the newsstands (the best being *Pro Football Weekly's Preview '95, Street and Smith's* and *The Sporting News*).

Injury Updates

Most daily newspapers list the official weekly NFL injury report in the agate section of Thursday's sports section, and *USA Today* runs it on Fridays. Remember that the "official" NFL injury report is not 100 percent accurate. Check your Saturday and Sunday newspapers, as well as the NFL pregame shows, for last-minute updates.

NFL News

You will also need to know the latest news about what's going on around the NFL — what lineup changes are about to occur, who's playing well and when a player is about to come off the injured reserve list. The best sources for NFL news are *USA Today*, *The Sporting News* and *Pro Football Weekly*.

Fantasy Tips

There are also several 900-number services available. One of the best is the one offered by *Pro Football Weekly*. The six editors offer their best fantasy football tips, injury updates and other late-breaking news on Fridays during the season. The number is 900/407-7004, and callers are charged $1.25 per minute.

Jack Pullman, who runs All Pro Publishing in Panorama City, Calif. (818/893-5055), also has a 900 number. His service, which is excellent, also offers a weekly newsletter during the season for fantasy football updates.

Other services are offered by the Franchise Football League (703/883-0029) and *Fantasy Football* magazine (206/487-9000).

Television

Last year, Rick Korch, the original author of this book, co-hosted the first nationwide television show ever on fantasy football. The show, called "Playoff Fantasy Football Weekly," was seen in 26 million homes on regional cable television. It was co-hosted by Norm Hitzges, the veteran ESPN broadcaster. The show will be back in 1995 in even more cities (although Rick Korch will be replaced by a new co-host). Check your regional sports network for the schedule.

On-line Services

There are several on-line computer services that serve as sources for fantasy football. If you have access to Prodigy, America Online, Compuserve or any of the other reliable on-line services, check to see if fantasy football is part of its menu. This is a growing field.

Chapter 2

PLAYER EVALUATIONS

The player evaluations in this book are intended as a guide to help you draft and put together your fantasy team before and during the season. But go ahead and make your own decisions. It's your team and you should have the biggest say-so in the makeup of it.

In writing the player evaluations, I have taken into consideration such factors as player performance over an entire career (not just last year's statistics), injury status, holdouts, the improvement and decline of players, age, changes in teams' game plans (and the players' roles in them), supporting cast, the movements of free agents and the 1995 drafts of every team.

But, since this book went to press in late spring, you will need to consider other factors, such as injuries suffered in the offseason and during training camp, depth chart changes and in-season coaching changes (for making roster transactions).

And, this year more than ever before, there was expected to be a large number of roster changes in June, many of them involving veteran players whom teams were going to cut because of salary-cap restrictions. Several dozen skill-position players might change teams in the six weeks between June 1 and the opening of training camps.

Players in this book are ranked by position under headings such as "Superstars," "Solid Picks" and "Could Come On." In most cases, players are ranked under each category in order of their talents and projected contribution to a fantasy football team, but quite often a player in a later category will actually be a better pick than one in a previous category. For example, Keith Byars is the first running back listed under "Best of the Rest," but he is certainly a better pick than Amp Lee and Derek Brown, two players listed as "Could Come On" ahead of him.

Since each fantasy football league differs in size and makes its own rules, it is difficult to make exact evaluations and suggestions. For example, a starting player in a 12-team league might be a backup in an eight-team league. So this book will mainly focus on average leagues — those with 8–10 teams that draft two quarterbacks, four running backs, four wide receivers, two tight ends and two kickers and that start one quarterback, two running backs, two wide receivers, one tight end and one kicker.

In Chapter 10, I rank the top players in every position regardless of which category they are listed in throughout the player evaluations. This is the list I will use going into my fantasy football draft (updating it, of course, with what happens during the preseason).

Tips for Choosing Players for Your Draft

Here are some general tips for any scoring method:

■ Don't draft only big-name players.

■ Remember that other players draft foolishly when a panic occurs. Just because everybody else is drafting kickers or quarterbacks, that doesn't mean you have to follow the trend. Be like an NFL coach — don't stray from your game plan.

■ Be careful when considering injury-prone players. If one of your top draft picks misses a large portion of the season, your team will suffer.

■ Know the status of players going into the season — who's injured and who's holding out. This is very important, because you don't want to draft a player who can't play.

Here's an example of your drafting strategy for the Basic Scoring Method:

■ Round 1 — Draft the player who will score the most touchdowns, usually Emmitt Smith or Jerry Rice. Remember, quarterbacks are awarded only three points for each touchdown pass thrown (in most leagues), and since quite a few of them can throw 20 touchdowns in a season, a running back or wide receiver who scores more than 10 or 12 touchdowns is very valuable — and very rare. (Suggested picks: Jerry Rice, Emmitt Smith, Natrone Means or Steve Young.)

■ Round 2 — Again, try to draft a running back or wide receiver who can score 10 or more touchdowns in a season. Don't panic and take a quarterback yet, unless all the good ones are going quickly. (Suggested picks: Jerome Bettis, Thurman Thomas, Andre Rison or Cris Carter.)

■ Round 3 — This is when you draft the best three-point player, a quarterback, or the best six-point player that is still available.

■ Rounds 4–5 — If you already have a quarterback, running back and wide receiver, take another running back, because there is little depth in the NFL at that position (there are a lot of good ones but only a few very good ones). But consider drafting another wide receiver, tight end Eric Green or Ben Coates or a kicker like John Carney or Pete Stoyanovich.

■ Rounds 6–8 — You will want to have all seven of your starting positions filled by the end of the eighth round, which allows you to draft one strong backup player (who will still play a lot if a starter is playing poorly). You might want to take your backup quarterback here, but not too early, because you might use him only once or twice all season. Also try to get one of the top tight ends. It might also be time to draft your first kicker.

■ Rounds 9–12 — Draft your backups, but try to get players who can step into your lineup if a starter is injured or playing poorly. Take the best available players, keeping in mind that you don't want to take too many from the same division (because of the byes). Draft seriously in the late rounds, because these players often are the determining factor between winning and losing. Also consider taking a rookie as your fourth running back or wide receiver in these rounds, because he may develop into an integral player on your team by the end of the season. Draft a defense in one of the final two rounds. The last round is also when you will want to gamble on a pick.

Rounds 6–10 are the most important of your draft. They are the ones that separate the contenders from the pretenders. Since most people will draft approximately the same in the early rounds, this is where you will pick up the players who will mean the difference between winning and losing. Pick some up-and-coming stars here, and, if they come through, so will your team.

Basic Scoring Method — This scoring system is the hardest to draft for, because luck more than skill determines how well your team will do.
■ Draft players solely on ability to score points.
■ Draft high-scoring running backs and wide receivers first.
■ Do not draft quarterbacks first.
■ Unless you have a chance for Ben Coates, Shannon Sharpe or Eric Green, don't draft a tight end until the second half of the draft.
■ Fill all of your starting positions by the end of Round 8.

Performance Scoring Method — This is the easiest scoring method to draft for, because it eliminates the luck factor more than the other methods — players are awarded points based purely on yards gained.
■ Draft players strictly on their potential for gaining yards.
■ Since quarterbacks pass for 300 yards more often than running backs or wide receivers accumulate 150 yards, go for a quarterback first.
■ Draft running backs and wide receivers in Rounds 2–5. Remember to take into consideration a running back's ability to gain yards receiving.
■ Draft your second quarterback no later than the end of Round 8 (and

earlier if there's a good one on the board).

■ Draft tight ends who gain yards rather than those who catch short touchdown passes at the goal line.

■ Fill all of your starting positions by the end of Round 8.

Distance Scoring Method — This method is a combination of the two above, since players are awarded points for scoring plays and the length of them. In other words, the longer the touchdown (or field goal), the more points awarded.

■ Focus on players who have big-play, long-distance abilities.

■ In the first round, draft either a running back or Jerry Rice. You want players who score from a long way out, rather than those players who see the ball mainly near the goal line (like Andre Rison or William Floyd).

■ In the second round, take your first wide receiver or one of the very top quarterbacks.

■ Wait until the third round before drafting a quarterback, and try to get one who throws to big-play receivers.

■ In the fourth round, draft the best available running back or receiver or one of the top three tight ends.

■ Go for a kicker in Round 5, one who has a strong leg and plays for a team that will give him a lot of opportunities for field goals (although a 1994 rule change will mean fewer 50-yard-plus field goals this year).

■ Fill all of your starting positions by the end of Round 8.

Combined Scoring Method — This method — which is the most used — combines many of the features of the above three systems, rewarding players who can score, score from long distances and pick up a lot of yardage.

■ In the first round, draft either a running back, a wide receiver or one of the two best quarterbacks.

■ In the second round, draft whichever of the two positions you didn't get in the first round or one of the top five quarterbacks.

■ By the third round, you should have a quarterback, running back and wide receiver.

■ Draft one of the top three tight ends by the end of the fifth round, and have your second running back and wide receiver by the end of the sixth round.

■ Don't draft a kicker too quickly, as there are at least a dozen every year who score 100 points. You will be better off stockpiling running backs and wide receivers.

Chapter 3
QUARTERBACKS

STEVE YOUNG

Not too many years ago, quarterback was the most consistent position with respect to production, but it isn't anymore. With the advent of free agency, quarterbacks now change teams at a pace never seen before in the history of the NFL. And that means it gets more difficult every year to predict performances of the NFL's passers.

In 1994, NFL teams made nearly 40 quarterback changes. In fact, only half a dozen teams retained the same starting and backup quarterbacks that they ended the season with in '93. This year, there won't be as many changes, because nearly every team had its starting quarterback set early

QUARTERBACKS 57

in the offseason. The few unsettled situations were in Arizona, Carolina, Chicago, Houston and Tampa Bay.

Another factor that causes big swings in quarterbacks' statistics every year is injuries. In most seasons, in fact, the most important quarterbacks are those who don't get injured — and the number seems to be decreasing every year. In 1990, 14 of the starting quarterbacks lasted the entire season. In 1991, 11 started every game; in '92 only eight did and in 1993 the number was down to seven. Last season again only seven quarterbacks started all 16 games — Jeff George, Brett Favre, Jeff Hostetler, Dan Marino, Drew Bledsoe, Jim Everett and Steve Young. It is very important to have a quality backup in fantasy football, because the chances are very good that your No. 1 man isn't going to start in every game.

Still, you shouldn't worry too much about getting a good quarterback, because there are at least 10 or 12 of them capable of putting up strong numbers. And that means, unless you blow your draft, you'll get one of them. After them, there is another group of six to eight quarterbacks also capable of good numbers. The talent pool is deep at quarterback, and, in an eight- or 10-team league, every team should get a good quarterback as well as a decent backup.

The most important rule in drafting a quarterback is to get a player who scores — either throwing the ball or running it in himself. Forget about completion percentage and other miscellaneous statistics that mean nothing in fantasy football.

Draft Tips for Choosing a Quarterback

■ Look at past performances, especially the last two or three seasons.

■ Look for quarterbacks who play for passing teams. They'll throw the most touchdown passes (especially near the goal line). The key is to get a quarterback who will throw 20 or more touchdown passes a season. And he doesn't necessarily have to play for a winning team.

■ Don't forget to consider a quarterback's running abilities. Steve Young and John Elway score several touchdowns themselves each season, and a few others, such as Randall Cunningham and Jeff Hostetler, also do pretty well. Since a touchdown is worth six points in the Basic Scoring Method, these quarterbacks are very important. Rushing yards are also very important in the Performance Scoring Method.

■ Do not draft a quarterback from a team where the situation is unsettled. Be sure that the first one you draft is going to start (and is healthy, too). If you are going to gamble, do it with your second quarterback.

■ If your league uses a scoring method that rewards yardage or distance, try to get a quarterback who has a big-play receiver on his team, such as Steve Young with Jerry Rice, John Elway with Anthony Miller and Scott Mitchell with Herman Moore.

■ Don't worry about drafting a quarterback from a losing team (if he's a good one). If his team lacks a running game, chances are he will throw a good percentage of touchdown passes, and that's what counts.

■ Make sure you have a quality backup who can take over if your starting quarterback is injured (or when your starter is out with a bye).

■ Don't pick a rookie quarterback unless you know he is going to see a lot of playing time.

■ Watch what is going on during training camp. Is Troy Aikman ever going to repeat his 1992 season, when he threw 23 touchdown passes? Can Scott Mitchell bounce back from an absolutely awful 1994 season? Will John Elway produce big numbers with the great receiving corps he has? Can Jeff Blake do it for 16 games? Does Warren Moon have another year or two left in him? Can Chris Miller ever stay healthy? If Drew Bledsoe cuts down on his interceptions in 1995 as Brett Favre did in '94, will Bledsoe throw 35 TD passes? Can Jim Everett repeat his fine 1994 season, when he tossed 22 TDs? Will Vinny Testaverde ever put it together? Is Stan Humphries really a Super Bowl quarterback? Can Jeff George do it again? Is Jim Kelly the most underrated quarterback in fantasy football? Will Rick Mirer progress this year under new coach Dennis Erickson? Who will start in Tampa Bay, Craig Erickson or Trent Dilfer? Can Steve Beuerlein bounce back? Can Dave Brown keep improving?

SUPERSTARS

STEVE YOUNG / 49ERS

Year	Att.	Cmp.	Pct.	Yds.	TDs	Int.	TD-R
1990	62	38	61.3	427	2	0	0
1991	279	180	64.5	2517	17	8	4
1992	402	268	66.7	3465	25	7	4
1993	462	314	68.0	4023	29	16	2
1994	461	324	70.3	3969	35	10	7

Comments: The best quarterback in the NFL, Young did everything last season in leading the 49ers to the Super Bowl championship. He led the NFL with a record 112.8 passer rating — the fourth straight year he has paced the league — and he had an NFL-high 35 touchdown passes and only 10 interceptions. He had more than 3,000 yards rushing for the third straight season and even scored seven touchdowns running himself. He had five 300-yard games and 10 multiple-TD outings. In fact, no quarterback in the NFL came close to Young's stats. He also threw nine TD passes and scored two more in the three postseason games. In 1993, he completed 68 percent of his passes for a club-record 4,023 yards and 29 TD passes, tops in the league. In '92, Young also led the league with 25 touchdown passes, and he had just seven interceptions. He also ran for four scores and was second on the team in rushing and second among NFL quarterbacks with a league-high 8.62 yards per rush. In 1991, Young missed six games and the 49ers missed the playoffs. He threw touchdown passes in all but one of his starts that year. Not only is Young the best, but he hasn't missed a game in the last three years.

The skinny: With 89 touchdown passes and 13 TDs himself the last three seasons, Young has 49ers fans asking, "Joe who?"

DAN MARINO / DOLPHINS

Year	Att.	Cmp.	Pct.	Yds.	TDs	Int.	TD-R
1990	531	306	57.6	3563	21	11	0
1991	549	318	57.9	3970	25	13	1
1992	554	330	59.6	4116	24	16	0
1993	150	91	60.7	1218	8	3	1
1994	615	385	62.6	4453	30	17	1

Comments: For consistency, you cannot go wrong with Marino, who is going to break every one of the NFL's career passing records in 1995. With the exception of the 1993 season, when he played in only five games because of injury, Marino has never thrown for fewer than 20 touchdowns in a season. Last year, he had a fine comeback season, leading the AFC in passing and throwing the third-most TD passes of any season in his career. He also threw his second-most attempts in a season, most completions and the third-most yards. He threw for TDs in all but the final two games, with nine multiple-TD games, three 300-yard games and two 400-yarders. Other than the 11 missed games in '93, he hasn't missed one since 1984. Going into 1995, Marino ranks second all-time in attempts, completions, yards and touchdowns. He has 10 3,000-yard passing seasons, the NFL record. The ultimate franchise quarterback, Marino has thrown at least one touchdown pass in 150 of the 172 regular-season games in which he has played. He has thrown three or more touchdowns in 53 games and four or more 19 times.

The skinny: Marino is definitely the No. 2 quarterback in fantasy football.

CAN'T MISS

DREW BLEDSOE / PATRIOTS

Year	Att.	Cmp.	Pct.	Yds.	TDs	Int.	TD-R
1993	429	214	49.9	2494	15	15	0
1994	691	400	57.9	4555	25	27	0

Comments: No quarterback in NFL history ever threw as many passes as Bledsoe did last year. While he threw too many interceptions, his 25 touchdowns ranked fourth in the league. He was one of only seven quarterbacks to start every game (the first Patriot to do so in 15 years), and he had six 300-yard games (two over 400) and TD passes in 13 games. His passing yardage and completions also led the NFL. However, he threw only one TD pass of more than 40 yards, so he is not yet a long-ball passer. In two seasons, Bledsoe has already passed for 7,049 yards and 40 TDs, a pace not too far off Dan Marino's. The first pick in the 1993 draft, Bledsoe had a slow rookie start, then got hot over the last four games. All he needs now is a better group of receivers, and he will probably throw close to 40 TD passes.

The skinny: Bledsoe is truly a franchise quarterback in both the NFL and fantasy football.

BRETT FAVRE / PACKERS

Year	Att.	Cmp.	Pct.	Yds.	TDs	Int.	TD-R
1991	5	0	0.0	0	0	2	0
1992	471	302	64.1	3227	18	13	1
1993	522	318	60.9	3303	19	24	1
1994	582	363	62.4	3882	33	14	2

Comments: Favre had a breakthrough season in 1994, cutting down on his interceptions and finishing second in the league in touchdown passes with a team-record 33. He was the second-highest-rated passer in the NFL and third in yards. He threw TD passes in all but one game, with two or more in 10 games, including the last eight straight. In fact, over the second half of the year, he threw 23 TDs, tops in the league. He had four 300-yard games. And he's durable, too, with a string of 45 consecutive starts, second longest in the NFL. In Packers history, he already ranks fourth in touchdown passes and fifth in yards. In 1993, Favre led the league in interceptions, though his 19 TD passes were fifth in the league and his 3,303 yards were sixth. In his first season as a starter in 1992, Favre became the youngest quarterback ever to play in a Pro Bowl, when he ranked sixth in pass rating and eighth in yardage.

The skinny: Favre is one of the top fantasy quarterbacks this year, but can he repeat 1994?

JOHN ELWAY / BRONCOS

Year	Att.	Cmp.	Pct.	Yds.	TDs	Int.	TD-R
1990	502	294	58.6	3526	15	14	3
1991	451	242	53.7	3253	13	12	6
1992	316	174	55.1	2242	10	17	2
1993	551	348	63.2	4030	25	10	0
1994	494	307	62.1	3490	16	10	4

Comments: Once again in 1994, Elway posted decent but not great statistics in fantasy football. In 1993, he was the second-best quarterback in the NFL after Steve Young. Last year, even though he was the NFL's fourth-ranked passing leader, he threw only 16 touchdown passes. He had four 300-yard games and five multiple-touchdown games, and ran for four TDs. He missed two of the last three games with a strained left knee. The 1993 season was the one in which he finally had the kind of which he is capable. He ranked first in the AFC in all six important statistical categories — passer rating, attempts, completions, completion percentage, touchdowns and yards. Four of those numbers were team records. Elway has thrown for over 3,000 yards in nine seasons (he and Dan Marino are the only quarterbacks ever with more than seven). Elway is a great runner, ranking fifth all-time among quarterbacks in yards rushing (2,670), and he has scored 26 touchdowns himself. In fact, in 12 NFL seasons, Elway has accounted for 225 touchdowns, an average of almost 19 a year.

The skinny: With such a great corps of receivers, Elway is capable of having another huge year.

WARREN MOON / VIKINGS

Year	Att.	Cmp.	Pct.	Yds.	TDs	Int.	TD-R
1990	584	362	62.0	4689	33	13	2
1991	655	404	61.7	4690	23	21	2
1992	346	224	64.7	2521	18	12	1
1993	520	303	58.3	3485	21	21	1
1994	601	371	61.7	4264	18	19	0

Comments: Moon wasn't exactly the savior in Minnesota last season, when the Vikings were knocked out of the playoffs in the first round. He threw more interceptions than touchdowns for the first time in nine years and ranked only seventh in the NFC in passing. However, he did finish ninth in TD passes and third in yards (with his third career 4,000-yard season). He set Vikings records for attempts and completions, and he had six 300-yard games. In 1993, his final year in Houston, Moon lost and regained his starting job in a year in which he ranked third in passing yards and fourth in TDs. The owner of virtually all of the Oilers' passing records, Moon is the NFL's sixth all-time passing-yardage leader and 12th in TD passes. In 1992, he ranked fourth in the AFC in passing, fifth in yards, fifth in completions, sixth in attempts, third in TD passes and first in TD passes per attempt — despite missing five games with an injury. In '91, Moon set NFL single-season records for completions (404) and attempts (655) and ranked first with 4,690 passing yards, the fifth-highest total ever.

The skinny: Moon has thrown the most interceptions in the NFL the last two years, but he also has 38 TDs in that time, sixth most.

JIM KELLY / BILLS

Year	Att.	Cmp.	Pct.	Yds.	TDs	Int.	TD-R
1990	346	219	63.3	2829	24	9	0
1991	474	304	64.1	3844	33	17	1
1992	462	269	58.2	3457	23	19	1
1993	470	288	61.3	3382	18	18	0
1994	448	285	63.6	3114	22	17	1

Comments: Kelly missed time with injuries last season, but he still is remarkably consistent, with an average of 24 touchdown passes the last six seasons. He has thrown for more than 3,000 yards six of the last seven seasons, with a high completion percentage. He missed the final two games with a left knee injury, but his TDs-to-attempts ratio is extremely high. He had two games with four TD passes last season, though only two 300-yard games, and he ranked third in the AFC in passing. The 18th player with 200 career touchdown passes, Kelly has started 46 of the Bills' last 48 regular-season games, so he is pretty durable. In 1993, some people said he was slipping, but his statistics said otherwise. In 1992, Kelly tied for third in TD passes. He was the top-rated passer in the AFC in 1990 and in the NFL in '91. His 33 TD passes in 1991 led the league. He holds nearly all of Buffalo's single-season and career passing records. His career completion percentage is third all-time.

The skinny: Kelly may be the most underrated quarterback in fantasy football.

RANDALL CUNNINGHAM / EAGLES

Year	Att.	Cmp.	Pct.	Yds.	TDs	Int.	TD-R
1990	465	271	58.3	3466	30	13	5
1991	4	1	25.0	19	0	0	0
1992	384	233	60.7	2775	19	11	5
1993	110	76	69.1	850	5	5	1
1994	490	265	54.1	3229	16	13	3

Comments: The Eagles' starting quarterback since 1987, Cunningham was replaced for the final two games of last season by Bubby Brister (who's now with the Jets), and his future is anything but secure. He threw 14 touchdown passes in the first nine games, then only two the rest of the year as he and the team slumped horribly. He did have four 300-yard games and his first 3,000-yard season since 1990, but he ranked only ninth in the conference in passing. Cunningham missed nearly all of the 1993 season after suffering a broken leg in the fourth game. That year he completed a fantastic 69.1 percent of his passes, and he threw five TD passes in his first three games. In 1992, he was the NFL's fifth-ranked passer, and he was the Eagles' third-leading rusher with 549 yards (tops among NFL quarterbacks), with five touchdowns. Cunningham missed all but one quarter of the 1991 season after suffering torn ligaments in his left knee. He is probably the most dangerous quarterback in the NFL because of his passing and running skills.

The skinny: Cunningham needs to bounce back with a stellar season.

TROY AIKMAN / COWBOYS

Year	Att.	Cmp.	Pct.	Yds.	TDs	Int.	TD-R
1990	399	226	56.6	2579	11	18	1
1991	363	237	65.3	2754	11	10	1
1992	473	302	63.8	3445	23	14	1
1993	392	271	69.1	3100	15	6	0
1994	361	233	64.5	2676	13	12	1

Comments: Aikman is one of the best quarterbacks in the NFL, but not in fantasy football, because he doesn't throw very many touchdown passes. Aikman did throw a TD pass in 16 straight games from 1993 until midway through '94, but rarely did he have more than one. In fact, Aikman hasn't thrown more than two TD passes in a game in three seasons — and that was with Michael Irvin, Alvin Harper and Jay Novacek as his receivers. Over the second half of last season, when he missed two games and struggled with a sprained knee, he threw only two TDs. One of the most accurate passers in NFL history, Aikman was the fourth-ranked passer in the NFC in 1994, but he ranked only eighth in yards and ninth in TD passes. In 1993, he led the NFL in passing and completion percentage and was second in interception percentage (only six all season), but he was just 10th in passing yards and 10th in touchdowns. And he had an incredible 69.1 completion percentage. Aikman had his best season in 1992, when he threw 23 touchdown passes, more than in the two previous seasons combined.

The skinny: Aikman is a great quarterback who's not as great in fantasy football.

SOLID PICKS

JIM EVERETT / SAINTS

Year	Att.	Cmp.	Pct.	Yds.	TDs	Int.	TD-R
1990	554	307	55.4	3989	23	17	1
1991	490	277	56.5	3438	11	20	0
1992	475	281	59.2	3323	22	18	0
1993	274	135	49.3	1652	8	12	0
1994	540	346	64.1	3855	22	18	0

Comments: Everett had a fantastic comeback season in 1994, when he set Saints single-season records for attempts, completions and yards, and he was just one TD pass shy of the team record. He ranked third in the NFC in passing and third in yards and TDs. He was one of only seven NFL quarterbacks to start all 16 games, and he threw at least one touchdown pass in 13 of them, with eight multiple-TD games. Everett was so bad in 1993 that the Rams, for whom he played the first eight years of his career, practically gave him away to New Orleans. In nine 1993 starts, he threw only eight touchdown passes, the fewest of his career. His streak of five consecutive 3,000-yard seasons, the fourth-longest streak in NFL history, was ended. Everett had a pretty good season in 1992, when he passed for 22 TDs, and his pass rating was his highest since 1989. He was pretty bad in 1991, throwing fewer than half the number of touchdown passes he had the previous three seasons. Everett led the NFL in TD passes in 1988 and '89.

The skinny: Everett looks as if he is back to where he was before.

JEFF HOSTETLER / RAIDERS

Year	Att.	Cmp.	Pct.	Yds.	TDs	Int.	TD-R
1990	87	47	54.0	614	3	1	2
1991	285	179	62.8	2032	5	4	2
1992	192	103	53.6	1225	8	3	3
1993	419	236	56.2	3242	14	10	5
1994	454	263	57.9	3334	20	16	2

Comments: Hostetler has had two very good seasons in a row for the Raiders, with 34 touchdown passes and seven TDs rushing. However, he struggled most of 1994 with too many costly interceptions and an inability to hit the deep passes, though he did lead the AFC in average yards per attempt. He had career highs in attempts, completions, yards (the second most in team history), TDs and interceptions. He had five multiple-TD games and three 300-yarders while starting all 16 games. In his first full season as a starter in 1993, Hostetler adapted well to his speed receivers and led all NFL quarterbacks with five rushing touchdowns (he has run for 16 TDs in limited action over the last six seasons). Hostetler was the success story of the NFL in 1990, going from backup to the winning quarterback in the Super Bowl for the Giants, though he didn't do much in '91 or '92.

The skinny: Hostetler's running TDs make him a pretty high fantasy draft choice.

JEFF GEORGE / FALCONS

Year	Att.	Cmp.	Pct.	Yds.	TDs	Int.	TD-R
1990	334	181	54.2	2152	16	13	1
1991	485	292	60.2	2910	10	12	0
1992	306	167	54.6	1963	7	15	1
1993	407	234	57.5	2526	8	6	0
1994	524	322	61.5	3734	23	18	0

Comments: In his first season with the Falcons, George had the best season of his career in 1994. He was the NFC's fifth-leading passer, with career highs in attempts, completions, completion percentage, yards and touchdowns. In fact, he finally reached his potential and can be considered one of the best quarterbacks in fantasy football. The only thing that separates him from the best NFL quarterbacks is consistency. He even had a streak of 279 attempts without an interception, the third longest in NFL history. George started all 16 games, six in which he had two or more TD passes, including four against Denver. With Indianapolis in '93, George started the final 11 games after holding out. Statistically, he set his second-highest season totals for attempts, completions and yards, but the Colts went 2–9 with him as a starter. In 1992, he had his worst season, missing six games with injuries and failing to throw a TD pass in six of 10 starts.

The skinny: By George, he turned into a good quarterback!

BEST OF THE REST

BOOMER ESIASON / JETS

Year	Att.	Cmp.	Pct.	Yds.	TDs	Int.	TD-R
1990	402	224	55.7	2931	24	22	0
1991	413	233	56.4	2883	13	16	0
1992	278	144	51.8	1407	11	15	0
1993	473	288	60.9	3421	16	11	1
1994	440	255	58.0	2782	17	13	0

Comments: Esiason started 14 games in 1994, though his better days seem to be behind him. In the final four games, he passed for only 484 yards and one touchdown. However, in the game before those four, he had his best passing game in five years, 382 yards. Esiason's season totals were fairly good for a backup fantasy quarterback, as he was fifth in the AFC in TD passes. In 1993, he nearly led the Jets to the playoffs, throwing for 3,421 yards (fourth in the NFL) and 16 touchdowns. He set career highs in attempts (473), completions (288) and completion percentage (60.9), and his 11 interceptions tied a career low. He is the 16th quarterback in the NFL with 200 TD passes and the 17th with 30,000 passing yards. Esiason has thrown for more than 3,000 yards seven times. In his final season with the Bengals in 1992, Esiason had his worst year ever, throwing for the fewest yards and touchdowns since he was a rookie in 1984. He has thrown more than 20 TD passes five times, but not since 1990. He led the AFC in passing in 1988 and '89.

The skinny: The greatest left-handed passer in NFL history, Esiason might still be able to put together another fine season.

VINNY TESTAVERDE / BROWNS

Year	Att.	Cmp.	Pct.	Yds.	TDs	Int.	TD-R
1990	365	203	55.6	2818	17	18	1
1991	326	166	50.9	1994	8	15	0
1992	358	206	57.5	2554	14	16	2
1993	230	130	56.5	1797	14	9	0
1994	377	207	54.9	2575	16	18	2

Comments: Testaverde might have led the Browns to their best season in years, but he is still an inconsistent quarterback who looks as if he will never reach his great potential. Last year he once again threw more interceptions than touchdowns (for the seventh time in eight pro seasons). He ranked only 11th in the AFC in passing. He did throw touchdown passes in 11 of the 14 games in which he played (he missed two starts with a concussion), but more than one only four times. He had no 300-yard games. In 1993, playing for Cleveland after six lousy seasons in Tampa Bay, Testaverde replaced Bernie Kosar as the Browns' starter and finished third in the AFC in passing. That's his only season with more TDs than interceptions. The owner of most of Tampa Bay's career passing marks, the 1986 Heisman Trophy winner threw an NFL-record 35 interceptions in 1988.

The skinny: Though inconsistent, Testaverde does throw a decent number of touchdown passes.

STAN HUMPHRIES / CHARGERS

Year	Att.	Cmp.	Pct.	Yds.	TDs	Int.	TD-R
1990	156	91	58.3	1015	3	10	2
1991	None						
1992	454	263	57.9	3356	16	18	4
1993	324	173	53.4	1981	12	10	0
1994	453	264	58.3	3209	17	12	0

Comments: Humphries may not have the statistics of most Super Bowl quarterbacks, but he sure does have the winning record of one (27–12 as a Charger). He had his best season in 1994, with career highs in completions, completion percentage and touchdowns. He was the AFC's fifth-ranked passer. He started 15 games last year, with two 300-yard games. Six of his TD passes were more than 40 yards. Only a midseason slump by the entire team hurt his stats. Humphries has sandwiched very good years around a mediocre one in 1993, when he was bothered by a shoulder injury. In '93, he threw only 12 touchdown passes, though he did come on late in the year. In 1992, Humphries led the Chargers to 11 victories in the last 12 games and a playoff berth. That year he ranked dead last in the NFL in passing after four weeks with eight interceptions and only one TD pass before he got hot. His 3,356 yards (third in the AFC and fifth in the NFL) were the most by a Chargers quarterback since 1985.

The skinny: Humphries is a pretty good fantasy backup.

CRAIG ERICKSON / COLTS

Year	Att.	Cmp.	Pct.	Yds.	TDs	Int.	TD-R
1992	26	15	57.7	121	0	0	0
1993	457	233	51.0	3054	18	21	0
1994	399	225	56.4	2919	16	10	1

Comments: Erickson was traded to Indianapolis in April, and he will be the Colts' starter over Jim Harbaugh. He started 15 games last season in Tampa Bay, finishing sixth in the NFC in passing with the second-best mark in Buccaneers history. He was the first Buc passer since 1987 to finish with more touchdowns than interceptions, and his average gain per pass attempt of 7.32 yards was fourth best in the NFL. Erickson came on the final seven games of the year, averaging 231 yards per game. In 1993, he took over for Steve DeBerg midway through the season opener and became the first Bucs passer other than Vinny Testaverde to win a game since 1987. His 18 touchdown passes were topped by only five other NFL quarterbacks. He threw for 3,054 yards, the most by a Tampa Bay passer since 1989, with touchdowns in 10 games. After sitting out the 1991 season with an injury suffered in college, Erickson played in six games in '92.

The skinny: With a good corps of receivers and a star runner, Erickson might have a banner season.

NEIL O'DONNELL / STEELERS

Year	Att.	Cmp.	Pct.	Yds.	TDs	Int.	TD-R
1990	DNP						
1991	286	156	54.5	1963	11	7	1
1992	313	185	59.1	2283	13	9	1
1993	486	270	55.6	3208	14	7	0
1994	370	212	57.3	2443	13	9	1

Comments: With an average of only 12 TD passes a season, O'Donnell will never be a top fantasy quarterback, but he is a statistically good one, especially since he throws few interceptions. In 1994, he ranked seventh in the AFC in passing, but his TD total ranked just 10th. He had only three games with more than 200 yards passing. He did show, however, in last year's AFC championship game, that he can put the ball in the air (54 attempts and 349 yards). O'Donnell ranked eighth in the AFC in passing in 1993, with career highs for attempts, completions, yards and touchdowns. The first two stats broke Terry Bradshaw's team records, and the yardage was third highest. He was the AFC's third-ranked passer in 1992. O'Donnell took over the starting job the second half of '91 when he replaced Bubby Brister. He ranked seventh in the AFC in passing that year.

The skinny: The Steelers win with O'Donnell, but his statistics will never make him a very good fantasy quarterback.

STEVE BONO / CHIEFS

Year	Att.	Cmp.	Pct.	Yds.	TDs	Int.	TD-R
1990	DNP						
1991	237	141	59.5	1617	11	4	0
1992	56	36	64.3	463	2	2	0
1993	61	39	63.9	416	0	1	1
1994	117	66	56.4	796	4	4	0

Comments: Now that Joe Montana has retired, Bono is the Chiefs' starting quarterback. He started two games in 1994 and played in five others. He had 300-plus yards passing in the two starts, with three TDs. Now 33 years old, Bono is 7–4 as an NFL starter, which means he is pretty much inexperienced (only 596 career pass attempts), but the Chiefs say they are comfortable with him as the No. 1 quarterback. Bono played in eight games for the 49ers in 1993 with good results. He was a disappointment for the first six years of his career, but in 1991 he looked very impressive in six starts for San Francisco. He threw back-to-back 300-yard games and passed for three touchdowns in three straight games that year. He also placed fourth in the NFL passing race.

The skinny: This is the year to finally find out if Bono is any good.

STEVE BEUERLEIN / JAGUARS

Year	Att.	Cmp.	Pct.	Yds.	TDs	Int.	TD-R
1990	DNP						
1991	137	68	49.6	909	5	2	0
1992	18	12	66.7	152	0	1	0
1993	418	258	61.7	3164	18	17	0
1994	255	130	51.0	1545	5	9	1

Comments: Beuerlein was the first player selected in the expansion draft and will start for Jacksonville, where he gets a fresh start — and gets away from Buddy Ryan. Last year, Beuerlein started the first two games for Arizona, then was benched for three games, then regained the starting job for five games, then was sidelined for the rest of the season. He was the second-worst-ranked passer in the NFC, with never more than one TD pass in a game. However, in 1993, his first full season as an NFL starter, he set career highs for attempts, completions, yards passing, touchdown passes, interceptions, completion percentage and passer rating. He threw three TD passes in three games. With Dallas in 1992, Beuerlein didn't play much, as Troy Aikman led Dallas to the Super Bowl. But in 1991, the year the Cowboys obtained him from the Raiders, he paid big dividends by taking over when Aikman was injured and leading them to the playoffs.

The skinny: With a good corps of receivers, don't be surprised if Beuerlein has a good season.

RICK MIRER / SEAHAWKS

Year	Att.	Cmp.	Pct.	Yds.	TDs	Int.	TD-R
1993	486	274	56.4	2833	12	17	3
1994	381	195	51.2	2151	11	7	0

Comments: Mirer didn't seem to progress very much in 1994, especially in relation to Drew Bledsoe, to whom he is often compared. Mirer did cut down on his interceptions, with an NFL low for full-time starters of only seven. Mirer has ended both of his NFL seasons with injuries, including a broken thumb in '94 that caused him to miss the final three games. In 1994, he threw touchdown passes in only seven games, more than one only three times, and he had just two games with more than 200 yards passing. Mirer was a big surprise in 1993, rewriting the record books for rookie quarterbacks. He set new marks for attempts, completions and yards, while starting all 16 games. He became the first rookie quarterback since 1973 to start all of his team's games. The downside of Mirer's rookie season was that he threw 17 interceptions against only 12 touchdowns. He has rushed for 496 yards and three touchdowns in two seasons.

The skinny: With Dennis Erickson as his head coach, Mirer will improve quickly.

FRANK REICH / PANTHERS

Year	Att.	Cmp.	Pct.	Yds.	TDs	Int.	TD-R
1990	63	36	57.1	469	2	0	0
1991	41	27	65.9	305	6	2	0
1992	47	24	51.1	221	0	2	0
1993	26	16	61.5	153	2	0	0
1994	93	56	60.2	568	1	4	0

Comments: Reich was signed as a free agent by Carolina on March 27 and will be the Panthers' starter. One of the best backup quarterbacks in the NFL, he usually did a fine job for Buffalo when replacing Jim Kelly over the last few seasons, and anybody who remembers how he led the Bills back from a 32-point deficit to beat Houston in the 1992 playoffs knows it. He has a 6–4 record as a starter (and 2–0 in the playoffs), but two losses came in the Bills' final two games of 1994 with the playoffs on the line. He played in all 16 games last season, throwing passes in five of them (he was the Bills' kick holder). His best season was 1991, when he threw six touchdown passes in only 41 attempts. He has 18 career TD passes and only 12 interceptions.

The skinny: For the first time, Reich gets a chance to show his stuff as a starter.

DAVE BROWN / GIANTS

Year	Att.	Cmp.	Pct.	Yds.	TDs	Int.	TD-R
1992	7	4	57.1	21	0	0	0
1993	0	0	0.0	0	0	0	0
1994	350	201	57.4	2536	12	16	2

Comments: Brown started 15 games for the Giants last season after replacing Phil Simms. He showed his inexperience early, then hit a midseason slump (with just one touchdown pass in seven games). But over the final six games of the year (including three final-minute victories), Brown showed tremendous improvement and solidified his position as the starter. He needs to get the ball into the end zone more and cut down on his interceptions, but he does well in a ball-control offense. His high game for the season was only 264 yards, and he had only three games with more than one TD pass. Brown played in only one game in 1993 (he was inactive in

13 others). He was drafted in the first round of the 1992 supplemental draft.
The skinny: Brown can make another big jump this year.

QUESTION MARKS

SCOTT MITCHELL / LIONS

Year	Att.	Cmp.	Pct.	Yds.	TDs	Int.	TD-R
1991	0	0	0.0	0	0	0	0
1992	8	2	25.0	32	0	1	0
1993	233	133	57.1	1773	12	8	0
1994	246	119	48.4	1456	10	11	1

Comments: One year ago, Mitchell was the biggest free-agent signing of the year. Within months, he was one of the biggest free-agent busts. He started nine games for Detroit, struggling mightily to prove himself but to no avail. He never passed for more than 246 yards in a game, and he seemed to throw either two TDs in a game or none, with too many interceptions. Coach Wayne Fontes was close to replacing Mitchell when the quarterback broke his right (non-throwing) wrist and was sidelined for the rest of the year. Mitchell got his first extended NFL action in 1993. He replaced an injured Dan Marino and completed 44-for-68 for 652 yards, six touchdowns and only one interception in October, with a 344-yard performance in just his second pro start. He then suffered a shoulder separation and missed four games. After returning, he looked only average in three starts, as Miami missed the playoffs.

The skinny: The jury is still out on the talented but inconsistent Mitchell.

CHRIS MILLER / RAMS

Year	Att.	Cmp.	Pct.	Yds.	TDs	Int.	TD-R
1990	388	222	57.2	2735	17	14	1
1991	413	220	53.3	3103	26	18	0
1992	253	152	60.1	1739	15	6	0
1993	66	32	48.5	345	1	3	0
1994	317	173	54.6	2104	16	14	0

Comments: The 1994 poster child for injured quarterbacks (two concussions, bruised ribs and a pinched nerve in his neck), Miller started only 10 games (playing in three others) but still managed to throw 16 touchdown passes, tied for sixth in the NFC. He threw passes in 10 games, but never more than two in a game. In 1993, he played in less than two full games because of an injured left knee. That same injury knocked him out for half of the '92 season. In '92, he was co-leading the NFL with 15 touchdown passes and only six interceptions before his injury. From 1989 to '92, Miller threw 26 more touchdowns than interceptions (74 to 48) and passed for over 11,000 yards. Over the last nine weeks of the '91 season, he threw 20 TDs and only six interceptions. That year he ranked third in the NFL in TD passes, behind Jim Kelly and Mark Rypien, the two Super Bowl quarterbacks. Miller played for new Rams head coach Rich Brooks in college at Oregon and will start this year as long as he can stay healthy.

The skinny: Miller has missed 28 games in the last two seasons. But, when healthy, he's one of the top fantasy quarterbacks.

CODY CARLSON / OILERS

Year	Att.	Cmp.	Pct.	Yds.	TDs	Int.	TD-R
1990	55	37	67.3	383	4	2	0
1991	12	7	58.3	114	1	0	0
1992	227	149	65.6	1710	9	11	1
1993	90	51	56.7	605	2	4	2
1994	132	59	44.7	727	1	4	0

Comments: Carlson blew it last year in his big chance as Houston's No. 1 quarterback. He started only five games because of at least five injuries (separated shoulder twice, broken nose and knee injuries). He completed fewer than 50 percent of his passes and threw just one touchdown pass. Though Carlson lacks durability, he does have very good ability. In seven NFL seasons prior to 1994, he started only 14 games and had a 10–4 record, usually looking pretty good. Carlson started the last six games of 1992 when Warren Moon was injured, completing nearly 66 percent of his passes (a team record), though he threw more interceptions than touchdowns. In 1990, he led the Oilers to a victory over Pittsburgh on 22-of-29 passing in the final game to clinch a playoff spot.

The skinny: Carlson was pretty bad in 1994, considering he was supposed to be a very capable replacement for Warren Moon. He'll get one more chance.

COULD COME ON

HEATH SHULER / REDSKINS

Year	Att.	Cmp.	Pct.	Yds.	TDs	Int.	TD-R
1994	265	120	45.3	1658	10	12	0

Comments: Shuler will be the starter for the Redskins this season, and steady improvement last December as a rookie showed that he will be a good quarterback in due time. However, he did struggle in three starts last October when he obviously was not ready for the pro game. In those three games, he completed only 36 percent of his passes and he threw seven interceptions, as the Redskins went 0–3. But he started the final five games, throwing six touchdown passes and averaging 229 yards in the last four contests. For the season, he ranked dead-last in the league in passing, but his December stint gives Redskins head coach Norv Turner a lot of hope for the future.

The skinny: Shuler might be ready to have a breakthrough season in 1995.

TRENT DILFER / BUCCANEERS

Year	Att.	Cmp.	Pct.	Yds.	TDs	Int.	TD-R
1994	82	38	46.3	433	1	6	0

Comments: The Buccaneers' No. 1 draft pick last season, Dilfer is the team's unquestioned starting quarterback, now that Craig Erickson is gone. He appeared in five games as a rookie in 1994, starting twice, but he produced only 19 points in three games of extended action and was banished to the bench. Dilfer completed fewer than 50 percent of his 82 passes, with six interceptions and only one touchdown. Of course, the two starts were against San Francisco and Chicago, two of the better defenses in the NFL.

The skinny: Dilfer has the tools and just needs the time. He'll get the time this season.

OTHERS

DAVE KRIEG / CARDINALS

Year	Att.	Cmp.	Pct.	Yds.	TDs	Int.	TD-R
1990	448	265	59.2	3194	15	20	0
1991	285	187	65.6	2080	11	12	0
1992	413	230	55.7	3115	15	12	2
1993	189	105	55.6	1238	7	3	0
1994	212	131	61.8	1629	14	3	0

Comments: Krieg had a great season in 1994, when he replaced Scott Mitchell and led Detroit to the playoffs. He played in the final eight games, with a great ratio of 14 TDs to only three interceptions. He didn't throw enough passes to qualify for the standings, but he would have ranked second behind Steve Young in passer ratings. Now the NFL's seventh all-time leading passer, the 36-year-old Krieg will get a chance to start for the Cardinals. He hasn't had a big year by fantasy standards since 1989, when he threw 21 TD passes for Seattle, but he would have surpassed that total last year if he had played 16 games. Krieg was Joe Montana's backup in Kansas City in 1993, following 12 years with the Seahawks. He ranks 11th on the career list for touchdown passes, 17th in attempts, 12th in completions and 15th in passing yards.

The skinny: A veteran who knows defenses, Krieg will do a good job if he doesn't have to carry the team.

ERIK KRAMER / BEARS

Year	Att.	Cmp.	Pct.	Yds.	TDs	Int.	TD-R
1990	Injured						
1991	265	136	51.3	1635	11	8	1
1992	106	58	54.7	771	4	8	0
1993	138	87	63.0	1002	8	3	0
1994	158	99	62.7	1129	8	8	0

Comments: Kramer had a great opportunity to quarterback the Bears last season, but he failed twice — because of a shoulder injury and then ineffectiveness. He started only five games, and the Bears lost four of them. However, Kramer did complete a high percentage of his passes (a team-record 62.7 percent) and he threw just one fewer TD pass than Steve Walsh, his replacement, who threw more than twice as many passes. Kramer had five TD passes in the first two games and the Bears' only 300-yard passing day of the season. Kramer led Detroit to division championships in 1991 and '93. In 1993, he started the last four games, going 3–1 with eight TDs and only two interceptions. In '91, he took over in Game 8 and led the Lions to five victories in their last five games (6–2 overall) and their first NFC Central title in eight years. He also led the team to an upset victory over Dallas in the divisional playoffs.

The skinny: Don't be surprised if Kramer wins the Bears' starting quarterback job in training camp, because he *is* better than Steve Walsh.

ROOKIES

See Chapter 12, Rookie Report.

1994 SURPRISE

JEFF BLAKE / BENGALS

Year	Att.	Cmp.	Pct.	Yds.	TDs	Int.	TD-R
1992	9	4	44.4	40	0	1	0
1993	DNP						
1994	306	156	51.0	2154	14	9	1

Comments: Blake was the biggest surprise at quarterback in 1994, going from an unknown third-stringer who had been cut by the Jets to Cincinnati's starter for the final nine games of the year. In his first start, he passed for the Bengals' most net yards in 16 games. A week later he passed for more yards (387) than any Cincinnati quarterback had in 68 games. And a week after that, he passed for 354 yards and four TDs. Blake was the AFC Offensive Player of the Month in November. Though he slowed down later in the season, his TDs-to-interceptions ratio was very good. Blake led Cincinnati to all three victories of the year, throwing at least one TD pass in eight of his nine games. He had thrown only 10 passes prior to 1994.

The skinny: Blake is a good quarterback in a fantasy league that uses a Distance Scoring System, because he throws a great deep pass.

BACKUPS

BOBBY HEBERT / FALCONS

Year	Att.	Cmp.	Pct.	Yds.	TDs	Int.	TD-R
1990	Holdout						
1991	248	149	60.1	1676	9	8	0
1992	422	249	59.0	3287	19	16	0
1993	430	263	61.2	2978	24	17	0
1994	103	52	50.5	610	2	6	0

Comments: Throwing 24 touchdown passes in 1993 wasn't enough for Hebert to continue as Atlanta's starter, as he backed up Jeff George in '94. He played in only eight games, with no starts, though he did see a lot of playing time. But Hebert threw too many interceptions and just two TD passes. In 1993, Hebert was third in the league with the most TD passes of his career after replacing an injured Chris Miller. Hebert finished fifth in the league in passing, seventh in yards and 10th in completions. He also had five games with three TD passes. With the Saints in 1992, Hebert set a career high in passing yards, ranked sixth in the NFL in touchdown passes and averaged over 200 passing yards per game. He was a contract holdout for the entire 1990 season.

The skinny: Despite having elbow trouble, Hebert can still be an effective starter.

BERNIE KOSAR / DOLPHINS

Year	Att.	Cmp.	Pct.	Yds.	TDs	Int.	TD-R
1990	423	230	54.4	2562	10	15	0
1991	494	307	62.1	3487	18	9	0
1992	155	103	66.5	1160	8	7	0
1993	201	115	60.5	1217	8	3	0
1994	12	7	58.3	80	1	1	0

Comments: Kosar didn't play much in 1994 while backing up ironman Dan Marino. He played in just two games and threw passes in only one of them. He has played relatively little since 1991, so he's not banged up. In 1993, Kosar was cut by the Browns and picked up two days later by

Dallas, where he played a key role and earned a Super Bowl ring. For the season he passed for 1,217 yards and threw eight touchdowns compared to only three interceptions. Kosar broke his right ankle twice in 1992 and started only seven games the entire season. He played well while he was in the lineup, with eight touchdown passes in only 155 attempts, a fine 5.2 percentage. When he plays a full season, Kosar averages 18 touchdown passes a year, a pretty good mark. In 1991, he threw 308 consecutive passes without an interception, a league record, and was the AFC's second-ranked passer.

The skinny: If Dan Marino were to get injured, Kosar would be a fine replacement.

BUBBY BRISTER / JETS

Year	Att.	Cmp.	Pct.	Yds.	TDs	Int.	TD-R
1990	387	223	57.6	2725	20	14	0
1991	190	103	54.2	1350	9	9	0
1992	116	63	54.3	719	2	5	0
1993	309	181	58.6	1905	14	5	0
1994	76	51	67.1	507	2	1	0

Comments: One of the best backup quarterbacks in the NFL, Brister replaced Randall Cunningham in the final two games of 1994 and had one 300-yard outing, though the Eagles lost both games. He signed with the Jets as a free agent and will back up Boomer Esiason this year. In 1993, Brister had the best season of his career when he started eight games after replacing an injured Cunningham in Philadelphia. An inconsistent passer who forced the long ball in seven seasons in Pittsburgh, Brister ranked seventh in the NFL in passing, setting an Eagles record for fewest interceptions in a season (five in 309 pass attempts). His 58.6 completion percentage was a career best. Brister lost his starting job to Neil O'Donnell in 1991.

The skinny: If Esiason were to struggle or get injured, Brister would do a decent job.

STEVE WALSH / BEARS

Year	Att.	Cmp.	Pct.	Yds.	TDs	Int.	TD-R
1990	336	179	53.3	2010	12	13	0
1991	255	141	55.3	1638	11	6	0
1992	DNP						
1993	38	20	52.6	271	2	3	0
1994	343	208	60.6	2078	10	8	1

Comments: Walsh was the Bears' savior last season, quarterbacking the team to a 9–4 record, including a big upset victory over Minnesota in the playoffs. He replaced Erik Kramer and played well — mostly by not making many mistakes. He set career highs for attempts, completions and passing yards. But he threw more than one touchdown pass only twice all season and had just two 200-yard games. A model quarterback for the Bears' short passing game, he will compete with Erik Kramer for the starting job during training camp, though most people think he will remain the backup. Walsh started the final game of 1993 for the Saints. He didn't play at all in '92, suiting up for only two games. Walsh started 11 games in 1990 after being acquired by the Saints from Dallas a month into the season, and led the team to a wild-card playoff berth.

The skinny: Walsh is the kind of quarterback a team can win with, but he cannot win by himself.

MARK RYPIEN / RAMS

Year	Att.	Cmp.	Pct.	Yds.	TDs	Int.	TD-R
1990	304	166	54.6	2070	16	11	0
1991	421	249	59.1	3564	28	11	1
1992	479	269	56.2	3282	13	17	2
1993	319	166	52.0	1514	4	10	3
1994	127	59	46.5	694	4	3	0

Comments: Rypien, who signed with St. Louis as a free agent in May, compiled a 2–1 record in the three games in which he subbed for Vinny Testaverde last season in Cleveland. However, Rypien wasn't really that good, as he threw only four touchdown passes and completed fewer than 50 percent of his passes. Rypien led Washington to a Super Bowl victory just over three years ago, but he seems to have lost it. In 1993, he started

10 games but ranked last in the NFL in passing, with only four touchdown passes (three of them in the season opener) and 10 interceptions. In 1992, Rypien held out, then suffered through a nightmarish season, declining to the NFC's lowest passer rating for all quarterbacks. He threw for a then career low in touchdowns and a career high in interceptions. In 1991, Rypien led the Redskins to a 17–2 record and the Super Bowl championship. He was second in the league in passing, and he led the NFC in touchdown passes (28, the second most in Redskins history) and passing yards (3,564).

The skinny: Rypien still has the potential to take over and play well if something were to happen to Chris Miller (and something most likely will).

RODNEY PEETE / EAGLES

Year	Att.	Cmp.	Pct.	Yds.	TDs	Int.	TD-R
1990	271	142	52.4	1974	13	8	6
1991	194	116	59.8	1339	5	9	2
1992	213	123	57.7	1702	9	9	0
1993	252	157	62.3	1670	6	14	1
1994	56	33	58.9	470	4	1	0

Comments: Peete signed with Philadelphia as a free agent and will back up Randall Cunningham. Last year, he replaced an injured Troy Aikman for part of one game, then sprained a thumb and missed a start before coming back to start one game. Playing for a team as good as the Cowboys certainly helped Peete's stats, as he threw more touchdown passes than interceptions for the first time since 1990. The Lions' No. 1 quarterback five straight years coming out of training camp, Peete never was able to hold down the starting job. In 1993, though healthy for a change, he threw 14 interceptions against only six touchdowns. In eight of his 10 starts, he failed to pass for even 200 yards. In 1992, he started 10 games but had a 2–8 record, and he averaged only 170 yards per start. In 1991, he started the first eight games before tearing his Achilles tendon. His best year was 1990, when he threw 13 TD passes and ran for six touchdowns.

The skinny: Peete couldn't stay healthy early in his career and couldn't play well enough when he did. But he is a pretty good backup quarterback.

ELVIS GRBAC / 49ERS

Year	Att.	Cmp.	Pct.	Yds.	TDs	Int.	TD-R
1993	DNP						
1994	50	35	70.0	393	2	1	0

Comments: Steve Young's backup, Grbac got his first NFL playing time last season, actually seeing quite a bit of mop-up duty during the year. He completed an impressive 70 percent of his passes. The 49ers' offense is so good that even their backup quarterbacks look good, and Grbac is no exception.

The skinny: The jury is still out on Grbac as a full-time replacement for Steve Young in the event Young went down with an injury. The 49ers hope they don't have to find out.

JAY SCHROEDER / CARDINALS

Year	Att.	Cmp.	Pct.	Yds.	TDs	Int.	TD-R
1990	334	182	54.5	2849	19	9	0
1991	357	189	52.9	2562	15	16	0
1992	253	123	48.6	1476	11	11	0
1993	159	78	49.1	832	5	2	0
1994	238	133	55.9	1510	4	7	0

Comments: After Buddy Ryan had given up on Steve Beuerlein and Jim McMahon in 1994, Schroeder was given the opportunity to start eight games, including the final six (winning five times). He threw only four TD passes all season, however, against seven interceptions, as he ranked 12th in the NFC in passing. In 1993, Schroeder started three games for Cincinnati while subbing for David Klingler. With the Raiders in 1992, Schroeder started nine games in another season in which he was unable to hold down the starting role. He led the team in passing but ranked only ninth in the AFC. In five seasons with the Raiders, he completed only 50 percent of his passes. In 1991, Schroeder started the first 15 games but then was benched in favor of Todd Marinovich for the last game and the playoffs. His best season was 1986, when he threw 22 TD passes for Washington.

The skinny: Schroeder has failed at too many starting opportunities during his career.

WADE WILSON / CUT BY SAINTS

Year	Att.	Cmp.	Pct.	Yds.	TDs	Int.	TD-R
1990	146	82	56.2	1155	9	8	0
1991	122	72	59.0	825	3	10	0
1992	163	111	68.1	1368	13	4	0
1993	388	221	57.0	2457	12	15	2
1994	28	20	71.4	172	0	0	0

Comments: Wilson has been cut by New Orleans the last two offseasons before being re-signed for less money. In 1994, he played in only four games, throwing his fewest passes since 1981. He did complete 71.4 percent of them. As the Saints' starter in 1993, Wilson started 14 games and finished 10th in the NFC in passing. He started the year off as one of the league's hottest passers, with seven TDs in the first five games. But he threw only five in the final 11 games and was replaced. In 1992, he was the hottest quarterback in the NFL over the last three games for Atlanta. He threw for over 1,000 yards and 10 TDs in that time, with a 300-yard game in every start. With the Vikings in '91, Wilson got off to a horrible start and lost his job after five games in which he had thrown 10 interceptions. He led the NFL in passing in 1988 while with Minnesota.

The skinny: Wilson is one of the best veteran backups in the NFL.

JIM HARBAUGH / COLTS

Year	Att.	Cmp.	Pct.	Yds.	TDs	Int.	TD-R
1990	312	180	57.7	2178	10	6	4
1991	478	275	57.5	3121	15	16	2
1992	358	202	56.4	2486	13	12	1
1993	325	200	61.5	2002	7	11	4
1994	202	125	61.9	1440	9	6	0

Comments: Harbaugh will finally be sent to the bench, now that Craig Erickson is on the Colts. Last year, Harbaugh was 4–5 as the team's starter, though he did set the Colts' single-season completion percentage record. He threw more than one TD pass in just three games and had a season high of only 206 yards passing. Harbaugh's rushing total of 223 yards was the most by a Colts quarterback since 1983. As the starting quarterback of the Bears in 1993, Harbaugh led the lowest-rated passing

QUARTERBACKS

offense in the NFL. Harbaugh is the all-time leader in Bears history in passing attempts and completions, but he has never thrown more than 15 TD passes in a season. He had his best season in 1991, when he set Bears records for attempts (478, second most in the NFC) and completions (275).

The skinny: Harbaugh is not even a good backup quarterback in the NFL.

CHRIS CHANDLER / OILERS

Year	Att.	Cmp.	Pct.	Yds.	TDs	Int.	TD-R
1990	83	42	50.6	464	1	6	1
1991	154	78	50.6	846	5	10	0
1992	413	245	59.3	2832	15	15	1
1993	103	52	50.5	471	3	2	0
1994	176	108	61.4	1352	7	2	1

Comments: Chandler was signed by the Oilers in March, though he will probably be a backup. In 1994, his only season with the Rams, Chandler started six games in place of Chris Miller and looked just average, though he had only two interceptions. He started two games for the Cardinals in 1993, though the team scored only 31 points in them. He held the starting job the final 14 games of '92, when he posted career highs in virtually every offensive category: pass attempts, completions, yards passing, completion percentage, touchdown passes and yards rushing. Chandler split the 1991 season in Tampa Bay and Phoenix. He was 0–6 as a starter in two years with the Buccaneers. He has a good arm but a big ego, which is why . . .

The skinny: . . . now with his fifth team, Chandler is a classic journeyman quarterback.

MIKE TOMCZAK / STEELERS

Year	Att.	Cmp.	Pct.	Yds.	TDs	Int.	TD-R
1990	104	39	37.5	521	3	5	2
1991	238	128	53.8	1490	11	9	1
1992	211	120	56.9	1693	7	7	0
1993	54	29	53.7	398	2	5	0
1994	93	54	58.1	804	4	0	0

Comments: Tomczak started two games in 1994, leading Pittsburgh to two victories. He threw for 343 yards in one start and two touchdowns in the other. He also passed for 248 yards and two touchdowns in the season finale after replacing Neil O'Donnell, the starter who was injured. A gambler, Tomczak played sparingly in 1993, his first season in Pittsburgh, throwing just 54 passes all season (two TDs and five interceptions). Tomczak started eight games in 1992, going 4–4 in Cleveland. In '91 he was 2–5 with Green Bay. He had a career-high 16 TDs in 1989 with Chicago.

The skinny: Tomczak has looked good in relief stints the last two seasons, but he isn't a quality starter, as he has proved many times in the past.

JOHN FRIESZ / SEAHAWKS

Year	Att.	Cmp.	Pct.	Yds.	TDs	Int.	TD-R
1990	22	11	50.0	98	1	1	0
1991	487	262	53.8	2896	12	15	0
1992	Injured						
1993	238	128	53.8	1402	6	4	0
1994	180	105	58.3	1266	10	9	0

Comments: Friesz was signed as a free agent in March and will back up Rick Mirer. In 1994 with Washington, he started the first four games of the season, then was replaced by rookies Heath Shuler and Gus Frerotte and saw very little action the rest of the season. However, he did have a good season, with eight touchdown passes in those four games, including four against the Saints. His problem was too many interceptions and having two high-priced rookies waiting to play. Friesz started six games for San Diego in '93, highlighted by a 152-pass streak without any interceptions. But he threw only six touchdowns in 238 passes, and the Chargers lost four of those six games. Friesz missed the entire 1992 season after suffering torn ligaments in his knee in the first preseason game. He started all 16 games for the Chargers in 1991, but he ranked last in passing in the conference.

The skinny: Friesz is a decent backup who throws too many interceptions as a starter.

HUGH MILLEN / BRONCOS

Year	Att.	Cmp.	Pct.	Yds.	TDs	Int.	TD-R
1990	63	34	54.0	427	1	0	0
1991	409	246	60.1	3073	9	18	1
1992	203	124	61.1	1203	8	10	0
1993	DNP						
1994	131	81	61.8	893	2	3	0

Comments: Millen started two games late last season in place of John Elway, completing 20 consecutive passes at one point, just two short of Joe Montana's NFL record. However, he threw only two touchdown passes in 131 attempts, a really bad figure considering the good corps of receivers on the Broncos. He did throw for a lot of yardage, picking up 242, 217 and 290 yards in the final three games. Millen was cut by New England in 1993 and picked up by Miami, though he did not play. He started the first five games of 1992 for New England, then suffered a shoulder separation and had only two more starts. He had his best season in 1991, when he passed for 3,073 yards.

The skinny: He could be fairly productive if pressed into service again in Denver.

BILLY JOE TOLLIVER / OILERS

Year	Att.	Cmp.	Pct.	Yds.	TDs	Int.	TD-R
1990	410	216	52.7	2574	16	16	0
1991	82	40	48.8	531	4	2	0
1992	131	73	55.7	787	5	5	0
1993	76	39	51.3	464	3	5	0
1994	240	121	50.4	1287	6	7	2

Comments: Tolliver was probably Houston's best quarterback last season, though his stats are hardly impressive. He started seven of the final nine games but generated very little offense. His best game produced only 226 yards and two touchdowns. Tolliver started two games for Atlanta in 1993, throwing three touchdown passes in one of them. He started five games in '92 but was benched in favor of Wade Wilson. At times, Tolliver wows you with his Sonny Jurgensen–type arm, but then he brings you down with an interception at a key time. Tolliver started for the Chargers in 1990 and part of '89 but lost his job there to John Friesz.

The skinny: If Tolliver is a starter, that means his team is not very good.

DAVID KLINGLER / BENGALS

Year	Att.	Cmp.	Pct.	Yds.	TDs	Int.	TD-R
1992	98	47	48.0	530	3	2	0
1993	343	190	55.4	1935	6	9	0
1994	231	131	56.7	1327	6	9	0

Comments: Klingler started the first seven games of 1994, then suffered a sprained knee and lost his starting job to Jeff Blake, probably for good. He saw action in only three games the rest of the season. Klingler did have career highs in attempts, completions and passing yards in the opener vs. Cleveland, and then came back with 266 yards and two TDs in Game 3. But in his last four starts, Klingler threw for only 646 yards and two TDs, and Bengals fans were relieved when he was relieved. He was given the starting job in 1993, but he never really has done much. He threw only six touchdown passes in 13 starts in '93, though he had only nine interceptions. In his rookie season of 1992, Klingler replaced Boomer Esiason and started four late games.

The skinny: Only 4–20 as a starter in Cincinnati, Klingler is probably another No. 1 pick who went bust.

JIM McMAHON / CARDINALS

Year	Att.	Cmp.	Pct.	Yds.	TDs	Int.	TD-R
1990	9	6	66.7	63	0	0	0
1991	311	187	60.1	2239	12	11	1
1992	43	22	51.2	279	1	2	0
1993	331	200	60.4	1976	9	8	0
1994	43	23	53.5	219	1	3	0

Comments: McMahon played in only the second and third games of 1994, starting once in a 32–0 loss to Cleveland. He was cut by the Vikings after leading them to the playoffs in 1993. He didn't have an exceptionally good season that year, but he did lead the team to victories in four of its final five games. McMahon sat on the bench most of the time from 1990 to '92, though he was 8–3 as a starter in 1991 with the Eagles when Randall Cunningham was injured, and he was named the Comeback Player in the NFL. His record as a starter in the NFL is 69–32.

The skinny: McMahon can always play well in stretches when given the chance.

GALE GILBERT / CHARGERS

Year	Att.	Cmp.	Pct.	Yds.	TDs	Int.	TD-R
1990	15	8	53.3	106	2	2	0
1991	DNP						
1992	DNP						
1993	0	0	0.0	0	0	0	0
1994	67	41	61.2	410	3	1	0

Comments: The Chargers' backup to Stan Humphries, Gilbert got one start (the third of his career) in 1994 but failed to generate much offense in a 10–9 loss to Atlanta. He was pretty good in his other playing time, however, with a good completion percentage and three TD passes compared to only one interception. Prior to joining San Diego, Gilbert was a rarely used No. 3 quarterback in Buffalo. He has thrown only 198 passes and nine TDs in nine pro seasons.

The skinny: A largely untested backup who appears to be steady.

SEAN SALISBURY / VIKINGS

Year	Att.	Cmp.	Pct.	Yds.	TDs	Int.	TD-R
1990	DNP						
1991	DNP						
1992	175	97	55.4	1203	5	2	0
1993	195	115	59.0	1413	9	6	0
1994	34	16	47.1	156	0	1	0

Comments: Salisbury started the final regular-season game of 1994 after Warren Moon was injured and the Vikings decided not to go with untested Brad Johnson. Salisbury had been inactive for the first 15 games of the season. He signed with Houston a year ago as a free agent but was cut before the start of the season and re-signed by Minnesota, where he played the previous two seasons. In 1993, Salisbury started four games and looked pretty impressive near midseason, especially when he had back-to-back 300-yard passing games, the first for the Vikings since 1985. But the Vikings lost three of those games and Salisbury lost his job. He started late in the 1992 season and also in the playoffs. He threw only two interceptions in 175 attempts, and his 1.1 interception percentage set a team record and led the league.

The skinny: Salisbury is 5–4 as an NFL starter and can post some pretty good stats.

JACK TRUDEAU / PANTHERS

Year	Att.	Cmp.	Pct.	Yds.	TDs	Int.	TD-R
1990	144	84	58.3	1078	6	6	0
1991	7	2	28.6	19	0	1	0
1992	181	105	58.0	1271	4	8	0
1993	162	85	52.5	992	2	7	0
1994	91	50	54.9	496	1	4	0

Comments: Trudeau was drafted by Carolina in the expansion draft, and he will back up Frank Reich, the ex-Bill, who will be the starter. Trudeau was the Jets' No. 2 quarterback in 1994. He started two games when Boomer Esiason was injured and appeared in five, but he couldn't produce much offense. He started the first five games of 1993 for Indianapolis — his ninth career installment as a starter but only the second time not dictated by a teammate's injury — before relinquishing the role to Jeff George. He led the Colts to a 2–3 record. Trudeau can get hot, but he just doesn't do it very often.

The skinny: Trudeau is a quality backup, but not much more.

GUS FREROTTE / REDSKINS

Year	Att.	Cmp.	Pct.	Yds.	TDs	Int.	TD-R
1994	100	46	46.0	600	5	5	0

Comments: Frerotte started four straight games as a rookie in the middle of last season, looking very impressive much of the time. However, Heath Shuler is the Redskins' quarterback of the present and future, and

Frerotte will be the backup. Frerotte threw two touchdown passes in his first start and three in the second, but he was benched after going 1 of 6 for 18 yards in the fourth start.

The skinny: Frerotte is a backup to keep an eye on.

VINCE EVANS / RAIDERS

Year	Att.	Cmp.	Pct.	Yds.	TDs	Int.	TD-R
1990	1	1	100.0	36	0	0	0
1991	14	6	42.9	127	1	2	0
1992	53	29	54.7	372	4	3	0
1993	76	45	59.2	640	3	4	0
1994	33	18	54.5	222	2	0	0

Comments: Still playing after all these years, the 40-year-old Evans is still pretty effective coming off the bench. He played in nine games in 1994, though he didn't get many snaps. In 1993, Evans started two games in relief of Jeff Hostetler, completing nearly 60 percent of his passes. His best outing was 247 yards and two touchdowns against the Jets. Evans came off the bench in the 1992 season finale and led the Raiders to a come-from-behind victory over Washington in which he threw two touchdown passes.

The skinny: Evans *is* playing well, but the Raiders would be in trouble if he had to start for a long stretch.

BUCKY RICHARDSON / OILERS

Year	Att.	Cmp.	Pct.	Yds.	TDs	Int.	TD-R
1992	0	0	0.0	0	0	0	0
1993	4	3	75.0	55	0	0	0
1994	181	94	51.9	1202	6	6	1

Comments: Richardson had the first extended action of his career in 1994, sometimes thrilling Oilers fans, although his statistics certainly don't show it. Subbing for an injured Cody Carlson, he threw for three touchdowns in the season opener and then started three of the next five games. However, he didn't move the offense very well and was replaced by Billy Joe Tolliver before starting again in the season finale (the team's second victory of the year). Richardson is a very good runner, with a 7.2-yard average (30 carries for 217 yards) that was the highest in the NFL for players with 15 or more carries. He was the NFL's fifth-leading rusher among quarterbacks, despite the lack of playing time.

The skinny: Richardson can run and throw the long pass, but he's not an NFL-caliber starter.

KENT GRAHAM / GIANTS

Year	Att.	Cmp.	Pct.	Yds.	TDs	Int.	TD-R
1992	97	42	43.3	470	1	4	0
1993	22	8	36.4	79	0	0	0
1994	53	24	45.3	295	3	2	0

Comments: Graham started one game last season in place of a struggling Dave Brown. But Graham struggled, too, completing only 9 of 26 passes for 92 yards against Arizona, and was sent back to the bench. He had his most playing time in 1992 when, as a rookie, he started three games when Phil Simms was injured. He has yet to complete 50 percent of his passes in a season.

The skinny: The Giants are in trouble if Graham has to start for an extended period.

DON MAJKOWSKI / LIONS

Year	Att.	Cmp.	Pct.	Yds.	TDs	Int.	TD-R
1990	264	150	56.8	1925	10	12	1
1991	226	115	50.9	1362	3	8	2
1992	55	38	69.1	271	2	2	0
1993	24	13	54.2	105	0	1	0
1994	152	84	55.3	1010	6	7	3

Comments: Majkowski started six games in relief of Jim Harbaugh last season in Indianapolis but was benched himself for the final two games because the Colts' offense was struggling. He signed with Detroit as an unrestricted free agent and will back up Scott Mitchell. He didn't have more than one touchdown pass in any game and his high game was just 186 yards. The good side is that he was 3–3 as the starter and he ran for three

QUARTERBACKS

touchdowns. Majkowski has never fully recovered from rotator cuff surgery in 1990, and it seems like a long time since he burst upon the scene in the NFL and threw 27 touchdown passes in 1989. Majkowski was being considered among the best quarterbacks in the NFL that year, when he led the league in attempts, completions and passing yards.

The skinny: It's too bad Majkowski ever got injured.

DAN McGWIRE / DOLPHINS

Year	Att.	Cmp.	Pct.	Yds.	TDs	Int.	TD-R
1991	7	3	42.9	27	0	1	0
1992	30	17	56.7	116	0	3	0
1993	5	3	60.0	24	1	0	0
1994	105	51	48.6	578	1	2	0

Comments: McGwire got the most playing time of his career in 1994, starting the final three games after Rick Mirer was injured. However, he didn't play well at all and was eventually signed as a free agent after the season by Miami, where he will have a tough time hanging on. He completed fewer than 50 percent of his passes, and he threw only one TD pass as the Seahawks lost two of the three games. McGwire played in three games in 1993, throwing only five passes. He had his best opportunity in 1992 but fractured his left hip and missed almost the entire season. At 6-foot-8, McGwire is the tallest quarterback ever to play professional football, which makes him . . .

The skinny: . . . a big bust in more ways than one.

. . . AND THE REST

MATT BLUNDIN, Chiefs — Blundin played in only one game in 1994, completing one of five passes for 13 yards, with one interception. At one time Kansas City's quarterback of the future, Blundin is still a huge question mark because he has played so little in three seasons (eight career passes).

MARK BRUNELL, Jaguars — Brunell won Green Bay's No. 2 quarterback job in 1994, although he played in only two games. He was traded to Jacksonville the day before this year's draft. After replacing an injured Brett Favre, he had a good performance against Minnesota that included a clutch quarterback draw for the team's only touchdown. For the season he completed 12 of 27 passes for 95 yards, with no touchdowns. He'll back up Steve Beuerlein this year — and he might give him a run for the job.

RICH GANNON, Chiefs — Gannon signed with Kansas City after being out of football all of 1994. He last played in 1993 for the Redskins, starting three games. His best season was 1990 with Minnesota, when he threw 16 touchdown passes. Gannon will be a pretty good backup for Steve Bono this season.

JASON GARRETT, Cowboys — Garrett started one game in 1994 against Green Bay when both Troy Aikman and Rodney Peete were injured. He played well, too, completing 16 of 31 passes for 315 yards, two touchdowns and only one interception. Garrett began 1993 as Dallas's No. 2 quarterback, but when Troy Aikman went down with an injury, Garrett was replaced by Bernie Kosar, a more capable and experienced quarterback. Though he is very inexperienced — he had thrown only 24 passes in two seasons prior to 1994 — he did show a lot of promise in 1994. With Rodney Peete's departure, Garrett becomes Aikman's backup.

STAN GELBAUGH, Seahawks — Gelbaugh played in only one game in 1994, the season finale, when he completed seven of 11 passes for 80 yards. He also played in just one game in 1993. He started eight games in '92 for Seattle and was the NFL's lowest-rated passer. The Seahawks were 1–7 in those games. In '91, Gelbaugh started three games for the Cardinals but had a 3:10 touchdowns-to-interceptions ratio.

BRAD JOHNSON, Vikings — Johnson was Minnesota's second-string quarterback in 1994, but the Vikings opted to start the more experienced third-stringer, Sean Salisbury, in the final game when Warren Moon was injured. Johnson saw action in four games, but his shaky performance in Game 15 against Detroit (14 of 29 for 104 yards and no touchdowns) doomed him a week later.

TOMMY MADDOX, Rams — Talented but inexperienced, Maddox becomes the Rams' No. 2 quarterback and might play a lot if Chris Miller gets injured (as Miller usually does). In 1994, Maddox completed 10 of 19 passes for 141 yards and two interceptions. His best season was in 1992 as a rookie, when he started four games for Denver in place of an injured John Elway. That season, he hit on 66 of 121 passes for 757 yards, five TDs and nine interceptions. He threw a TD pass on his only pass attempt in 1993 for the Broncos.

BROWNING NAGLE, Colts — Nagle got his only action of 1994 when he started the final game, but he completed only 8 of 21 passes for 69 yards and was replaced. He also bombed as a starter with the Jets in 1992, when he completed 192 of 387 passes for 2,280 yards, seven touchdowns and 17 interceptions. He threw only 14 passes in 1993. Nagle had loads of potential coming out of college, but he has yet to show it in the pros.

TODD PHILCOX, Buccaneers — Philcox did not play in 1994 after being cut by Cleveland. In 1993, he suddenly found himself as the Browns' starter midway through the season after Vinny Testaverde was injured and Bernie Kosar was cut. He started four games, throwing for 316 yards in one of them and four TDs overall (but also seven interceptions). However, the Browns lost three of those games. Philcox also started one game in 1992, throwing three TD passes to Eric Metcalf. Then he suffered a broken thumb and was knocked out of the lineup.

ANDRE WARE, Jaguars — Ware spent the 1994 season out of football after getting cut by Minnesota. He got another opportunity to start for Detroit in 1993 and once again he failed to take advantage of it. In two starts, he was ineffective then benched. For the season, he completed 20 of 45 passes for 271 yards. He started the last three games of 1992 and played the best football of his career. He threw two touchdowns in his first start and passed for 290 yards in the next game, both victories. He'll probably be cut by Jacksonville.

SCOTT ZOLAK, Patriots — A pretty good backup, Zolak played very little in 1994 behind Drew Bledsoe, and he has thrown only 10 passes in the last two seasons. In 1992, he started in the Patriots' only two victories of the season.

Other Quarterbacks on Rosters

Jeff Brohm, Chargers
Mike Buck, Cardinals
Ty Detmer, Packers
Jay Fiedler, Eagles
Glenn Foley, Jets
Will Furrer, Broncos
Bob Gagliano, 49ers
Brad Goebel, Browns
Jeff Graham, Raiders
Trent Green, Redskins
Billy Joe Hobert, Raiders
Don Hollas, Lions

Perry Klein, Falcons
Chuck Long, Lions
Jamie Martin, Rams
Shane Matthews, Bears
Jim Miller, Steelers
Bill Musgrave, Broncos
Doug Nussmeier, Saints
Doug Pederson, Panthers
T.J. Rubley, Packers
Rick Strom, Bills
Gino Torretta, Lions
Tom Tupa, Browns
Jay Walker, Patriots
Casey Weldon, Buccaneers
Stan White, Giants
Erik Wilhelm, Bengals
Peter Tom Willis, Buccaneers

Chapter 4
RUNNING BACKS

EMMITT SMITH

The most important players on your fantasy teams are always the running backs. It is the one position at which you need the most consistent play, because it's the one with the biggest gap in point production between the superstars and the next level.

Running backs in the NFL and fantasy football are a dime a dozen, but there are several premier backs who should be among your first picks. Draft one of them and you are almost assured of a touchdown every week.

The two best running backs in the NFL are Barry Sanders and Emmitt Smith, although that's not necessarily the case in fantasy football. Both will get you 100 yards a game, and Smith is usually good for a touchdown or two as well. Sanders? Only time will tell if he will get the ball near the goal line often in 1995.

Running back is again the deepest position this year, as there are about a dozen other backs very capable of scoring 10 touchdowns. Two or three of them won't do much this year, but going into a fantasy draft they are certainly outstanding choices at the time. The problem is that this year there are a lot of questions about many of the running backs, and that will make it much harder on Draft Day.

After the second tier of backs, there is another group of about a dozen backs who stand very good chances of coming on this year, scoring six to eight touchdowns and rushing for 600–800 yards — or more. They are great choices for your second pick at the position.

What is impossible to tell is which backs will come out of nowhere. Every year there's a Bernie Parmalee or Leroy Hoard who doesn't get drafted but ends up being one of the highest-scoring players in the league. Try to find out who some of this year's sleepers might be, then draft them in the later rounds of your draft.

Draft Tips for Choosing Running Backs

■ Look at past performances, especially the last two or three seasons, rather than just last season.

■ Draft running backs from run-oriented teams.

■ In the Basic Scoring Method, look for each team's designated scorers. Players such as Brad Baxter and William Floyd may not gain a lot of yards but they do get into the end zone a lot. A consistent scorer is the first priority.

■ In the Performance Scoring Method, draft runners strictly by their ability to gain yards rushing and receiving. The combination of the two categories often equals one very good player, such as Thurman Thomas or Johnny Johnson. But don't discount running backs who are primarily receivers, such as Ronnie Harmon, Dave Meggett and Glyn Milburn.

■ In the Distance Scoring Method, look for backs who score consistently and do so on long runs (or pass plays), such as Barry Sanders and Marshall Faulk. Under this scoring method, scatbacks are better picks than big backs. Forget about the big backs who score touchdowns but don't gain much yardage (such as Marion Butts and Leonard Russell).

■ Try to determine who will be the featured running backs for the following teams: Dolphins, Browns, Bengals, Raiders, Broncos, Chiefs, Patriots, Redskins, Bears, 49ers, Packers and Saints. None of that group — one-third of the teams in the NFL — has a definite top running back.

■ Remember to draft rookies who might break into the starting lineup, such as Ki-Jana Carter, James Stewart and Tyrone Wheatley. Several rookies always have big years, and it's up to you to figure out which ones will do it in 1995.

■ Consider drafting big, durable backs rather than smaller scatbacks who often come out in goal-line situations and might be more injury-prone.

■ Make sure you have capable backups who can take over if one of your starters is injured or out of the lineup on a bye.

■ Know what is going on during training camp. Will Jerome Bettis bounce back and score more than he did in 1994? Will Mario Bates give the Saints the featured ball carrier they have lacked for years? Will Terry Allen carry the load, or will he share it with Amp Lee? Can Gary Brown bounce back in Houston? Will Lorenzo White be Cleveland's much-needed featured back? Can Rod Bernstine stay healthy for an entire season in Denver? Is the Raiders' Harvey Williams for real? Will Kansas City's Marcus Allen ever grow old? Will Barry Sanders be Detroit's goal-line ball carrier now that Derrick Moore is in San Francisco? Who will be the 49ers' featured back? Will rookies Ki-Jana Carter and James Stewart post good numbers for expansion teams? Can Garrison Hearst come through for the Cardinals? Is Ronald Moore getting a new lease on life with the Jets? What will become of Barry Foster and Johnny Johnson? Who will emerge as the top back in Washington? Can Miami's running backs stay healthy and, if so, who will get the bulk of the carries?

SUPERSTARS

EMMITT SMITH / COWBOYS

Year	Rush	Yards	TDs	Rec.	Yards	TDs
1990	241	937	11	24	228	0
1991	365	1563	12	49	258	1
1992	373	1713	18	59	335	1
1993	283	1486	9	57	414	1
1994	368	1484	21	50	341	1

Comments: In 1994, Smith became the first player in NFL history to rush for 1,400 or more yards in four consecutive seasons. Despite hamstring, turf toe and foot injuries, he finished third in the league with 1,484 yards. He scored a phenomenal 22 touchdowns, the fourth most in NFL history. His 21 rushing TDs tied him for the second most in league history and set a team record. Among his six 100-yard games were 171-yard and 163-yard performances, giving Smith 11 career games with at least 150 rushing yards. In 1993, despite missing the first two games in a contract holdout, he won his third consecutive NFL rushing title. He joined Earl Campbell, Jim Brown and Steve Van Buren as the only NFL players to accomplish that feat. The NFL and Super Bowl MVP that year, he was also the Cowboys' second-leading receiver. He led the league in total yards and average yards per carry. Smith has rushed for 100 yards in 35 of his 84 regular-season games as a Cowboy. Already Dallas's second-leading career rusher (behind Tony Dorsett) with 7,183 yards, Smith rushed for a club-record 1,713 yards in 1992. That was more yards than eight AFC teams and seven NFC teams! In the playoffs, Smith has 919 rushing yards, a 4.48 average per carry and 10 TDs. He simply dominates.

The skinny: Smith is every fantasy player's dream pick.

BARRY SANDERS / LIONS

Year	Rush	Yards	TDs	Rec.	Yards	TDs
1990	255	1304	13	35	462	3
1991	342	1548	16	41	307	1
1992	312	1352	9	29	225	1
1993	243	1115	3	36	305	0
1994	331	1883	7	44	283	1

Comments: Sanders was on pace to gain 2,000 yards during much of the 1994 season. He was held under 50 yards for three out of four games but still finished with 1,883 yards, the fourth-highest total in NFL history. Sanders became the second player in history to tally more than 1,000 yards in each of his first six seasons. He had 10 100-yard games in '94 and now has 40 in his career. With his 237 yards rushing vs. Tampa Bay Nov. 13, Sanders established a Lions single-game mark and became the first player in history to gain 200 yards in one half. Incredibly, Sanders has a string of 732 consecutive attempts (runs and receptions) without fumbling the ball. His 44 pass receptions last year are a personal best, and he now has 10,436 combined yards. He was having a great year in 1993 until suffering a knee injury in the 11th game and missing the remainder of the regular season. In 1992, because of a bad offensive line, Sanders had only 367 rushing yards in the first six games before finishing fast (985 yards in 10 games) to rank fourth in the NFL. In 1991, Sanders finished second in the NFL in rushing. He led the league in 1990 and was second as a rookie in '89. Detroit's all-time rushing leader with 6,789 yards in five seasons, Sanders has rushed for 100 yards in 30 of 73 career games. He has 68 career TDs.

The skinny: Sanders is arguably the best runner in football, although not in fantasy football because he is too often replaced near the goal line.

CAN'T MISS

NATRONE MEANS / CHARGERS

Year	Rush	Yards	TDs	Rec.	Yards	TDs
1993	160	645	8	10	59	0
1994	343	1350	12	39	235	0

Comments: In his first season as a starter in 1994, Means set the Chargers' single-season rushing record with 1,350 yards, San Diego's first 1,000-yard effort since 1990. He recorded a team-record five consecutive 100-yard performances in Games 5–9, and his 12 TDs were the most by a Chargers running back since Chuck Muncie had 19 in 1981. Means finished second in the AFC in rushing and third in the AFC with 1,585 total yards from scrimmage. He started off slowly as a rookie in 1993 but came on very strong at the end of the season. He led the Chargers in touchdowns with eight, including a 65-yard run that was the team's longest run from scrimmage since 1981. Though he didn't start any games as a rookie, Means ranked fifth among rookie runners and second on the Chargers, and he had two 100-yard games. He now has eight 100-yard games.

The skinny: He Means even more business in '95.

MARSHALL FAULK / COLTS

Year	Rush	Yards	TDs	Rec.	Yards	TDs
1994	314	1282	11	52	522	1

Comments: Faulk more than lived up to his advance billing with an outstanding rookie season in 1994. He rushed for 1,282 yards, the 10th-highest rookie total in NFL history and the best ever by a Colts rookie. His rushing total ranked third in the AFC and fifth in the NFL. He was a consensus Rookie of the Year pick and was named to the Pro Bowl. Faulk started out with an excellent pro debut and never slowed down. He rushed for 143 yards and three touchdowns against Houston in his first game and finished with four 100-yard games. He also caught 52 passes. Faulk accumulated 1,804 combined yards, second in the AFC and fourth in the NFL, and his 11 rushing TDs ranked third in the league. Faulk's impact on the Indianapolis ground game was enormous: The four previous seasons, the Colts ranked 27th and 28th in the league in rushing. Last year, they ranked fourth.

The skinny: Faulk will only get better and better.

CHRIS WARREN / SEAHAWKS

Year	Rush	Yards	TDs	Rec.	Yards	TDs
1990	6	11	1	0	0	0
1991	11	13	0	2	9	0
1992	223	1017	3	16	134	0
1993	273	1072	7	15	99	0
1994	333	1545	9	41	323	2

Comments: One of the NFL's best young runners, Warren goes too much unnoticed on a losing team. In 1994, he became the first back in NFL history to gain 1,000 yards in three straight seasons for losing teams. His career-high 1,545 yards led the AFC, ranked second in the league and set a team record. Warren had an excellent 4.6-yard average and posted seven 100-yard games. He had by far his best season as a receiver, with 41 catches. Despite playing with two fractured ribs, Warren finished 1994 strong, gaining 449 yards in his last four games. His 185-yard game in Week 15 was his personal high and the best in the AFC last year, and his 1,868 combined yards led the conference. In 1993, he had three 100-yard games and topped 1,000 yards for the second consecutive season. Warren was a remarkable success story in 1992, going from the Seahawks' No. 3 halfback to becoming only the second player in team history to reach the 1,000-yard rushing mark. In 1991, he made one start but rushed for only 13 yards on 11 carries.

The skinny: Don't overlook Warren, as a lot of fans do.

RUNNING BACKS

RICKY WATTERS / EAGLES

Year	Rush	Yards	TDs	Rec.	Yards	TDs
1991	Injured					
1992	206	1013	9	43	405	2
1993	208	950	10	31	326	1
1994	239	877	6	66	719	5

Comments: The man whom 49ers coach George Siefert called the best all-around back in football left the Super Bowl champions and signed with the Eagles in the offseason. He'll take over as the Eagles' featured back after piling up his most total yardage yet in 1994. Watters finished eighth in the NFC in rushing and third in combined yards with 1,596. He caught a career-high 66 passes for 719 yards, both figures ranking second on the 49ers. Watters had two 100-yard rushing game and one 100-yard receiving effort. Watters had almost identical years in 1992 and '93 — about 1,000 yards and 11 touchdowns, and he was injured late in the season. Despite sitting out Games 13–15 of the regular season in '93 with stretched knee ligaments, he led the 49ers in rushing. He returned for the playoffs and scored an NFL-record five touchdowns against the Giants. In '92, Watters gained 1,013 yards to establish a 49ers rushing record for first-year backs — despite the fact he missed almost five full games because of injuries. As a rookie in '91, he suffered a broken right foot at the beginning of training camp and missed the entire season.

The skinny: Watters has scored 11 touchdowns in each of his three NFL seasons.

SOLID PICKS

THURMAN THOMAS / BILLS

Year	Rush	Yards	TDs	Rec.	Yards	TDs
1990	271	1297	11	49	532	2
1991	288	1407	7	62	631	5
1992	312	1487	9	58	626	3
1993	355	1315	6	48	387	0
1994	287	1093	7	50	349	2

Comments: For a player who had his least productive season since his rookie year in 1988, Thomas still posted some impressive numbers in 1994. He finished seventh in the NFL in rushing and became the fifth player in NFL history to gain 1,000 rushing yards in five straight seasons. He had 1,442 combined yards, seventh among running backs, and scored nine TDs. Thomas had three straight 100-yard games, missed Week 5 with a sprained knee and returned the next week with another 100-yard effort. His numbers tailed off in the second half of the season, but he still finished with solid stats. In 1993, Thomas fell short of the 2,000-yard mark in total yards after reaching it in 1991 and '92, and he scored only six touchdowns. Thomas is still among the league's best pass-receiving backs. He led the NFL in combined yards from scrimmage (rushing and receiving) from 1989 to '92, breaking a league record held by Jim Brown. In 1992, Thomas gained a career-high 2,113 total yards, the ninth-highest total in NFL history. In 1991, he was named the NFL's Most Valuable Player, and only an ankle injury in the last game kept him from leading the league in rushing. In six seasons, Thomas has rushed for 8,724 yards. He has 40 100-yard rushing games in his career.

The skinny: Thomas is still among the best all-around running backs.

RODNEY HAMPTON / GIANTS

Year	Rush	Yards	TDs	Rec.	Yards	TDs
1990	109	455	2	32	274	2
1991	256	1059	10	43	283	0
1992	257	1141	14	28	215	0
1993	292	1077	5	18	210	0
1994	327	1075	6	14	103	0

Comments: The first Giants player to rush for 1,000 yards in four consecutive seasons, Hampton's 1994 performance moved him into second place on the team's all-time rushing list, with 4,807 yards. He added four 100-yard games last year and now has 16 in his career. Despite missing two games due to a bruised back and kidney, he was the third-leading rusher in the NFC and ranked sixth in the NFL. He has handled the ball 466 straight times without fumbling. In 1993, Hampton hit the 100-yard mark five times, despite missing four games with a knee injury after getting off to a great start (430 yards in the first four games). His touchdown production, however, has fallen off the past two seasons. In 1992, Hampton scored 14 touchdowns, third in the league. In '91, he was the third-leading rusher in the NFC and tied for eighth in TDs with 10. In 1990, he finished second on the Giants in rushing and third in receiving, though he fractured his left ankle in the first playoff game and missed the NFC championship game and the Super Bowl.

The skinny: Though not a big breakaway threat, the consistent Hampton is still one of the top fantasy backs, even though rookie Tyrone Wheatley might take away some of Hampton's carries.

TERRY ALLEN / CUT BY VIKINGS

Year	Rush	Yards	TDs	Rec.	Yards	TDs
1991	120	563	2	6	49	1
1992	266	1201	13	49	478	2
1993	Injured					
1994	255	1031	8	17	148	0

Comments: In 1994, Allen made his second miraculous recovery from a serious knee injury, a feat never before done in the NFL. He rushed for 1,031 yards, fourth best in the NFC and eighth in the NFL. However, he was cut by Minnesota in early May (though he might be re-signed). In 1994, he was second in the NFC with eight rushing TDs. Just one year after suffering a ruptured anterior cruciate ligament that sidelined him the entire '93 season, Allen led the team in rushing in all but one 1994 game and he had three 100-yard games. In 1992, he was one of the top players in both the NFL and fantasy football. He broke Chuck Foreman's team record by rushing for 1,201 yards to rank third in the NFC. He also scored 13 touchdowns on the ground to tie a team record, and two through the air. A ninth-round draft pick, Allen gave a preview of things to come late in 1991 when he rushed for 563 yards and replaced Herschel Walker.

The skinny: The first player in NFL history to play on two reconstructed knees, Allen is one of the game's better running backs.

JEROME BETTIS / RAMS

Year	Rush	Yards	TDs	Rec.	Yards	TDs
1993	294	1429	7	26	244	0
1994	319	1025	3	31	293	1

Comments: One of the game's best young power backs, Bettis really struggled to gain 1,000 yards behind a rebuilding offensive line in 1994. His 3.2-yard average per carry was the lowest among the top 20 ground-gainers, and he gained only 211 yards during the final seven weeks. Still, Bettis did register his second straight 1,000-yard season and he finished fourth in the NFC in rushing. He was fifth in the conference in total yardage with 1,318, and he made the Pro Bowl. Bettis had four 100-yard games, but all of them were in the first five weeks. The Rookie of the Year in 1993, Bettis showed glimpses of being the next Earl Campbell when he was the league's second-leading rusher, just 57 yards behind Emmitt Smith. He also had an excellent 4.9-yard average, seven 100-yard games, seven touchdowns and 26 pass receptions. His 1,429 yards was the seventh-highest total in NFL history for a rookie and fourth highest for a Rams player. Bettis's high game of 212 yards against New Orleans was only the eighth time a rookie rusher has hit the 200-yard mark.

The skinny: This battering Ram needs better blocking to produce more by fantasy football standards.

BAM MORRIS / STEELERS

Year	Rush	Yards	TDs	Rec.	Yards	TDs
1994	198	836	7	22	204	0

Comments: The third-leading rookie rusher in 1994 with 836 yards, Morris picked right up where the injured Barry Foster left off. He's a bowling ball who takes on tacklers, and he had a very good 4.2-yard average per carry. His 1,040 combined yards led the team. He finished second on the Steelers in rushing, fourth in receiving and first in touchdowns. In Game 7 against the Giants, Morris rushed for 146 yards and a touchdown, and he added a 108-yard game in Game 13. Morris was a steal as the 14th running back chosen in the '94 draft.

The skinny: Morris will be Pittsburgh's featured back in 1995, and Foster will most likely be elsewhere.

WILLIAM FLOYD / 49ERS

Year	Rush	Yards	TDs	Rec.	Yards	TDs
1994	87	305	6	19	145	0

Comments: Once Floyd worked his way into the starting lineup six weeks into the 1994 season he began establishing himself as one of the premier fullbacks in the league. For the season, he finished second on the team in rushing with 305 yards, caught 19 passes for 145 yards, and was fifth on the high-scoring 49ers with six touchdowns. The first-round pick added moxie and swagger to the league's best team and was an All-Madden Team pick. In the playoffs, Floyd ran wild, scoring three times against the Bears and one each against the Cowboys and Chargers.

The skinny: With Ricky Watters gone, expect a huge year from Floyd in 1995.

RONALD MOORE / JETS

Year	Rush	Yards	TDs	Rec.	Yards	TDs
1993	263	1018	9	3	16	0
1994	232	780	4	8	52	1

Comments: Moore led the Cardinals in rushing in 12 games in 1994, but Garrison Hearst is their man for 1995, so Moore was sent packing to the Jets for wide receiver Rob Moore. He should be able to beat out Johnny Johnson for the starting job. Moore started all 16 games and led Arizona with 780 rushing yards in '94. He scored five TDs and a two-point conversion, and posted the team's only 100-yard rushing effort with 118 yards in 28 carries at Washington October 16. During a midseason stretch, he had 82 carries for 227 yards. A big surprise in 1993, Moore didn't start the first five games but still rushed for 1,018 yards, the first Cardinals player to hit that mark since 1985 and the first rookie since '79. His nine rushing touchdowns led all rookies and set a team record.

The skinny: Moore might gain a lot of yards this year, but he needs to get back into the end zone.

LORENZO WHITE / BROWNS

Year	Rush	Yards	TDs	Rec.	Yards	TDs
1990	168	702	8	39	368	4
1991	110	465	4	27	211	0
1992	265	1226	7	57	641	1
1993	131	465	2	34	229	0
1994	191	757	3	21	188	1

Comments: White signed with division-rival Cleveland as a free agent and will be that team's No. 1 back this year. In 1994, when Jeff Fisher took over as the Oilers' head coach before Week 11, he made White Houston's starting runner, and White became the team's only consistent offensive weapon. Despite just eight starts, he led the Oilers in rushing with 757 yards. He was the team's fourth-leading receiver. He moved into second place on the team's all-time rushing list with 4,079 yards and became Houston's all-time leading receiver among running backs with 184 career receptions. In 1993, he was plagued by strained hamstrings, lost his starting job to Gary Brown and finished with just 465 rushing yards. He emerged as one of the NFL's top backs in 1992, rushing for 1,226 yards, fifth in the NFL, on a fine 4.6-yard average. He also caught 57 passes and had 1,867 total yards from scrimmage. In 1991, White was second on the team in rushing and sixth in receiving, despite not starting a game.

The skinny: White should end Cleveland's woes at running back.

ERRICT RHETT / BUCCANEERS

Year	Rush	Yards	TDs	Rec.	Yards	TDs
1994	284	1011	7	22	119	0

Comments: The NFC Offensive Rookie of the Year in 1994, Rhett ran wild once he took over the starting job halfway through the season. He gained 707 yards in the final seven games and had four 100-yard games, including a 192-yard, 40-carry effort against Washington in Game 13. Rhett became just the fourth Buccaneer to rush for 1,000 yards, joining Ricky Bell, James Wilder and Reggie Cobb, and he established a team rushing record for rookies. He finished sixth in the NFC in rushing and 10th in the NFL. Rhett scored all but one of the team's rushing TDs.

The skinny: Rhett should post pretty good numbers in 1995 because he will most likely start all season.

MARCUS ALLEN / CHIEFS

Year	Rush	Yards	TDs	Rec.	Yards	TDs
1990	179	682	12	15	189	1
1991	63	287	2	15	131	0
1992	67	301	2	28	277	1
1993	206	764	12	34	238	3
1994	189	709	7	42	349	0

Comments: Allen has been the Chiefs' most consistent offensive player the last two years after being nearly forgotten by the Raiders. In 1994, he bypassed Earl Campbell for ninth place on the NFL's all-time rushing list. He led the Chiefs in rushing for the second straight season and now has 10,018 career rushing yards. Allen has scored 22 touchdowns over the past two seasons, the most in the AFC. He had his most pass receptions last year, 42, in seven seasons. Allen had his finest game in a playoff-clinching win over the Raiders, when he rushed for 132 yards on 33 attempts. It was his 23rd 100-yard game. The NFL's Comeback Player of the Year in 1993, Allen was the first Chiefs player since 1963 to lead the league in touchdowns. His 15 TDs were the second most ever by a Chief. He set a team record by scoring a touchdown in seven straight games (just the kind of production fantasy players want). In 12 seasons, Allen has been one of the league's best all-around backs, and he will likely enter the Hall of Fame someday. He has 120 career TDs, the fourth most ever, and he ranks sixth with 14,622 career combined yards.

The skinny: Allen somehow seems to get better with age, so don't write him off yet.

EDGAR BENNETT / PACKERS

Year	Rush	Yards	TDs	Rec.	Yards	TDs
1992	61	214	0	13	93	0
1993	159	550	9	59	457	1
1994	178	623	5	78	546	4

Comments: After leading the Packers in rushing and finishing second in receiving in 1994, Bennett seems poised to become the team's featured back this year. Perhaps the most underrated fantasy football player, he finished eighth in the NFC among nonkickers with nine touchdowns. His 78 receptions set a team record for running backs and stands as the fifth-highest total in team history. His career-best 623 rushing yards ranked 12th in the NFC. Bennett had three 100-yard rushing efforts last season. In 1993, Bennett finished second on the Packers in both rushing and receiving, and his 10 touchdowns ranked sixth in the NFL. A starter in 14 games, his reception total was third among NFC running backs. His 3.5-yard-per-carry rushing average the past two seasons isn't great, but he seldom fumbles.

The skinny: With 19 touchdowns the last two years, Bennett is one of the best fantasy picks that few people know much about.

JOHNNY JOHNSON / JETS

Year	Rush	Yards	TDs	Rec.	Yards	TDs
1990	234	926	5	25	241	0
1991	196	666	4	29	225	2
1992	178	734	6	14	103	0
1993	198	821	3	67	641	1
1994	240	931	3	42	303	2

Comments: Johnson has probably lost his starting job to trade acquisition Ronald Moore. In 1994, a hamstring injury in Game 8 slowed Johnson after a great start. In the first seven games, he rushed for 548 yards and had 25 catches for 201 yards. Although he tailed off after the injury, he finished sixth in the AFC in rushing with 931 yards and was 10th in combined yards with 1,234. He led the team in rushing for the second straight year and eclipsed the 4,000-yard career rushing mark. And his 42 catches ranked fourth on the team. In 1993, he was the only back in the league to lead his team in both rushing and receiving. He set a club record for most receptions (67) and receiving yards (641) in a single season by a back. His 1,462 total yards ranked sixth in the NFL and second in team history. With the Cardinals in 1992, Johnson held out but then came on strong to rush for 734 rushing yards in the final nine games. A seventh-round pick, he made a huge impact in '90 when he led all rookies in rushing.

The skinny: Johnson is a good all-around runner who will most likely play elsewhere in 1995.

MARIO BATES / SAINTS

Year	Rush	Yards	TDs	Rec.	Yards	TDs
1994	151	579	6	8	62	0

Comments: In 1994, Bates continued a trend that has followed the Saints throughout the 1990s — he was the fourth straight rookie back to lead the team in rushing. He's also the sixth player to lead the team in rushing the past six seasons. Despite missing Games 3–7 when teammate Lorenzo Neal broke Bates's jaw, the second-rounder led the team with 579 yards and six rushing touchdowns. He came on very strong with 543 yards in the second half of the season and was second among rookie rushers in the NFC. In Game 10 against Atlanta, Bates rushed for 141 yards and two TDs and caught three passes for 28 yards.

The skinny: Bates might be the answer on a team with a revolving-door backfield.

LEROY HOARD / BROWNS

Year	Rush	Yards	TDs	Rec.	Yards	TDs
1990	58	149	3	10	73	0
1991	37	154	2	48	567	9
1992	54	236	0	26	310	1
1993	56	227	0	35	351	0
1994	209	890	5	45	445	4

Comments: Hoard had a great season in 1994, with 890 rushing yards, the most by a Browns player in nine years. He earned a Pro Bowl berth with a huge late surge, plowing for 623 yards in the final eight games. He had 1,335 combined yards, seventh in the AFC, and nine touchdowns. His 4.3-yard-per-carry average was tied for third in the NFL among backs with 750 or more yards. Hoard had two 100-yard rushing games and a 99-yard game. In 1992 and '93, he scored only one TD. In 1991, Hoard came out of nowhere, and his nine TD receptions were the most in one season by an NFL running back since official statistics were first recorded in 1932.

The skinny: Look for another productive season from Hoard, although Lorenzo White will be the featured back.

1994 SURPRISES

HARVEY WILLIAMS / RAIDERS

Year	Rush	Yards	TDs	Rec.	Yards	TDs
1991	97	447	1	16	147	2
1992	78	262	1	5	24	0
1993	42	149	0	7	42	0
1994	282	983	4	47	391	3

Comments: Williams came to the Raiders with a chip on his shoulder after Kansas City gave up on him and posted his best season as a pro in

1994. He was brought in to jump-start a lethargic running game, took over the starting job before Game 7 and finished fifth in the AFC in rushing with 983 yards. Williams caught 47 passes, the most by a Raiders running back in seven years. His 1,374 combined yards ranked sixth in the AFC and 11th in the NFL, and he added seven touchdowns. A highly touted rookie in 1991, Williams flashed a lot of promise with 447 rushing yards and a 4.6-yard average per carry. But he landed in Chiefs coach Marty Schottenheimer's doghouse and did little in 1992 and '93.

The skinny: A change of scenery can sometimes do wonders.

BERNIE PARMALEE / DOLPHINS

Year	Rush	Yards	TDs	Rec.	Yards	TDs
1992	6	38	0	0	0	0
1993	4	16	0	0	0	0
1994	216	868	6	34	249	1

Comments: Three years after sorting packages for UPS, Parmalee came out of nowhere in 1994 to rank eighth in the AFC in rushing with 868 yards. His dream season included 1,117 combined yards. Parmalee built his reputation as a special-teams standout until injuries depleted Miami's running back corps. He made the most of his 10 starts, with seven touchdowns, a 4.0-yard average per rush and 34 pass receptions. His increase of 854 yards from his 1993 total represented the largest single-season rushing improvement in Dolphins history and the best in the NFL last year. Parmalee had three 100-yard games.

The skinny: Don't expect the same numbers from Parmalee in 1995.

CRAIG HEYWARD / FALCONS

Year	Rush	Yards	TDs	Rec.	Yards	TDs
1990	129	599	4	18	121	0
1991	76	260	4	4	34	1
1992	104	416	3	19	159	0
1993	68	206	0	16	132	0
1994	183	779	7	32	335	1

Comments: In 1994, Heyward had a great comeback season and the best season of his career in yards rushing, receptions and touchdowns. He overcame weight and alcohol problems to take the starting job from Erric Pegram in the sixth game and bulled for 124 combined yards and two touchdowns in his first start. Heyward gained 4.3 yards per carry for the season, tying for third among running backs with 160 or more carries. He also showed surprising versatility by catching 32 passes for 335 yards, giving him 1,014 combined yards. After a steady, if unspectacular, career in New Orleans, Heyward was a bust with Chicago in 1993.

The skinny: Now Heyward is no longer a big, fat bust.

ROOKIES

See Chapter 12, Rookie Report.

SLIPPED IN 1994

GARY BROWN / OILERS

Year	Rush	Yards	TDs	Rec.	Yards	TDs
1991	8	85	1	2	1	0
1992	19	87	1	1	5	0
1993	195	1002	6	21	240	2
1994	169	648	4	18	194	1

Comments: A classic rags-to-riches story in 1993, Brown was plagued by injuries, a weight problem and fumbleitis in 1994. He missed Games 5 and 6 due to a sprained ankle, and lost his starting job in Game 11 when Jeff Fisher replaced Jack Pardee as head coach. Now, with Lorenzo White out of the picture, Brown takes over again. He still posted respectable numbers in '94, with 648 rushing yards, a 3.8-yard average per carry, 18 pass receptions, 842 combined yards and five TDs. He had more than 100 combined yards in three straight early-season games. In 1993, Brown gave the Oilers the kind of running game they haven't had since Earl Campbell. The lowest-paid player on the Oilers, he replaced Lorenzo White in Game 9 and went on to rush for 1,002 yards with an outstanding 5.1-yard average per carry. Only eight backs in NFL history have ever gained 1,000 yards on fewer carries.

The skinny: Brown should easily bounce back with a 1,000-yard season.

REGGIE BROOKS / REDSKINS

Year	Rush	Yards	TDs	Rec.	Yards	TDs
1993	223	1063	3	21	186	0
1994	100	297	2	13	68	0

Comments: Brooks started the first five games of 1994, then missed two games due to a pulled rib cage muscle. When he returned in Week 8, Brooks found himelf benched in favor of Ricky Ervins. After an excellent rookie 1993 season, Brooks averaged just 2.97 yards per rush last year. He virtually disappeared in the middle part of the season, but he will compete for the starting job in 1995. In 1993, Brooks was the only bright spot on a dismal Redskins offense. He was the first Redskins rookie to top 1,000 yards in rushing when he averaged 4.8 yards per carry. He had four 100-yard games, as well as the league's two longest runs of the season, 85 and 78 yards. He took over a starting role in the fourth game of '93.

The skinny: Stay tuned to the battle for the starting job in Washington in '95.

ERRIC PEGRAM / STEELERS

Year	Rush	Yards	TDs	Rec.	Yards	TDs
1991	101	349	1	1	−1	0
1992	21	89	0	2	25	0
1993	292	1185	3	33	302	0
1994	103	358	1	16	99	0

Comments: In 1994, Pegram got off to a good start, then struggled and lost his starting job to Craig Heyward in Game 6. He had 212 yards, a 4.4-yard average per carry, and a touchdown in the first three games, but he gained just 146 yards the rest of the season. He signed with Pittsburgh as a free agent and will back up Bam Morris. In 1993, Pegram gave the Falcons a solid running game, although he won't ever scare opposing teams because he's not a breakaway threat. His 1,185 yards was the seventh-best total in Atlanta history and fourth most in the league. Pegram had four 100-yard games, including 192- and 180-yard outings. After coming out of nowhere in 1991 as an unknown rookie to gain 349 yards, Pegram didn't get the ball much in '92.

The skinny: The change of scenery should help Pegram get more playing time.

HAROLD GREEN / BENGALS

Year	Rush	Yards	TDs	Rec.	Yards	TDs
1990	83	353	1	12	90	1
1991	158	731	2	16	136	0
1992	265	1170	2	41	214	0
1993	215	589	0	22	115	0
1994	76	223	1	27	267	1

Comments: Green continued his downslide in '94, with his lowest rushing output as a pro. He did catch 27 passes for 267 yards, leading Bengals running backs with a 9.9-yard average. But, for the second straight year, his average per carry was under 3.0. Green had his best game of '94 in the finale vs. the Eagles, rushing for 70 yards and catching three passes for 57 yards. After a career year in 1992, Green had a horrible 2.7-yard rushing average in '93, despite leading the team in rushing with 589 yards. In fact, he became the first runner in NFL history to carry the ball at least 200 times and average less than three yards an attempt. In '92, Green led the Bengals in both rushing and receiving and was moving up to the top tier of backs in the NFL. However, he scored the fewest touchdowns out of all players who rushed for over 1,000 yards.

The skinny: In the last five seasons, Green has scored only eight touchdowns.

DERRICK MOORE / 49ERS

Year	Rush	Yards	TDs	Rec.	Yards	TDs
1993	88	405	3	21	169	1
1994	27	52	4	1	10	0

Comments: Moore was acquired by San Francisco in a trade with Detroit in April. One of the NFL's best goal-line runners, he will get a chance to start for the 49ers, who have lost Ricky Watters. In 1993 and '94, if you had Barry Sanders on your fantasy team, Moore was the guy you hated. Whenever Detroit got near the goal line, it was Moore — not Sanders — who carried the ball. He scored four TDs in both '93 and '94. The Lions liked to deploy him near the goal line, where he could use his size and leaping ability. In 1993, when Sanders was injured for the last five games, Moore rushed for 259 yards in three starts before he, too, was injured.

The skinny: Moore would post great numbers if he were to start for the 49ers.

CHARLIE GARNER / EAGLES

Year	Rush	Yards	TDs	Rec.	Yards	TDs
1994	109	399	3	8	74	0

Comments: Sidelined early and late in the 1994 season, Garner excelled in between in his rookie campaign. He missed the first three games due to a rib injury, then became the seventh rookie in NFL history to rush for 100 yards in his first two games. But in Game 9, he fumbled twice, then left with thigh and hand injuries. Against the Giants in Game 15, Garner suffered a ruptured tendon in his left knee. He finished second on the Eagles in rushing. The knock on him is a lack of durability.

The skinny: The acquisition of Ricky Watters will probably put Garner on the bench in '95.

MARK HIGGS / CARDINALS

Year	Rush	Yards	TDs	Rec.	Yards	TDs
1990	10	67	0	0	0	0
1991	231	905	4	11	80	0
1992	256	915	7	16	142	0
1993	186	693	3	10	72	0
1994	62	195	0	0	0	0

Comments: Higgs had a disappointing season in 1994 after being cut by Miami and picked up by the Cardinals. He led the Dolphins in rushing from 1991 to '93, though Don Shula never really considered Higgs his top back. In 1993, Higgs had 559 yards rushing in the first 10 games but only 134 in the last six. He rushed for over 900 yards in both 1991 and '92, and his 1,820 rushing yards in that time ranked fourth among AFC backs. His career-best 915 yards in 1992 was the most by a Miami back since 1978. In '91, he rushed for over 100 yards in each of his first two NFL starts, with more yards in those games than in his previous three years combined.

The skinny: Higgs has seen his best days.

FADING VETERANS

EARNEST BYNER / BROWNS

Year	Rush	Yards	TDs	Rec.	Yards	TDs
1990	297	1219	6	26	248	1
1991	274	1048	5	34	308	0
1992	262	998	6	39	338	1
1993	23	105	1	27	194	0
1994	75	219	2	11	102	0

Comments: Byner contributed modestly to Cleveland's ground game in 1994. He gained 219 yards and started one game, but he averaged only 2.9 yards a carry, a far cry from his prime. He returned for his second stint in Cleveland after signing as a free agent. He was rarely on the field in 1993 for the Redskins; his primary role was as a third-down back. After three seasons totaling 3,265 yards from 1990 to '92, Byner has really slipped since then. In 1992, he just missed gaining 1,000 yards rushing, which would have given him three consecutive 1,000-yard seasons and established him as only the 11th NFL player to reach the mark at age 30 or older. He had the best season of his career in 1990, with 1,219 yards.

The skinny: Byner is near the end of a long, great career.

TOM RATHMAN / RAIDERS

Year	Rush	Yards	TDs	Rec.	Yards	TDs
1990	101	318	7	48	327	0
1991	63	183	6	34	286	0
1992	57	194	5	44	343	4
1993	19	80	3	10	86	0
1994	28	118	0	26	194	0

Comments: Rathman has a reputation as a quality blocker and dependable pass receiver, but he didn't do either well last season. Now, with Derrick Fenner likely to become the Raiders' starting fullback, Rathman faces an uncertain future. In '94, he rushed just 28 times for 118 yards — third on the team — and caught 26 passes. Known throughout his career as a prolific touchdown scorer, he was shut out last season. He was injured for half of 1993, which accounts for that dismal season. In 1992, he scored nine times, although he had only 537 yards from scrimmage. He scored six touchdowns in 1991.

The skinny: Rathman's best days are behind him.

CLEVELAND GARY / RAMS

Year	Rush	Yards	TDs	Rec.	Yards	TDs
1990	204	808	14	30	150	1
1991	68	245	1	13	110	0
1992	279	1125	7	52	293	3
1993	79	293	1	36	289	1
1994	7	11	0	2	19	0

Comments: Gary rejoined the Rams during the offseason after one year in Miami. He was waived by the Rams just before the '94 season. He played in two midseason games but suffered a hamstring injury and missed the last six games. In 1993, Gary was coming off the best year of his career but lost his job to rookie Jerome Bettis. In 1992, he led the Rams in both rushing and receiving. Gary was 10th in the NFL in rushing with 1,125 yards, eighth with 1,418 total yards from scrimmage and 11th in scoring with 10 touchdowns. He set career highs for rushing yards, receptions (52) and yards in a game (144). After a great 1990 season in which he scored 15 touchdowns, Gary sat on the bench most of the time in '91. Gary is still a chronic fumbler.

The skinny: Gary should switch teams again if he wants to play much.

QUESTION MARKS

BARRY FOSTER / STEELERS

Year	Rush	Yards	TDs	Rec.	Yards	TDs
1990	36	203	1	1	2	0
1991	96	488	1	9	117	1
1992	390	1690	11	36	344	0
1993	177	711	8	27	217	1
1994	216	851	5	20	124	0

Comments: Foster was averaging better than 100 yards a game through Week 5 of the 1994 season, then sprained a knee and sat out three weeks. He missed Game 13 due to broken bones in his lower back but returned with his third 100-yard game of the year. With Bam Morris taking over the starting job and Erric Pegram now the backup, Foster will probably be traded. In 1994, he led the Steelers with 851 rushing yards, ninth best in the AFC. He teamed with Morris to form the league's best running back duo, with 1,687 rushing yards and 2,015 combined yards. After getting off to a fantastic start in 1993, Foster missed the final seven games of the season with ligament damage in his left ankle. Still, he finished second on the Steelers in rushing and first in touchdowns. Foster had the greatest season ever for a Steelers back in '92, when he was second in the NFL in rushing with 1,690 yards. He led the AFC with 11 rushing TDs and tied Eric Dickerson's NFL record with 12 100-yard games. A fifth-round steal in the 1990 draft, Foster became a starter in '91.

The skinny: In the right situation, Foster could have another huge year if he stays healthy.

BRAD MUSTER / SAINTS

Year	Rush	Yards	TDs	Rec.	Yards	TDs
1990	141	664	6	47	452	0
1991	90	412	6	35	287	1
1992	98	414	3	34	389	2
1993	64	214	3	23	195	0
1994	1	3	1	10	88	0

Comments: Once one of the game's better fullbacks during his

Chicago days, Muster has suffered a slew of injuries in New Orleans. In 1994, he pulled a hamstring in Game 3, reaggravated it four times and missed eight games in all. He did score on his only carry of the season, and he caught 10 passes for 88 yards. Muster missed the first three games of 1993 and never really got on track. His rushing total of 214 yards was a then career low, as were his three TDs. In 1992, when he started all 16 games, Muster was the Bears' second-leading rusher. Muster really came into his own in 1990, rushing for 664 yards, leading the Bears in receiving with 47 catches and scoring six touchdowns.

The skinny: If only Muster could stay healthy . . .

TOMMY VARDELL / BROWNS

Year	Rush	Yards	TDs	Rec.	Yards	TDs
1992	99	369	0	13	128	0
1993	171	644	3	19	151	1
1994	15	48	0	16	137	1

Comments: "Touchdown Tommy" Vardell got off to a good start last year, then suffered a season-ending knee injury while trying to catch a pass on the third play of Cleveland's fifth game. At the time, he was leading the Browns with 16 receptions for 137 yards. He now faces an uncertain future after undergoing surgery twice on his left knee. Vardell scored his first pro TD in the first game of 1993 after having been shut out of the end zone as a rookie. He led the Browns in rushing in '93 and had the team's first 100-yard rushing game since 1988.

The skinny: If his knee holds up, Touchdown Tommy could be heard from again.

LᴇSHON JOHNSON / PACKERS

Year	Rush	Yards	TDs	Rec.	Yards	TDs
1994	26	99	0	13	168	0

Comments: In his rookie season of 1994, Johnson gave few indications of how he had led the nation in rushing during his senior year of college. But he was hampered by hamstring injuries in preseason camps, then he tore the anterior cruciate ligament in his left knee in practice December 27. He hopes to return to the field sometime during the '95

RUNNING BACKS

season. Before the knee injury, Johnson was a backup running back who saw action as a sometimes third-down back. He averaged a promising 12.9 yards per catch. Johnson finished fourth on the Packers in rushing.

The skinny: Johnson faces uncertain rehabilitation, but he could be a star someday.

COULD COME ON

GARRISON HEARST / CARDINALS

Year	Rush	Yards	TDs	Rec.	Yards	TDs
1993	76	264	1	6	18	0
1994	37	169	1	6	49	0

Comments: In the final month of 1994, Hearst flashed the brilliance that made him the third player picked in the 1993 draft. He gained 56 yards on just three carries December 4, then turned a swing pass into a 29-yard play the next week to set up a game-winning field goal. In Week 15, Hearst scored on a one-yard run, threw a 10-yard TD pass to Larry Centers and rushed for 62 yards. He improved his average per carry from 3.5 in '93 to 4.6 last year. After missing the first six weeks of the season, Hearst returned to the field on October 16, almost a year to the day after suffering a season-ending knee injury as a rookie in 1993. At the time of the injury, he was having a pretty good rookie campaign, with 264 yards in five starts and six games.

The skinny: Hearst will be the Cardinals' featured back — and a good fantasy pick — this year.

TERRY KIRBY / DOLPHINS

Year	Rush	Yards	TDs	Rec.	Yards	TDs
1993	119	390	3	75	874	3
1994	60	233	2	14	154	0

Comments: Kirby got off to a good start in 1994, then tore the anterior cruciate ligament in his right knee in Game 4 and spent the rest of the season on injured reserve. At the time of his injury, Kirby was tied for seventh in the AFC with 233 rushing yards, and he averaged 3.9 yards per carry. Kirby showed more skills as a pass-receiving back in his rookie season of '93, but proved he could run last year. In a game against the Jets, he gained 100 rushing yards — the first 100-yard game of his career — on just 15 carries. As a rookie third-round draft choice in 1993, Kirby had an unimpressive 3.3-yard average running the ball, but he did lead the Dolphins in receiving and he tied for the NFL lead among running backs. His 75 catches was the second-highest single-season total in Miami history.

The skinny: If Kirby's knee holds up and he regains his starting job, he'll produce.

AMP LEE / VIKINGS

Year	Rush	Yards	TDs	Rec.	Yards	TDs
1992	91	362	2	20	102	2
1993	72	230	1	16	115	2
1994	29	104	0	45	368	2

Comments: Used mainly in passing situations in 1994, Lee caught 45 passes, tying for third on the Vikings and ranking first among running backs. He was slowed by an early-season knee injury, but he came on strong late in the season. He had 25 receptions over the last seven games. One of the best backup backs in the NFL the past three seasons, Lee will share starting time with Terry Allen in '95. In three 1993 starts for the injured Ricky Watters in San Francisco, he gained 290 yards rushing and receiving and scored three touchdowns. The rest of the year he knew he didn't have a chance to even compete for a starting job and asked to be traded. A second-round draft choice in 1992, Lee started three games (again for an injured Watters) and scored four touchdowns.

The skinny: Lee's salary quadrupled in the offseason, and he appears primed for his best year yet.

GREG HILL / CHIEFS

Year	Rush	Yards	TDs	Rec.	Yards	TDs
1994	141	574	1	16	92	0

Comments: Despite finishing third in the AFC and fifth in the NFL among rookie running backs in 1994, Hill had trouble displacing Marcus Allen. Hill, who rushed for 574 yards, led the team in rushing in five games and did have the Chiefs' best average per carry, 4.1. He caught 16 passes for 92 yards. In his best game, against Seattle October 23, Hill gained 74 yards in 17 attempts.

The skinny: In 1995, Hill will get his second chance to replace a legend.

BEST OF THE REST

MARION BUTTS / PATRIOTS

Year	Rush	Yards	TDs	Rec.	Yards	TDs
1990	265	1225	8	16	117	0
1991	193	834	6	10	91	1
1992	218	809	4	9	73	0
1993	185	746	4	15	105	0
1994	243	703	8	9	54	0

Comments: Butts had the worst year of his career in 1994 and his lowest rushing output since his rookie season of 1989. In New England's playoff game at Cleveland, he was benched in favor of Corey Croom, who had not run a play from scrimmage all season. Thus, Butts is clearly not in the team's plans. He started all 16 regular-season games and scored eight TDs (five of them were in the first four games), his most in four years. However, Butts's 2.9-yard average per rush was horrendous. He did finish '94 with exactly 5,000 career rushing yards, seventh among active rushers. Butts was traded to New England on Draft Day in 1994 after another solid season for the Chargers in 1993. The Chargers' leading rusher for five straight seasons, Butts is their No. 2 career rusher. In his best season, 1990, he was second in the AFC in rushing while breaking the single-season team record with 1,225 yards.

The skinny: No Butts about it — it's time for another change of scenery if he is going to get much playing time this season.

LEONARD RUSSELL / BRONCOS

Year	Rush	Yards	TDs	Rec.	Yards	TDs
1991	266	959	4	18	81	0
1992	123	390	2	11	24	0
1993	300	1088	7	26	245	0
1994	190	620	9	38	227	0

Comments: Russell led the Broncos with 620 rushing yards and nine touchdowns in 1994, but his 3.3-yard average per carry was indicative of the AFC's second-worst ground game. Russell did have two 100-yard games, and he finished fourth on the team with a career-high 38 receptions. In the 15th game he ruptured a disk in his neck and was placed on injured reserve. He appears to have recovered from surgery. With New England in 1993, Russell was the featured ball carrier for Bill Parcells, and he posted his best season, with career highs in touchdowns, rushing attempts, rushing yards, receptions, receiving yards and total yards. His rushing total was sixth in the NFL and second in the AFC. After a Rookie of the Year season in 1991, the sophomore jinx hit Russell in '92, when he had a low 3.2-yard average and missed five games with injuries. In '91, he led all rookie rushers with 959 yards and ranked fourth in the AFC.

The skinny: Russell's 1995 production for Denver will largely depend on the status of Rod Bernstine.

ROD BERNSTINE / BRONCOS

Year	Rush	Yards	TDs	Rec.	Yards	TDs
1990	124	589	4	8	40	0
1991	159	766	8	11	124	0
1992	106	499	4	12	86	0
1993	223	816	4	44	372	0
1994	17	91	0	9	70	0

Comments: Injuries have prevented Bernstine from giving the Broncos the ground game they had expected. In 1994, his second season with the team, he had a big season opener, with 55 yards rushing and eight receptions for 67 yards. But in Week 2, he suffered a hamstring injury. After sitting out a week, Bernstine returned but then suffered a severe knee injury and missed the rest of the season. In 1993, he didn't have the kind of season that was expected of him after being obtained from the Chargers. Still, he led Denver in rushing with a career-high 816 yards, sixth in the AFC, and two 100-yard games. He ended the season on injured reserve with a dislocated right shoulder (the second straight year he has suffered that injury). In '92, his rushing total was his lowest since he switched to running back from tight end. In 1991, Bernstine finished second on the Chargers in rushing, with more yards than he had in his first four seasons combined, and he scored eight touchdowns.

The skinny: If only Bernstine could stay healthy . . .

HERSCHEL WALKER / GIANTS

Year	Rush	Yards	TDs	Rec.	Yards	TDs
1990	184	770	5	35	315	4
1991	198	825	10	33	204	0
1992	267	1070	8	38	278	2
1993	174	746	1	75	610	3
1994	113	528	5	50	500	2

Comments: Walker could become a bigger version of a Dave Meggett in New York this year. With Meggett gone and Rodney Hampton the team's steady every-down back, the Giants may utilize Walker's versatility. In 1994 while with the Eagles, he became the only player in NFL history to record 90-yard plays via a rush, reception and kickoff return in the same season. Only one other player had accomplished the feat in an entire career. Walker led the team in touchdowns with eight, in rushing with 528 yards, finished third in receiving with 50 catches and had 1,028 combined yards. His 1,609 all-purpose yards moved him into seventh place on the all-time list. In 1993, Walker ranked seventh in the NFL with 1,356 total yards. In 1992, Walker's 1,070 rushing yards and 10 touchdowns led the Eagles, and he became the first Eagles running back to surpass 1,000 yards since 1985. It was the second time in his career he hit the 1,000-yard mark.

The skinny: Forget the fact that Walker is 33 years old — he's still an excellent player.

BRAD BAXTER / JETS

Year	Rush	Yards	TDs	Rec.	Yards	TDs
1990	124	539	6	8	73	0
1991	184	666	11	12	124	0
1992	152	698	6	4	32	0
1993	174	559	7	20	158	0
1994	60	170	4	10	40	0

Comments: Baxter started nine games in 1994 but was benched in favor of Richie Anderson late in the season. One of the league's best goal-line runners, Baxter scored four TDs last year and finished third on the team in rushing wth 170 yards, moving him into eighth place on the team's all-time list. He missed one game with a turf toe injury. In Game 7 against New England, he ran for two TDs and 38 yards in 12 attempts. In 1993, Baxter was second on the Jets in rushing but was the leading touchdown scorer. He also set career highs as a receiver with 20 catches for 158 yards. In 1992, he led the Jets in rushing with 698 yards. In 1991, Baxter's 11 rushing touchdowns led the AFC and tied a team record.

The skinny: In the last five years, Baxter has scored 34 touchdowns on the ground, an average of nearly seven per season.

DERRICK FENNER / RAIDERS

Year	Rush	Yards	TDs	Rec.	Yards	TDs
1990	215	859	14	17	143	1
1991	91	267	4	11	72	0
1992	112	500	7	7	41	1
1993	121	482	1	48	427	0
1994	141	468	1	36	276	1

Comments: Fenner signed with the Raiders in April after leading the Bengals in rushing in 1994. He also led the team's running backs in receptions and reception yardage. However, he was benched for the final three games, as Cincinnati coach Dave Shula continued his desperate search for a running game. In 1993 he was used mostly as a receiver until late in the season, when he took over as the No. 1 ball carrier. However, he scored only once in 169 times handling the ball. He very quietly had a fine comeback season in 1992 after being acquired by Cincinnati. Playing mostly in short-yardage situations, he was the team's No. 2 rusher and

RUNNING BACKS

leading TD scorer. Fenner had come out of nowhere in 1990 with Seattle to score 15 times, which tied for the NFL lead. In 1991 he lost his starting job after six games, because he was averaging only 3.1 yards a carry.

The skinny: Fenner fills a void for the Raiders and could be a sleeper as a fantasy pick.

LEWIS TILLMAN / BEARS

Year	Rush	Yards	TDs	Rec.	Yards	TDs
1990	84	231	1	8	18	0
1991	65	287	1	5	30	0
1992	6	13	0	1	15	0
1993	121	585	3	1	21	0
1994	275	899	7	27	222	0

Comments: The Bears' featured back in 1994, Tillman was adequate but unspectacular. He is not the outside running threat the Bears need, as his 3.3-yard average per carry last season attested. Tillman had 1,121 combined yards, ninth in the NFC, and posted two 100-yard rushing games. His 899 rushing yards were the most by a Bear in four years. In Game 4, Tillman gained 96 yards and two touchdowns in 32 carries. He signed with the Bears as a free agent last year after an impressive 1993 season with the Giants. In '93, he looked excellent in the four games he started in place of Rodney Hampton, rushing for 425 yards, with a couple of 100-yard games. Tillman has 2,305 career yards.

The skinny: Tillman will be fighting for his starting job in '95.

SPECIALISTS

LARRY CENTERS / CARDINALS

Year	Rush	Yards	TDs	Rec.	Yards	TDs
1990	0	0	0	0	0	0
1991	14	44	0	19	176	0
1992	37	139	0	50	417	2
1993	25	152	0	66	603	3
1994	115	336	5	77	647	2

Comments: A pass-catching specialist, Centers set a team record in

1994 with 77 catches for 647 yards. He scored seven touchdowns, including five on the ground. Centers, who tied for second among NFL running backs in pass receptions, had at least two catches in every game, including 10 receptions in one contest. He had nine games with at least 66 combined rushing and receiving yards and led the Cardinals in combined yards with 983. In 1993, Centers caught 66 passes to lead the Cardinals in receiving, the team's first running back to do so since Terry Metcalf in 1974. He ranked fifth among NFL backs in receiving, sporting a 9.1-yard average. In '92, he ranked sixth in the league among running backs in receiving.

The skinny: Centers is the perfect third-down back, and he is starting to run the ball more, too.

RONNIE HARMON / CHARGERS

Year	Rush	Yards	TDs	Rec.	Yards	TDs
1990	66	363	0	46	511	2
1991	89	544	1	59	555	1
1992	55	235	3	79	914	1
1993	46	216	1	73	671	2
1994	25	94	1	58	615	1

Comments: One of the premier pass-catching running backs in the NFL, Harmon tied for the team lead with 58 receptions in 1994. He averaged an exceptional 10.6 yards per catch, accumulated 36 first downs and extended his streak to 67 games with at least one reception. His 484 career receptions ranks third in the AFC and fifth in the entire NFL among all active running backs. Harmon's 210 pass receptions from 1992 to '94 also leads active running backs. In 1993 he caught more than 70 passes for the second consecutive season. Harmon led all backs with his 79 catches in '92 and had a career high of 914 receiving yards. In 1991, he led the Chargers with 1,099 yards from scrimmage, and he was third on the team in rushing with 544 yards and a 6.1-yard average, which led all NFL running backs.

The skinny: Harmon is not a threat in fantasy football but is down-right dangerous in real football.

DAVE MEGGETT / PATRIOTS

Year	Rush	Yards	TDs	Rec.	Yards	TDs
1990	22	164	0	39	410	1
1991	29	153	1	50	412	3
1992	32	167	0	38	229	2
1993	69	329	0	38	319	0
1994	91	298	4	32	293	0

Comments: Signed as a free agent in the offseason, Meggett has a shot at becoming New England's featured back this season. A superb third-down specialist and kick returner, Meggett got a chance to show what he can do as a runner in 1994. In two starts in place of the injured Rodney Hampton, he rushed for 122 yards and two touchdowns in 42 carries. Meggett's 1994 rushing average of 3.3 yards was nothing special, but he's still one of the top pass receivers among running backs. He has excelled when given the ball on a regular basis. In 1993, he rushed for a career-high 329 yards, although he did not score. He did, however, throw two TD passes. In 1991, he led the Giants in receptions, and in '92 he was second. Meggett, who has five career TDs on punt returns, finished second in the NFC and third in the NFL last season with a 12.4-yard average. In '90, he led the NFC in kickoff returns and was second in punt returns.

The skinny: Don't be surprised if Meggett has his best season yet.

KEITH BYARS / DOLPHINS

Year	Rush	Yards	TDs	Rec.	Yards	TDs
1990	37	141	0	81	819	3
1991	94	383	1	62	564	3
1992	41	176	1	56	502	2
1993	64	269	3	61	613	3
1994	19	64	2	49	418	5

Comments: In the midst of an excellent 1994 season, Byars tore cartilage and ligaments in his right knee November 6 and underwent reconstructive knee surgery. At the time, he had 49 pass receptions to lead the Dolphins and rank fourth in the AFC. He became the first back in NFL history to catch at least one pass in 100 straight games, and now has a streak of 112. Only six receivers have ever had longer streaks. His seven touchdowns tied for 11th in the conference last year. One of the top active receivers in the league, Byars has 481 career catches for 4,563 yards and 21 TDs. He was the lone fullback named to the AFC's Pro Bowl squad in 1993, when he had one of his finest seasons. He was third on the team in rushing, third in receiving and tied for second in scoring. His receiving total ranked seventh among all backs. A tight end in Philadelphia in 1992, Byars left that team so he could return to running back. In 1991, he tied for both the Eagles' lead in receiving and the NFL title among running backs.

The skinny: Byars's legs might be slower, but his hands are as great as ever.

GLYN MILBURN / BRONCOS

Year	Rush	Yards	TDs	Rec.	Yards	TDs
1993	52	231	0	38	300	3
1994	58	201	1	77	549	3

Comments: The Broncos' second-leading receiver in 1994, Milburn led AFC running backs with 77 catches. The mighty mite caught at least two passes in every game and at least five passes in nine games to become one of the league's best all-purpose backs. The Broncos had never before had two receivers with 60 or more receptions in a season, but Milburn, Shannon Sharpe and Anthony Miller all surpassed that total in '94. Milburn averaged 7.1 yards per catch and 3.5 yards per rushing attempt. He also finished sixth in the AFC in punt returns with a 9.2-yard average. Milburn looked great early on as a rookie in 1993 but faded dramatically as the season went along. He scored a touchdown in his first pro game, but had only two more the rest of the year.

The skinny: Milburn adds the excitement lacking in the rest of the Bronco backfield.

LEROY THOMPSON / PATRIOTS

Year	Rush	Yards	TDs	Rec.	Yards	TDs
1991	20	60	0	14	118	0
1992	35	157	1	22	278	0
1993	205	763	3	38	259	0
1994	102	312	2	65	465	5

Comments: A third-down specialist in 1994, Thompson was an ineffective runner but a good receiver. He caught 65 passes, third most among AFC backs and sixth most among NFL backs. He also scored seven regular-season touchdowns, including five TD catches, and added a sixth TD catch in the playoffs. But his rushing average was only 3.1 yards per carry. With Pittsburgh in 1993, Thompson capably replaced an injured Barry Foster midway through the season. He rushed for 108 yards in his first start and led the Steelers in rushing. However, he scored only three times all season and the Steelers were 3–4 in games he started. His 205 rushes, 763 rushing yards and 38 receptions all were career highs. In 1992, he ranked second on the Steelers in rushing with a club-best 4.7-yard average per carry.

The skinny: With Drew Bledsoe at quarterback for the Patriots, Thompson could have another big season ahead coming out of the backfield.

KEVIN TURNER / EAGLES

Year	Rush	Yards	TDs	Rec.	Yards	TDs
1992	10	40	0	7	52	2
1993	50	231	0	39	333	2
1994	36	111	1	52	471	2

Comments: After joining Leroy Thompson to form the best pass-catching backfield duo in the NFL in 1994, Turner signed with Philadelphia in the offseason. He caught 52 passes on the only team in NFL history to have five receivers with 50 or more receptions. Turner started the first nine games at fullback but averaged just 3.1 yards a carry and lost his job. In 1993, Turner carried the ball only 50 times but averaged 4.6 yards a carry and led the team's backs in receiving. Turner, who has been compared to Dallas's Daryl Johnston, has scored six of his seven career touchdowns on pass receptions. As a rookie in 1992, he played in all 16 games but didn't see the ball much.

The skinny: Turner gives the Eagles a big blocking back with great pass-catching skills.

KIMBLE ANDERS / CHIEFS

Year	Rush	Yards	TDs	Rec.	Yards	TDs
1991	0	0	0	2	30	0
1992	1	1	0	5	65	0
1993	75	291	0	40	326	1
1994	62	231	2	67	525	1

Comments: Anders set a Kansas City record for catches by a back with a team-high 67 receptions in 1994. He caught at least one pass in all but one game, had at least five grabs in nine games and averaged 7.8 yards per catch. One of the best fullbacks and pass-receiving backs in the league, Anders finished third on the Chiefs in rushing with 231 yards, and finished with 756 combined yards and three TDs. He had a stellar playoff game against Miami, catching six passes for 103 yards, including a 57-yard TD. After logging two injury-filled seasons, he had his best year in 1993, starting 13 games and rushing for 291 yards, second on the team. He was third on the team in receptions.

The skinny: Anders is an excellent role player who produces.

JOHNNY BAILEY / RAMS

Year	Rush	Yards	TDs	Rec.	Yards	TDs
1990	26	86	0	0	0	0
1991	15	43	1	0	0	0
1992	52	233	1	33	331	1
1993	49	253	1	32	243	0
1994	11	35	1	58	516	0

Comments: Known primarily in the past as an excellent kick returner, Bailey came into his own in 1994 as an excellent pass-receiving running back. He led the Rams with 58 receptions and averaged 8.9 yards per catch. He became the sixth running back to lead the Rams in receiving, and he caught at least one pass in 13 games, despite missing two games with an abdominal pull. Bailey pretty much matched his 1992 stats in '93. He got his first real chance to show what he could do as a running back in 1992, when he was the Cardinals' second-leading rusher and No. 5 receiver. Bailey led the NFL in punt returns in 1992.

The skinny: Bailey doesn't score enough to be a fantasy consideration.

OTHERS

RICKY ERVINS / REDSKINS

Year	Rush	Yards	TDs	Rec.	Yards	TDs
1991	145	680	3	16	181	1
1992	151	495	2	32	252	0
1993	50	201	0	16	123	0
1994	185	650	3	51	293	1

Comments: Washington's leading rusher and second-leading receiver in 1994, Ervins regained the starting job he had lost to Reggie Brooks the year before. He averaged 3.5 yards per carry, accumulated 943 combined yards and scored four touchdowns. He had 99 combined yards and two TDs in Game 8 at Indianapolis, and helped revive a ground game that was awful early in the season before improving considerably. After a very good rookie year in 1991, Ervins's stats slipped the next two seasons. In 1993, he was the team's third-leading rusher, though 98 yards rushing in one outing was nearly half of his rushing total. In '92, Ervins had a bad 3.3-yard average and rushed for almost 200 fewer yards than he did in '91. He was the NFC's top rookie rusher in 1991.

The skinny: Ervins might be a good late-round gamble.

JOHN L. WILLIAMS / STEELERS

Year	Rush	Yards	TDs	Rec.	Yards	TDs
1990	187	714	3	73	699	0
1991	188	741	4	61	499	1
1992	114	339	1	74	556	2
1993	82	371	3	58	450	1
1994	68	317	1	51	378	2

Comments: A good blocking fullback and a great receiver, Williams provided a perfect complement to Pittsburgh's power running game in 1994. He led the Steelers in receiving with 51 catches and finished third in rushing with 317 yards and an excellent 4.7-yard average per carry. In his best game, against the Eagles in Week 15, he rushed for 94 yards and a touchdown and caught four passes for 17 yards. Williams was Seattle's second-leading rusher and pass receiver in 1993. Seen more as a pass receiver, with seven consecutive seasons of 50-plus catches, he is tied with Marcus Allen for the second-most pass receptions in NFL history among backs (522). Since he entered the NFL in '86, no other back has more receptions for more yards (4,629) than Williams.

The skinny: Williams is not a good fantasy player, but he needs only 45 catches to become the most prolific pass-catching back ever.

REGGIE COBB / JAGUARS

Year	Rush	Yards	TDs	Rec.	Yards	TDs
1990	151	480	2	39	299	0
1991	196	752	7	15	111	0
1992	310	1171	9	21	156	0
1993	221	658	3	9	61	1
1994	153	579	3	35	299	1

Comments: Cobb says he can be a 1,000-yard rusher in Jacksonville, but that's what the Packers had expected when they signed him as a free agent last year. And, with rookie James Stewart expected to be Jacksonville's featured back, Cobb will most likely be the backup. He is steady and dependable, if unspectacular, but he has never averaged more than 3.8 yards per carry during his career. In 1994, Cobb was second on the Packers in rushing with 579 yards, and he had 878 combined yards and four TDs. After an outstanding 1992, Cobb was very disappointing in '93. He had a lousy 3.0-yard rushing average, with only one 100-yard game. In 1992, Cobb finished eighth in the NFL in rushing with 1,171 yards, fifth in attempts and fifth in rushing touchdowns. He scored a single touchdown in nine games. In 1991, he also led Tampa Bay in rushing.

The skinny: Cobb will be lucky to remain a starter this season.

RAYMONT HARRIS / BEARS

Year	Rush	Yards	TDs	Rec.	Yards	TDs
1994	123	464	1	39	236	0

Comments: Harris played little in September before starting the final 11 games at fullback after injuries forced Merril Hoge to retire. The Bears' most productive rookie, Harris finished second on the team in rushing yards and third in receiving. A self-proclaimed "ultra back," Harris doesn't go down on the initial hit, rarely is stopped behind the line and is equally adept at running and pass catching. He led Chicago ball carriers in yards three times. In the 15th game, he had 92 rushing yards and a TD.

The skinny: Harris could be worth a late-round fantasy draft pick.

BRIAN MITCHELL / REDSKINS

Year	Rush	Yards	TDs	Rec.	Yards	TDs
1990	15	81	1	2	5	0
1991	3	14	0	0	0	0
1992	6	70	0	3	30	0
1993	43	246	3	20	157	0
1994	78	311	0	26	236	1

Comments: A kick returner extraordinaire, Mitchell set or tied six Redskins records in 1994. His 2,477 combined yards left him with the second-highest total in league history. Nobody returned punts like Mitchell last year, when he ran back two for touchdowns and led the NFL with a 14.1-yard average, the second best in team history. He now has five TDs on punt returns, one off the NFL record. He finished fourth in the NFC and sixth in the NFL in kickoff returns with a 25.5-yard average, and his 1,478 kickoff return yards broke a team record. Mitchell looked great in the 1993 season opener, when he rushed for 116 yards and scored two TDs in a Monday night win over Dallas. That was almost as many yards as he would gain the rest of the season, because he was relegated to kick-return duties.

The skinny: A lucrative offseason contract means Mitchell will be a big part of the team's plans this year.

KENNETH DAVIS / BILLS

Year	Rush	Yards	TDs	Rec.	Yards	TDs
1990	64	302	4	9	78	1
1991	129	624	4	20	118	1
1992	139	613	6	15	80	0
1993	109	391	6	21	95	0
1994	91	381	2	18	82	0

Comments: Davis had another effective season as Thurman Thomas's backup in 1994, although he scored just two touchdowns after two straight six-TD seasons. He had Buffalo's longest run, a 60-yarder against Kansas City in Game 8. Davis started one game, in place of the injured Thomas in Week 5, and gained 78 yards in 18 attempts. He again showed more explosiveness than Thomas, leading the Bills rushers with 4.2 yards per carry. One of the best backups in the NFL, Davis rushed for more yards than starters on some teams in 1991 and '92. He set career single-season highs for rushing and receiving in 1991, and he nearly equaled them in '92.

The skinny: Davis still runs well after nine seasons.

IRVING SPIKES / DOLPHINS

Year	Rush	Yards	TDs	Rec.	Yards	TDs
1994	70	312	2	4	16	0

Comments: Despite just one start, Spikes finished second on the Dolphins in rushing with 312 yards. He missed four games due to a knee injury sustained in Week 2, his best game, when he ran for 70 yards in 13 attempts. His 4.5-yard average per carry led Dolphins regulars. In his only start, November 13 against Chicago, Spikes had 74 combined yards. With one more attempt, Spikes's 22.8-yard average per kickoff return would have ranked fourth in the AFC.

The skinny: Spikes has some big-play potential but plays on a team loaded with running backs.

ROBERT SMITH / VIKINGS

Year	Rush	Yards	TDs	Rec.	Yards	TDs
1993	82	399	2	24	111	0
1994	31	106	1	15	105	0

Comments: A good pass receiver, Smith finished third on the Vikings in rushing last season with 106 yards, and caught 15 passes. He replaced Qadry Ismail as the team's main kickoff returner late in the '94 season and posted an excellent 26.2-yard average in 16 returns. Smith missed one game due to a hip injury. When the Vikings were looking for running backs in 1993, they turned for a time to Smith, their first-round draft pick. He

RUNNING BACKS

started two games in the second half of the season, rushing for 94 yards in his first start. But he suffered a serious knee injury in the next game and missed the rest of the season.

The skinny: This is the year we find out if Smith is a first-round bust.

DEREK BROWN / SAINTS

Year	Rush	Yards	TDs	Rec.	Yards	TDs
1993	180	705	2	21	170	1
1994	146	489	3	44	428	1

Comments: Brown carried the ball 111 times for 340 yards and two touchdowns in the first eight games of 1994, then lost his starting tailback job to rookie Mario Bates. He finished second on the team in rushing with 489 yards, but he averaged just 3.3 yards per carry. He ranked fourth on the Saints with 44 pass receptions for 428 yards. Brown led the Saints in rushing in 1993, ranking fifth among all rookies. His rushing total was the most by a Saints player since 1989. He scored a touchdown in his first game and three in the first five, but then failed to get into the end zone the rest of the season as the team slumped.

The skinny: Brown is a second-stringer until further notice.

ROOSEVELT POTTS / COLTS

Year	Rush	Yards	TDs	Rec.	Yards	TDs
1993	179	711	0	26	189	0
1994	77	336	1	26	251	1

Comments: Primarily a lead blocker for Marshall Faulk, Potts is a good, hard runner. He finished second on the Colts in rushing and averaged 4.4 yards per attempt. Potts was fourth on the team in pass receptions with 26. He was the team's leading rusher twice, including a 74-yard, six-carry performance in one game. A rookie second-round draft choice in 1993, Potts led the Colts in rushing with 711 yards. But he did not score a touchdown and was prone to fumble. He was slowed by a hamstring injury in November, but he performed best against conference champions Buffalo and Dallas, rushing for more than 100 yards against each team.

The skinny: Potts could be good for a few short touchdown runs.

VINCE WORKMAN / BUCCANEERS

Year	Rush	Yards	TDs	Rec.	Yards	TDs
1990	8	51	0	4	30	1
1991	71	237	7	46	371	4
1992	159	631	2	47	290	0
1993	78	284	2	54	411	2
1994	79	291	0	11	82	0

Comments: Workman started the first eight games of 1994 while rookie Errict Rhett was broken in slowly. Workman finished second on the Buccaneers in rushing with 291 yards and had the best average, 3.7 yards per carry, among the backs. Known as a good pass receiver, Workman caught only 11 passes in 1994, his lowest total in four seasons. A role-type player who can play any spot in the backfield, Workman was second on the Buccaneers in both rushing and receiving in 1993. He notched a career-high 54 receptions, the best total by a Tampa Bay running back since 1984. In 1992, Workman's 631 rushing yards were the most by a Green Bay back since 1989 and led the squad. In 1991, he scored 11 touchdowns, but he has only six scores since then.

The skinny: Workman might become Tampa Bay's third-down specialist.

VAUGHN HEBRON / EAGLES

Year	Rush	Yards	TDs	Rec.	Yards	TDs
1993	84	297	3	11	82	0
1994	83	325	2	18	137	0

Comments: Hebron was a solid contributor in 1994 on a team that was very deep at running back. He did well in the second half of four midseason games. In his first start, against Cleveland in Game 10, Hebron caught six passes for 54 yards and rushed for 39 yards and a touchdown. Hebron led the Eagles in rushing in five games and finished third in rushing with 325 yards. He had a solid rookie season, finishing third on the Eagles in rushing and first in rushing touchdowns. He started four games late, though 66 yards in the season opener was his best outing.

The skinny: Hebron could get buried in the Eagles' depth chart this season.

BLAIR THOMAS / COWBOYS

Year	Rush	Yards	TDs	Rec.	Yards	TDs
1990	123	620	1	20	204	1
1991	189	728	3	30	195	1
1992	97	440	0	7	49	0
1993	59	221	1	7	25	0
1994	24	70	1	2	1	0

Comments: Signed late in the 1994 season when Emmitt Smith was hobbled by injuries, Thomas started the final regular-season game at New York, rushing for 63 yards and a touchdown in 18 carries. He also scored two TDs against the Packers in Dallas's playoff opener. He began the season in New England and gained 63 yards in 14 attempts against the Jets, but he had only five carries in the next 10 games and was waived. A bust in four seasons with the Jets, Thomas hardly resembles the breakaway back who starred at Penn State, or even the modestly successful runner he was in his prime with the Jets. Thomas averaged five yards a carry as a rookie, and in 1991 he led the team in rushing.

The skinny: Thomas could be one injury away from a starting job in Dallas, but the chances are better that he will lose his No. 2 role to rookie Sherman Williams.

ERIC LYNCH / LIONS

Year	Rush	Yards	TDs	Rec.	Yards	TDs
1993	53	207	2	13	82	0
1994	1	0	0	2	18	0

Comments: With Barry Sanders healthy, Lynch is relegated to short-yardage blocking and special-teams play. He touched the ball just three times in 1994 after being pressed into a starting role due to injuries the previous year. At the end of 1993, Lynch was the Lions' starting halfback, and the team's running game didn't miss a beat. He gained 115 yards in 30 carries in the 1993 regular-season finale against Green Bay. He made his first start that season against Chicago and responded with 85 yards.

The skinny: Lynch won't repeat his rookie stats as long as Barry Sanders is around, but the departure of Derrick Moore thrusts him into the backup role.

ERIC BIENIEMY / BENGALS

Year	Rush	Yards	TDs	Rec.	Yards	TDs
1991	3	17	0	0	0	0
1992	74	264	3	5	49	0
1993	33	135	1	1	0	0
1994	73	295	0	5	48	0

Comments: Signed by Cincinnati in the offseason, Bieniemy gets a chance to earn what he's always wanted: a starting job in the NFL. He's coming off a productive 1994 season in which he finished second on the Chargers in rushing with a career-high 295 yards in a backup role. Bieniemy rushed for 33 yards in four carries against Pittsburgh in the AFC title game. He has averaged better than four yards a carry the past two seasons.

The skinny: Bieniemy has as good a shot as anybody to carry the load in Cincinnati this year.

DARYL JOHNSTON / COWBOYS

Year	Rush	Yards	TDs	Rec.	Yards	TDs
1990	10	35	1	14	148	1
1991	17	54	0	28	244	1
1992	17	61	0	32	249	2
1993	24	74	3	50	372	1
1994	40	138	2	44	325	2

Comments: Johnston has always been a devastating blocker, and his productivity has increased the past two seasons. He has four touchdowns each of the last two seasons, and in 1994 he had 463 combined yards. He was fourth on the Cowboys in receptions with 44. In 1993, Johnston rushed for only 74 yards (he had only seven carries in the last eight games), but he ranked third on the team in receiving and had 446 total yards. Johnston has never missed a game during his career and he never takes off a down. In 1992, he finished fifth on the team in receiving and first among the team's backs. Most important, he is an excellent lead blocker for Emmitt Smith.

The skinny: The "Moose" is loose, and his numbers will only get better.

RUNNING BACKS

CARWELL GARDNER / BILLS

Year	Rush	Yards	TDs	Rec.	Yards	TDs
1990	Injured					
1991	42	146	4	3	20	0
1992	40	166	2	7	67	0
1993	20	56	0	4	50	1
1994	41	135	4	11	89	0

Comments: Gardner is utilized for his goal-line running and short-yardage blocking. After a disappointing 1993 season, Gardner last year matched his production of 1991 and '92. He scored three of his four touchdowns in the final four games, including a pair of scores in a comeback win over Miami. Gardner's rookie season of 1990 was a washout because of a knee injury. He has a reputation as a fumbler.

The skinny: Gardner is the Bills' short-yardage specialist and might see more playing time.

MACK STRONG / SEAHAWKS

Year	Rush	Yards	TDs	Rec.	Yards	TDs
1994	27	114	2	3	3	0

Comments: Chris Warren's backup and a special-teams player, Strong gained 114 yards and averaged 4.2 yards per carry last season. He started Game 13 in place of the injured Warren but rushed for only 17 yards and quickly made way for the Seattle star. Strong gained all of his yards in the final six games.

The skinny: He came on Strong in the last half of '94.

DERRICK CLARK / BRONCOS

Year	Rush	Yards	TDs	Rec.	Yards	TDs
1994	56	168	3	9	47	0

Comments: A free-agent rookie in 1994, Clark won a job with the Broncos in the preseason by displaying excellent catching and running ability for a big back. He was used on special teams and in goal-line situations, and he scored three touchdowns. He started four games due to injuries to Rod Bernstine and Leonard Russell. In the season finale, Clark rushed for 55 yards and two TDs on 15 carries.

The skinny: Clark may be the Broncos' goal-line runner in '95.

ADRIAN MURRELL / JETS

Year	Rush	Yards	TDs	Rec.	Yards	TDs
1993	34	157	1	5	12	0
1994	33	160	0	7	76	0

Comments: Shifty and explosive, Murrell was slowed by a sprained knee that sidelined him for six 1994 games. He tied for the team lead with a 4.8-yard average per carry and he also caught seven passes for 76 yards. Murrell sparked the Jets' offense in Game 6 against Indianapolis by rushing for 65 yards and making a key third-down reception. A rookie in 1993, he was fourth on the team in rushing with 157 yards, though he seemed to spend more time running east and west rather than taking the ball upfield.

The skinny: Murrell is a player to keep an eye on.

SCOTTIE GRAHAM / VIKINGS

Year	Rush	Yards	TDs	Rec.	Yards	TDs
1992	14	29	0	0	0	0
1993	118	487	3	7	46	0
1994	64	207	2	1	1	0

Comments: The Vikings' second-leading rusher in 1994, Graham played his best game in the regular-season finale against San Francisco, when he gained 70 yards on 17 rushing attempts. His average per carry of only 3.2 yards was no bargain, however. In 1993, Graham started the final three games and helped revive the Vikings' slim playoff hopes. A free-agent signee who had been out of football, he rushed for 79 yards in his first start, then 139 more yards a week later and then another 166 yards. Graham also scored three times in the final four games. He played very little as a rookie.

The skinny: Graham is a capable, if unspectacular, backup.

LORENZO NEAL / SAINTS

Year	Rush	Yards	TDs	Rec.	Yards	TDs
1993	21	175	1	0	0	0
1994	30	90	1	2	9	0

Comments: The Saints' starting fullback, Neal had just one good game carrying the ball in 1994, rushing for 63 yards in 14 attempts in Game 6. Otherwise he did little, with just 90 yards in 30 attempts and two pass receptions. As a rookie in 1993, Neal averaged 8.3 yards while rushing for 175 yards (89 and 86 yards) in the first two games. But he broke his right ankle in that second game and was sidelined for the rest of the season.

The skinny: Neal's most notable accomplishment in 1994 was breaking the jaw of his teammate, Mario Bates, in a fight, then starting alongside him late last season.

LINCOLN COLEMAN / COWBOYS

Year	Rush	Yards	TDs	Rec.	Yards	TDs
1993	34	132	2	4	24	0
1994	64	180	1	8	46	0

Comments: Coleman was the Cowboys' second-leading rusher in 1994, but he was demoted to third string late in the season. In Weeks 4 and 5, he led the Cowboys in rushing yards with 74 and 57, respectively, but his role diminished after that. In 1993, everyone asked, "Who's he?" when Dallas started to play Coleman a lot late in the season and in the Super Bowl. A former Arena League player, Coleman provided the answer by rushing for 132 yards, 57 in the first pro game in which he touched the ball.

The skinny: Coleman may not last another year in Dallas.

DERRICK LASSIC / PANTHERS

Year	Rush	Yards	TDs	Rec.	Yards	TDs
1993	75	269	3	9	37	0
1994	Injured					

Comments: Carolina obtained Lassic in the expansion draft. He missed the entire 1994 season with a quadriceps injury, although he wasn't placed on injured reserve until December. A rookie in 1993, he started the first two games of the season when Emmitt Smith was a contract holdout. In fact, he was the first rookie running back to ever start a season opener for a defending Super Bowl champion. A fourth-round draft pick, Lassic ranked second on the Cowboys in rushing.

The skinny: Lassic will battle for a starting job if he's healthy.

DONNELL BENNETT / CHIEFS

Year	Rush	Yards	TDs	Rec.	Yards	TDs
1994	46	178	2	7	53	0

Comments: Bennett was starting to roll late in his rookie season until he suffered a season-ending knee injury December 18. He had gained 135 yards on 31 rushing attempts and had six catches for 38 yards in his last five games. A second-round draft pick, he finished fourth on the Chiefs in rushing and scored two touchdowns.

The skinny: Bennett gives the Chiefs a second good young fullback.

ANTHONY JOHNSON / BEARS

Year	Rush	Yards	TDs	Rec.	Yards	TDs
1990	0	0	0	5	32	2
1991	22	94	0	42	344	0
1992	178	592	0	49	517	3
1993	95	331	1	55	443	0
1994	5	12	0	5	31	0

Comments: After gaining over 1,000 total yards in 1992, Johnson played a lesser role in '93 and barely played at all in '94 except on special teams. Now he has a chance to become the Bears' third-down specialist. Johnson finished third on the Jets in special-teams tackles last year. In 1993, he caught a career-high 55 passes for Indianapolis, but he fell out of favor with the coaching staff late in the season. At the time he was leading all running backs with 48 receptions. He still led the Colts in rushing and was third in receiving for a career-best 1,109 total yards from scrimmage, which ranked seventh in the AFC and 20th in the NFL.

The skinny: Johnson is a good all-purpose running back.

RODNEY CULVER / CHARGERS

Year	Rush	Yards	TDs	Rec.	Yards	TDs
1992	121	321	7	26	210	2
1993	65	150	3	11	112	1
1994	8	63	0	0	0	0

Comments: Acquired on waivers just before the 1994 season, Culver rode the pines behind Natrone Means. He made his first carries as a Charger in Game 15 and gained 63 yards in eight attempts. Culver isn't all that good, but he has been a touchdown scorer. In his first two seasons, he had 14 touchdowns while serving as the Colts' short-yardage back (he scored once on a fumble recovery). In three years, however, he has rushed for only 534 yards and a lousy 2.75-yard average.

The skinny: Don't expect much in 1995, either.

JAMES JOSEPH / BENGALS

Year	Rush	Yards	TDs	Rec.	Yards	TDs
1991	135	440	3	10	64	0
1992	0	0	0	0	0	0
1993	39	140	0	29	291	1
1994	60	203	1	43	344	2

Comments: The multifaceted Joseph saw action at fullback, tailback, tight end and H-back last year in Philadelphia but was signed by the Bengals in the offseason as a free agent. He was fourth on the Eagles in pass receptions and fifth in rushing. Joseph scored on a career-long 34-yard run against Dallas in Game 6, then had a 35-yard TD catch the next week. He missed two games due to a sprained knee but returned and had a big day against the Cowboys in Week 13, with 82 combined yards. In 1993, Joseph gained 294 of his 431 total yards in the final three games. After leading the Eagles in rushing in 1991, Joseph played all 16 games in '92 but didn't carry the ball from scrimmage. He was the main ball carrier the second half of 1991.

The skinny: A change of scenery would suit Joseph well.

STEVE SMITH / SEAHAWKS

Year	Rush	Yards	TDs	Rec.	Yards	TDs
1990	81	327	2	4	30	3
1991	62	265	1	15	130	1
1992	44	129	0	28	217	1
1993	47	156	0	18	187	0
1994	26	80	2	11	142	1

Comments: A backup fullback, Smith has always been a devastating blocker with good pass-receiving hands. He scored three touchdowns and caught 11 passes for 142 yards last year. He averaged only 3.0 yards per carry last year, however, and just 1.9 yards per carry in 1993. Smith started 13 games at fullback for the Raiders in '93. He was hampered by injuries late in the season and in the playoffs.

The skinny: Smith is purely a blocker and not much of a runner, though he did score two TDs rushing last season.

REGGIE RIVERS / BRONCOS

Year	Rush	Yards	TDs	Rec.	Yards	TDs
1991	2	5	0	0	0	0
1992	74	282	3	45	449	1
1993	15	50	1	6	59	1
1994	43	83	2	20	136	0

Comments: Rivers has not shown much since 1992. In '94, he contributed mostly as a pass-receiving back and on special teams, where he excels. Rivers caught 20 passes for 136 yards, a 6.8-yard average, but his rushing average of 1.9 yards per attempt was terrible. He had four catches for 37 yards in Week 4 and 47 combined yards in the eighth game. In 1993, Rivers carried the ball just 15 times and caught just six passes after career highs of 282 yards rushing and 45 receptions as a rookie the year before.

The skinny: Rivers may never match his 1992 production.

RUNNING BACKS

DEXTER CARTER / JETS

Year	Rush	Yards	TDs	Rec.	Yards	TDs
1990	114	460	1	25	217	0
1991	85	379	2	23	253	1
1992	4	9	0	1	43	1
1993	10	72	1	3	40	0
1994	8	34	0	7	99	0

Comments: The forgotten man in San Francisco's juggernaut 1994 offense, Carter gets a new lease on life with the Jets, although he'll have plenty of competition. He was the 49ers' top punt and kickoff returner the past three seasons. He caught only nine passes and ran for 34 yards in eight attempts last year, but he set a club record with 48 kickoff returns. His 1,105 kickoff-return yards ranked second in team history. He didn't get many opportunities from scrimmage the past three seasons, mostly because he's a fumbler. He was injured most of '92, but in 1991, he was third on the team in rushing and seventh in receiving. In '90, Carter led the 49ers in rushing because both Roger Craig and Tom Rathman had subpar seasons.

The skinny: Carter will be the Jets' return specialist and battle for playing time in the offense.

ROBERT GREEN / BEARS

Year	Rush	Yards	TDs	Rec.	Yards	TDs
1992	8	46	0	1	5	0
1993	15	29	0	13	63	0
1994	25	122	0	24	199	2

Comments: A versatile third-down specialist and special-teams player for Chicago, Green was third on the Bears in rushing and sixth in receiving in 1994. In a Halloween night game against Green Bay, Green had 96 all-purpose yards. In Minnesota a month later, Green had six receptions for 69 yards, including a sensational tackle-breaking 39-yard touchdown.

The skinny: Green will be pressed for the Bears' pass-receiving role by Anthony Johnson.

CALVIN JONES / RAIDERS

Year	Rush	Yards	TDs	Rec.	Yards	TDs
1994	22	93	0	2	6	0

Comments: His rookie season was largely a learning experience from the bench, although Jones got some action in the Raiders offense in the last half of 1994. He posted a respectable 4.2-yard average per rush. In Game 10, Jones rushed for 32 yards in six attempts.

The skinny: Jones could see more action in '95.

RICHIE ANDERSON / JETS

Year	Rush	Yards	TDs	Rec.	Yards	TDs
1993	0	0	0	0	0	0
1994	43	207	1	25	212	0

Comments: Anderson took the starting fullback job away from Brad Baxter late in 1994 and led the Jets in rushing and receiving with 87 combined yards in his first start. He finished second on the team in rushing with 207 yards and a fine 4.8-yard average per carry. He was also fifth on the team in receiving and receiving yards. Anderson had a career day in Game 10 at Green Bay with 74 rushing yards, including a 55-yard gallop. He missed two games with a dislocated finger.

The skinny: Anderson's late-season surge last year bears watching. He could become a productive player by fantasy standards.

ANTHONY McDOWELL / BUCCANEERS

Year	Rush	Yards	TDs	Rec.	Yards	TDs
1992	14	81	0	27	258	2
1993	2	6	0	8	26	1
1994	21	58	0	29	193	1

Comments: The Buccaneers' leading receiver among backs last year with 29 catches, McDowell is the blocking back for Errict Rhett. McDowell, who started 11 games at fullback, was ineffective as a ball carrier, rushing for just 58 yards in 21 attempts. Out the last third of the 1993 season with a sprained ankle, he certainly didn't improve upon his 1992 season. That year he came out of nowhere as an eighth-round draft pick, turning into a pretty good pass receiver out of the backfield and averaging 5.8 yards per rush.

The skinny: McDowell has yet to prove he can be a good goal-line runner.

DARRELL THOMPSON / BEARS

Year	Rush	Yards	TDs	Rec.	Yards	TDs
1990	76	264	1	3	1	0
1991	141	471	1	7	71	0
1992	76	255	2	13	129	1
1993	169	654	3	18	129	0
1994	2	–2	0	0	0	0

Comments: Thompson was signed by the Bears in March. In 1994, he was bounced around the Packers like a Ping-Pong ball, getting cut three times and picked up twice. He was a major disappointment in Green Bay, which drafted him in the first round of the 1990 draft. In 1993, Thompson was handed the team's starting job after John Stephens was traded and Eric Dickerson failed a physical. He responded with the best year of his career. His 654 yards ranked 12th in the NFC in rushing and were the most by a Green Bay back since 1989. Thompson rushed for less than 1,000 yards total in his first three seasons, though he did have a handful of good games, showing that he possesses some talent.

The skinny: This may be one final chance for Thompson.

. . . AND THE REST

(listed in alphabetical order)

RANDY BALDWIN, Panthers — Baldwin led the AFC in kickoff returns in 1994 with a 26.9-yard average, third best in the NFL. He played sparingly otherwise, with 23 rushing attempts for 78 yards and three pass receptions.

PAT CHAFFEY, Packers — Chaffey was signed by the Packers in the offseason after not playing anywhere in 1994. The Jets' backup fullback in '93, he suffered torn knee ligaments in Game 3 and underwent reconstructive knee surgery. In '92, he played in 14 games and had a fine 6.9-yard rushing average, finishing third on the team with 186 yards.

BOB CHRISTIAN, Panthers — A fine third-down pass receiver, Christian played on every special-teams unit for Chicago last year. He had a 21-yard pass reception and 20-yard run in '94. The previous year, he caught 16 passes for 160 yards and was terrific on special teams.

JEFF COTHRAN, Bengals — A bruising rookie, Cothran progressed steadily and finished the 1994 season as a starter. He scored the first time he touched the ball, a seven-yard run on a fake field goal. He tied for second on the team in special-teams tackles.

AARON CRAVER, Broncos — Four weeks after getting waived by the Dolphins, Craver was re-signed when Terry Kirby was injured four games into the 1994 season. Craver, who has great pass-catching skills, caught 24 passes for 237 yards and rushed for 43 yards in just six attempts last year. He missed the 1993 season due to a knee injury. He was signed by Denver as a free agent.

COREY CROOM, Patriots — After playing only on special teams in 1994, Croom started in the backfield in New England's playoff game when Marion Butts was benched. In the loss at Cleveland, Croom led the Patriots with 35 rushing yards on nine attempts and caught a five-yard pass. A rookie free agent in 1993, Croom rushed for 198 yards (third on the team) and one touchdown. He also caught eight passes.

GARY DOWNS, Giants — Mainly a special-teams player in 1994, Downs appeared offensively in some third-down situations. The rookie gained 51 yards in 15 carries and caught two passes for 15 yards.

VAUGHN DUNBAR, Saints — Dunbar hasn't done much since his fine first season of 1992, when he rushed for 565 yards, second most among rookies. He suffered torn knee ligaments in the 1993 training camp and missed the entire season, and last year he carried the ball only three times for nine yards. Dunbar appears to have joined Craig Heyward as another first-round back who didn't last long in New Orleans.

SAM GASH, Patriots — The team's top blocking back, Gash rushed for 86 yards on 30 attempts in 1994. He caught nine passes for 61 yards. A good special-teams player, Gash rushed for 149 yards (48 carries) in 1993 and caught 14 passes.

HOWARD GRIFFITH, Panthers — Griffith started the last 10 games of 1994 at fullback. He proved to be a capable receiver, catching 16 passes for 113 yards and a touchdown. He also rushed for 30 yards in nine attempts. In Game 12, he had six catches for 41 yards and a 6-yard run.

BOBBY HUMPHREY, Bills — After being out of football for two seasons, Humphrey signed with Buffalo in the offseason. In his last season, 1992, Humphrey led the Dolphins in receiving and was second in rushing. He had 1,000-yard seasons for the Broncos in 1989 and '90, but was beset by a drug charge and was shot in the thigh. In his prime, Humphrey was a strong, quick runner who made good cuts and had good balance. He has one last chance.

RONALD HUMPHREY, Colts — Humphrey played little on offense but was the Colts' best kickoff returner, finishing sixth in the AFC with a 22.4-yard average on 35 returns, including a 95-yard touchdown. He rushed 18 times for 85 yards and caught three passes for 19 yards.

TRACY JOHNSON, Seahawks — Seattle's starting fullback for 10 games in 1994, Johnson rushed for 44 yards in 12 attempts and caught 10 passes for 91 yards. He scored two touchdowns. A decent fullback and a good blocker, he rushed only five times for 34 yards in 1992 and '93.

YONEL JOURDAIN, Bills — Signed as a free agent in 1993, Jourdain became the Bills' top kick returner last year, with 27 returns for 601 yards, seventh in the AFC. He had three rushes for 24 yards and three catches for 28 yards in Game 12, and finished the year with 17 carries for 56 yards and 56 yards in 10 receptions, seeing a lot of action as Thurman Thomas's backup .

TIM LESTER, Rams — Lester lost his starting fullback job to Howard Griffith in November of '94. He ran seven times for 14 yards and caught just one pass for 1 yard. In 1993, Lester rushed 11 times for 74 yards and caught 18 passes for 154 more in '93, excellent averages either way he got the ball.

DORSEY LEVENS, Packers — A promising rookie who beat veteran Dexter McNabb out of a backup fullback spot, Levens played in short-yardage situations and had a TD run in the playoffs.

MARC LOGAN, Redskins — Logan was signed by Washington after being cut by San Francisco, where he lost his starting job to rookie William Floyd in 1994. For the year, he rushed 33 times for 143 yards and one touchdown. His best season was in 1993, when he scored seven TDs.

DEREK LOVILLE, 49ers — A third-string tailback in 1994, Loville finished sixth on the 49ers in special-teams tackles. He rushed for 99 yards in 31 carries and caught two passes for 26 yards. With Ricky Watters gone, the 49ers say they would be happy with Loville and Derrick Moore in the backfield.

FRED McAFEE, Steelers — McAfee played in six games with the Steelers in 1994. He rushed for 51 yards in 18 carries late in the season, and caught a four-yard pass. His best year was his rookie season of 1991 with the Saints, when he rushed for 494 yards in 109 carries.

TODD McNAIR, Oilers — Once a vital part of Kansas City's offense, the versatile McNair was obtained on waivers by the Oilers last year and was third string. He caught eight passes for 78 yards, including a fine five-catch, 77-yard performance in the 13th game. He mostly played on special teams. In 1993, he was third on the Chiefs in rushing, with 51 carries for 278 yards and a superb 5.5-yard average per carry, all career bests. From 1989 to '92, McNair rushed for only 357 yards and one touchdown, but he was the Chiefs' leading receiver, with 155 catches.

TYRONE MONTGOMERY, Raiders — Montgomery started the first six games of 1994 at halfback but didn't produce, then found himself at the end of the bench. He was deactivated the rest of the season. He did catch eight passes for 126 yards, including 93 yards in just three catches and 13 rushes for 55 yards in Week 3. A versatile player, Montgomery's stock rose in the 1993 playoffs. Seldom used until late in the season (37 carries for 106 yards), he proved to be a good pass-catcher but an inconsistent performer.

DERRICK NED, Saints — Ned contributed in Weeks 3–5 of 1994, then disappeared into a backup fullback role. A decent swing back, he caught 13 passes for 86 yards and rushed for 36 yards in 11 carries. He accumulated 66 combined yards at Tampa Bay in Week 3. In 1993, Ned carried nine times for 71 yards and caught nine passes for 54 yards.

KENYON RASHEED, Giants — A solid blocker, Rasheed started seven times in 1994 and played in every game. He gained 44 yards in 17 carries and caught 10 passes for 97 yards. He caught three passes for 47 yards against Arizona in Week 2. The Giants' backup fullback as a rookie in 1993, Rasheed rushed for 42 yards on nine carries and scored one TD.

GREG ROBINSON, Raiders — Robinson was one of six rookie runners to lead his team in rushing in 1993, when he gained 591 yards. An eighth-round draft pick, he injured his knee and missed the last four games of the season and all of 1994. He's not a super-talented back, but his stats certainly raised a few eyebrows. He is a question mark heading into 1995.

MAZIO ROYSTER, Jaguars — The 17th player picked in the expansion draft, Roster caught seven passes for 36 yards in Tampa Bay last year. He also rushed for seven yards in nine attempts. He has 42 career rushing attempts for 142 yards and a touchdown, 13 receptions for 62 yards and a 12.8-yard average in eight kickoff returns.

JAMES SAXON, Dolphins — In 1994, Saxon helped fill the void after pass-receiving specialist Keith Byars went down with a knee injury.

Saxon caught 27 passes for 151 yards, all in the last half of the season. In his last five seasons, though, Saxon has only 64 rushing yards in 26 attempts.

CEDRIC SMITH, Redskins — Smith was a big part of Washington's improved ground game in the second half of 1994. He started the final eight games as the blocking back, and gained 48 yards in 10 rushes. He caught 15 passes for 188 yards and a touchdown.

ADAM WALKER, 49ers — A special-teams regular in 1994, Walker rushed for 54 yards in 13 attempts. He rushed three times for 23 yards in the season finale. In San Francisco's playoff opener, Walker scored a touchdown against the Bears.

LAMONT WARREN, Colts — Warren showed promise as a rookie with two fine rushing performances late in the season. He gained 50 yards in five carries in Game 13, then ran for 28 yards in three carries in Week 15. He rushed 18 times for 80 yards and caught three passes for 47 yards.

Other Running Backs on Rosters
Tommie Agee, Cowboys
Jamal Anderson, Falcons
Steve Avery, Steelers
Eric Ball, Panthers
Wes Bender, Raiders
Dewell Brewer, Panthers
Leon Brown, Jaguars
Tony Carter, Bears
Randy Cuthbert, Panthers
Bobby Joe Edmonds, Buccaneers
Keith Elias, Giants
Charles Evans, Vikings
Eddie Fuller, Panthers
Gary Harrell, Giants
Rudy Harris, Buccaneers
Frank Harvey, Browns
Brian Henesey, Eagles
John Ivlow, Broncos
Randy Jordan, Jaguars
David Lang, Rams
Le'Shai Maston, Jaguars
Dexter McNabb, Jaguars
Brian O'Neal, Panthers

Tyrone Rush, Redskins
Lamar Smith, Seahawks
Tony Smith, Panthers
Deon Strothers, Broncos
Tim Tindale, Bills
Ed Toner, Steelers
Nate Turner, Bills
Vernon Turner, Panthers
Jon Vaughn, Chiefs
Russell White, Packers
Marcus Wilson, Jaguars
Frank Wycheck, Redskins

Chapter 5
WIDE RECEIVERS

JERRY RICE

It's another year of fantasy football and another season with Jerry Rice clearly the top pick at wide receiver in fantasy football. At no other position in pro football does one player so clearly dominate his peers as Rice does. In the five years of this book, Rice hasn't always been the leading scorer among receivers, but he has always been the No. 1 fantasy pick at his position. And it is for that reason that Rice should again be strongly considered for the No. 1 overall pick in many fantasy drafts.

In some years, wide receiver has been the deepest of the five main positions in fantasy football. Although not extremely deep this year, the depth of quality receivers increased in 1994 due to the emergence of several young, rising stars. There are perhaps a dozen receivers capable of scoring at least 10 touchdowns this season, with the most likely being Rice, Carl Pickens, Andre Rison, Tim Brown, Herman Moore and Cris Carter.

After them comes a group of solid receivers that includes Michael Irvin, Andre Reed, Rob Moore, Irving Fryar, Anthony Miller, Terance Mathis, Henry Ellard, Alvin Harper and Michael Haynes before you get to a large group of players who could get anywhere from eight touchdowns to only one or two. And that is the group of receivers that is going to be so important this year. The team that drafts one or two of those receivers who have career years will be in contention for a fantasy league championship.

Draft Tips for Choosing Wide Receivers

■ Look at past performances, especially the last two or three seasons, rather than just last season.

■ Draft receivers from pass-oriented teams, such as the Dolphins, 49ers, Patriots, Bengals, Raiders and Broncos. Forget about running teams like the Steelers, Giants and Colts.

■ Draft receivers who are favorite targets of a good quarterback, such as Jerry Rice, Irving Fryar, Cris Carter, Tim Brown or Michael Irvin.

■ Don't overlook the secondary receivers, such as Calvin Williams, Mike Pritchard, Darnay Scott, Jake Reed, John Taylor and Randal Hill, because they occasionally play better over an entire season (and certainly in stretches) than the main receiver. Also, if the primary receiver gets injured, the secondary receiver becomes the main target.

■ Remember that in today's era of three- and four-wide-receiver formations, a receiver does not have to be a starter to make a big contribution. Many backup wideouts catch half a dozen touchdown passes each season, which is as many as — or more than — a lot of the good starters will catch.

■ Remember to draft rookies who might break into the starting lineup, such as Michael Westbrook, J.J. Stokes and Joey Galloway. Several rookies always have big years, and it's up to you to determine which ones will do it in 1995. And, because wide receivers are often so hard to judge, one or two rookies might come through in big ways.

■ Look for speed receivers who make the big plays, rather than possession receivers (especially in the Performance Scoring Method).

■ Make sure you have capable backups who can take over if one of your starters is injured or out of the lineup on a bye.

■ If a team has just made a quarterback change, or it looks as if a team will have inconsistent quarterbacking throughout the season, take that into consideration. Last year's Oilers and Colts were perfect examples. With three quarterbacks starting for both of those teams during last season, the statistics of their teams' receivers were affected. In other words, stay away from quarterback controversies.

■ Take into consideration that receivers are often double-teamed, so you will want to know which players will be affected by that and which ones can beat the double-team.

■ Be aware of what is going on during training camp. Will Vincent Brisby become Drew Bledsoe's main receiver in New England now that Michael Timpson is gone? Can Henry Ellard defy his age another year or two in Washington? Will Kevin Williams take a step up into the No. 2 receiver role in Dallas? Will Terance Mathis prove that his outstanding 1994 season was no fluke? Do the Bears have a quarterback who can get the ball to what has become a very solid receiving corps? Who will emerge as Brett Favre's go-to receiver in Green Bay? Who will get the ball to Rob Moore in Arizona? Will J.J. Stokes step right into the forefront of the 49ers' offense in his rookie season? Who will be the main receivers on the two expansion teams, and will they score enough to become productive by fantasy football standards? In their second season together, will Anthony Miller hook up with John Elway to become one of the league's best combinations? Can Alvin Harper do in Tampa Bay what he did in Dallas, or will Trent Dilfer's growing pains take their toll on Harper's production? Will Carl Pickens and Darnay Scott again team up to become one of the league's most dangerous duos? Will the old-guard receivers be pushed out of Houston by their young protégés?

THE SUPERSTAR

JERRY RICE / 49ERS

Year	Rec.	Yards	Avg.	TDs
1990	100	1502	15.0	13
1991	80	1206	15.1	14
1992	84	1201	14.3	10
1993	98	1503	15.3	15
1994	112	1499	13.4	13

Comments: Without question the greatest receiver in NFL history, Rice hasn't slowed down a bit in 10 illustrious seasons. He had one of his best years in 1994, with a club-record 112 receptions for 1,499 yards. Rice led all receivers in passing yardage and in touchdowns with 15 (he had two running the ball). He set an NFL record with his ninth 1,000-yard season, and he added five 100-yard games to give him 49, the second most ever. In Game 11 against the Rams, Rice set a single-game record and tied the No. 3 performance in NFL history with 16 catches for 165 yards and three TDs. Rice is virtually unstoppable on short passes near the goal line. He's still on pace to shatter every career receiving record in the NFL record books. In 1993, he led the NFL in receiving yards, tied for the lead in touchdowns and was second in catches. He now ranks first on the all-time list in reception touchdowns (131), is second in receiving yards with 13,275 and second in catches with 820. He has a team- and NFL-record 139 total TDs. Rice has caught at least one pass in every game during his career, 143 straight, dating back to 1985. It is his ability to kick into some kind of otherworld, warp-speed gear in just one step that makes him so great.

The skinny: Rice is one of the best players the game has ever seen at any position.

CAN'T MISS

ANDRE RISON / BROWNS

Year	Rec.	Yards	Avg.	TDs
1990	82	1208	14.7	10
1991	81	976	12.0	12
1992	93	1121	12.1	11
1993	86	1242	14.4	15
1994	81	1088	13.4	8

Comments: The most talented free agent in the 1995 market, Rison signed with the team he liked most as a boy, the Browns. His big-play ability should open up the offense, although the Browns might be hard-pressed in their conservative attack to get him enough balls to keep him happy. In 1994, Rison scored his fewest touchdowns since his rookie season. His production may have been subpar by Rison's standards, but he still ranked seventh in the NFC in catches and 10th in receiving yards. He actually started out red-hot, with 26 catches for 316 yards and four TDs in the first two games. But he dug himself into June Jones' doghouse and was suspended for one game. He averaged 85 catches and more than 11 touchdowns in five seasons in Atlanta, but he wasn't re-signed because of off-field problems and rules violations. Only one other player, Sterling Sharpe, has caught more passes in his first six seasons than Rison's 475 receptions. In 1993, he finished fourth in receptions and set a team record for TD receptions with 15, tying Jerry Rice for the league lead. In 1992, Rison ranked second in the NFL in receiving and fourth in receiving yards. Rison doesn't break too many long ones, as his average per catch is not all that high, but he's practically impossible to stop near the goal line.

The skinny: Will a change of scenery bring out the best — or the worst — in "Bad Moon" Rison?

CRIS CARTER / VIKINGS

Year	Rec.	Yards	Avg.	TDs
1990	27	413	15.3	3
1991	72	962	13.4	5
1992	53	681	12.8	6
1993	86	1071	12.5	9
1994	122	1256	10.3	7

Comments: Nobody makes more acrobatic catches than Carter, and nobody has ever caught passes like he did in 1994. Carter hauled in 122 passes to break Sterling Sharpe's one-year-old NFL record by 10. That's an average of more than seven receptions a game. Carter averaged only 10.3 yards a catch, but he proved to be the ultimate possession receiver. He caught 10 or more passes in four games and had five 100-yard days. His 1,256 receiving yards set a team record and ranked fourth in the NFC. Carter teamed with Jake Reed to form the most prolific receiving tandem in NFL history, with 207 catches. The nine-year veteran had three touchdown catches in Game 4, then caught 14 passes for 167 yards a week later. Carter had 86 catches in 1993, the most ever by a Vikings wide receiver and the second most in team history at the time. He also totaled 1,071 receiving yards, the most by a Viking since Anthony Carter in 1988. Carter caught 72 passes in 1991 and would have hit the 70 mark in '92 except for a shoulder injury that forced him to miss the final four games. In other words, he has turned into one of the best wide receivers in the NFL and in fantasy football.

The skinny: . . . and Buddy Ryan once waived him, saying all Carter could do was catch touchdown passes.

HERMAN MOORE / LIONS

Year	Rec.	Yards	Avg.	TDs
1991	11	135	12.3	0
1992	51	966	18.9	4
1993	61	935	15.3	6
1994	72	1173	16.3	11

Comments: In 1994, Moore ascended into the elite group of NFL wide receivers. His 72 receptions were the most ever by a Detroit wide receiver and his 1,173 receiving yards ranked seventh in the NFC and second in team history. Moore scored 11 touchdowns, which tied for third among all receivers. He tied a team record with at least one TD pass in six straight games. In Game 8, Moore caught nine passes for 106 yards and two TDs. The next week, he caught eight passes for 151 yards and two scores. Moore caught five or more passes in nine games and has caught at least one pass in 46 straight contests. Throughout 1993, Moore was hampered by nagging injuries as well as the Lions' who's-going-to-start-at-quarterback-this-week? problem. Still, he led the team in receiving, receiving yards and touchdowns. In 1992, Moore missed four games but accumulated statistics that would have translated to 67 catches and 1,265 yards over a full season.

The skinny: Hardly a defensive back in football can stop Moore one-on-one.

TIM BROWN / RAIDERS

Year	Rec.	Yards	Avg.	TDs
1990	18	265	14.7	3
1991	36	554	15.4	5
1992	49	693	14.1	7
1993	80	1180	14.8	7
1994	89	1309	14.7	9

Comments: Brown followed up a great 1993 season with an even greater 1994 season. His 89 catches was the most ever by a Raiders wide receiver and six short of Todd Christensen's team record. Brown ranked third in the AFC in receptions and caught more passes than the rest of the Raiders' receivers combined. His career-high 1,309 receiving yards ranked

WIDE RECEIVERS

first in the AFC and fourth in the NFL, and he ranked second in the conference in TD receptions with nine. He had four games with 100 receiving yards, and ranked second in the AFC and fourth in the NFL in punt-return average, 12.2 yards. Brown had an outstanding season in 1993, catching 80 passes for 1,180 yards (first in the AFC) and seven touchdowns (tied for third in the AFC). He was the first Raider to record a 1,000-yard season since 1989. The Raiders' leading receiver in 1992, Brown has fully recovered from a 1989 knee injury that almost ended his career. In 1991, Brown led the team's wide receivers with five touchdowns on only 36 receptions (he also had one TD on a punt return).

The skinny: Brown is the ultimate go-to receiver in the AFC.

MICHAEL IRVIN / COWBOYS

Year	Rec.	Yards	Avg.	TDs
1990	20	413	20.7	5
1991	93	1523	16.4	8
1992	78	1396	17.9	7
1993	88	1330	15.1	7
1994	79	1241	15.7	6

Comments: Irvin had one of his typically great, consistent seasons in 1994. He caught at least two passes in every game and finished fifth in the NFC and eighth in the NFL in receiving yards. His reception total ranked eighth in the conference and marked his fourth straight season with at least 78 catches. Irvin, who had six 100-yard games in the '94 regular season, added two more in the postseason and now has a team-record four 100-yard playoff games. He has 15 games with eight or more pass receptions. The only Cowboy to ever post four straight 1,000-yard seasons, Irvin owns the top four single-season reception and yardage totals in Cowboys history. His 416 career receptions rank third in team history. In 1993 he was second in the league in receiving yards (1,330) and third in receptions (88). He has a career receiving average of 16.67 yards, and has caught at least one pass in 65 straight games. In 1991, he finished second in the NFL in receptions with 93 and first in receiving yards with 1,523, the sixth-best total ever.

The skinny: It's a sure bet that Irvin will catch about 80 passes for 1,300 yards and seven TDs this season. But, with Alvin Harper gone, Irvin might score double-digit touchdowns.

CARL PICKENS / BENGALS

Year	Rec.	Yards	Avg.	TDs
1992	26	326	12.5	1
1993	43	565	13.1	6
1994	71	1127	15.9	11

Comments: Pickens emerged in 1994 as one of the NFL's top young receivers. His 11 touchdown catches led the AFC and his 1,127 receiving yards was fourth best in team history and ranked fifth in the AFC. His 71 catches tied a team record and ranked 10th in the conference. Pickens started somewhat slowly, missed Game 7 due to a shoulder injury then caught fire and had a phenomenal second half. In the final seven games, he caught 48 passes for 785 yards and nine touchdowns. He became the first NFL player in four years to record four straight 100-yard receiving games. Pickens had an excellent season in 1993, considering the Bengals' quarterbacking woes. He started 14 games (missing two), finishing fourth in receptions on the team but first in receiving touchdowns with six. In 1992, though his statistics were merely average, he was one of two wide receivers on most All-Rookie teams.

The skinny: Expect nothing less than huge numbers from Pickens.

TERANCE MATHIS / FALCONS

Year	Rec.	Yards	Avg.	TDs
1990	19	245	12.9	0
1991	28	329	11.8	1
1992	22	316	14.4	3
1993	24	352	14.7	0
1994	111	1342	12.1	11

Comments: One of the free-agent finds of all time, Mathis posted phenomenal numbers in Atlanta last season. He set a team record for catches with 111, the fourth-highest total in league history. After four quiet years as a backup and kick returner with the Jets, Mathis flourished in Atlanta's run-and-shoot attack. While Andre Rison drew double teams, Mathis used his running back–like moves to roll up 1,342 yards, the third-highest total in the league and second most in Falcons history. Mathis tied a team record with five 100-yard games, including a 13-catch, 163-yard performance against Denver in Game 11. His 11 TDs tied for third in the league. In 1993, Mathis was the Jets' No. 3 receiver, finishing fifth on the team in receiving. He has never missed a game in six pro seasons. In 1992, he had three TDs among his 22 receptions, and he also scored on a 10-yard run.

The skinny: Mathis probably won't repeat his 1994 numbers, but he won't be too far off, either.

JAKE REED / VIKINGS

Year	Rec.	Yards	Avg.	TDs
1991	0	0	0.0	0
1992	6	142	23.7	0
1993	5	65	13.0	0
1994	85	1175	13.8	4

Comments: In one season, Reed transformed promise into incredible production. After having caught just 11 passes in his first three seasons, Reed stayed healthy in 1994 and developed rapidly. The result was 85 receptions to rank fifth in the NFC and ninth in the league. His 1,175 receiving yards ranked sixth in the conference. Reed and teammate Cris Carter set an NFL record for most receptions by a tandem (207) in a single season. In a year in which Carter set the all-time record for catches, Reed still led the Vikings in receiving yards in six games and in catches three times. He had three 100-yard receiving games, including an eight-catch, 157-yard day in Game 9. Reed was expected to make a big contribution in 1993, but he was injured the first one-third of the season and caught only five passes. Reed was a highly regarded third-round draft pick in 1991.

The skinny: Reed gives new meaning to the term "quantum leap."

ANDRE REED / BILLS

Year	Rec.	Yards	Avg.	TDs
1990	71	945	13.3	8
1991	81	1113	13.7	10
1992	65	913	14.0	3
1993	52	854	16.4	6
1994	90	1303	14.5	8

Comments: One of the league's most consistent receivers for years,

Reed may have had his best season ever in 1994. He became the first Buffalo player to catch 90 passes in a season, and he now owns the top five catch totals in team history. He fell nine yards short of his team record for yardage in a season, 1,312. On a team that has struggled the past couple of years with its deep passing game, Reed caught an 83-yard TD pass and averaged 14.5 yards per catch. On November 20 against Green Bay, Reed caught a team-record 15 passes for 191 yards and two touchdowns. In 1993, he didn't lead the Bills in receiving for the first time in eight years, but he did lead the team in receiving yards and tied for first in receiving touchdowns. In 1991, Reed scored touchdowns in nine games, and his 10 receiving TDs tied a team record. He has caught 50-plus passes in nine consecutive seasons. Reed also has 28 100-yard games during his career, 16 multi-touchdown games and 65 TDs. Reed is a fine runner on end-arounds (39 carries for 309 yards the last four years). He now has 676 career catches, sixth on the NFL's all-time list.

The skinny: Still a great fantasy pick, Reed is truly among the best all-time receivers.

IRVING FRYAR / DOLPHINS

Year	Rec.	Yards	Avg.	TDs
1990	54	856	15.9	4
1991	68	1014	14.9	3
1992	55	791	14.4	4
1993	64	1010	15.8	5
1994	73	1270	17.4	7

Comments: Over the past two seasons, Fryar and Dan Marino have become one of the league's top passing combinations. Fryar has caught at least one pass in all 32 games as a Dolphin. In 1994, he finished third in the AFC in receiving yards with a career-high 1,270. He finished ninth in the conference in receptions, fourth in yards per catch and tied for fourth in receiving touchdowns with seven. Between Games 10 and 13, Fryar logged four straight 100-yard receiving games, a club record. His six 100-yard games for the season tied for second in team history. He didn't have the great 1993 season that many expected, but it wasn't bad, either. Fryar ranked No. 2 on the Dolphins in receiving, No. 1 among wideouts. His 64 catches and 1,010 yards were both the second-highest figures of his career. After several seasons of unrealized potential, Fryar has played very well the last five years. In 1991, he became just the third 1,000-yard receiver in Patriots history, and his 68 catches — fourth most in team history — moved him into second place on the team's all-time receiving list.

The skinny: The Marino-to-Fryar connection will continue to flourish.

ANTHONY MILLER / BRONCOS

Year	Rec.	Yards	Avg.	TDs
1990	63	933	14.8	7
1991	44	649	14.8	3
1992	72	1060	14.7	7
1993	84	1162	13.8	7
1994	60	1107	18.5	5

Comments: When Miller signed with the Broncos in 1994, pairing the speedster with John Elway, Jerry Rice–type numbers were expected. That didn't happen, at least not until the final six weeks. Miller took a while to learn the system and started slowly, with just 12 catches for 162 yards through five games. He hit full stride the final six games, when he had four 100-yard games while catching 27 passes. Miller finished sixth in the AFC with 1,107 receiving yards and second among leaders in average per catch, 18.5. But his 60 catches ranked just 15th in the conference. In 1993, his final season in San Diego, Miller finished second in the AFC in receptions and yards. He had a career-high 84 catches for 1,162 yards and seven touchdowns. Miller has 25 career 100-yard games. In 1989 and '90, he caught 138 passes for 2,185 yards and 17 touchdowns, but quarterbacking problems ruined his '91 season.

The skinny: With a year in Denver under his belt, Miller may produce Rice-type numbers.

MICHAEL HAYNES / SAINTS

Year	Rec.	Yards	Avg.	TDs
1990	31	445	14.4	0
1991	50	1122	22.4	11
1992	48	808	16.8	10
1993	72	778	10.8	4
1994	77	985	12.8	5

Comments: Besides providing the big plays New Orleans has lacked for years, Haynes also showed remarkable consistency in 1994, his first season as a Saint. He caught at least two passes in every game and caught a career-high 77 passes. He placed 11th in the NFC in catches and in receiving yards with 985. Haynes had the team's longest play from scrimmage, a 78-yard TD catch at Atlanta in Game 14. In 1993, he came back to earth after two sensational seasons. He caught 72 passes, but his 778 yards and 10.8-yard average were both ordinary. In 1991 and '92, Haynes scored 21 touchdowns on 98 receptions, a fantastic 21 percent rate, higher than anyone else in the league. Only former teammate Andre Rison and San Francisco's Jerry Rice had more TD catches in that span. Haynes had only moderate success in his first three seasons. But in 1991, he emerged as one of the NFL's top deep threats, with 11 touchdowns and a league-best 22.4-yard average per catch. A former Olympic Trials speedster, he is among the league's fastest players in pads.

The skinny: Haynes should be able to improve on his TD production of the past two seasons.

FRED BARNETT / EAGLES

Year	Rec.	Yards	Avg.	TDs
1990	36	721	20.0	8
1991	62	948	15.3	4
1992	67	1083	16.2	6
1993	17	170	10.0	0
1994	78	1127	14.4	5

Comments: A year after torn knee ligaments wrecked his 1993 season, Barnett rebounded with his best season ever in 1994. He caught 78 passes, the most ever by an Eagles wide receiver. His 1,127 passing yards was the most by an Eagle in nine years. He tied for ninth in the NFC in catches and placed eighth in receiving yards. One of the game's best deep threats, Barnett had six receptions of 47 yards or more (four went for touchdowns). He added three 100-yard receiving days to his career total of 13. In Game 7, he caught five passes for 187 yards. Barnett has quietly turned into one of the best receivers in the NFL. In 1992, he led the Eagles in receptions and receiving yards, ranking 13th and fifth in the NFL, respectively, in those categories. His 16.2-yard average was the second best of all receivers with 55 or more catches. In his first three seasons, 18

of Barnett's 165 catches went for TDs, including eight of 35 yards or more.
The skinny: Only injuries seem to be able to stop Barnett.

ALVIN HARPER / BUCCANEERS

Year	Rec.	Yards	Avg.	TDs
1991	20	326	16.3	1
1992	35	562	16.1	4
1993	36	777	21.6	5
1994	33	821	24.9	8

Comments: Although he had only 33 catches in 1994, Harper gained 821 yards to rank 16th in the NFC. The ultimate big-play, burn-'em-deep receiver, Harper was unhappy with his limited role in Dallas and took a hike, signing with the Buccaneers in the offseason. He led the Cowboys in touchdown catches last season with eight and registered three 100-yard games. Harper is the NFL's all-time leading yards-per-catch leader in the playoffs with a phenomenal 27.9-yard average. He saves his best for when he plays against the best — in four games against the 49ers, Harper has 11 receptions for 367 yards. In 1993, his average per catch of 21.6 yards led the NFC. That was the highest mark for a Dallas receiver since Bob Hayes in 1971. Although he has yet to have a breakthrough season in the NFL, that's because he was overshadowed in Dallas by Michael Irvin.

The skinny: Harper's presence will greatly help his new teammates by spreading defenses thin. But can Trent Dilfer get him the ball?

SOLID PICKS

CALVIN WILLIAMS / EAGLES

Year	Rec.	Yards	Avg.	TDs
1990	37	602	16.3	9
1991	33	326	9.9	3
1992	42	598	14.2	7
1993	60	725	12.1	10
1994	58	813	14.0	3

Comments: Williams's 1994 production was good by NFL standards but not very good by fantasy football standards. He caught 58 passes and his career-high 813 receiving yards ranked 17th in the NFC, but Williams uncharacteristically scored only three touchdowns — and they were all in the first two games. Williams had averaged more than seven touchdowns a season in the first four years of his career. But he ranked second on the Eagles in every receiving category, and 41 of his receptions resulted in first downs. With Fred Barnett out of the lineup in 1993, Williams had career highs for receptions, yards and touchdowns, and he led the Eagles in scoring and receiving yards. His 10 TD receptions ranked fourth in the league. In 1992, he led the Eagles with seven TD receptions and finished third in receiving. A dislocated left shoulder sidelined Williams for a month in 1991, when he had the lowest figures of his career. In '90, he set a team record for rookies with nine TD receptions.

The skinny: Look beyond last season's stats to determine Williams's value on your draft day.

HENRY ELLARD / REDSKINS

Year	Rec.	Yards	Avg.	TDs
1990	76	1294	17.0	4
1991	64	1052	16.4	3
1992	47	727	15.5	3
1993	61	945	15.5	2
1994	74	1397	18.9	6

Comments: A free-agent steal in 1994, Ellard had a phenomenal year despite the absence of a consistent quarterback throwing to him. He finished second in the NFL in receiving yards with 1,397. That ranks second in Redskins history. At age 33, Ellard was the oldest player in history to amass that many receiving yards in a season. His average per catch of 18.9 yards was the highest among the league's 56 receivers with 50 or more catches. Ellard ranked 13th in the conference in catches with 74, and all but three of them were good for first downs. He raced out of the gate with three 100-yard games in the first four weeks and finished '94 with five 100-yard games. In fact, he starred on a team that until December had no other credible receiving threat. In 1993, Ellard's 11th season as a Ram, he led the team in catches and yards receiving. He is the Rams' all-time leading receiver, with 593 catches for 9,761 yards and 48 touchdowns. Ellard has at least 50 receptions in eight seasons, and he ranks second in the league in receiving yards between 1988 and '94 with 8,211.

The skinny: There may still be a couple of good seasons left in the ageless Ellard.

JOHN TAYLOR / 49ERS

Year	Rec.	Yards	Avg.	TDs
1990	49	748	15.3	7
1991	64	1011	15.8	9
1992	25	428	17.1	3
1993	56	940	16.8	5
1994	41	531	13.0	5

Comments: Taylor had another steady season in 1994, finishing fourth on the 49ers in receptions (41) and yards (531), and tying for third in touchdown catches with five. However, for the third straight season he was slowed by injury. Last year, he was bothered by an arthritic condition in his right knee and he sat out the regular-season finale. He caught seven passes for 103 yards and a touchdown in Week 3. In 1993, he finished third on the 49ers in receiving and second in yards and receiving touchdowns. Overshadowed by Jerry Rice, Taylor has the ability to take control of a game all by himself. In fact, if Rice weren't on the 49ers, Taylor might have been able to catch 90 passes and score 15 touchdowns a season, because he has been that good at times. His trademark is the big play, and he is still among the most dangerous after-the-catch receivers in pro football. In 1991, his last healthy season, he caught a career-high 64 passes, and in 1989 he had 60 receptions, 1,077 yards and 10 TDs.

The skinny: Taylor is one of the better No. 2 receivers in NFL history.

DARNAY SCOTT / BENGALS

Year	Rec.	Yards	Avg.	TDs
1994	46	866	18.8	5

Comments: An apparent second-round steal, Scott teamed with Carl Pickens to form one of the most dangerous duos in the NFL in 1994. Scott led the AFC with an average of 18.8 yards per catch, and he tied Pickens for the NFL lead in receptions of 50 or more yards, five. In Games 8 and 9, Scott became the first receiver in Bengals history to record back-to-back

150-yard receiving games. In Game 11, he even completed a 53-yard bomb to Pickens. His 866 receiving yards ranked 13th in the AFC. Scott caught a pass in every game.

The skinny: There's danger lurking in every Scott pass pattern.

WILLIE ANDERSON / COLTS

Year	Rec.	Yards	Avg.	TDs
1990	51	1097	21.5	4
1991	32	530	16.6	1
1992	38	657	17.3	7
1993	37	552	14.9	4
1994	46	945	20.5	5

Comments: One of the NFL's premier home-run threats, Anderson signed with the Colts as a free agent after an excellent 1994 season with the Rams. "Flipper" ranks third in NFL history in average gain per catch, 20.25 yards (for players with a minimum of 200 catches). He had his best season in four years in 1994, when his 20.5-yard average ranked second in the NFL. Anderson led the Rams in receiving yards with 945 (12th best in the NFC), and his five TDs ranked second on the team. His 46 receptions were the third most in his career. In Week 2, Anderson caught five passes for 154 yards, his most single-game receiving yards in five years. In 1993, he missed five games with injuries but finished second on the Rams with 37 catches, 552 yards and four TDs. His production tailed off from 1991 to '93, when he failed to approach the 1,000-yard seasons he put together in 1989 and '90 (though he did score seven times in '92). He has big-play potential and can reach the end zone every time the ball is headed his way.

The skinny: Will Anderson and Craig Erickson turn into a TD combination?

MIKE PRITCHARD / BRONCOS

Year	Rec.	Yards	Avg.	TDs
1991	50	624	12.5	2
1992	77	827	10.7	5
1993	74	736	9.9	7
1994	19	271	14.3	1

Comments: Off to a flying start with 19 catches for 271 yards in three games, Pritchard suffered a lacerated kidney and missed the remainder of the 1994 season. Six weeks after the injury, when hopes of a December return evaporated, Pritchard was placed on injured reserve. He appears to be back at full strength for his second season in Denver. He is one of the best possession receivers in the NFL. In his first three seasons, he averaged only 10.9 yards per catch. But he does have the fifth-most receptions ever for a player in his first three years, 201, and he has caught at least one pass in 50 of the 51 games in which he has played. His 77 catches in 1992 is the fifth-highest total in Falcons history and ranked eighth in the NFL. Pritchard was named to the All-Rookie team in 1991.

The skinny: Figure on Pritchard to come back strong in 1995.

J.J. BIRDEN / FALCONS

Year	Rec.	Yards	Avg.	TDs
1990	15	352	23.5	3
1991	27	465	17.2	2
1992	42	644	15.3	3
1993	51	721	14.1	2
1994	48	637	13.3	4

Comments: Signed as a free agent in the offseason, Birden is tailor-made for Atlanta's run-and-shoot offense. He is a big-play threat, averaging 40.2 yards in his 14 career TDs and 15.4 yards per catch overall. Birden led the Chiefs the past three seasons with 141 catches. Despite missing three games in 1994 with a back injury, Birden was second on the Chiefs in receiving yards and third in receptions. He had back-to-back 100-yard games late in the season. One of the NFL's most underrated receivers, Birden is tied with Otis Taylor for the most catches (27) in Chiefs playoff history. In 1993, he set career highs and was second on the team with 51 receptions for 721 yards. He started all 16 games. A true deep threat, his average per catch is coming down each year, but it's still pretty good.

The skinny: Birden should hook up with Jeff George on a few bombs.

VINCENT BRISBY / PATRIOTS

Year	Rec.	Yards	Avg.	TDs
1993	45	626	13.9	2
1994	58	904	15.6	5

Comments: Despite hobbling through much of the 1994 season with a serious hamstring injury, Brisby finished third in receiving yards and fourth in catches on the Patriots' aerial brigade. He missed two midseason games but still led the team's wide receivers in touchdown catches with five. He caught at least two passes in every game he played in, and in Week 5 he caught six aerials for 117 yards and two TDs. The Patriots' second-leading receiver as a rookie in 1993, Brisby started 13 games. He led all rookie wide receivers in catches with 45, the third most in team history for rookies behind Randy Vataha and Hart Lee Dykes. He has excellent raw physical skills, and displayed better consistency in his second season

The skinny: With Michael Timpson gone, Brisby will make for a great second receiver on a fantasy team this year.

ROB MOORE / CARDINALS

Year	Rec.	Yards	Avg.	TDs
1990	44	692	15.7	6
1991	70	987	14.1	5
1992	50	726	14.5	4
1993	64	843	13.2	1
1994	78	1010	12.9	6

Comments: Arizona made Moore the second-highest-paid receiver in the league when it obtained him in an offseason trade. A broken left wrist hardly slowed Moore in the first two games of 1994, his best season. He broke the wrist in the second preseason game and wore a cast for the season opener, when he caught five passes for 83 yards, and for Game 2, when he caught nine aerials for 147 yards and a touchdown. Moore caught a pass in every game, finished sixth in the AFC in catches with 78 and tied for eighth in yardage with 1,010. Both totals are career highs, and his catch total ranks third in Jets history. His six TD catches tied for seventh in the conference. In 1993, when Moore was slowed by a knee surgery, ankle injuries and then bruised ribs, he still led Jets wide receivers in receptions, though he scored only one touchdown. After just five seasons, he is the team's seventh-leading career receiver (306) and is eighth in receiving yards (4,258). In five NFL seasons, Moore has yet to turn into the kind of gamebreaker he was expected to be.

The skinny: Moore is a solid possession receiver who lacks big-play ability.

BRIAN BLADES / SEAHAWKS

Year	Rec.	Yards	Avg.	TDs
1990	49	525	10.7	3
1991	70	1003	14.3	2
1992	19	256	13.5	1
1993	80	945	11.8	3
1994	81	1086	13.4	4

Comments: In 1994, his seventh season, Blades set career highs in receptions with 81 and yards with 1,086. A Pro Bowl alternate for the second straight season, he finished fifth in the AFC in catches and seventh in yards. In Week 12 he caught seven passes for 141 yards, the 14th 100-yard game of his career. Blades caught a pass in every 1994 game. He had a fine comeback season in 1993, when he broke Steve Largent's team record of 79 receptions in a single season. Blades and Largent are the only Seahawks to ever have 1,000-yard receiving seasons (Blades has three). He now has four seasons with at least 70 receptions, and he possesses three of the team's top four single-season catch totals. Blades played in only six games in 1992 because of a broken collarbone. In 1991, he finished with 70 receptions and over 1,000 yards for the second time in three years.

The skinny: Few receivers have ever caught more passes for fewer touchdowns than Blades.

DERRICK ALEXANDER / BROWNS

Year	Rec.	Yards	Avg.	TDs
1994	48	828	17.3	2

Comments: Despite playing sparingly early in the 1994 season, Alexander led the Browns with 48 receptions and 828 yards. His yardage ranked second among rookies and 15th overall in the AFC, and his 17.3-yard average ranked fifth among the top 20 receivers in the AFC. Alexander missed Game 10 with a twisted ankle. Three weeks later, he caught seven passes for 171 yards, his third 100-yard game of the season. In his first pro start, Alexander caught six passes for 136 yards, including an 81-yard touchdown catch that tied for the sixth longest in team history.

The skinny: But can Alexander turn his big-play ability into TD production?

WILLIE DAVIS / CHIEFS

Year	Rec.	Yards	Avg.	TDs
1992	36	756	21.0	3
1993	52	909	17.5	7
1994	51	822	16.1	5

Comments: In the past three seasons, only Alvin Harper has averaged more yards per catch than Davis among receivers who have had 100 or more receptions. Davis, who in 1994 led the Chiefs with 16.1 yards per catch, has a 17.9-yard average since 1992. He led the team's receivers with 51 catches, second on the team, in 1994. He also led the team in receiving touchdowns and receiving yards. In the season opener, Davis set a career high with seven catches, then matched the feat five games later. Davis, who missed two 1994 games due to a knee injury, has 27 catches of 20 yards or more in the past two seasons. In 1993, he topped the Chiefs in receptions (52), yards (909) and TD catches (7). The TD total was the most by a Kansas City wide receiver since 1988 and was the fourth most in the conference. Davis came out of relative obscurity in 1992, when he led the NFL in yards per catch with a lofty 21.0-yard average.

The skinny: Can Davis still flourish without Joe Montana on the throwing end of his passes?

MIKE SHERRARD / GIANTS

Year	Rec.	Yards	Avg.	TDs
1990	17	264	15.5	2
1991	24	296	12.3	2
1992	38	607	16.0	0
1993	24	433	18.0	2
1994	53	825	15.6	6

Comments: Sherrard had the best season of his injury-plagued nine-year career in 1994. He complained he wasn't used enough, but on a running team without a great quarterback he did well to catch a career-high 53 passes for 825 yards and six touchdowns. He caught a pass in all but one game and had two 100-yard receiving days. Sherrard got off to a great start in 1993 before injury struck once again. He broke his right hip in Game 6 and was then hospitalized with a blood clot. He had been the Giants'

WIDE RECEIVERS

leading receiver with 24 catches when he was injured, ranking third in the NFL in receiving yards at the time. A big-play wideout, Sherrard has the full package of size, speed and consistency. A twice-broken leg sidelined Sherrard for three years, but in 1990 he rebounded nicely.

The skinny: Sherrard could make your draft if he stays healthy — or break your heart if the injury bug strikes again.

TONY MARTIN / CHARGERS

Year	Rec.	Yards	Avg.	TDs
1990	29	388	13.4	2
1991	27	434	16.1	2
1992	33	553	16.8	2
1993	20	347	17.4	3
1994	50	885	17.7	7

Comments: Only three receivers in the AFC topped Martin's seven touchdown catches in 1994. Three of his TD catches went for 40 or more yards, including an NFL record–tying 99-yard touchdown catch in Week 3. He replaced the departed Anthony Miller as the Chargers' big-play threat in 1994, when he led the team in receiving yards with 885 (which ranked 12th in the AFC), and in average per catch, 17.7 yards. Martin finished third on the team in receptions with 50 and he had three 100-yard games. Shut out in the season opener, Martin caught a pass in every other game. He was traded from Miami to San Diego in 1994 after the Chargers lost Anthony Miller in free agency. In 1993, Martin was Miami's sixth-leading receiver, but he led the team with a 17.4-yard average per catch.

The skinny: Martin's career year in '94 was no fluke.

RICKY PROEHL / SEAHAWKS

Year	Rec.	Yards	Avg.	TDs
1990	56	802	14.3	4
1991	55	766	13.9	2
1992	60	744	12.4	3
1993	65	877	13.5	7
1994	51	651	12.8	5

Comments: Lacking a consistent receiver with great hands, the

Seahawks filled a need by trading a fifth-round draft choice for Proehl during the offseason. In 1994, for the fourth time in five years, he led the Cardinals in catches with 51 and he gained 651 yards, the second most on the team. Proehl also led the Cardinals with five touchdown catches. Remarkably consistent and durable (he has never missed a game), Proehl had an outstanding season in 1993, leading Cardinals wideouts in catches, yards and touchdowns. He caught TD passes in five straight games to match a team record — and that's the kind of consistency you want in fantasy football.

The skinny: Proehl is a perfect fit for Seattle quarterback Rick Mirer.

QUINN EARLY / SAINTS

Year	Rec.	Yards	Avg.	TDs
1990	15	238	15.9	1
1991	32	541	16.9	2
1992	30	566	18.9	5
1993	45	670	14.9	6
1994	82	894	10.9	4

Comments: Early paired with Michael Haynes in 1994 to form the most productive receiving tandem in Saints history. The two players combined for 159 receptions and 1,879 yards. The addition of a quality quarterback, Jim Everett, helped Early come of age last season. The seven-year veteran established career highs in catches (82) and yards (894), ranking sixth in the NFC in catches and 14th in yards. Early caught at least three passes in 15 games and started the season off with eight catches for 101 yards, the first of four games with eight receptions. He also started out hot in 1993, with six TDs in the first nine games, but then he was shut out of the end zone the rest of the year. Still, he led the team in TDs. Early first started to show something in 1992, when he caught five touchdown passes on 30 receptions.

The skinny: Early is a fine possession receiver who complements the Saints' long-ball threats.

CHARLES JOHNSON / STEELERS

Year	Rec.	Yards	Avg.	TDs
1994	38	577	15.2	3

WIDE RECEIVERS

Comments: Johnson broke in slowly with the Steelers and their four-wide-receiver rotation in 1994, then was benched in late November. But his four-catch, 165-yard, two-TD effort in the final game may be a sign of things to come. A first-round pick in the 1994 draft, Johnson finished fourth among rookie receivers with 38 catches, and he averaged 15.2 yards per catch. He had two games with seven receptions in each. Johnson averaged 21.6 yards in 16 kickoff returns and 6.0 yards on punt returns.

The skinny: Expect Johnson to emerge as Pittsburgh's No. 1 receiver.

SEAN DAWKINS / COLTS

Year	Rec.	Yards	Avg.	TDs
1993	26	430	16.5	1
1994	51	742	14.5	5

Comments: Dawkins was the closest thing to a gamebreaker in the Colts' receiving corps in 1994. He led the team in receiving yards (742) and average yards per catch (14.5), and finished third in catches. He caught a pass in every game and logged the only 100-yard game among Indianapolis wide receivers. A first-round draft choice in 1993, he started seven of 16 games in his rookie season (though only when the Colts employed three-wide-receiver sets). Dawkins caught passes in only nine games, but a high of eight catches for 144 yards against the Cowboys showed lots of potential. He led the team with a 16.5-yard average per catch.

The skinny: Dawkins will team with Willie Anderson to give the Colts a good pair of starting receivers in 1995.

BEST OF THE REST

MARK INGRAM / PACKERS

Year	Rec.	Yards	Avg.	TDs
1990	26	499	19.2	5
1991	51	824	16.2	3
1992	27	408	15.1	1
1993	44	707	16.1	6
1994	44	506	11.5	6

Comments: Obtained from Miami in an offseason trade, Ingram will move right into Green Bay's starting lineup. In 1994, he ranked fourth on the Dolphins in receptions, third in receiving yardage and sixth in scoring. He has two straight seasons with 44 catches and six touchdowns. Ingram had a career game November 27, when he came off the bench to catch nine passes for 117 yards and four touchdowns. It was only the second time in his career that he had more than one TD catch. Ingram missed one 1994 game due to a shin injury. Early in 1993, he really struggled to learn the Miami offense, but he was an integral part of it late in the year. His six TDs tied for the team lead, and he was fourth in receiving. He had six modestly productive seasons with the Giants before signing with Miami as a free agent a year ago. A speedster who excels on posts and outs, Ingram had the best season of his career in 1991, leading the Giants with 51 receptions.

The skinny: Ingram is adequate, but don't expect him to even begin filling Sterling Sharpe's shoes.

WEBSTER SLAUGHTER / OILERS

Year	Rec.	Yards	Avg.	TDs
1990	59	847	14.4	4
1991	64	906	14.2	3
1992	39	486	12.5	4
1993	77	904	11.7	5
1994	68	846	12.4	2

Comments: Slaughter tied for the team lead in receptions and led the Oilers in receiving yards in 1994. His 68 catches ranked 11th in the AFC, but his 12.4-yard average per catch won't scare many secondaries. Slaughter started 12 games and caught a pass in all but one game. He finished 1994 with his second 100-yard game of the season. In 1993, Slaughter led the Oilers in receiving despite missing the last two-plus games of the year. At the time, he was leading the AFC in receiving and was bidding to become only the seventh person ever to make 100 receptions. It was the most productive season of his nine-year career. He signed with Houston as an unconditional free agent in 1992, immediately making a huge impact. One of the NFL's most underrated wide receivers, he always knew he would be a star on a passing team, which is why he wanted out of Cleveland. He is the Browns' sixth-leading receiver ever.

The skinny: No more run-and-shoot bonanza for Slaughter.

WIDE RECEIVERS

GARY CLARK / DOLPHINS

Year	Rec.	Yards	Avg.	TDs
1990	75	1112	14.8	8
1991	70	1340	19.1	10
1992	64	912	14.3	5
1993	63	818	13.0	4
1994	50	771	15.4	1

Comments: Clark signed with Miami as a free agent in the offseason. Despite nagging groin and leg injuries and only two starts in 1994, Clark led the Cardinals in receiving yardage, and with his 50 receptions became the first player in NFL history to catch 50 or more passes in his first 10 seasons. Clark finished the season tied with Henry Ellard for eighth place on the all-time receptions list with 662 catches. He finished 1994 strong, with two 100-yard games and a 96-yard effort in the final four weeks. Clark took a while to get used to the Cardinals' offense in 1993, but he came on like gangbusters, with 45 catches for 601 yards and four TDs in the final eight games. He ranked third on the Cardinals in receiving. In his last year with the Redskins in 1992, he failed to reach 1,000 yards receiving after three consecutive seasons of doing so. In the last nine seasons, Clark is fourth among active players in receiving yards, and he's tied for fourth in catches. In 1991, he finished second in the NFL in receiving yardage (1,340) and second with a 19.1-yard average.

The skinny: Clark is not done yet, and he might be a big surprise in Miami.

MICHAEL TIMPSON / BEARS

Year	Rec.	Yards	Avg.	TDs
1990	5	91	18.2	0
1991	25	471	18.8	2
1992	26	315	12.1	1
1993	42	654	15.6	2
1994	74	941	12.7	3

Comments: Timpson was signed in the offseason to step right into Chicago's starting lineup. He brings speed, experience and a knack for getting open. In 1994, Timpson led New England's wide receivers with a career-high 74 catches to finish eighth in the AFC. His career-high 941 receiving yards ranked 10th in the conference. He caught a career-high 10 catches in Week 3, then repeated the feat in Game 10. In 1993, Timpson finished third on the team in receiving. He caught at least one pass in 14 of 16 games, and both of his TDs were in the final two games. He has lots of speed and big-play potential but little knack for finding the end zone.

The skinny: Timpson probably had a career year in '94.

LAKE DAWSON / CHIEFS

Year	Rec.	Yards	Avg.	TDs
1994	37	537	14.5	2

Comments: A third-round steal, Dawson had a solid rookie season in 1994. He finished third on the Chiefs in receiving yards with 537 and fifth in catches, 37, despite missing three games with a shoulder injury and one with a knee ailment. In Game 15, Dawson became the first Chiefs rookie in 13 years to reach 100 receiving yards in a game. He started six games, became a permanent part of the offense at midseason, and finished second on the team with 10 catches of 20 yards or more.

The skinny: Dawson's numbers will get better and better.

QADRY ISMAIL / VIKINGS

Year	Rec.	Yards	Avg.	TDs
1993	19	212	11.2	1
1994	45	696	15.5	5

Comments: While his older brother, Rocket, has always received more attention, Qadry is developing into a better NFL player. Ismail was a big-play threat for the Vikings in 1994. He led the team's outstanding starting receivers in average per catch, 15.5 yards. His 65-yard TD catch at New England on November 13 was the team's longest play from scrimmage in three years. Ismail led the team in receiving in Game 6 with seven catches for 117 yards, and he had two 100-yard receiving games. He tied a team record by catching a TD pass in four consecutive games. Ismail finished 10th in the NFC and 14th in the league in kickoff returns with a 23.1-yard average. As a rookie in 1993, he was Minnesota's third wide receiver and finished fifth on the team in receptions. He played just like a rookie — meaning he had flashes of brilliance but lacked consistency and dropped too many passes.

The skinny: "The Missile" will soar higher in '95.

BERT EMANUEL / FALCONS

Year	Rec.	Yards	Avg.	TDs
1994	46	649	14.1	4

Comments: An immediate starter in Atlanta's four-wideout offense, Emanuel tied for second among rookie receivers in 1994 with 46 catches, fourth on the team. He led the Falcons in average per catch at 14.1 yards, and he caught an 85-yard touchdown pass in the season finale, when he had four catches for 136 yards. Emanuel caught at least one pass in 14 games.

The skinny: Emanuel will get better with more experience.

RAGHIB "ROCKET" ISMAIL / RAIDERS

Year	Rec.	Yards	Avg.	TDs
1993	26	353	13.6	1
1994	34	513	15.1	5

Comments: In his second year in the league, Ismail ranked second on the Raiders with five touchdown catches, second in receiving yards with 513 and third in receptions with 34. In Game 13 at San Diego, he caught two TD passes. He finished 10th in the AFC in kickoff returns with a 21.5-yard average. The "Rocket" finally landed in the NFL in 1993 and had a pretty good year. He made a moderate impact as a receiver but was excellent as a kick returner.

The skinny: Ismail is a pretty good player, but he will never approach the potential he exhibited in college.

COURTNEY HAWKINS / BUCCANEERS

Year	Rec.	Yards	Avg.	TDs
1992	20	336	16.8	2
1993	62	933	15.0	5
1994	37	438	11.8	5

Comments: Injuries slowed but didn't stop Hawkins, who in 1994 finished second on the Buccaneers in catches with 37 and touchdown catches with five. A broken hand sustained in the preseason sidelined Hawkins in the opener, and a sprained knee ligament ended his season in the 14th game. After a disappointing rookie campaign, he took advantage of the absence of Lawrence Dawsey to lead the team in receptions, yards and receiving touchdowns in 1993. Over the last six games of '93, he scored four touchdowns on 35 receptions and 565 yards. His 933 yards was ninth in the league and the most by a Buccaneers receiver since 1989.

The skinny: A good receiver on a team loaded with good receivers, Hawkins may become the No. 3 man.

BRETT PERRIMAN / LIONS

Year	Rec.	Yards	Avg.	TDs
1990	36	382	10.6	2
1991	52	668	12.8	1
1992	69	810	11.7	4
1993	49	496	10.1	2
1994	56	761	13.6	4

Comments: The Lions' second-leading receiver the past two years, Perriman had led the club in 1991 and '92. He's a possession receiver who moved from the slot to the outside when Anthony Carter was injured early in '94. He caught a pass in every game. Detroit's best receiver at running after the catch, he also ran nine reverses for 86 yards to rank second on the Lions in rushing. His 69 catches in 1992 were the third-highest single-season total in team history. He ranked sixth in the NFC in receptions and 11th in yards. He was the only Lions player to catch a pass in all 16 games.

The skinny: He'll never be great, but Perriman is consistent.

RICKY SANDERS / FALCONS

Year	Rec.	Yards	Avg.	TDs
1990	56	727	13.0	3
1991	45	580	12.9	5
1992	51	707	13.9	3
1993	58	638	11.0	4
1994	67	599	8.9	1

Comments: The offseason trade acquisition of Eric Metcalf might put Sanders on the sidelines. He did produce in 1994, finishing third on the Falcons in receptions with 67 (his highest total since 1989), but he ran short routes and averaged just 8.9 yards per catch. He caught six or more passes in nine games last year but clearly is no longer the top receiver he once was. Sanders was the Redskins' leading receiver in 1993, though their quarterbacking problems left him with an 11-yard average per catch and only four TDs (all in the first four games). Sanders has caught more than 50 passes in six of the last seven seasons. After two excellent seasons in 1988 and '89, he has been just mediocre since, averaging 55 catches for 650 yards and 3.2 scores. He has never been much of a deep threat (except in Super Bowl XXII).

The skinny: After 10 years, Sanders is slowing down.

DESMOND HOWARD / JAGUARS

Year	Rec.	Yards	Avg.	TDs
1992	3	20	6.7	0
1993	23	286	12.4	0
1994	40	727	18.2	5

Comments: A major disappointment in his first two pro seasons, Howard had a pretty good 1994 season. He ranked third on the Redskins with 40 receptions, second with 727 receiving yards and an excellent 18.2-yard average, and second with five TD catches. He caught a pass in 14 games and finished with 24 catches in his last six games, including two 100-yard outings. The 1991 Heisman Trophy winner started to show some signs of improvement in the final seven games of 1993, when he made 16 of his 23 catches. Howard has a reputation for coasting through practices.

The skinny: The Redskins gave up on Howard, so perhaps a fresh start in Jacksonsville can restore his collegiate form.

LAWRENCE DAWSEY / BUCCANEERS

Year	Rec.	Yards	Avg.	TDs
1991	55	818	14.9	3
1992	60	776	12.9	1
1993	15	203	13.5	0
1994	46	673	14.6	1

Comments: Dawsey returned from a serious knee injury to lead the Buccaneers in receiving last season despite missing the first six games. He had torn ligaments in his left knee in the fourth game of 1993 and missed the remainder of that season, but he has fully recovered. Upon returning, Dawsey caught four passes for 65 yards and a touchdown against the 49ers in Game 7. He finished strong down the stretch like the sure-handed receiver he was before the knee injury, and he has now caught a pass in the last 43 games in which he played. Dawsey led the Buccaneers in receiving in both 1991 and '92, although he scored only four times. A steal in the third round, he made the All-Rookie team when he led all first-year receivers in catches (55) and yards receiving (818).

The skinny: If quarterback Trent Dilfer develops quickly, Dawsey will likely post excellent numbers in 1995.

ROOKIES

See Chapter 12, Rookie Report.

COULD COME ON

KEVIN WILLIAMS / COWBOYS

Year	Rec.	Yards	Avg.	TDs
1993	20	151	7.6	2
1994	13	181	13.9	0

Comments: One of the top kick returners in the NFL, Williams will likely assume a starting job in 1995 due to the departure of Alvin Harper. In 1994, Williams finished third in the NFC and fourth in the NFL in kickoff returns with a 26.7-yard average. Williams finished sixth in the NFC in punt returns with an 8.9-yard average and was sixth on the team in receptions. As a rookie in 1993, Williams scored six TDs — two on receptions, two on end-arounds and two on punt returns. He finished sixth on the team in receiving, though he averaged only 7.6 yards per catch. He also led the team in punt and kickoff returns.

The skinny: Look for a big increase in production in 1995.

ISAAC BRUCE / RAMS

Year	Rec.	Yards	Avg.	TDs
1994	21	272	13.0	3

Comments: Bruce's first NFL reception, a 34-yard touchdown pass in Week 2 of the 1994 season, may be an indication of things to come. The Rams believe he has the tools to become a great receiver. A second-round draft pick in 1994, Bruce caught a pass in 11 straight games but sprained his right knee and missed the final four games. Bruce tied for third place in touchdown catches among rookie wide receivers with three. He finished seventh on the Rams in catches and reception yards.

The skinny: Bruce will replace Willie Anderson and become a major player.

RANDAL HILL / DOLPHINS

Year	Rec.	Yards	Avg.	TDs
1991	43	495	11.5	1
1992	58	861	14.8	3
1993	35	519	14.8	4
1994	38	544	14.3	0

Comments: The speedy Hill has returned to the team that drafted him four years ago after three mediocre seasons in Arizona. In 1994, he wrestled a starting job away from Gary Clark and was fourth on the team in catches and reception yards. In 1993, he made three of his four TD receptions over the final three weeks. He was fourth on the Cardinals in receiving, with at least one catch in 14 games. In 1992, Hill led the team in receiving yardage with 861, and he finished as the team's second-leading receiver. After coming to the Cardinals in an early-season trade in '91, he started only five games but was the team's third-leading receiver.

The skinny: Hill could be primed for a career year.

CURTIS CONWAY / BEARS

Year	Rec.	Yards	Avg.	TDs
1993	19	231	12.2	2
1994	39	546	14.0	2

Comments: In 1994, Conway became the first Bear in 14 years to have a rush, reception, pass, kickoff return and punt return in one season. He was having a fairly good sophomore season until a thigh injury in Game 10 sidelined him the next three weeks. Conway tied for second in receptions, was second in receiving yardage and led the team with a 14.0-yard average per catch. He had a fine 22.8-yard kickoff-return average. In Week 2, Conway caught seven passes for 148 yards and a touchdown. The sixth pick in the 1993 draft, Conway had a disappointing rookie season, although the Bears' woes on offense were much to blame. The speedster was to be brought along slowly, but Wendell Davis's injury forced him into the lineup for seven starts.

The skinny: It's time for Conway to realize his great potential.

ROBERT BROOKS / PACKERS

Year	Rec.	Yards	Avg.	TDs
1992	12	126	10.5	1
1993	20	180	9.0	0
1994	58	648	11.2	4

Comments: Brooks emerged as a solid starting receiver opposite Sterling Sharpe in 1994. His 58 catches, which tied for 18th in the NFC, nearly doubled his two-year career total entering the season. He started every game for the first time in his career and teamed with Sharpe to give the Packers their first pair of receivers in 11 years to catch 50 or more passes. In Game 14 against the Bears, Brooks recorded his first 100-yard receiving game, but he is much more explosive as a kick returner than as a receiver. He had touchdown returns of 96 yards on a kickoff and 85 yards on a punt. Brooks averaged 8.8 yards per punt return to rank seventh in the NFC. He returned only nine kickoffs last year, but led the NFL in kickoff returns in 1993 with a 26.6-yard average.

The skinny: Brooks is a good starting receiver but is not the No. 1 guy the Packers need.

RAY CRITTENDEN / PATRIOTS

Year	Rec.	Yards	Avg.	TDs
1993	16	293	18.3	1
1994	26	379	13.5	3

Comments: The departure of Michael Timpson paves the way for Crittenden to fight for a starting job in 1995. Last year, he caught a pass in nine of the first 10 games but often disappeared in the final six outings. He placed sixth on the Patriots in receptions with 26 and in receiving yards with 379. Crittenden's 19.2-yard kickoff-return average in 1994 was not very good, but he did better on punt returns, averaging 8.6 yards. He had a highlight film–type diving 23-yard TD catch against Miami in the season opener. A rookie free agent in 1993, Crittenden finished eighth on the team in receiving and had an excellent 18.3-yard average per catch.

The skinny: Crittenden is definitely a player to watch in '95.

RYAN YARBOROUGH / JETS

Year	Rec.	Yards	Avg.	TDs
1994	6	42	7.0	1

Comments: Yarborough played in 13 games but made little impact in his rookie season of 1994. He caught six passes for just 42 yards. In Game 11, he caught an 11-yard touchdown pass. A second-round pick out of Wyoming, Yarborough was tremendously productive in college. In 1995, he'll get a golden opportunity to start, because Rob Moore and Art Monk are gone.

The skinny: A much bigger role is planned for Yarborough in 1995.

JOHNNIE MORTON / LIONS

Year	Rec.	Yards	Avg.	TDs
1994	3	39	13.0	1

Comments: While several other top wide receiver prospects had good rookie seasons in 1994, Morton struggled. Although he played in 14 games, he didn't catch a pass until Week 13, and he finished with only three catches. Morton did score on an 18-yard touchdown pass and a 93-yard kickoff return, but he mostly sat on the bench behind consistent veteran Aubrey Matthews. The offseason departure of Mel Gray may result in greatly increased kick-return responsibilities for Morton this year.

The skinny: It's too early to call Morton a bust, but it is time for him to step up.

1994 SURPRISES

MARK SEAY / CHARGERS

Year	Rec.	Yards	Avg.	TDs
1993	0	0	0.0	0
1994	58	645	11.1	6

Comments: Seay came out of nowhere to catch three touchdown passes in the first two games of 1994, then slowed his TD pace but developed into a fairly solid possession receiver. Seay tied Ronnie Harmon for the Chargers' lead in catches, and he finished second on the team in receiving yardage with 645. He was also second in TD catches with six and he caught a pass in 14 games. In the team's playoff opener against Miami, he caught six passes for 61 yards and a score. Seay earned a starting job with a strong showing in training camp. In Week 2, he caught eight passes for 119 yards and two TDs. But later in the season, he dropped too many passes. In 1993, San Diego picked up Seay on waivers from the 49ers, where he had been sitting on the bench.

The skinny: Watch closely in the preseason to see if Seay opens the 1995 season as a starter.

JEFF GRAHAM / BEARS

Year	Rec.	Yards	Avg.	TDs
1991	2	21	10.5	0
1992	49	711	14.5	1
1993	38	579	15.2	0
1994	68	944	13.9	4

Comments: In 1994, his first year with the Bears, Graham had a breakthrough season, with career highs in catches, yards and touchdowns. He caught at least two passes in every game and filled a gaping hole in the team's offense. His 68 receptions were the most by a Bear in 24 years. Graham finished 56 yards short of becoming Chicago's first 1,000-yard receiver since 1970, and he had two 100-yard receiving games. Notorious for failing to produce touchdowns in the first three years of his career, Graham scored five last season. With Pittsburgh in 1993, he caught 38 passes (third on the team) and had a pretty good 15.2-yard average per catch, but he still dropped too many catchable balls. In 1992, he had a fine sophomore season after doing little as a rookie the season before. In the first two games of 1992, he caught 13 passes for 235 yards and one touchdown.

The skinny: Graham has developed into a dependable go-to receiver, but he might be relegated to playing the slot in passing situations in '95.

TORRANCE SMALL / SAINTS

Year	Rec.	Yards	Avg.	TDs
1992	23	278	12.1	3
1993	16	164	10.3	1
1994	49	719	14.7	5

Comments: Small heads into the 1995 season coming off a career game. In the 1994 season finale, he caught six passes for 200 yards — the second-highest receiving-yardage total in Saints history — and scored on touchdown passes of 75 and 36 yards. He led the Saints in average per catch, 14.7 yards, and placed third in receptions and yardage. Small's penchant for clutch catches — he caught 20 passes on third downs last season — helped make him a hot commodity on the free-agent market, but the Saints matched Seattle's offer. Just when he was coming on in 1993 with 14 catches in Games 3–7, Small was injured and caught only one pass the rest of the year. A great fifth-round draft pick in 1992, he was a pleasant surprise as a rookie, catching 23 passes and scoring three touchdowns.

The skinny: At 6-foot-3, Small looms much larger than his name suggests.

CHARLES WILSON / BUCCANEERS

Year	Rec.	Yards	Avg.	TDs
1990	7	84	12.0	0
1991	19	305	16.1	1
1992	0	0	0.0	0
1993	15	225	15.0	0
1994	31	652	21.0	6

Comments: Wilson was best known as a kickoff returner before last year, when he developed into a dangerous and explosive pass receiver. He led Tampa Bay with six touchdown passes — four of which went for 40 or more yards. He had an outstanding 21.0-yard average per catch and he also averaged 25.1 yards on 10 kickoff returns. In a game against the Rams, Wilson caught four passes for 176 yards and two touchdowns. As a kick returner, he ranked third in the NFC in both 1990 and '91, when he was with Green Bay. As a receiver, he caught 15 passes for 225 yards in 1993.

The skinny: With Alvin Harper now a Buccaneer, don't expect repeat production from Wilson.

FLOYD TURNER / COLTS

Year	Rec.	Yards	Avg.	TDs
1990	21	396	18.9	4
1991	64	927	14.5	8
1992	5	43	8.6	0
1993	12	163	13.6	1
1994	52	593	11.4	6

Comments: In 1994, his first season with the Colts, Turner started all 16 games for the first time in his career, and his numbers showed it. He led the team's receivers with six TDs, tied for the team lead in receptions with 52 and finished second in receiving yards. Turner caught a pass in all but one game and had three or more catches in 12 games. An up-and-coming star in 1991, he really struggled to recover from a 1992 injury when he broke his left thigh. He caught only 17 passes in the two seasons that followed the injury. In 1991, he went from a backup to the Saints' top pass catcher, with a career-high 64 catches for 927 yards and eight scores.

The skinny: Turner will round out a fine Colts receiving corps as the No. 3 man.

1994 DISAPPOINTMENTS

MICHAEL JACKSON / BROWNS

Year	Rec.	Yards	Avg.	TDs
1991	17	268	15.8	2
1992	47	755	16.1	7
1993	41	756	18.4	8
1994	21	304	14.5	2

Comments: After missing half of the 1994 season with a hamstring pull, Jackson came alive in the playoffs, leading the Browns with 10 catches for 169 yards. He recorded the team's fourth-best single-game playoff receiving-yardage total, 122 yards, against New England. Jackson made the most of his 21 regular-season catches, as 18 went for first downs. He is fast and gets open, but he is inconsistent and was benched for the 1994 regular-season finale. In his two previous seasons, Jackson had emerged as one of the best wide receivers in fantasy football, catching 15 touchdown passes. His eight TDs in 1993 tied for second in the AFC, as did his 18.4-yard average per catch (for players with at least 700 receiving yards). Jackson came out of nowhere in '92, when his seven TDs surprised nearly everybody.

The skinny: The acquisition of Andre Rison may reduce Jackson's role to that of a third-down specialist.

ERNEST GIVINS / CUT BY OILERS

Year	Rec.	Yards	Avg.	TDs
1990	72	979	13.6	9
1991	70	996	14.2	5
1992	67	787	11.7	10
1993	68	887	13.0	4
1994	36	521	14.5	1

Comments: The most productive receiver in Oilers history, Givins was cut on May 15, not long after posting the worst season of his career in 1994. He caught only 36 passes, a single-season low, and he scored only two touchdowns. In fact, Givins caught only eight passes over the last five weeks of the season. He led the team in punt returns with 37, but averaged a dismal 5.7 yards despite a 78-yard touchdown runback. Givins owns team records in career receptions with 542, and career receiving yards, 7,935. He ranked second on the team in receptions and yards in 1993, and he scored four touchdowns. Along with Gary Clark, he is the only player in NFL history to catch at least 50 passes in each of his first eight seasons. Durable, he has missed only two games in nine seasons. He set a personal high with 10 touchdown catches in 1992, first in the AFC and third most in the NFL.

The skinny: Givins is not quite done yet, but he does need a new address.

MARK CARRIER / PANTHERS

Year	Rec.	Yards	Avg.	TDs
1990	49	813	16.6	4
1991	47	698	14.9	2
1992	56	692	12.4	4
1993	43	746	17.3	3
1994	29	452	15.6	5

Comments: Carrier struggled in 1994, his second season with the Browns. He was not a favorite target of Vinny Testaverde, Carrier's former quarterback in Tampa Bay. The Panthers selected Carrier in the 16th round of the expension draft. In '94, Carrier ranked second among Cleveland receivers in receptions with 29, but he struggled with a hamstring injury after midseason. All but five of his catches were good for first downs. The reception total, though, was his lowest since his rookie season of 1987. In 1993, his first season in Cleveland, Carrier was the team's second-leading receiver and tops among wideouts. He had a career-high 17.3-yard average per catch and three TDs. The Buccaneers' all-time leading receiver, he has 17 career 100-yard games. It's likely Carrier won't ever repeat the excellent season he had in 1989 in Tampa Bay (86 catches for 1,422 yards and nine touchdowns), but he is a solid starter.

The skinny: Carrier should be the top Carolina receivers.

JAMES JETT / RAIDERS

Year	Rec.	Yards	Avg.	TDs
1993	33	771	23.4	3
1994	15	253	16.9	0

Comments: Jett is one of the league's fastest players, but he did little in 1994 as the Raiders' third wide receiver. He dropped some passes early and often disappeared, with no catches in eight games. An undrafted rookie free agent in 1993, Jett had an excellent 23.4-yard average per catch, the best mark in the NFL. He was third on the team in receiving, though he started just one game. He was a member of the 1992 Olympic Gold Medal–winning 400-meter relay team.

The skinny: Speed kills, but in the NFL it only kills if you can catch the ball.

QUESTION MARKS

ERIC METCALF / FALCONS

Year	Rush	Yards	TDs	Rec.	Yards	TDs
1990	80	248	1	57	452	1
1991	30	107	0	29	294	0
1992	73	301	1	47	614	5
1993	129	611	1	63	539	2
1994	93	329	2	47	436	3

Comments: Atlanta swapped first-round draft picks with the Browns to obtain Metcalf, an all-purpose standout who is being switched from running back to slot receiver. In 1994, Metcalf became the second player in Browns history to be listed among the top 10 rushers, receivers, kickoff returners, punt returners and combined yardage leaders. He finished second on the team with seven total touchdowns, second in rushing and second in receiving. He became the fourth player in NFL history to return at least two punts for TDs in successive seasons, and he finished fifth in the AFC in punt returns with a 9.9-yard average. The top multipurpose threat in the NFL in 1993 (1,932 combined yards), Metcalf was second on the Browns in rushing and first in receiving. Following two subpar seasons, he made a fine comeback in 1992. He was the Browns' second-leading receiver with 47 catches and third-leading rusher with 301 yards, and he scored seven TDs. As a rookie in 1989, Metcalf scored 10 TDs.

The skinny: The Falcons will try to find many ways of getting the ball in Metcalf's hands in 1995.

HAYWOOD JEFFIRES / OILERS

Year	Rec.	Yards	Avg.	TDs
1990	74	1048	14.2	8
1991	100	1181	11.8	7
1992	90	913	10.1	9
1993	66	753	11.4	6
1994	68	783	11.5	6

Comments: Despite tying for the team lead in receptions in 1994, Jeffires was cut by the Oilers in early March due to salary considerations and then re-signed. Last year, Jeffires led the team with six touchdowns and tied for the NFL lead in two-point conversions with three. He tied Webster Slaughter for the team lead in receptions with 68, Jeffires's fifth consecutive season with 50 or more catches. He caught at least one pass in every game. Since 1990, Jeffires has averaged 80 receptions and 7.2 touchdowns per season. The fifth Houston receiver to surpass 400 career receptions, he now ranks third on the team's all-time list with 454. In 1993, he caught only 66 passes and slipped to third on the Oilers in receiving. That snapped his streak of three straight years as the AFC pass-catching champ. Still, he led the Oilers with six TD catches. He has caught at least one pass in 79 of the last 80 games. In 1991, he became only the fifth player in pro football history to amass 100 receptions in one season.

The skinny: One of the game's best possession receivers, in 1995 Jeffires will make the Oilers glad they re-signed him during the offseason.

ANTHONY CARTER / LIONS

Year	Rec.	Yards	Avg.	TDs
1990	70	1008	14.4	8
1991	51	553	10.8	5
1992	41	580	14.1	2
1993	60	774	12.9	5
1994	8	97	12.1	3

Comments: After catching five passes for 61 yards and a pair of touchdowns in the Lions' 1994 season opener, Carter broke his collarbone the next week and missed 11 games. He returned for the final three games but played sparingly. Thought to be getting too old just two years ago, Carter resurrected his career in 1993 with the Vikings. He finished second on the team in receiving, receiving yardage and receiving touchdowns and first in average per catch. At midseason, he had successive games of 8 catches for 86 yards, 10 for 164, 4 for 111 and 9 for 104, with three touchdowns — proving he can still play with the best. Carter had disappointing seasons in 1991 and '92. He had three consecutive 1,000-yard seasons from 1988 to '90, and he averaged nearly seven touchdowns a season until '92.

The skinny: Carter might have to call it a career after 10 seasons.

WIDE RECEIVERS

VANCE JOHNSON / BRONCOS

Year	Rec.	Yards	Avg.	TDs
1989	76	1095	14.4	7
1990	54	747	13.8	3
1991	21	208	9.9	3
1992	24	294	12.3	2
1993	36	517	14.4	5

Comments: Given the choice between making more money in Seattle or staying home and going back to his old team, Johnson chose the latter, signing a one-year contract with the Broncos during the offseason. He sat out all of 1994 after being cut by the Chargers. Now he'll be reunited with John Elway, a pairing that connected on 35 touchdown passes between 1985 and '93. With the Broncos in 1993, Johnson was having his best season in several years before breaking his ankle in Game 11. In the 10 games he played, he caught 36 passes and scored five touchdowns. He had disappointing seasons in 1991 and '92.

The skinny: Can the old Elway-to-Johnson magic return?

OTHERS

KELVIN MARTIN / JAGUARS

Year	Rec.	Yards	Avg.	TDs
1990	64	732	11.4	0
1991	16	243	15.2	0
1992	32	359	11.2	3
1993	57	798	14.0	5
1994	56	681	12.2	1

Comments: The most experienced player on Jacksonville (he's played nine pro seasons), Martin was acquired with the 29th pick in the expansion draft. He is coming off a good 1994 season with the Seahawks. He finished second on the team in receptions (56) and in reception yards (681). Martin caught a pass in all but one game, and in Week 5 he caught eight passes for 104 yards and a touchdown. In 1993, he was a welcome addition to a team looking for a complementary receiver to Brian Blades.

He led the team with five receiving TDs and a 14.0-yard average per catch, with at least one reception in all 16 games. Martin led the Cowboys in receiving in '90 with a career-high 64 catches.

The skinny: Martin is a good catch who should catch quite a few for the Jaguars, but he doesn't score very often.

O.J. McDUFFIE / DOLPHINS

Year	Rec.	Yards	Avg.	TDs
1993	19	197	10.4	0
1994	37	488	13.2	3

Comments: In 1994, McDuffie finished fifth on the Dolphins in receptions and fourth in reception yards. His penchant for producing first downs is uncannny; last year, he touched the ball 42 times and picked up 31 first downs. On third down, McDuffie made a first down all 16 times he touched the ball. In Game 9, he caught seven passes for 108 yards, both career highs. McDuffie led Miami in punt and kickoff returns the last two seasons, although his respective 1994 averages of 7.1 yards and 21.3 yards are mediocre. In 1993, he ranked seventh on the team with 19 catches, but had only a 10.4-yard average per catch and no scores (he had two TDs on punt returns). He caught passes in the final nine games.

The skinny: With just three touchdowns in two seasons, "Mr. First Down" is far from becoming "Mr. Touchdown."

SHAWN JEFFERSON / CHARGERS

Year	Rec.	Yards	Avg.	TDs
1991	12	125	10.4	1
1992	29	377	13.0	2
1993	30	391	13.0	2
1994	43	627	14.6	3

Comments: In 1994, Jefferson set career highs for the third year in a row, catching 43 passes for 627 yards and three touchdowns. He started all 16 games and caught a pass in all but one. But, although he has great speed, he did not have more than 79 receiving yards in a 1994 game. He did, however, catch TD passes of 47, 52 and 29 yards and rush three times for 40 yards.

The skinny: Jefferson may be better suited for the No. 3 receiver slot.

WIDE RECEIVERS

BILL BROOKS / CUT BY BILLS

Year	Rec.	Yards	Avg.	TDs
1990	62	823	13.3	5
1991	72	888	12.3	4
1992	44	468	10.6	1
1993	60	714	11.9	5
1994	42	482	11.5	2

Comments: In 1994, Brooks had the fewest pass receptions, 42, in his nine-year career. He finished fourth on the Bills in catches and third in receiving yards, but he was let go in late April. He started nine of 1994's 16 games and had seven receptions in two games. In 1993, his first season with the Bills, Brooks finished second on the team with 60 receptions, the fifth time in his career he has caught at least that many. In 1992, Brooks was demoted by the Colts to second string. Prior to that year, Brooks had led Colts receivers in receiving four times in six years. He had caught at least one pass in 118 of 122 career games until 1994, when he was shut out in three games.

The skinny: Brooks seems to be on the backside of an excellent career.

YANCEY THIGPEN / STEELERS

Year	Rec.	Yards	Avg.	TDs
1991	0	0	0.0	0
1992	1	2	2.0	0
1993	9	154	17.1	3
1994	36	546	15.2	4

Comments: Despite starting just five games in 1994, Thigpen was the Steelers' most consistent wide receiver. He caught a pass in 14 games, finished fourth on the team in receptions and yardage and he led the receiving corps with four touchdown passes. His steady play put Andre Hastings on the bench for the final five regular-season games. He also averaged 24.2 yards in five kickoff returns. Thigpen caught only nine passes in 1993, but three of them went for touchdowns. He was injury-plagued early in his career.

The skinny: Thigpen enters 1995 as Pittsburgh's starter opposite Charles Johnson.

TODD KINCHEN / RAMS

Year	Rec.	Yards	Avg.	TDs
1992	0	0	0.0	0
1993	8	137	17.1	1
1994	23	352	15.3	3

Comments: Kinchen's pro career has sure gotten off to a rocky start, but he shows signs of being a big-play man. The Rams released Kinchen two days after the 1994 season opener, then re-signed him 15 days later. He caught 23 passes for 352 yards and three touchdowns, all in the final 11 games. In San Francisco on November 20, Kinchen scored on a 44-yard end-around. Two weeks later, he caught five passes for 76 yards and a TD. In 1993, he caught eight passes for 137 yards and a TD, then tore ligaments in his left knee in a basketball game. Kinchen drew attention when he returned two punts for touchdowns in the final game of 1992.

The skinny: A player worth watching, Kinchen could be a good midseason fantasy pickup.

DON BEEBE / PANTHERS

Year	Rec.	Yards	Avg.	TDs
1990	11	221	20.1	1
1991	32	414	12.9	6
1992	33	554	16.8	2
1993	31	504	16.3	3
1994	40	527	13.2	4

Comments: Beebe was another free agent who signed with Carolina during the offseason. Despite sitting out three games due to a concussion, he had his most consistent season in 1994 for the Bills. He caught at least one pass in every game he played, and had a career-high 40 catches, fifth on the team. Buffalo's No. 3 receiver most of his career, Beebe ranked third on the team in yards with 527. In 1993, he ranked fifth in catches and second in yards per catch. He caught passes in 13 games and gained his sixth career 100-yard game. Beebe set personal highs in 1992 with 33 catches for 554 yards. He is one of the fastest players in the NFL, but his problem is that he always seems to get injured.

The skinny: In a 1991 game, Beebe caught four touchdown passes.

CHRIS CALLOWAY / GIANTS

Year	Rec.	Yards	Avg.	TDs
1990	10	124	12.4	1
1991	15	254	10.9	1
1992	27	335	12.4	1
1993	35	513	14.7	3
1994	43	666	15.5	2

Comments: In his first season as a full-time starter, Calloway took a step up in 1994. He set career highs in catches (43), receiving yards (666) and average per catch (15.5 yards). He ranked second on the Giants in all three of those categories. He caught at least one pass in every game and had a career-high 93 yards on three receptions in Week 7. The Giants' third-leading receiver in '93, Calloway caught 31 of his 35 passes in the last nine games after Mike Sherrard was injured. The year before, he finished sixth in receiving.

The skinny: Calloway's numbers could improve as Giants quarterback Dave Brown improves.

JESSIE HESTER / RAMS

Year	Rec.	Yards	Avg.	TDs
1990	54	924	17.1	6
1991	60	753	12.6	5
1992	52	792	15.2	1
1993	64	835	13.0	1
1994	45	644	14.3	3

Comments: A good free-agent pickup in 1994, Hester ranked third on the Rams in catches with 45 and second in receiving yards with 644. He caught a pass in every game, extending his streak of at least one reception to 78 games. That streak ranks sixth among active players. In his best game, at Tampa Bay December 11, Hester caught six passes for 82 yards and a touchdown. He now has 5,451 career receiving yards. Hester was a first-round bust with the Raiders and retired in 1989, but the Colts saw something in him, giving him another chance, and he gave them four good, consistent seasons in return, averaging 57 receptions and 826 yards.

The skinny: Hester's career has had almost as many lives as a cat.

ANTHONY MORGAN / PACKERS

Year	Rec.	Yards	Avg.	TDs
1991	13	211	16.2	2
1992	14	323	23.1	2
1993	1	8	8.0	0
1994	28	397	14.2	4

Comments: The Packers' third wide receiver in 1994, Morgan logged career highs in catches and receiving yards. He played in every game for the first time in his injury-riddled career and finished fourth on the team in receiving yards and sixth in receptions. He came on strong during the final 10 games with 23 catches. He caught six passes for 103 yards and two touchdowns — both were career highs — against Detroit in Game 13. Morgan was signed by Green Bay midway through the 1993 season right after he was cut by Chicago, where he was continually beset by injuries. In two and a half seasons in Chicago, the speedy Morgan caught only 27 passes, though he was supposed to begin 1993 as the Bears' starter.

The skinny: With Sterling Sharpe forced to retire, Morgan will battle for a starting job. But he will most likely be Green Bay's third or fourth receiver.

ANDRE HASTINGS / STEELERS

Year	Rec.	Yards	Avg.	TDs
1993	3	44	14.7	0
1994	20	281	14.1	2

Comments: Hastings started 1994 by splitting starting time with Yancey Thigpen in the Steelers' four-receiver rotation. Halfway through the season, Thigpen became the full-time starter and Hastings saw less action. He did finish with eight catches for 105 yards and two touchdowns in the final three games. A possession receiver who lacks deep speed, Hastings did very little as a rookie after dropping two passes in the season opener.

The skinny: Hastings could develop into a reliable No. 3 receiver for the Steelers.

TIM McGEE / BENGALS

Year	Rec.	Yards	Avg.	TDs
1990	43	737	17.1	1
1991	51	802	14.7	4
1992	35	408	11.7	3
1993	39	500	12.8	3
1994	13	175	13.5	1

Comments: After only one year in Washington, McGee re-signed with Cincinnati in April and spent the 1994 season as a second-stringer. He started one game in place of an injured Carl Pickens and caught four passes for 72 yards and a touchdown. McGee didn't do much in his only season as a Redskin in 1993, especially since the team had big problems at quarterback. In his last year with the Bengals, 1992, McGee slipped to 35 catches, his worst season in five years. In 1991, he was the Bengals' second-leading receiver and he topped the team in receiving touchdowns. McGee was Cincinnati's featured receiver in 1989, when Eddie Brown was slowed by injuries, and he had his best pro season, with 65 catches for 1,211 yards and eight touchdowns.

The skinny: It's too bad McGee can't turn back the clock six years.

NATE LEWIS / FALCONS

Year	Rec.	Yards	Avg.	TDs
1990	14	192	13.7	1
1991	42	554	13.2	3
1992	34	580	17.1	4
1993	38	463	12.2	4
1994	2	13	6.5	1

Comments: Obtained on waivers by the Bears from the Rams just before the 1994 season, Lewis earned a job only because he is a good kickoff returner. He finished eighth in the league with a 25.0-yard kick-return average, though he caught only two passes. In Game 13 at Minnesota, Lewis set a Chicago record with 221 kickoff-return yards in a game. In 10 starts with the Chargers in 1993, he was the team's third-leading receiver, though he never was the complement to Anthony Miller that the team wanted. In '92, he was third on the team in receiving, second in TD receptions and first in average yards per catch.

The skinny: Good kickoff returners aren't good fantasy players unless they play more downs than Lewis does.

DEREK RUSSELL / BRONCOS

Year	Rec.	Yards	Avg.	TDs
1991	21	317	15.1	1
1992	12	140	11.7	0
1993	44	719	16.3	3
1994	25	342	13.7	1

Comments: An injury to Mike Pritchard elevated Russell to Denver's starting lineup, but injuries plagued Russell's 1994 season, too. A sprained knee sidelined him for three games early in the season, and he missed Week 12 with a neck injury. Russell finished sixth on the Broncos in receptions and fifth in receiving yards. He caught three passes for 65 yards in the final game. In 1993, he was the Broncos' leading pass-catcher among wide receivers and led the team in kickoff returns. He caught a pass in the first 12 games, then sprained his ankle and missed the rest of the season. He had an up-and-down 1992 season in which he started, then was replaced and finally injured. Russell did have a good rookie campaign in '91.

The skinny: The addition of Ed McCaffrey hurts Russell's chances of playing much in Denver.

JEFF QUERY / BENGALS

Year	Rec.	Yards	Avg.	TDs
1990	34	458	13.5	2
1991	7	94	13.4	0
1992	16	265	16.6	3
1993	56	654	11.7	4
1994	5	44	8.8	0

Comments: The Bengals' leading receiver in 1993, Query sat on the bench most of '94. He did start four games, but he caught just five passes all season and was inactive for four games. In '93, Query enjoyed his best season as a pro. He caught at least one pass in 15 games, three or more in

11 of them, and he scored four touchdowns. A former Packer, he joined the Bengals in midseason of 1992, finishing seventh on the team in receiving but tying for the team lead with three receiving touchdowns.

The skinny: Query has great speed but little chance of getting much playing time.

ERNIE MILLS / STEELERS

Year	Rec.	Yards	Avg.	TDs
1991	3	79	26.3	1
1992	30	383	12.8	3
1993	29	386	13.3	1
1994	19	384	20.2	1

Comments: Mills put highly touted rookie Charles Johnson on the bench for the final six games of 1994 and led the Steelers with an excellent 20.2 yards per catch. He didn't catch enough of those long passes, though, and his 19 receptions ranked just eighth on the team. Mills caught a pass in each of the final seven games (he started the final six). In 1993, Mills was the team's sixth-leading receiver, making at least one catch in 13 games before missing the season finale. A third-round draft pick in 1991 who didn't do much as a rookie, Mills was the team's fourth-ranked receiver with 30 catches in '92, although he started only four games.

The skinny: Mills will take Johnson's seat on the bench this year.

THOMAS LEWIS / GIANTS

Year	Rec.	Yards	Avg.	TDs
1994	4	46	11.5	0

Comments: A season-ending knee injury in Week 9 ruined half of Lewis's rookie season in 1994. He caught just four passes but has an opportunity to become an integral part of the 1995 offense. He averaged 12.8 yards in five punt returns and returned 26 kickoffs for 509 yards, 19.6 yards per attempt. He will get many more opportunities to return kicks due to Dave Meggett's departure.

The skinny: Considered a reach in the first round of the 1994 draft, Lewis can now prove his skeptics wrong.

ED McCAFFREY / BRONCOS

Year	Rec.	Yards	Avg.	TDs
1991	16	146	9.1	0
1992	49	610	12.4	5
1993	27	335	12.4	2
1994	11	131	11.9	2

Comments: Mainly a special-teams player with the 49ers in 1994, McCaffrey backed up Jerry Rice and, not surprisingly, played little on offense. He signed with the Broncos during the offseason and may play a more prominent role as a possession receiver. Last year, he caught 11 passes for 131 yards and two touchdowns. McCaffrey seems to play well when given the opportunity. Despite starting just two games in 1993, he ranked fourth on the team in receptions. In 1992, he started just three games but led the Giants with 49 catches and five receiving touchdowns. A third-round draft choice in 1991 — he was called the steal of the round by Bill Walsh — McCaffrey was the Giants' No. 4 wide receiver as a rookie in 1991.

The skinny: McCaffrey could be good for 30 or 40 catches and three or four TDs in 1995.

CEDRIC TILLMAN / JAGUARS

Year	Rec.	Yards	Avg.	TDs
1992	12	211	17.6	1
1993	17	193	11.4	2
1994	28	455	16.3	1

Comments: Tillman flashes big-play ability at times but disappears at other times. He was obtained by the Jaguars in the expansion draft. In his first three starts of 1994, Tillman caught just three passes for 52 yards. But when he started in Game 11 in place of the injured Derek Russell, he exploded for an eight-catch, 175-yard day, the best all season by a Broncos receiver. Overall, he ranked fifth on the team in receptions and fourth in passing yards. In the final game of 1993, he caught five passes for 91 yards and one touchdown, and in a 1992 game he caught an 81-yard TD. As a rookie, he caught 11 of his 12 passes in the final four games.

The skinny: Tillman just needs to become more consistent.

TOM WADDLE / BENGALS

Year	Rec.	Yards	Avg.	TDs
1990	2	32	16.0	0
1991	55	599	10.9	3
1992	46	674	14.7	4
1993	44	552	12.5	1
1994	25	244	9.8	1

Comments: A blue-collar favorite in Chicago for the last four seasons, Waddle was signed by the Bengals as a free agent in the offseason. He has built a reputation as a clutch third-down receiver who rarely drops a pass. From 1991 to '93, Waddle caught more passes than any other Bears player. Last year he missed two games with a pulled hamstring and four games due to arthroscopic knee surgery, but he still finished fifth on the team in catches and third in receiving yards. Waddle is a possession receiver who can catch in a crowd, but he won't go far once he gets the ball and has had trouble staying healthy because he is so frail. He was a good pickup for Cincinnati.

The skinny: Waddle should be the perfect possession-type complement to Cincinnati's bombs-away passing attack.

NATE SINGLETON / 49ERS

Year	Rec.	Yards	Avg.	TDs
1993	8	126	15.8	1
1994	21	294	14.0	2

Comments: Singleton had a good sophomore season as John Taylor's backup in 1994. He started for the injured Taylor in the final regular-season game and led the team in receiving with six catches for 74 yards. Singleton finished fifth on the team in catches with 21 and in yards with 294, and he led the receivers in yards per catch, 14.0. In Game 12, Singleton caught a 43-yard touchdown pass.

The skinny: Rookie J.J. Stokes will place Singleton deep on the 49ers bench.

AUBREY MATTHEWS / LIONS

Year	Rec.	Yards	Avg.	TDs
1990	30	349	11.6	1
1991	3	21	7.0	0
1992	9	137	15.2	0
1993	11	171	15.5	0
1994	29	359	12.4	3

Comments: A dependable, productive veteran who can play any receiver spot, Matthews last year had his best season since 1990. He started three games, kept rookie Johnnie Morton on the bench and finished fourth on the Lions in receptions and third in receiving yards. A versatile player who can fill in at all four wide receiver spots in Detroit, Matthews didn't play much in the previous three seasons.

The skinny: Matthews probably won't play as much in 1995 as he did in '94.

HORACE COPELAND / BUCCANEERS

Year	Rec.	Yards	Avg.	TDs
1993	30	633	21.1	4
1994	17	308	18.1	0

Comments: Copeland settled into a more limited role last year than he had in his rookie season of 1993. He started just two games in '94 and caught more than one pass in only four games. His fine average per catch of 18.1 yards did approach his rookie average of 21.1 yards per grab. In Game 10, Copeland caught three passes for 98 yards, including a 65-yard touchdown play. As a rookie in 1993, Copeland emerged as a big-play receiver. How big? In successive games near midseason, he scored touchdowns on four consecutive passes, of 26, 67, 60 and 44 yards (juking Deion Sanders for the final score).

The skinny: Copeland will be hard-pressed to get on the field much in '95.

VICTOR BAILEY / CHIEFS

Year	Rec.	Yards	Avg.	TDs
1993	41	545	13.3	1
1994	20	311	15.6	1

Comments: Bailey was acquired by Kansas City in a Draft Day trade. In Philadelphia in 1994, his role was limited in 1994 because of Fred Barnett's return, and he couldn't match his rookie production of '93. Bailey served as the third wide receiver, playing in all 16 games but starting none. He did catch a pass in 12 games. Bailey was among the top rookie receivers in 1993, when he finished second among all first-year wideouts in receptions and fourth in receiving yards. He started the final 10 games after Barnett was injured, missing two starts himself with a hamstring injury.

The skinny: With no star receivers on Kansas City, Bailey gets a new chance.

ARTHUR MARSHALL / GIANTS

Year	Rec.	Yards	Avg.	TDs
1992	26	493	19.0	1
1993	28	360	12.9	2
1994	16	219	13.7	0

Comments: A versatile performer, Marshall played in all 16 Giants games in 1994. He caught 16 passes, ran the ball twice from scrimmage, returned kickoffs and a punt, and even faded back to pass, although he was sacked. He caught more than one pass in only two games, though. Marshall was traded to the Giants on Draft Day of 1994. He was a true free-agent find for Denver in 1992, making most of the All-Rookie teams. In '93, he started nine of 16 games, most of them when Vance Johnson was injured. He was the team's sixth-leading receiver, and he also threw a touchdown pass.

The skinny: Marshall is possibly the Giants' No. 4 wide receiver in '95.

TYDUS WINANS / REDSKINS

Year	Rec.	Yards	Avg.	TDs
1994	19	344	18.1	2

Comments: Winans joined Henry Ellard and Desmond Howard to form the only trio in the NFL in 1994 to average at least 18 yards per catch (players with a minimum of 16 catches). Winans displayed good hands in his limited role as a rookie. He caught passes in 10 games, and in Game 6 he caught two touchdown passes totaling 68 yards. Four weeks later, he had four catches for 52 yards and scored on a two-point conversion play.

The skinny: Winans will battle for the Nos. 2 and 3 receiver positions.

RUSSELL COPELAND / BILLS

Year	Rec.	Yards	Avg.	TDs
1993	13	242	18.6	0
1994	21	255	12.1	1

Comments: Copeland started slowly in 1995 but did much better in the second half of the season. In a four-game stretch, he caught 14 passes for 188 yards and a touchdown. He finished sixth on the team in catches and receiving yards. The Bills' best rookie in 1993, Copeland specialized as a kick returner, leading the team in both punt and kickoff returns. He finished second to Thurman Thomas in combined yards (rushing, receiving and returns). Copeland shows a lot of promise as a receiver, as he averaged a team-high 18.6 yards in '93. But he didn't really improve in his second year.

The skinny: The 1995 season will be a crossroads one for Copeland.

GARY WELLMAN / OILERS

Year	Rec.	Yards	Avg.	TDs
1992	0	0	0.0	0
1993	31	430	13.9	1
1994	10	112	11.2	0

Comments: Coming off a 1993 success story, Wellman missed the first six games of 1994 due to a knee injury. He played in eight games as a substitute but caught just 10 passes for 112 yards. In 1993, Wellman played very well in the final three games while subbing for the injured Webster Slaughter. He finished sixth on the team with 31 catches for 430 yards and one TD. His average per catch of 13.9 yards led the Oilers. He spent most of 1991 on the practice squad and all of '92 on the roster, but he didn't make his first pro catch until '93.

The skinny: Wellman will battle for a roster spot.

ALEXANDER WRIGHT / RAMS

Year	Rec.	Yards	Avg.	TDs
1990	11	104	9.5	0
1991	10	170	17.0	0
1992	12	175	14.6	2
1993	27	462	17.1	4
1994	16	294	18.4	2

Comments: The Rams signed Wright in the offseason to fill the vacancy of gamebreaker Willie Anderson, and he will get an opportunity to become the Rams' big-play threat. Wright did a lot once he got the ball in 1994, but he has trouble getting open. He led the Raiders with an 18.4-yard average, but he caught only 16 passes. A starter in 15 games each of the past two seasons, Wright had a career year in 1993 with 27 receptions, a 17.1-yard average per catch and four TD receptions. After two years as a big bust in Dallas, where he was a second-round draft pick, Wright was acquired by the Raiders in an early-season trade in '92.

The skinny: Time is running out on the six-year veteran to turn potential into big-play ability.

WILLIE GREEN / PANTHERS

Year	Rec.	Yards	Avg.	TDs
1990	Injured			
1991	39	592	15.2	7
1992	33	586	17.8	5
1993	28	462	16.5	2
1994	9	150	16.7	0

Comments: Green began the 1994 season with Tampa Bay and ended it as one of the first players to be signed by the expansion Panthers. He caught nine passes for 150 yards in five games with the Buccaneers, then was waived October 11. A touchdown-maker in 1991, Green hasn't done very much since early 1992. He was signed by the Buccaneers as a free agent after the 1993 season. In '91, he came out of nowhere to score seven times during the regular season and three more in two playoff games. In '92 he followed that up by scoring in each of the first three games. He has a high average per catch and 14 touchdowns over his four-year career, but he really disappears for long stretches.

The skinny: Green is no longer a useful fantasy football pick.

. . . AND THE REST

(listed in alphabetical order)

STEVIE ANDERSON, Jets — Anderson caught a pass in five straight games early in 1994 but had just one catch in the final 10 games and finished the season on the inactive list. He caught nine passes for 90 yards.

MICHAEL BATES, Seahawks — Seattle's primary kick returner, Bates averaged 19.5 yards in 26 kickoff returns in 1994. He caught five passes for 112 yards — an excellent 22.4-yard average. Bates also caught a 40-yard touchdown pass in Week 2.

BUCKY BROOKS, Bills — A knee injury sidelined Brooks for much of his 1994 rookie season. He played in three games and returned nine kickoffs for 162 yards. The speedster will get a chance to earn much more playing time in '95.

REGGIE BROWN, Oilers — In the 1994 season opener, Brown came off the bench to catch four passes for 34 yards and score on a two-point conversion. After that, he did nothing all season. He played in four games.

WESLEY CARROLL, Chiefs — Carroll was waived by the Colts before the 1994 season after three disappointing years in New Orleans and Cincinnati. In 1993, he played in 12 games but caught only six passes. In '92, he caught touchdown passes in each of the first two games, then was shut out of the end zone the rest of the season.

PAT COLEMAN, Oilers — Coleman started two games early in the 1994 season, then was benched and finished the season on the inactive list. In the two games he started, he caught six passes for 78 yards. In Week 4,

Coleman grabbed four passes for 112 yards and a touchdown. But he caught just one pass in the final 10 games and 20 for the season. In 1993, he caught nine passes for 129 yards.

CHARLES DAVENPORT, Jaguars — Davenport was the 19th pick in the expansion draft after sitting on the end of the Steelers' bench in 1994. He played in seven games but caught no passes. In his first two seasons, he caught 13 passes for 187 yards and no scores.

ANTHONY EDWARDS, Cardinals — Edwards spent the 1994 season on injured reserve after suffering a knee injury. In 1993, he turned into a big-play specialist in limited time at wide receiver. He had receptions of 65 yards (touchdown), 55 and 49. That added up to a 25.1-yard average on 13 catches.

LEONARD HARRIS, Falcons — A backup in 1994, Harris caught nine passes for 113 yards. He is a quick 10-year veteran who was signed as a free agent in 1994. His best season was 1992, when he caught 35 passes for 435 yards and three TDs in Houston.

DANAN HUGHES, Chiefs — Hughes caught seven passes for 80 yards in 1994 but is mainly a special-teams player. He led the Chiefs in punt returns with 27 for a 7.1-yard average, and averaged 21.1 yards in nine kickoff returns. He didn't catch a pass in his rookie season of 1993.

KEVIN LEE, Patriots — Lee missed his entire rookie season in 1994 because of a broken jaw suffered in the preseason. However, because of the departure of Michael Timpson, Lee will get a shot at starting in '95. He came out of college as a highly touted speedster. Keep an eye on him.

CHUCK LEVY, Cardinals — In his rookie season of 1994, Levy crawled in and out of Buddy Ryan's doghouse. The team's top kickoff returner with a 19.7-yard average, Levy was moved from running back to wide receiver in late November. Ryan likes the way Levy runs after the catch. Levy could give the Cardinals the big-play threat they sorely lacked in '94.

KEENAN McCARDELL, Browns — McCardell flashes big-play ability, as his gaudy average-per-catch suggests (18.1 yards). He posted career highs with four catches for 80 yards in Week 9, his first of three starts. He also caught a 20-yard pass for Cleveland's only TD against Pittsburgh in the playoffs. In his last four games of 1993, he caught 13 passes for 234 yards and scored four touchdowns. He had two-TD games in consecutive weeks against the Patriots and Rams.

GREG McMURTRY, Bears — McMurtry was picked up on waivers from the Rams and started four games for the Bears in 1994 when Curtis Conway was injured. He caught eight passes for 112 yards, all in the final seven games. McMurtry started the first eight games of 1993 for New England, then lost his starting job to rookie Vincent Brisby. In fact, he didn't catch a pass in any of the last nine games and finished sixth on the team in receiving. He had started 29 of 32 games the previous two seasons, finishing third on the Patriots in receptions both years.

TERRY MICKENS, Packers — Mickens showed some potential as a rookie in 1994. He caught four passes for 31 yards, all in the final eight games. He saw increased playing time as the season progressed and might play more this season.

SCOTT MILLER, Dolphins — Miller scored his first career touchdown, on a one-yard pass, in Game 13. He caught six passes for 94 yards in 1994. In 1993, he caught two passes for 15 yards.

DAVID MIMS, Panthers — Mims started the first two games of 1994 for Atlanta and caught a pass in each, but did almost nothing the rest of the season. A free-agent rookie in 1993, he caught 12 passes for 107 yards and one TD.

TERRY OBEE, Bears — A broken leg sidelined Obee for the entire 1994 season. On a team depleted of wide receivers the previous year, Obee was the third-leading receiver on the Bears (26 catches for 351 yards) and scored the team's most receiving touchdowns (three). A sure-handed overachiever, he moved up from the No. 5 wide-receiver spot in training camp to start five games. If healthy, Obee is a dependable backup, and nothing more.

DAVID PALMER, Vikings — A midseason toe injury slowed Palmer after a decent start to his rookie season of 1994. He caught four passes for 70 yards and a touchdown in a three-week period to earn his first NFL start, but then he did little the rest of the year and was even inactive for three weeks. Palmer led the team in punt returns.

CHRIS PENN, Chiefs — A rookie third-round pick in 1994, Penn caught three passes for 24 yards and returned nine kickoffs for a 21.6-yard average. He has good size but not that much speed.

BRYAN REEVES, Cardinals — A sure-handed possession receiver, Reeves caught on as a rookie free agent and grabbed 14 passes for a 14.4-yard average in 1994. He caught a nine-yard TD pass and had the team's longest kickoff return of the season (53 yards).

PATRICK ROBINSON, Cardinals — Robinson was picked up on waivers early in the 1994 season and finished ninth in the NFC in punt returns with a 7.0-yard average. He averaged 19.3 yards per kickoff return and caught one pass. A rookie in 1993, Robinson caught eight passes for 72 yards. He led the team in both punt and kickoff returns.

RICO SMITH, Browns — Smith started four games in 1994 when Michael Jackson injured his knee. Smith caught two passes for 61 yards, including a 50-yarder. In 1993 he caught four passes for 55 yards. He has exceptional raw speed.

DWIGHT STONE, Panthers — Primarily a special-teams standout, Stone was the odd-man-out of the Steelers' offense in 1994, when he caught just seven passes for 81 yards, so he signed with Carolina as a free agent. In 1993, Stone made a career-high 41 receptions, second on the Steelers, for 587 yards and two TDs. Stone had the most productive year of his career in 1991, when he led Pittsburgh's wideouts with five touchdowns, all of them for more than 40 yards.

LAMAR THOMAS, Buccaneers — Thomas caught seven passes for 94 yards in 1994. He started strong out of the gate as a rookie in 1993, then dropped a few passes and lost his confidence. For the season he caught eight passes for 186 yards and two TDs.

ROBB THOMAS, Seahawks — Thomas spent most of 1994 on the Seahawks' bench. He caught four passes for 70 yards and started one game while backing up Brian Blades. He had pretty good seasons with Kansas City in 1991, when he caught 43 catches for 495 yards, and in 1990. But, in three seasons in Seattle, Thomas has just 22 catches.

MIKE WILLIAMS, Jaguars — Williams had by far his best season in 1994, with 15 catches for 221 yards. In the 12th game, against the Jets, he hauled in three passes for a career-high 62 yards. He caught a pass in nine games. Williams's speed is sorely needed in Jacksonville.

Other Wide Receivers on Rosters

Aaron Bailey, Colts
Shannon Baker, Jaguars
Chris Brantley, Rams
Troy Brown, Patriots
Richard Buchanan, Panthers
Jeff Campbell, Broncos
Greg Clifton, Panthers
Keith Crawford, Packers
Tyree Davis, Buccaneers
Cory Fleming, Cowboys
Daryl Frazier, Panthers
Mel Gray, Oilers
Eric Guliford, Panthers
Travis Hannah, Oilers

Ronnie Harris, Seahawks
Willie Harris, Jaguars
Steve Hawkins, Panthers
Jeff Hill, Bengals
Daryl Hobbs, Raiders
Harrison Houston, Chiefs
Willie Jackson, Jaguars
Hassan Jones, Raiders
Charles Jordan, Packers
Tony Kimbrough, Broncos
Kevin Knox, Cardinals
Sean LaChappelle, Chiefs
Damon Mays, Steelers
Derrell Mitchell, Saints

Orlando Parker, Jets
Greg Primus, Bears
Barry Rose, Panthers
Jermaine Ross, Rams
Larry Ryans, Panthers
Bill Schroeder, Packers
Malcom Seabron, Oilers
Leslie Shepherd, Redskins
Jimmy Smith, Jaguars
Daryl Spencer, Falcons

Milt Stegall, Packers
Charles Swann, Panthers
Jeff Sydner, Eagles
Steve Tasker, Bills
David Thomas, Bills
Doug Thomas, Redskins
Olanda Truitt, Redskins
Clarence Verdin, Buccaneers
Terrence Warren, Seahawks
Eric Weier, Panthers

Chapter 6
TIGHT ENDS

BEN COATES

Tight ends score fewer points in fantasy football than players at any other position, but they still can mean the difference between winning and losing any particular week. And that's why drafting the right tight ends is so valuable.

Every year there are a precious few NFL tight ends who are every bit as good as many wide receivers, players who are capable of scoring up to 10 touchdowns in a season. This year's top receivers are Ben Coates, Eric Green and Shannon Sharpe. Along with Keith Jackson, whose 1995 status is a big question mark, each of them has been considered the best tight end in the league at different times over the last four years.

Coates emerged last year as the game's most dominant tight end since Kellen Winslow. He is the preferred target of a top quarterback in Drew Bledsoe. And tight ends are a major part of coach Bill Parcells's game plan.

Jackson has shown consistency over the years and can score from anywhere. But he has been contemplating retirement and may no longer have the desire to play at the same level that once established him as a star.

Green has apparently put personal troubles behind him, and should be expected to have one of his best seasons — possibly a career year — in 1995 now that he's with Miami. If Green scored 10 or 12 touchdowns in 1995, it wouldn't surprise too many people.

Sharpe is a tight end with the skills of a wide receiver. He will likely produce somewhere between last year's four touchdowns and his nine-TD season of 1993.

After Coates, Green, Jackson and Sharpe, there are several tight ends who are capable of making 40 or so receptions and scoring five or six TDs this season. They are Brent Jones, Troy Drayton, Jay Novacek, Jackie Harris and Pete Metzelaars. These players might not score as much as the top three tight ends, but some of them might catch as many or more passes.

Several other tight ends are capable of producing four or five TDs. They include rookies Kyle Brady and Mark Bruener, Tony McGee and Chris Gedney, Keith and Kerry Cash, Irv Smith and Howard Cross.

So there are enough good or very good tight ends for every team in any fantasy football league, even in today's era of sophisticated offenses and multiple-receiver formations, in which tight ends are too often relegated to blocking duties.

Draft Tips for Choosing Tight Ends

■ Look at past performances, especially the last two or three seasons, rather than just last season (although tight end might be the one position where last year's performance should weigh heaviest).

■ Draft tight ends from predominantly passing teams that spread the ball around, because they are likely to catch more passes. And, on these teams, look for tight ends who are integral parts of a team's passing attack. Those teams are Miami, San Francisco, Pittsburgh, Green Bay, Denver, Dallas, New England, Chicago, St. Louis and the Jets. Stay away from them and other teams that don't throw to their tight ends enough, like San Diego and Arizona. Draft tight ends who play during goal-line situations and ones who run deep pass patterns, because both are apt to get into the end zone.

■ At the same time, if a tight end is on a team with two very good wide

TIGHT ENDS

receivers, he might be apt to catch more passes because those other players will draw more double coverage.

■ Don't draft tight ends who are basically blockers. Know which tight ends are receivers and which ones are blockers.

■ Consider matching a tight end with your quarterback when putting together your team. It's worth more points if you have both players from one team when they score.

■ Take into consideration tight ends on teams that are likely to have a quarterback change during the season. The switching of quarterbacks often means a change in a team's offensive scheme, and thus it could change the production of the player you want to pick.

■ A tight end you draft in the last round won't be much different in terms of scoring capability than one you might draft in the middle rounds, so don't choose one too early if you can stock up on other positions.

■ Watch what is going on during training camp. Has Keith Jackson decided to play for Green Bay, or is he going to call it quits? Will the Jets find a way to utilize both rookie Kyle Brady and veteran Johnny Mitchell in their lineup? Who will be the starters in Buffalo, Arizona, Indianapolis, Minnesota, Philadelphia and Washington? Can Pete Metzelaars still produce on an expansion team? Will Chris Gedney finally stay healthy in Chicago? Will a change of scenery make the difference for Derek Brown in Jacksonville? How good can Jackie Harris be if he stays healthy for an entire season? Can Tony McGee raise his play up to the top level he sometimes flashes? Will Brent Jones approach his nine-touchdown total of 1994? Will Eric Green connect with Dan Marino for huge numbers?

SUPERSTARS

BEN COATES / PATRIOTS

Year	Rec.	Yards	Avg.	TDs
1991	10	95	9.5	1
1992	20	171	8.6	3
1993	53	659	12.4	8
1994	96	1174	12.2	7

Comments: The ultimate third-down option, Coates caught more passes in 1994 than any tight end in NFL history, breaking Todd Christensen's record of 95 by one. Coates set a team single-season receiving record, and his 1,174 receiving yards ranks second in team history. In Week 12, he caught a team-record 12 passes for 123 yards against the Raiders. He caught at least two passes in every game, extending his consecutive game receiving streak to 33. He ranked fourth in the league in catches and fourth in the conference in yardage. Coates became the Patriots' starter in 1993 and led the team in receptions, receiving yards and touchdowns. His eight TD catches ranked second among NFL tight ends, the most for a Patriot at the position since 1980 and most on the team since '86. In 1992, he doubled his output of his rookie season with 20 receptions. Coates can find the seam in any zone defense.

The skinny: Coates is simply the best tight end in the NFL.

SHANNON SHARPE / BRONCOS

Year	Rec.	Yards	Avg.	TDs
1990	7	99	14.1	1
1991	22	322	14.6	1
1992	53	640	12.1	2
1993	81	995	12.3	9
1994	87	1010	11.6	4

Comments: Sharpe had a better year in 1994 than he did in '93, except he didn't get into the end zone as much. The fact that he missed two games due to a sprained knee and still caught a career-high 87 passes shows his dominance. He ranked fourth in the AFC in receptions and tied for eighth in receiving yards with 1,010. He caught at least three passes in the 14 games in which he played. Sharpe caught six aerials for 121 yards and a touchdown in Game 7, then grabbed a season-high 10 passes for 95 yards in the 13th game. Sharpe is no longer referred to as Sterling's younger brother. In 1993, he led the Broncos in receptions, yards and touchdowns and was named All-Pro. His 81 receptions ranked eighth in the NFL, and his nine TD passes tied for second in the AFC and first among receivers. He plays the old Kellen Winslow slot position, swinging between tight end, H-back and wide receiver.

The skinny: Ten touchdowns, 100 catches and 1,000 yards are within Sharpe's sure-handed grasp in 1994.

ERIC GREEN / DOLPHINS

Year	Rec.	Yards	Avg.	TDs
1990	34	387	11.4	7
1991	41	582	14.2	6
1992	14	152	10.9	2
1993	63	942	15.0	5
1994	46	618	13.4	4

Comments: In one of the biggest offseason transactions, Green left the Steelers and signed as a free agent with Miami, where he should flourish in 1995. With Dan Marino on the other end, Green has a good shot at career receiving highs. But Green's blocking might prove to be even more valuable, as the Dolphins will try to use his massive size to bolster the ground game. In 1994, Green finished second on the Steelers in receiving with 46 catches and led the team in receiving yards with 618. His four touchdown catches tied for the team lead. Green had the most consistent season of his career in 1993, leading the Steelers in receiving and yards. His 63 receptions ranked third among NFL tight ends. However, he does have his past troubles. In 1992, Green missed three weeks with an injury and then was suspended by the NFL for six weeks for substance abuse. In 1990, he was the last first-round draft choice to sign a contract but finished with seven TDs, tops among NFL tight ends.

The skinny: Green's numbers could nearly double in '95.

CAN'T MISS

BRENT JONES / 49ERS

Year	Rec.	Yards	Avg.	TDs
1990	56	747	13.3	5
1991	27	417	15.4	0
1992	45	628	14.0	4
1993	68	735	10.8	3
1994	49	670	13.7	9

Comments: Jones led all NFL tight ends in touchdowns in 1994 with a career-high nine, and he also added a two-point conversion to give him

56 points, great by fantasy football standards. He ranked third on the 49ers in catches with 49 and yards with 670. His 13.7-yard average per catch is very good for a tight end. Jones caught a pass in every game except the regular-season finale, when the team rested its starters for the playoffs and Jones rested a thigh injury. He made the Pro Bowl for the third straight season. The 49ers' second-leading receiver in 1992 and '93, Jones set a team record for tight ends with 68 catches in '93. He gives the 49ers a great receiving trio along with Jerry Rice and either John Taylor or J.J. Stokes (whichever one is the secondary wideout), though Jones is the one who gets overshadowed. Jones is actually the player Steve Young goes to on third-and-three.

The skinny: Jones is a tight end you can count on.

JACKIE HARRIS / BUCCANEERS

Year	Rec.	Yards	Avg.	TDs
1990	12	157	13.1	0
1991	24	264	11.0	3
1992	55	595	10.8	2
1993	42	604	14.4	4
1994	26	337	13.0	3

Comments: In his first season as a Buccaneer in 1994, Harris was on pace to challenge the team's tight end receiving records until injuring a shoulder in Week 9. That sidelined him for the rest of the season. At the time of his injury, Harris was leading the team in receiving with 26 catches, second among tight ends in the NFC. In Week 2, his best game, he caught four passes for 96 yards and a touchdown against the Colts. Harris is a deep threat who knows how to find the seams in a zone defense. He moved into the forefront of NFL tight ends in 1992, when he caught 55 passes. In 1993, he was slowed by injuries but still caught 42 passes for 604 yards to rank third on the Packers in receptions and first in yards per catch. In 1992, Harris caught at least one pass in all 16 games, and his 55 catches ranked second only to Dallas's Jay Novacek among the league's tight ends.

The skinny: If Buccaneers quarterback Trent Dilfer has a good year, Harris will have a great one.

JAY NOVACEK / COWBOYS

Year	Rec.	Yards	Avg.	TDs
1990	59	657	11.1	4
1991	59	664	11.3	4
1992	68	630	9.3	6
1993	44	445	10.1	1
1994	47	475	10.1	2

Comments: Novacek's fantasy football productivity has slipped the past two seasons, but he's still Troy Aikman's go-to receiver when it's third-and-five. He's still among the league's top tight ends and finished the 1994 season third on the Cowboys in receptions with 47 and in yards with 475. Novacek missed two games due to a strained abdominal muscle but caught a pass in every other game. He saved his best for the postseason, catching 15 passes for 176 yards in two playoff games. He was the best tight end in the NFL in 1992, but his statistics slipped a bit in '93. Since 1990, Novacek has the most catches (277) and the fourth-most receiving yards (2,871) among NFL tight ends.

The skinny: Novacek is due for at least a few TD receptions this season.

TROY DRAYTON / RAMS

Year	Rec.	Yards	Avg.	TDs
1993	27	319	11.8	4
1994	32	276	8.6	6

Comments: Drayton led the Rams in touchdowns with six in 1994 despite not even being involved in the offense early in the season. He didn't catch a pass in the first two games but became a scoring weapon from short range. Drayton placed fourth on the team in receptions with 32 and sixth in receiving yards. But he never gained more than 40 yards in a game. A second-round draft pick in 1993, Drayton was fourth on the Rams in receiving despite starting only two games. He scored four touchdowns and was one of the top rookie tight ends in the league. He started to come on late in the season, scoring three times in the last seven games.

The skinny: One of the game's best young tight ends, there's no telling how well Drayton could do with a good quarterback.

SOLID PICKS

JOHNNY MITCHELL / JETS

Year	Rec.	Yards	Avg.	TDs
1992	16	210	13.1	1
1993	39	630	16.2	6
1994	58	749	12.9	4

Comments: Mitchell says he's the best tight end since Kellen Winslow, but might not even play that position this year. His big-play capabilities are often overshadowed by errors and dropped passes. The surprising selection of Kyle Brady in this year's draft gives the Jets a wealth of tight ends, and Mitchell may move to wide receiver to help shore up a serious weakness there. In 1994, he finished 18th in the AFC in catches with 58 and in yards with 749. He ranked fourth among AFC tight ends in catches and third in yards, and finished second on the Jets in catches. In Game 11, he caught a career-high 11 passes for 120 yards. Mitchell broke out like gangbusters in 1993, catching all six of his TD passes in the first eight games. Though his pace slowed a bit, he finished fourth on the team in receiving and third in yards. Drafted for his big-play reputation, Mitchell has the body of a linebacker and the ability of a wide receiver.

The skinny: Pay attention to how Mitchell is utilized in the preseason.

PETE METZELAARS / PANTHERS

Year	Rec.	Yards	Avg.	TDs
1990	10	60	6.0	1
1991	5	54	10.8	2
1992	30	298	9.9	6
1993	68	609	9.0	4
1994	49	428	8.7	5

Comments: Metzelaars was signed as a free agent by the Panthers and will move into a starting job. Remarkably consistent during his days in Buffalo, Metzelaars showed no signs of slowing down in 1994, his 13th NFL season. He caught a pass in all but one game and finished third on the team in catches with 49, which ranked fifth among AFC tight ends. One

TIGHT ENDS

of the league's most productive tight ends, Metzelaars has more than 300 career receptions. In 1993, he led the Bills in receiving, the first tight end to pace the club since 1962. He had an excellent season in '92 after a few years in which he lost his starting job and didn't contribute much.

The skinny: Even on an expansion team, Metzelaars should be good for a few TDs, especially if former Bills teammate Frank Reich is the starting quarterback.

HOWARD CROSS / GIANTS

Year	Rec.	Yards	Avg.	TDs
1990	8	106	13.3	0
1991	20	283	14.2	2
1992	27	357	13.2	2
1993	21	272	13.0	5
1994	31	364	11.7	4

Comments: The quality consistency of Cross helped lead to the departure of Derek Brown, a former No. 1 pick, in the offseason. In his sixth season in 1994, Cross set career highs with 31 receptions for 364 yards. He ranked fourth on the team in catches, third in receiving yards and tied for second in touchdown catches with four. He caught a pass in every game. Cross has started 64 consecutive games and played in 96 straight. In 1993, he ranked among the tight end leaders in TD catches with five. Cross is a stationary blocker who has developed into a pretty good receiver, though he's not a deep threat. He is especially effective inside the 20-yard line.

The skinny: Cross seems to be getting better every year.

IRV SMITH / SAINTS

Year	Rec.	Yards	Avg.	TDs
1993	16	180	11.3	2
1994	41	330	8.0	3

Comments: In 1994, his second season, Smith caught the most passes of any Saints tight end in nine years. He finished fifth on the team in receptions with 41 and caught a pass in all but three contests. Smith had six catches in Week 5 and seven in the 10th game. One of two first-round draft choices by New Orleans in 1993, Smith finished his rookie season with 16 catches for 180 yards and two touchdowns. He started eight of the 16 games.

The skinny: Smith should have an even better season this year.

ED WEST / COLTS

Year	Rec.	Yards	Avg.	TDs
1990	27	356	13.2	5
1991	15	151	10.1	3
1992	4	30	7.5	0
1993	25	253	10.1	0
1994	31	377	12.2	2

Comments: West signed with the Colts as a free agent after one of his best seasons. In 1994, he established career highs in catches (31) and yards (377). He will provide experienced insurance while the Colts wait for rookie second-round pick Ken Dilger to develop. West is an excellent blocker who has little speed but good hands. He started 12 games for Green Bay in 1994 and played in 12, but he missed two due to an ankle injury. He ranks 10th on the Packers' all-time receiving list with 202 catches (second among tight ends) for 3,221 yards and 25 touchdowns. West scored 16 touchdowns from 1988 to '91, which was the third most in the NFL those four seasons. He is still one of the steadiest tight ends around.

The skinny: West remains a solid goal-line receiver.

TONY McGEE / BENGALS

Year	Rec.	Yards	Avg.	TDs
1993	44	525	11.9	0
1994	40	492	12.3	1

Comments: In 1994, McGee finished third on the Bengals in receiving for the second straight season, this time with 40 catches for 492 yards. He caught a pass in 14 games and had three games with five receptions. McGee led all rookie tight ends in receptions in 1993 with 44 catches. He can really run after the catch, but he dropped too many balls last season. McGee has started every game in his career except one missed due to an injury.

The skinny: With 84 career receptions, McGee has found the end zone only once.

KEITH CASH / CHIEFS

Year	Rec.	Yards	Avg.	TDs
1992	12	113	9.4	2
1993	24	242	10.1	4
1994	19	192	10.1	2

Comments: In the midst of a breakthrough season in 1994, Cash suffered a season-ending knee sprain in Week 5. He caught 19 passes for 192 yards and two scores before the injury and was easily on pace to establish career highs. Cash caught a touchdown pass in each of the first two games, then caught seven passes for 73 yards, both career highs, the next week. Cash has some big-play ability and can turn underneath passes into big gains. He has 21 career postseason receptions, the third most in team history. In 1993, he finished tied for fifth on the team with 24 catches, and his four touchdowns were second on the team.

The skinny: Barring another injury, Cash will have a breakthrough season.

COULD COME ON

ANDREW JORDAN / VIKINGS

Year	Rec.	Yards	Avg.	TDs
1994	35	336	9.6	0

Comments: In 1994, Jordan caught the most passes, 35, of any Vikings rookie in 18 years. He started seven of the first 12 games as a second tight end, then became the sole starter when Adrian Cooper was injured. Jordan caught passes in all but three games, scored on a two-point conversion pass, and had eight catches of 17 yards or more. He finished fifth on the team in receptions.

The skinny: Jordan is a sixth-round steal with a lot of potential.

DEREK BROWN / JAGUARS

Year	Rec.	Yards	Avg.	TDs
1992	4	31	7.8	0
1993	7	56	8.0	0
1994	0	0	0.0	0

Comments: A total bust with the Giants, Brown was taken in the expansion draft by the Jaguars, who hope a change of scenery can tap the potential of a first-round pick in the 1992 draft. Brown can't block well, which is why he didn't play much in New York. But he can catch the ball and could be a surprise because Jacksonville plans to utilize him a lot — even downfield. In three seasons, Brown has just seven starts, 11 catches for 87 yards and no touchdowns.

The skinny: If ever there was a viable second chance for success, this is it.

CHRIS GEDNEY / BEARS

Year	Rec.	Yards	Avg.	TDs
1993	10	98	9.8	0
1994	13	157	12.1	3

Comments: Gedney has all the talent to be a top receiving tight end, but his first two seasons have been slowed by injuries. Last season, a broken fibula in Week 7 ended his season. Gedney got off to a good start, as his two touchdown catches in the season opener were the most by a Bears tight end in one game in 19 years. He added a spectacular one-handed TD grab in Game 5. As a rookie in '93, Gedney missed the first five games after breaking a collarbone in training camp. He eventually caught 10 passes for 98 yards.

The skinny: Gedney could be a steal in your fantasy draft — or a wasted pick.

MARK CHMURA / PACKERS

Year	Rec.	Yards	Avg.	TDs
1992	Injured			
1993	2	13	6.5	0
1994	14	165	11.8	0

Comments: Almost by default, Chmura enters the 1995 season as the starter because Keith Jackson has refused to report to the team. A sure-handed career backup, Chmura started four games in place of the injured Ed West last season and placed seventh on the club with 14 receptions — all in the final five games. He had his best performance as a pro in Game 15, with five catches for 63 yards against Atlanta.

The skinny: In Mike Holmgren's passing offense, Chmura could post some pretty good numbers.

1994 SURPRISES

WESLEY WALLS / SAINTS

Year	Rec.	Yards	Avg.	TDs
1990	5	27	5.4	0
1991	2	24	12.0	0
1992	Injured			
1993	0	0	0.0	0
1994	38	406	10.7	4

Comments: A free-agent steal, Walls was a pleasant surprise in 1994. He tied for third on the Saints in touchdown catches with four, finished fifth in receiving yards with 406 and sixth in catches with 38. He caught a pass in the first 13 games of the season, then was hampered by a separated shoulder. Walls was signed by New Orleans before the 1994 season after three undistinguished seasons in San Francisco. He missed the entire '92 season with a shoulder injury.

The skinny: Walls might be the real deal, not a flash in the pan.

AARON PIERCE / GIANTS

Year	Rec.	Yards	Avg.	TDs
1992	0	0	0.0	0
1993	12	212	17.7	0
1994	20	214	10.7	4

Comments: Pierce combined with teammate Howard Cross last season to give the Giants eight touchdown catches from their tight ends, a remarkable achievement. The team's H-back, he caught a career-high 20 passes. He started 11 games — six at tight end, two at wide receiver and three at H-back. In 1993, Pierce started six times at H-back. Injuries slowed his rookie season of 1992, when he played in only one game.

The skinny: Pierce is a versatile and productive performer.

ALFRED PUPUNU / CHARGERS

Year	Rec.	Yards	Avg.	TDs
1992	0	0	0.0	0
1993	13	142	10.9	0
1994	21	214	10.2	2

Comments: Football fans were asking "Who's the guy with the funny name?" when Pupunu helped rally the Chargers to an upset win over the Steelers in last season's AFC title game. Pupunu caught a 43-yard TD pass in the third quarter and had four receptions for 76 yards in the game. He led Charger tight ends with 21 catches in 1994. A rapidly developing H-back, Pupunu started 13 games and missed the other three due to injuries last year. In 1993, he had a career high of six catches in one game.

The skinny: Pupunu may be a decent fantasy backup.

JAMES JENKINS / REDSKINS

Year	Rec.	Yards	Avg.	TDs
1991	0	0	0.0	0
1992	0	0	0.0	0
1993	0	0	0.0	0
1994	8	32	4.0	4

Comments: A backup to Ethan Horton in 1994, Jenkins will get a chance to become the starter this season. After three seasons of inactivity, Jenkins became a legitimate option near the goal line in 1995. He caught four touchdown passes — all in goal-line situations — and finished with eight receptions for 32 yards. In Game 8, Jenkins caught two TD passes from Gus Frerotte. He had not caught a pass prior to 1994.

The skinny: Jenkins will greatly increase his production this year, but he will be hard-pressed to exceed last year's TD production.

QUESTION MARKS

KEITH JACKSON / PACKERS

Year	Rec.	Yards	Avg.	TDs
1990	50	670	13.4	6
1991	48	569	11.9	5
1992	48	594	12.4	5
1993	39	613	10.0	6
1994	59	673	11.4	7

Comments: After an outstanding seven-year career, Jackson's heart apparently is no longer into the game. The Packers traded a second-round draft pick to the Dolphins for Jackson in the offseason, but he doesn't want to play in Green Bay. The offseason acquisition of Eric Green rendered Jackson expendable in Miami, where he had an excellent 1994 season. Jackson set team tight end records for receptions (59), reception yards (673) and touchdown catches (seven). His seven TDs tied for second among NFL tight ends, and he placed 16th in the conference in receptions. He caught a pass in every game and had two TD receptions in the team's playoff game. In his first full season with Miami in 1993, Jackson had what was for him a subpar season. He was fifth on the Dolphins in catches and second in touchdowns. A five-time Pro Bowler, Jackson has been the most productive tight end in the NFL over the last seven years, with 388 receptions and 35 touchdowns.

The skinny: Jackson is among the very best — when he wants to be.

WALTER REEVES / BROWNS

Year	Rec.	Yards	Avg.	TDs
1990	18	190	10.6	0
1991	8	45	5.6	0
1992	6	28	4.7	0
1993	9	67	7.4	1
1994	6	61	10.2	1

Comments: A lower-back injury sidelined Reeves for all but five 1994 games, as he spent much of the season on injured reserve. In the first three games, he caught six passes for 61 yards and a touchdown. Reeves signed with Cleveland as a free agent before the 1994 season and he will probably start again if his back holds up. He was an underachiever in Phoenix for three years, although he is more of a blocker than a receiver.

The skinny: Reeves's preseason health and performance may speak volumes.

BEST OF THE REST

ADRIAN COOPER / VIKINGS

Year	Rec.	Yards	Avg.	TDs
1991	11	147	13.4	2
1992	16	197	12.3	3
1993	9	112	12.4	0
1994	32	363	11.3	0

Comments: Cooper was finishing a good first season with the Vikings when he injured a shoulder and missed the final four games. At the time, he was leading the team's tight ends with 32 receptions. He ranked sixth on the Vikings in catches and fifth in receiving yards, but he failed to score. Cooper caught a pass in all 12 games in which he played. He was a malcontent in Pittsburgh who didn't give 100 percent because he was unhappy with his contract. He started 14 of 16 games in 1992 when Eric Green was out of the lineup. He caught only 16 passes but did score three TDs.

The skinny: Cooper will battle Andrew Jordan for the Vikings' starting job, and he'll certainly be used in double-tight-end sets.

DERRICK WALKER / CHIEFS

Year	Rec.	Yards	Avg.	TDs
1990	23	240	10.4	1
1991	20	134	6.7	0
1992	34	393	11.6	2
1993	21	212	10.1	1
1994	36	382	10.6	2

Comments: With just 11 starts in 1994, Walker recorded the fourth-most receptions ever by a Chiefs tight end and the most in 16 years. His 36 catches ranked sixth on the team, and his 382 yards ranked fifth. An injury to Keith Cash pressed Walker into a starting job, and he made the most of the opportunity. In his first start, against Denver, he caught eight passes — the most ever by a Chiefs tight end in one game — and gained 98 yards. He caught three passes for 27 yards and a touchdown in Kansas City's playoff loss to Miami. Walker joined the Chiefs just before the 1994 regular season after spending his first four seasons with San Diego.

The skinny: Walker is an outstanding blocker and excellent backup.

PAUL GREEN / SEAHAWKS

Year	Rec.	Yards	Avg.	TDs
1992	9	67	7.4	1
1993	23	178	7.7	1
1994	30	208	6.9	1

Comments: Green finished the 1994 season with 30 receptions, the most by a Seattle tight end in 10 years and just seven shy of the team's single-season record for the position. He started 11 games and did well enough to make Ferrell Edmunds expendable. In the final six games, Green caught 21 passes. He's a talented receiver, though he doesn't do much after he gets the ball.

The skinny: Green will battle rookie Christian Fauria for the starting job.

ANDREW GLOVER / RAIDERS

Year	Rec.	Yards	Avg.	TDs
1991	5	45	9.0	3
1992	15	178	11.9	1
1993	4	55	13.8	1
1994	33	371	11.2	2

Comments: Glover had a good 1994 season, ranking fourth on the Raiders in receptions and receiving yards with 33 catches for 371 yards, both career highs. Glover caught a pass in all but two games and had a season-high five catches in Game 5. He caught only four passes in '93, but he did show a lot of potential in '92, when he caught 15 balls. Glover scored three touchdowns on five receptions as a rookie in 1991. At nearly 6-foot-

7, he is great near the goal line because he can jump and outmuscle defensive backs for the ball.

The skinny: The addition of Kerry Cash will reduce Glover's playing time this season.

BRIAN KINCHEN / BROWNS

Year	Rec.	Yards	Avg.	TDs
1990	0	0	0.0	0
1991	0	0	0.0	0
1992	0	0	0.0	0
1993	29	347	12.0	2
1994	24	232	9.7	1

Comments: Kinchen started the final 11 games of 1994 when starter Walter Reeves was injured. He caught 24 passes to rank fifth on the Browns, catching at least one pass in each of the last nine games. A long snapper in his first five seasons, Kinchen performed better than anyone might have expected in 1993, when he started 14 games and was the Browns' fifth-leading receiver. He caught 21 passes in the last seven games. But he isn't a dominant blocker and provides little speed at the position.

The skinny: Kinchen will return to his backup role in '95.

PAT CARTER / OILERS

Year	Rec.	Yards	Avg.	TDs
1990	8	58	7.3	0
1991	8	69	8.6	2
1992	20	232	11.6	3
1993	14	166	11.9	1
1994	11	74	6.7	1

Comments: The Oilers' attempt to utilize the tight end position was a failure in 1994. As a result, they wasted Carter's good receiving talents. Carter caught only 11 passes for 74 yards and a touchdown. However, the midseason coaching change resulted in more pass routes and a little less pass blocking for Carter. In Week 14, he caught four passes for 49 yards.

With the Rams, Carter caught six TD passes from 1991 to '93. He had his best season in '92, with 20 catches for 232 yards and three touchdowns.

The skinny: Owner Bud Adams's insistence on more use of the tight end should result in much better numbers for Carter this season.

REGGIE JOHNSON / EAGLES

Year	Rec.	Yards	Avg.	TDs
1991	6	73	12.2	1
1992	10	139	13.9	1
1993	20	243	12.2	1
1994	7	79	11.3	0

Comments: Johnson was signed by Green Bay as a free agent early in the 1994 season after three years in Denver. Slowed by a hamstring injury early in the season, he played in nine of the final 10 games, started twice and caught seven passes for 79 yards. He got off to a good start in 1993, catching six passes and scoring one touchdown in the first three games. But then Shannon Sharpe took over and Johnson was the forgotten man. In 1992, he caught six of his 10 receptions in the final two games, with his only touchdown coming in the season finale.

The skinny: Johnson may be the Eagles' starter in 1995.

SLIPPED IN 1994

KERRY CASH / RAIDERS

Year	Rec.	Yards	Avg.	TDs
1991	1	18	18.0	0
1992	43	521	12.1	3
1993	43	402	9.3	3
1994	16	190	11.9	1

Comments: Cash signed with the Raiders as a free agent after a very disappointing 1994 season with the Colts that began with a holdout. On a team that got poor production out of its tight ends, Cash led the group with 16 catches for 190 yards. Despite starting every game, he was slowed by an ankle injury, played five games without catching a pass and never caught more than three in a game. The Colts weren't very satisfied with Cash's production, even when he put up pretty good numbers for two straight seasons, catching 43 passes in both 1992 and '93. In fact, he became the first Colts tight end to post consecutive 40-catch seasons since John Mackey in the 1960s.

The skinny: The Raiders will try to utilize Cash better than the Colts did.

ETHAN HORTON / CUT BY REDSKINS

Year	Rec.	Yards	Avg.	TDs
1990	33	404	12.2	3
1991	53	650	12.3	5
1992	33	409	12.4	2
1993	43	467	10.9	1
1994	15	157	10.5	3

Comments: Horton was waived by the Redskins in the offseason after his subpar 1994 season. He caught just 15 passes for 157 yards in 15 starts, but he did score three touchdowns, fourth among the team's pass receivers. The Raiders' second-leading receiver in 1993, Horton signed with Washington as a free agent. He had been pretty consistent the previous four years, although he has yet to reach the potential some people expected of him. Horton was a bust as a running back with Kansas City before being converted to tight end by the Raiders. He was a Pro Bowler in 1991, when he led the Raiders in receiving and scored five touchdowns.

The skinny: Don't write off Horton yet.

RON HALL / LIONS

Year	Rec.	Yards	Avg.	TDs
1990	31	464	15.0	2
1991	31	284	9.2	0
1992	39	351	9.0	4
1993	23	268	11.7	1
1994	10	106	10.6	0

Comments: Injuries accounted for a subpar 1994 season for Hall,

TIGHT ENDS

who started 10 games and played in 13. The team's top blocking tight end, he caught 10 passes for 106 yards but was nagged by several foot and knee injuries and finished the season on injured reserve. Hall signed with Detroit as a free agent before the 1994 season. In 1993, he was fourth on the Buccaneers in receiving, though he did drop a lot of passes. From 1988 to '92, he joined Keith Jackson as the only two tight ends in the league with at least 30 receptions every year. Hall is still a deep threat.

The skinny: If the Lions go to their tight ends more, Hall could have a big comeback season.

ROOKIES

See Chapter 12, Rookie Report.

OTHERS

MAURICE JOHNSON / EAGLES

Year	Rec.	Yards	Avg.	TDs
1991	6	70	11.7	2
1992	2	16	8.0	0
1993	10	81	8.1	0
1994	21	204	9.7	2

Comments: A career backup, Johnson started five 1994 games in double-tight-end situations, then earned five starts in place of the injured Mark Bavaro. He caught a pass in all but one game and ranked fifth on the team in receptions with 21. Johnson caught 10 passes for 81 yards in 1993. He played in all 16 games and earned two starts.

The skinny: Johnson will battle Reggie Johnson for the starting job.

KEITH JENNINGS / BEARS

Year	Rec.	Yards	Avg.	TDs
1991	8	109	13.6	0
1992	23	264	11.5	1
1993	14	150	10.7	0
1994	11	75	6.8	3

Comments: Jennings was waived in the final cutdown of 1994 but re-signed when Chris Gedney was injured in October. He caught 11 passes and was a part of a Bears tight end corps that caught a very respectable eight touchdown passes. A solid blocker but pedestrian receiver, Jennings has been the Bears' healthiest tight end the past two seasons. He started 14 games in 1992, putting up pretty good numbers.

The skinny: Jennings will back up Chris Gedney in '95.

TYJI ARMSTRONG / BUCCANEERS

Year	Rec.	Yards	Avg.	TDs
1992	7	138	19.7	1
1993	9	86	9.6	1
1994	22	265	12.0	1

Comments: Known mostly for his blocking prowess, Armstrong moved into the starting lineup for the final seven games of 1994 because Jackie Harris was injured. Armstrong caught 22 passes for 265 yards (both figures more than doubled his previous career totals). He is a tenacious blocker who has started 24 games in three seasons.

The skinny: Armstrong is a better blocker than pass receiver.

JAMES THORNTON / JETS

Year	Rec.	Yards	Avg.	TDs
1990	19	254	13.4	1
1991	17	278	16.4	1
1992	Injured			
1993	12	108	9.0	2
1994	20	171	8.6	0

Comments: Thornton registered the second-highest receiving total of his career, 20, in 1994. He started two games, including Game 9, when he hauled in six passes. He finished sixth on the team in receptions. In 1993, his numbers slipped from what he used to compile with the Bears. Thornton had started 55 straight games at tight end for Chicago until missing the last three of 1991 and then all of '92 with an arch injury. A bruiser, he is more of a blocker.

The skinny: Thornton is at best the Jets' No. 3 tight end.

RODNEY HOLMAN / LIONS

Year	Rec.	Yards	Avg.	TDs
1990	40	596	14.9	5
1991	31	445	14.4	2
1992	26	266	10.2	2
1993	25	244	9.8	2
1994	17	163	9.6	0

Comments: In 1994, his 13th season, Holman led the Lions' tight ends in receiving with 17 catches for 163 yards. He started six games and played in 15, but his streak of 191 consecutive games played in was broken. He has played in 196 games, the third most among tight ends in NFL history. In 1993, Holman's 25 receptions were the most by a Detroit tight end since 1985.

The skinny: These days, Holman barely resembles the player that was among the best at his position five years ago.

JONATHAN HAYES / STEELERS

Year	Rec.	Yards	Avg.	TDs
1990	9	83	9.2	1
1991	19	208	10.9	2
1992	9	77	8.6	2
1993	24	331	13.8	1
1994	5	50	10.0	1

Comments: Hayes started four games with the Steelers in 1994 in double-tight-end formations. He caught just five passes and doesn't figure to play much more this year because rookie Mark Bruener is the team's future tight end.

The skinny: Hayes is a backup, nothing more.

DUANE YOUNG / CHARGERS

Year	Rec.	Yards	Avg.	TDs
1991	2	12	6.0	0
1992	4	45	11.3	0
1993	6	41	6.8	2
1994	17	217	12.8	1

Comments: Known for his dominating blocking skills, the massive 270-pound Young set career highs last season with 17 catches for 217 yards. He started 14 games in 1994. In 1993, he set a career high with two touchdown catches.

The skinny: Young won't do much for your fantasy team unless you have Natrone Means, who utilizes Young's great blocks.

RON MIDDLETON / RAMS

Year	Rec.	Yards	Avg.	TDs
1990	0	0	0.0	0
1991	3	25	8.3	0
1992	7	50	7.1	0
1993	24	154	6.4	2
1994	0	0	0.0	0

Comments: Middleton started three games as a second blocking tight end and played in all 16 in 1994. However, he failed to catch a pass after posting a career year in '93. Though he excels as a run blocker, Middleton caught 24 passes in 1993 — more than three times his previous single-season best — because the Redskins were so beset by injuries.

The skinny: Middleton is strictly an extra blocker for Jerome Bettis.

TED POPSON / 49ERS

Year	Rec.	Yards	Avg.	TDs
1994	13	141	10.8	0

Comments: Popson appears to be solid insurance in the event of a Brent Jones injury. When Jones sat out the 1994 regular-season finale, Popson led the 49ers in receiving with eight catches for 80 yards. He finished eighth on the team in receptions with 13 and seventh in reception yards with 141.

The skinny: Popson might be groomed to become Jones's successor.

JERRY EVANS / BRONCOS

Year	Rec.	Yards	Avg.	TDs
1993	0	0	0.0	0
1994	13	127	9.8	2

Comments: In the 1994 preseason, Evans beat out veterans Keith McKeller and Reggie Johnson for the Broncos' blocking-tight-end position. He caught 13 passes for 127 yards and two touchdowns. Evans started 11 games, mostly in double-tight-end sets.

The skinny: Evans is a player to keep an eye on.

SHANNON MITCHELL / CHARGERS

Year	Rec.	Yards	Avg.	TDs
1994	11	105	9.5	0

Comments: Mitchell started seven games in his rookie season of 1994. He caught 11 passes for 105 yards, all in Games 10–14. He caught three passes for 44 yards against the 49ers December 11, then caught a 19-yard pass in the AFC championship game against Pittsburgh.

The skinny: Mitchell is a free-agent find who has good size and good hands.

. . . AND THE REST

(listed in alphabetical order)

CHARLES ARBUCKLE, Colts — Arbuckle made the rounds in 1994 from the Colts to the Packers and back to the Colts, who waived him in the preseason and picked him back up during the regular season. He started one game, played in seven and caught one seven-yard pass. In 1993, he caught 14 of his 15 receptions in the final five games, with one eight-catch game.

GREG BATY, Dolphins — In 1994, Baty played in all 16 games for the second straight season and caught two passes for 11 yards and a touchdown. Primarily a special-teams player, he caught five passes for 78 yards and a TD in 1993. It doesn't look as if Baty will ever catch 37 passes in a season again, as he did as a rookie in 1986 in New England.

FRED BAXTER, Jets — Baxter played in 11 games last season, catching three passes for 11 yards and a touchdown. A sprained ankle sidelined him for five games. A rookie fifth-round draft choice in 1993, he caught only three passes for 48 yards and one touchdown, although he missed six games with a hamstring injury.

JOHN BURKE, Patriots — Burke started six games in double-tight-end formations in 1994, his rookie season. He caught nine passes for 86 yards, but Burke is a Patriot for one reason — Bill Parcells loves his ability to drive defenders off the ball.

FERRELL EDMUNDS, cut by Seahawks — Edmunds was waived by the Seahawks in the offseason after two bulging disks in his back sidelined him for half of the 1994 season. He caught just seven passes for 43 yards in '94. In 1993, he caught 24 passes for 239 yards. He drops too many passes. Edmunds' career may be over.

CHAD FANN, Cardinals — Fann beat Derek Ware out of a job in the midseason of 1994. Fann caught 12 passes for 96 yards, all in the final five games after Ware was waived. He started nine games and played in all 16.

SCOTT GALBRAITH, Cowboys — Galbraith caught four passes for 31 yards last year and only one pass for one yard and a touchdown in 1993. Most of his playing time comes in two-tight-end formations. He is a better blocker than receiver. Galbraith's best season was 1991, when he caught 27 passes for 328 yards in Cleveland.

TRACY GREENE, Chiefs — As a rookie seventh-round draft choice, Green caught six passes for 69 yards and a touchdown in 1994. He started two games in double-tight-end sets. In Week 6, his crucial 19-yard catch with 13 seconds left set up the winning touchdown against the Broncos.

TY HALLOCK, Lions — Hallock started 11 games last season. Converted from linebacker to tight end in the 1993 preseason, he is sometimes utilized as a blocking back. He caught seven passes for 75 yards last season and had eight grabs (two TDs) in his rookie season of 1993.

LONNIE JOHNSON, Bills — The offseason departure of Pete Metzelaars means Johnson will get a chance to earn the starting job in 1995. In 1994, his rookie season, Johnson caught three passes for 42 yards. He's a bit undersized but has displayed good blocking and pass-catching skills.

MITCH LYONS, Falcons — Tight ends don't play very much in Atlanta's offense, and Lyons led Falcons receivers in 1994 with just seven catches for 54 yards. A rookie in '93, Lyons started eight games, playing in 16. A superb blocker, he caught eight passes for 63 yards.

VINCE MARROW, Panthers — After two years on practice squads, Marrow caught five passes for 44 yards in 1994, when he was a backup on the Bills. He was selected in the 23rd round of the expansion draft.

DAVE MOORE, Buccaneers — Moore caught four passes for 57 yards in 1994. He started five games late in the season when the Buccaneers ran the ball more and utilized double-tight-end sets. In 1993, Moore caught four passes for 47 yards and a touchdown.

TROY SADOWSKI, Bengals — A five-year veteran, Sadowski played in 15 games and started one in 1994. He is mainly used as a blocker, although he had a career-high 15 receptions for 54 yards.

TERRY SAMUELS, Cardinals — Samuels started six games at three different positions — tight end, H-back and fullback — in his rookie season of 1994. He caught eight passes for 57 yards and proved to be a versatile player.

CRAIG THOMPSON, Steelers — After a year out of the NFL, Thompson was signed by the Steelers in the offseason. In 1993, he caught 17 passes for 81 yards and a touchdown in Cincinnati. The year before, Thompson had 19 catches for 194 yards and two TDs.

LAWYER TILLMAN, Panthers — Tillman hasn't played a down since fracturing an ankle in the ninth game of the 1993 season in Cleveland. He was signed as a free agent in December and will battle for a roster spot. A bust as a second-round pick in the 1989 draft, Tillman's best season was 1992, when he caught 25 passes for 498 yards. He missed the entire 1990 and 1991 seasons due to injuries.

DEREK WARE, Bengals — Ware was cut by Arizona late in the 1994 season and picked up by the Bengals December 21. He played in 15 games for the third time in his three-year career. With 17 receptions, Ware more than quadrupled his output of the two previous seasons.

RYAN WETNIGHT, Bears — Wetnight played in 11 games in 1994, catching 11 passes for 104 yards. He made a one-handed touchdown catch of a tipped pass while lying on his back in Game 12, but he dropped two easy TD catches the season before. Wetnight caught nine passes for 93 yards and one score in 1993.

JAMIE WILLIAMS, Raiders — Williams played in every 1994 game, mainly on special teams. He caught just three passes and doesn't figure to play much on offense this year, either. Williams has played with four NFL teams in his 12-year career. In 1992, he had 22 receptions.

JEFF WILNER, Packers — Wilner made the Packers' roster last season as a rookie free agent. Injuries thrust him into the team's picture, and Wilner caught five passes for 31 yards. He played in 11 games, starting one.

Other Tight Ends on Rosters

Bradford Banta, Colts	Yonnie Jackson, Seahawks
Harold Bishop, Buccaneers	Craig Keith, Steelers
Kirk Botkin, Saints	Brian Kozlowski, Giants
Rickey Brady, Rams	Aaron Laing, Chargers
Brett Carolan, 49ers	Harper LeBel, Falcons
Rob Coons, Bills	Thomas McLemore, Colts
Carlester Crumpler, Seahawks	John Henry Mills, Oilers
Carlos Etheredge, Jaguars	Brent Novoselsky, Vikings
Paul Francisco, Patriots	A.J. Ofodile, Bills
David Frisch, Bengals	Greg Schorp, Jaguars
Richard Griffith, Jaguars	Tommie Stowers, Chiefs
Frank Hartley, Browns	Jeff Thomason, Packers
Kurt Haws, Panthers	Frank Wainright, Broncos

Chapter 7
KICKERS

JOHN CARNEY

Kickers always play a big role in pro football. Nearly half of all games in the NFL are decided by less than a touchdown, and kickers are almost always a team's leading scorer. In fact, the 10 most-accurate field goal kickers in NFL history are all active players.

Kickers are also very valuable in fantasy football. However, there are a lot of very good ones in the NFL, so drafting one need not be a top priority for fantasy players until the middle rounds. More than a dozen kickers score 100 or more points every season. In 1994, 13 of the 28 kickers scored at least 100 points; the year before, 18 of them did it.

Last year, teams attempted fewer field goals because of a new rule that places missed field goals at the spot the ball was kicked rather than at the line of scrimmage. Thus, even though the 10 most-accurate field goal kickers in NFL history are all active players, there were 43 fewer field goals and 78 fewer attempts, as coaches often chose a pooch punt over a long field goal attempt.

The best kickers are not necessarily those who score the most points. Nick Lowery and Morten Andersen are two of the best kickers in NFL history. But they play for teams that usually don't score a lot of points, and they usually don't score as many points as some of the other kickers.

In 1994, the leading scorers among kickers were Fuad Reveiz and John Carney. After them was a second tier of high-scoring kickers, including Jason Elam, Matt Bahr, Andersen and Chris Boniol. Reveiz and Bahr probably weren't starters for a lot of fantasy teams at the start of the season, and most fans had never heard of Boniol before last year.

Picking this year's top fantasy kickers is going to be a toss-up. The best advice, obviously, is to go with the kickers who play for the highest-scoring teams. They figure to be Carney, Pete Stoyanovich, Boniol, Brien, Elam, Jason Hanson, Steve Christie, Nick Lowery, Morten Andersen, Jeff Jaeger, Gary Anderson, Norm Johnson and Chris Jacke. That's a lot of kickers, so you can't help but have a good one on your fantasy team.

The best long-distance kickers are Nick Lowery, Pete Stoyanovich, Morten Andersen, Steve Christie, Norm Johnson and Tony Zendejas,

Remember that kickers are probably the least reliable players in the NFL. Every year, two or three of them have bad seasons (like Detroit's Jason Hanson last year). The key to a fantasy season could be not having one — or two — of the bad kickers on your team.

Draft Tips for Choosing Kickers

■ Look at past performances, especially the last three or four seasons, rather than just last year. Far too often, a kicker's most recent season is not indicative of his true abilities (whether he had a good season or a poor one).

■ The biggest consideration for a kicker is the team he plays on. Therefore, be sure to draft those kickers who will get the most opportunities to score — not necessary the team with the most touchdowns like San Francisco, but teams that attempt a lot of field goals (San Diego). The best guide here is a team's performance from the previous season.

■ Be sure to have a very good backup kicker who can take over if your starter is injured or is having a bad season. Don't be forced to go through the season with a kicker having an off year.

■ A kicker's longevity with a team is important, because some teams don't have any continuity at the position and thus change kickers often (even in midseason). If a kicker has played for the same team for several years, that team usually has a lot of confidence in that kicker.

■ If your league's scoring system rewards long field goals, know which kickers are reliable on the long kicks (40 yards or longer). However, consider the new rule that places the ball after missed field goals at the spot of the kick, not the previous line of scrimmage. That resulted in 49 fewer field goal attempts from 50-plus yards last year. Prior to 1993, only 10 players in NFL history had converted four or more field goals of 50 yards or more in a single season. That feat was accomplished by seven kickers in 1993, but none in '94.

■ Know what is going on during training camp. What kickers have been cut? Is Brad Daluiso now the field goal kicker for the Giants? Will Chris Boniol and Doug Brien cement their job status for two of the highest-scoring teams? Can John Carney continue to carry fantasy teams? Will Jason Hanson regain his form of 1993? Will Chip Lohmiller ever get back into the 100-point column? Are Eddie Murray and Norm Johnson ever going to age? Will Greg Davis get within range enough to score? Shouldn't Pete Stoyanovich score more points than he does? Is Jason Elam going to score 119 points every year? Can Fuad Reveiz keep on kicking field goals without a miss? Is Jeff Jaeger going to continue his every-other-year streak of high scoring? Did John Kasay make a mistake by signing with the expansion Panthers? Is Doug Pelfrey really a 100-point kicker?

CAN'T MISS

JOHN CARNEY / CHARGERS

Year	XP	XPA	FG	FGA	Pts.
1990	27	28	19	21	84
1991	31	31	19	29	88
1992	35	35	26	32	113
1993	31	33	31	40	124
1994	33	33	34	38	135

Distance	1–19	20–29	30–39	40–49	50+
1994	0/0	12/12	15/15	5/9	2/2

Comments: In 1994, Carney posted his third straight excellent season to prove he's among the elite kickers. He had a streak of 21 consecutive field goals that included back-to-back five-for-five performances. In 1994, Carney set a team record for field goals in a season with 34 — only one behind the league record — and led the NFL in scoring with 135 points, one of his 10 team records. He now ranks second in team history with 543 points. His 89.5 percent field goal accuracy ranked second in the league, and he hit all four of his postseason field goal attempts. The surprise kicker in the NFL in 1993, Carney set a league record with 29 consecutive field goals dating back to 1992. He had two games in which he kicked six field goals. In '91, Carney set a team record with a 54-yard field goal, and he also had a 53-yarder. In 1990, he set a club record for accuracy by hitting 19 of his 21 field goal attempts (90.5 percent). Overall, he ranks third on the NFL's all-time list in accuracy (131 of 165 for 79.39 percent).

The skinny: Carney can literally carry a fantasy team for weeks at a time.

PETE STOYANOVICH / DOLPHINS

Year	XP	XPA	FG	FGA	Pts.
1990	37	37	21	25	100
1991	28	29	31	37	121
1992	34	36	30	37	124
1993	37	37	24	32	109
1994	35	35	24	31	107

Distance	1–19	20–29	30–39	40–49	50+
1994	1/1	8/8	6/10	8/10	1/2

Comments: A consistent 100-point scorer, Stoyanovich is one of the best long-range kickers. The NFL's scoring and field goal leader in 1992, Stoyanovich has averaged 109.5 points a year during his six NFL seasons. In 1994, Stoyanovich had a hot streak with 16 field goals in six midseason games. Miami's fourth all-time leading scorer, Stoyanovich's 79.26 accuracy rate (149 of 188) on field goals ranks fourth in NFL history. In 1991, he missed the first two games, but he still finished first in the AFC and second in the NFL in scoring with 121 points. Stoyanovich already has 13 career field goals of 50 yards or longer, including a 59-yarder in 1989, which is the fourth longest in NFL history, and an NFL playoff-record 58-yarder in 1990. He missed the longest field goal attempt of the '94 season, a 63-yarder.

KICKERS

The skinny: Stoyanovich will again finish among the highest-scoring kickers in 1995.

JASON ELAM / BRONCOS

Year	XP	XPA	FG	FGA	Pts.
1993	41	42	26	35	119
1994	29	29	30	37	119

Distance	1–19	20–29	30–39	40–49	50+
1994	0/0	11/11	11/11	7/12	1/3

Comments: Elam followed up a solid rookie season with an excellent 1994. He is almost automatic from inside 40 yards, having missed just one in two years. Elam booted at least one field goal in all but one game last season. He kicked a 34-yard overtime game winner in Week 14, and had a 54-yarder in Week 8. He was the third-leading scorer among kickers last year. His second straight 119-point output matched the fourth-highest mark in Broncos history. He has made five of nine career attempts from beyond 50 yards. As a rookie, Elam kicked field goals in 13 of 16 games.

The skinny: There's no reason to think Elam won't be among the league leaders again.

FUAD REVEIZ / VIKINGS

Year	XP	XPA	FG	FGA	Pts.
1990	26	27	13	19	65
1991	34	35	17	24	85
1992	45	45	19	25	102
1993	27	28	26	35	105
1994	30	30	34	39	132

Distance	1–19	20–29	30–39	40–49	50+
1994	0/0	13/13	12/13	8/10	1/3

Comments: Reveiz had an outstanding 1994 season, finishing in a first-place tie in the NFC in scoring with 132 points. He connected on his last 28 field goal attempts, one shy of the league record and the longest ever in one season. The streak includes a pair of five-for-five performances. His 87.2 percent accuracy ranked first in the conference and third overall. Reveiz has made 54 of his last 55 field goal tries from 45 yards or closer. After making just three of 11 attempts from beyond 40 in 1993, Reveiz made nine of 13 from that distance last season. He missed the 1989 season with a groin injury, and in 1990 he lost his job in San Diego after hitting only two of seven field goals. He was signed by the Vikings midway through the '90 season. He used to be considered a streak kicker but is now one of the league's best.

The skinny: Can Reveiz match his great 1994 season?

CHRIS BONIOL / COWBOYS

Year	XP	XPA	FG	FGA	Pts.
1994	48	48	22	29	114

Distance	1–19	20–29	30–39	40–49	50+
1994	3/3	3/4	10/12	6/9	0/1

Comments: After winning a wide-open preseason battle for the kicking job, Boniol quickly earned his keep by making the first nine regular-season attempts of his professional career. His longest field goal was a 47-yarder. The rookie missed his only playoff field goal attempt, a 27-yarder, but he was nine of nine in postseason extra points and never missed during the regular season. He finished fourth in the NFC in scoring and seventh in the NFL with 114 points. And he proved to be pretty good on the long kicks, hitting six of 10 from 40 yards and beyond.

The skinny: Boniol will consistently be among the top scorers as long as he's a Cowboy.

DOUG BRIEN / 49ERS

Year	XP	XPA	FG	FGA	Pts.
1994	60	62	15	20	105

Distance	1–19	20–29	30–39	40–49	50+
1994	1/1	4/4	5/6	5/8	0/1

Comments: Brien led one of the highest-scoring teams in NFL history in points with 105 last season, despite having the second-fewest field goal attempts among starting kickers. He did set a team record with 60 extra points in 62 attempts. Brien's 75 percent field goal accuracy was the best by a 49er since 1989. He kicked field goals of 40 and 48 yards against New Orleans November 28. He made both of his field goal attempts and was four of four on his extra points against Tampa Bay October 23 to earn the NFC Special Teams Player of the Week honors.

The skinny: Brien is bound to score often on this juggernaut team.

MORTEN ANDERSEN / SAINTS

Year	XP	XPA	FG	FGA	Pts.
1990	29	29	21	27	92
1991	38	38	25	32	113
1992	33	34	29	34	120
1993	33	33	28	35	117
1994	32	32	28	39	116

Distance	1–19	20–29	30–39	40–49	50+
1994	0/0	9/9	11/14	8/10	0/6

Comments: The NFL recordholder with 22 field goals of 50 yards or longer, Andersen was zip for six from 50 and beyond last year. He was a very effective 28 of 33 otherwise, and he made all five of his attempts at Atlanta in Week 14. Considered by many the best kicker in the NFL, Andersen was 16 of 16 on field goals inside the 40-yard line in 1993. He has scored 100 or more points in four straight seasons and nine times in the last 10 seasons. Andersen ranks sixth all-time on the field goal accuracy list (302 of 389 for 77.63 percent). He has scored in 174 consecutive games, the second longest streak ever, and he had a streak of 25 straight field goals in 1992 and '93. In 1992, Andersen was second in the NFL in scoring with 120 points (one point off his career high). Andersen's 60-yarder in 1991 is tied for the second longest in NFL history. The fifth-highest-scoring active player, he has kicked the seventh-most field goals in NFL history.

The skinny: Andersen will be among the top NFC scorers if the Saints match their improved point production of last year.

STEVE CHRISTIE / BILLS

Year	XP	XPA	FG	FGA	Pts.
1990	27	27	23	27	96
1991	22	22	15	20	67
1992	43	44	24	30	115
1993	36	37	23	32	105
1994	38	38	24	28	110
Distance	1–19	20–29	30–39	40–49	50+
1994	0/0	11/12	6/7	5/7	2/2

Comments: Christie started the 1994 season with a team-record 16 straight field goals, including a five-of-five performance in Week 3. He was the last kicker in the league to miss a field goal. He finished tied for fourth in the AFC in scoring and was fifth in the league in field goal accuracy at 85.7 percent. That moved him into second place in all-time NFL field goal accuracy at 79.56 percent. Christie set a team record by making all 38 of his extra points. In 1993, he was inconsistent and downright bad beyond the 50-yard line. His 59-yard field goal against Miami in 1993 is the fourth longest in league history. In two seasons with the Buccaneers, he connected on 38 of 47 field goal attempts (81 percent).

The skinny: The Bills may be on a downswing, but Christie isn't.

GARY ANDERSON / STEELERS

Year	XP	XPA	FG	FGA	Pts.
1990	32	32	20	25	92
1991	31	31	23	33	100
1992	29	31	28	36	113
1993	32	32	28	30	116
1994	32	32	24	29	104
Distance	1–19	20–29	30–39	40–49	50+
1994	1/1	7/8	8/9	7/9	1/2

Comments: Coming off another solid season, Anderson consistently scores more than 100 points. He had a midseason streak of 18 straight field goals, including 10 in three games, in 1994. He booted two overtime game-winners (one a 51-yarder). In 1993, Anderson's 93.3 accuracy rate on field

KICKERS

goals (28 of 30) led the AFC. He ranks fifth all-time in field goal accuracy (309 of 394 for 78.23 percent). Anderson has the fourth-most field goals in NFL history (309) and ranks 11th on the NFL's all-time scoring list with 1,343 points. His only weakness is that he doesn't kick the long ones anymore (he has just one over 50 yards in four years). In 1990, he became only the second kicker to hit 200 field goals in less than 10 seasons (Jan Stenerud was the other). Anderson might be starting to show some age, but he has the second-highest field goal percentage (88.1 percent) over the last two years.

The skinny: Anderson should continue to post big numbers on one of the AFC's best teams.

MATT STOVER / BROWNS

Year	XP	XPA	FG	FGA	Pts.
1990	Injured				
1991	33	34	16	22	81
1992	29	30	21	29	92
1993	36	36	16	22	84
1994	32	32	26	28	110
Distance	1–19	20–29	30–39	40–49	50+
1994	1/1	7/7	10/11	8/8	0/1

Comments: In one sensational season in 1994, Stover turned around a mediocre career and entrenched himself as a top kicker. He led the NFL in field goal percentage with a 92.8 percent accuracy mark. He finished the season with 20 consecutive field goals, a team record, and he scored 110 points, the fourth-best total in team history. His only misses were from 32 and 50 yards. His 26 field goals set another team record. Stover has the highest field goal accuracy rate, 78.2 percent, in Cleveland history. He got off to a good start in 1993 (seven of seven) before going cold (five of eleven) for a short spell. He had a pretty good season in 1992, when he scored 92 points, though only three of his kicks were over 40 yards. Stover was shaky going into '92 after missing clutch field goal attempts in two 1991 games.

The skinny: Stover should be good for another 100-point season for Cleveland in 1995.

SOLID PICKS

CHRIS JACKE / PACKERS

Year	XP	XPA	FG	FGA	Pts.
1990	28	29	23	30	97
1991	31	31	18	24	85
1992	30	30	22	29	96
1993	35	35	31	37	128
1994	41	43	19	26	98
Distance	**1–19**	**20–29**	**30–39**	**40–49**	**50+**
1994	1/1	11/11	4/6	2/5	1/3

Comments: Jacke ranks seventh on the NFL's all-time field goal accuracy list with 116 kicks in 148 attempts, a 77.6 percent mark. Last year was perhaps Jacke's worst season, despite a 73.8 percent field goal accuracy. In 1994, he missed the first two extra points of his career and for the first time in his six-year career had a kick of any kind blocked (339 total attempts up to that point). In Week 14 against Chicago, Jacke made all four field goal tries and was four-of-four on extra points. He has 13 career field goals from 50 or more yards and he has played in 96 straight games. In 1993 he kicked 17 straight field goals and had six kicks from 50 yards and beyond to tie Dean Biasucci's NFL record. His 128 points were a career high and tied a team record. He is the Packers' third all-time leading scorer.

The skinny: Jacke is among the league's elite kickers but usually not among the top scorers.

NORM JOHNSON / FALCONS

Year	XP	XPA	FG	FGA	Pts.
1990	33	34	23	32	102
1991	38	39	19	23	95
1992	39	39	18	22	93
1993	34	34	26	27	112
1994	32	32	21	25	95
Distance	**1–19**	**20–29**	**30–39**	**40–49**	**50+**
1994	0/0	9/9	7/7	4/4	1/5

Comments: In 1994, Johnson made 20 of 20 field goal attempts from inside the 50. He made his final 14 field goal tries over the final nine games, and his last miss was a 53-yarder that hit the upright. In Week 10 in New Orleans, Johnson hit six of six attempts, one shy of the NFL record. He extended his PAT streak to 139, the third-longest active streak. Johnson has made 52 of his last 57 field goal attempts. In 1993 he had an almost-perfect season, hitting 26 of 27 field goal attempts (96.3 percent) for the second-best field goal accuracy percentage ever. Johnson also kicked 26 straight field goals from 1992 to '93 for the second-longest streak in league history. He is rewriting the Falcons' record book with four excellent seasons — 63 of 72 on field goals for 87.5 percent, and the three best single-season marks in team history. Johnson ranks 16th on the NFL's all-time scoring list, 14th in field goals and 13th in extra points. He has 18 field goals of 50 or more yards.

The skinny: For a player cut by Seattle because he missed too many big kicks, Johnson has some great stats.

JASON HANSON / LIONS

Year	XP	XPA	FG	FGA	Pts.
1992	30	30	21	26	93
1993	28	28	34	43	130
1994	39	40	18	27	93

Distance	1–19	20–29	30–39	40–49	50+
1994	0/0	6/7	7/7	5/8	0/5

Comments: Hanson did not have a bad 1994 season if you consider he was zero for five from 50 yards and beyond and was 18 of 22 otherwise. Hanson has proven to be a solid short-range kicker (he has missed only one from inside 42 yards in three professional seasons). After the Lions changed holders for Week 7, Hanson converted 13 of 15 field goals, including his final 10 attempts. He followed up an excellent rookie season by hitting 24 of 24 inside the 40-yard line in 1993 while scoring a club-record 130 points and hitting 34 field goals. Hanson led the NFC in scoring that year and was second in the league in field goals. In 1992, Hanson was the Offensive Rookie of the Year after hitting 18 of his last 19 field goals.

The skinny: Hanson needs to bounce back this season to prove he's among the elite kickers.

NICK LOWERY / JETS

Year	XP	XPA	FG	FGA	Pts.
1990	37	38	34	37	139
1991	35	35	25	30	110
1992	39	39	22	24	105
1993	37	37	23	29	106
1994	26	27	20	23	86
Distance	1–19	20–29	30–39	40–49	50+
1994	0/0	8/8	6/7	6/8	0/0

Comments: Lowery's point production dropped in 1994 but his accuracy didn't. He finished the season with a string of 13 successful field goal attempts, including kicks of 49, 46, 45 and 41 yards. He was successful on 87 percent of his kicks, fourth-best mark in the league. Lowery is still the NFL's all-time leader in field goal accuracy (349 of 433 for 80.41 percent). He has scored more than 100 points in 11 seasons, another league record. Now the third-highest scorer in NFL history with 1,559 points, Lowery needs just 24 field goals to tie the all-time field goal record of 373. The 39-year-old kicker hasn't slowed with age. He led the NFL again in field goal percentage in 1992, hitting 22 of 24 attempts for 91.7 percent. He has 20 career field goals from 50 yards or more, a record that was broken in 1992 by Morten Andersen. In both 1990 and '91, he had streaks of 21 consecutive field goals. In 1990, Lowery scored 139 points and hit 34 of 37 field goals.

The skinny: Lowery is arguably the best ever, though he is certainly not the highest-scoring placekicker these days.

MATT BAHR / PATRIOTS

Year	XP	XPA	FG	FGA	Pts.
1990	29	30	17	23	80
1991	24	25	22	29	90
1992	29	29	16	21	77
1993	28	29	13	18	67
1994	36	36	27	34	117
Distance	1–19	20–29	30–39	40–49	50+
1994	0/0	14/14	9/12	4/8	0/0

Comments: At age 39, the 16-year veteran shows no signs of fading. Bahr had one of the best seasons of his career in 1994. He made 27 of 34 field goal attempts for 79.4 percent. His career percentage is 72.7 (277 of 382). His 117 points ranked fourth in the NFL and established his career high. Bahr is now 12th on the league's all-time scoring list with 1,326 points. In 1993, he replaced Scott Sisson for the final three games after he had kicked for Philadelphia the previous 11 weeks. He is well-liked by Patriots coach Bill Parcells, which means that even if he struggles he should be around in 1995. In 14 career playoff games, Bahr has kicked 40 of 41 extra-point attempts and 21 of 25 field goals for 103 points, second among kickers in NFL playoff history.

The skinny: Bahr keeps rolling along like Old Man River.

JEFF JAEGER / RAIDERS

Year	XP	XPA	FG	FGA	Pts.
1990	40	42	15	20	85
1991	29	30	29	34	116
1992	28	29	15	26	73
1993	27	29	35	44	132
1994	31	31	22	28	97
Distance	1–19	20–29	30–39	40–49	50+
1994	1/1	5/5	6/9	8/11	2/2

Comments: Jaeger ended his odd year good, even year bad quirk by having a consistent 1994 season, although he didn't score 100 points. He made five of five field goal attempts against Denver in Week 14, and hit his final nine attempts of the season. He was two-for-two from beyond 50 yards for the year. With 606 points scored as a Raider, Jaeger ranks third in team history, and he has led the Raiders in scoring for six straight seasons. In 1993, Jaeger tied Ali Haji-Sheikh's NFL record with 35 field goals, and his 132 points led the NFL that year. Jaeger constantly bailed out the Raiders' offense in 1993, when he hit on 11 straight field goal attempts. He had a miserable season in 1992, but in 1991 he was the NFL's most-honored kicker with an 85.3 percent accuracy that ranked second. Jaeger is reliable inside the 40, hitting 89 of 105 the last five years. He had never kicked one longer than 50 yards until '91; he now has 11.

The skinny: Jaeger is capable of ranking among 1995's top scorers.

LIN ELLIOTT / CHIEFS

Year	XP	XPA	FG	FGA	Pts.
1992	47	48	24	35	119
1993	2	3	2	4	8
1994	30	30	25	30	105

Distance	1–19	20–29	30–39	40–49	50+
1994	3/3	15/17	4/6	3/4	0/0

Comments: Elliott had a fine first season with the Chiefs in 1994, connecting on 83.3 percent of his field goal attempts, the ninth-best accuracy mark in the NFL. He finished eighth in the AFC with 105 points, his second career 100-point year in his three professional seasons. The former Cowboy made all three of his attempts from 45-plus yards out. His long was 49 yards in Week 7. Elliott has a career field goal percentage of 73.9 percent (51 of 69) and has converted 79 of 81 extra-point tries for 97.5 percent. He had a great season in 1992 with Dallas.

The skinny: Elliott should finish near the middle of the pack in point production among kickers.

EDDIE MURRAY / EAGLES

Year	XP	XPA	FG	FGA	Pts.
1990	34	34	13	19	73
1991	40	40	19	28	97
1992	13	13	5	9	28
1993	38	38	28	33	122
1994	33	33	21	25	96

Distance	1–19	20–29	30–39	40–49	50+
1994	1/1	8/8	10/10	2/6	0/0

Comments: Murray solidified Philadelphia's kicking game last year. He hit his first nine field goal attempts to extend his string of successful attempts to 19 (dating back to the 1993 regular season and postseason when he was with Dallas). Murray finished second in the NFC in field goal accuracy (84 percent). He was 19-of-19 from inside the 40-yard line and extended his extra-point streak to 195, just 36 short of the NFL record. In

1993, he scored 122 points in the last 14 games with the Super Bowl champion Cowboys, but then signed with Philadelphia, so his point production slipped in '94. The second-leading active scorer in the NFL with 1,359 points, Murray is 10th all-time in scoring and is the ninth-most accurate field goal kicker ever. He has 20 field goals of 50-yards-plus, second most ever. Murray was the best field goal kicker in the NFL in 1988 and '89, when he hit on 20 of 21 attempts in both seasons. But his short kickoffs are a concern, and he was replaced on kickoffs late last season.

The skinny: Murray is still one of the most accurate kickers and he will score 100 points again, but not much more.

DOUG PELFREY / BENGALS

Year	XP	XPA	FG	FGA	Pts.
1993	13	16	24	31	85
1994	24	25	28	33	108

Distance	1–19	20–29	30–39	40–49	50+
1994	1/1	8/8	8/10	9/10	2/4

Comments: A Pelfrey field goal was the final play in all three Cincinnati victories in 1994. He has the unusual distinction of having kicked two field goals in the final three seconds of a game, last year's season-ending win over the Eagles. Pelfrey produced arguably the best field goal performance in Bengals history, hitting a club-record 28 of 33 for a team-record 84.8 percent. He's deadly inside 49 yards, and his 108 points was the Bengals' most in nine years. He set a team single-game record with six field goals in six attempts in Week 9. Pelfrey had a so-so rookie season in 1993. He missed three extra points but was pretty good on field goals and long kicks (10 of 13 from 40 and beyond).

The skinny: Pelfrey could score 100 points again due to the team's improving offense.

BEST OF THE REST

CHIP LOHMILLER / REDSKINS

Year	XP	XPA	FG	FGA	Pts.
1990	41	41	30	40	131
1991	56	56	31	43	149
1992	30	30	30	40	120
1993	24	26	16	28	72
1994	30	32	20	28	90
Distance	1–19	20–29	30–39	40–49	50+
1994	0/0	9/11	5/6	5/8	1/3

Comments: Lohmiller improved upon his horrible 1993 season but still finished near the bottom in field goal accuracy, 71.4 percent. After missing three of his first seven 1994 attempts, he almost lost his job. However, he then made nine of his next 11 attempts. After averaging 125 points a year in his first five seasons, Lohmiller was the second-lowest-scoring full-time kicker in the league in 1993. He had averaged more points than any other player in NFL history after five years in the league (1988–92), and his career 71.4 percent accuracy rate is pretty good. In 1994, Lohmiller kicked field goals in only nine games as the Redskins suffered through their second straight bad season.

The skinny: As the Redskins improve, Lohmiller's fantasy productivity should as well.

KEVIN BUTLER / BEARS

Year	XP	XPA	FG	FGA	Pts.
1990	36	37	26	37	114
1991	32	34	19	29	89
1992	34	34	19	26	91
1993	21	22	27	36	102
1994	24	24	21	29	87
Distance	1–19	20–29	30–39	40–49	50+
1994	1/1	7/7	6/9	5/8	2/4

Comments: Butler became only the fourth player in NFL history to reach 1,000 points before the end of his 10th season. He is the Bears' all-time leading scorer with 1,002 points, a fine average of 100.2 points a year. Even so, Butler may have lost the confidence of his coaches. He missed a 40-yarder that would have beaten Minnesota in Week 13, and two short misses cost the Bears a victory in 1993. Once one of the league's most consistent kickers, his 72.4 percent field goal accuracy rate ranked 23rd in the league last year. Still, he was named NFC Special Teams Player of the Month in November when he made nine of 10 field goals. Butler hit on 5 of 8 from 50 yards and beyond in 1993 (the third-highest total in the entire league) — including two 55-yarders, which were personal bests and team records. In 1988 and '89 he set a league record with 24 consecutive field goals. He has 16 career 50-yard field goals, a club record.

The skinny: Butler is a decent backup kicker in fantasy football if he holds on to his job.

BRAD DALUISO / GIANTS

Year	XP	XPA	FG	FGA	Pts.
1991	2	2	2	3	8
1992	0	0	0	1	0
1993	0	0	1	3	3
1994	5	5	11	11	38
Distance	1–19	20–29	30–39	40–49	50+
1994	2/2	1/1	5/5	2/2	1/1

Comments: In his first three years in the NFL, Daluiso made a living solely due to his long kickoffs. Last year, he replaced David Treadwell as the field goal kicker at halftime in Game 13. Daluiso made the most of his opportunity by converting all 10 of his attempts in the final four games. He also had a 49-yarder in Week 7. He led the NFL in 1994 in touchbacks with 19. Daluiso has attempted only 18 field goals in four NFL seasons, but for his career, he has connected on 14 of them for a 77.78 percent accuracy mark.

The skinny: His long kickoffs will keep him employed. Now we'll see if he can kick field goals consistently, too.

GREG DAVIS / CARDINALS

Year	XP	XPA	FG	FGA	Pts.
1990	40	40	22	33	106
1991	19	19	21	30	82
1992	28	28	13	26	67
1993	37	37	21	28	100
1994	17	17	20	26	77

Distance	1–19	20–29	30–39	40–49	50+
1994	0/0	10/11	3/4	6/7	1/4

Comments: Davis had a pretty good 1994 season, but he kicked for the league's second-lowest-scoring team and finished with the second fewest points among full-time kickers. He thrived on pressure kicks, winning two games with last-minute field goals and sending another into overtime. Davis converted on 13 of his last 14 field goal attempts. After a hamstring injury sidelined him for two games, he put together a late-season streak of 11 straight field goals, a club record. His 76.9 percent accuracy rate ranked fifth in the NFC and was the team's best mark since 1975. In 1993, he became just the third Cardinal since 1970 to score 100 points. Davis had a miserable year in 1992, missing half of his 26 field goal attempts and ranking last in the league in accuracy.

The skinny: Davis's point total could really improve in '95 if the Cardinals find an offense.

AL DEL GRECO / OILERS

Year	XP	XPA	FG	FGA	Pts.
1990	31	31	17	27	82
1991	16	16	10	13	46
1992	41	41	21	27	104
1993	39	40	29	34	126
1994	18	18	16	20	66

Distance	1–19	20–29	30–39	40–49	50+
1994	0/0	4/5	4/4	7/8	1/3

Comments: Del Greco's fortunes plummeted with the collapse of the

Oilers in 1994, as he scored only 66 points despite another solid season. His 85 percent field goal accuracy mark remains among the all-time best. He finished the 1994 season with 11 straight field goals to tie a team record. Del Greco is the most accurate kicker in franchise history (80.9 percent). In 1994, he led the NFL in average per make (37.4). His 126 points in 1993 (a team record) broke his career best of the previous season. Del Greco has solidified his position as the Oilers' kicker after a shaky career (he had only a 66 percent career mark heading into '92).

The skinny: Del Greco is not likely to score a lot of points until the Oilers improve.

OTHERS

JOHN KASAY / PANTHERS

Year	XP	XPA	FG	FGA	Pts.
1991	27	28	25	31	102
1992	14	14	14	22	56
1993	29	29	23	28	98
1994	25	26	20	24	85
Distance	1–19	20–29	30–39	40–49	50+
1994	1/1	1/1	11/11	6/9	1/2

Comments: Signed by Carolina as a free agent this year, Kasay has one of the strongest young legs in the NFL. He made all 18 of his field goal attempts from 42 yards or less in 1994, and his long kickoffs helped the Seahawks lead the AFC in kickoff coverage. Kasay's field goal percentage (83.33) equaled Norm Johnson's team record. His career percentage, 78.1 (82 of 105), is a Seattle record. He made 11 straight to start the '94 season. Kasay had a fine comeback season in 1993, with three 50-yarders and a fourth-place accuracy rate, 82.1 percent. In 1992, Kasay scored the second-fewest points of any kicker who played in all 16 games, with barely half of the 102 points he had in 1991 because of a very inept Seattle offense.

The skinny: Kasay won't score a lot of points for the first-year Panthers.

DEAN BIASUCCI / COLTS

Year	XP	XPA	FG	FGA	Pts.
1990	32	33	17	24	83
1991	14	14	15	26	59
1992	24	24	16	29	72
1993	15	16	26	31	93
1994	37	37	16	24	85
Distance	1–19	20–29	30–39	40–49	50+
1994	1/1	5/5	3/7	5/9	2/2

Comments: Biasucci had a pretty good season going until finishing 1994 with four misses in his final six attempts. He had more than one field goal in a game only four times last year. Biasucci was two-of-two from 50-plus yards and is tied for fourth in NFL history with 18 career field goals from 50 and beyond. The Colts' all-time scoring leader, he has led the team in scoring for nine straight seasons. He holds the team record with 176 career field goals. After several subpar seasons, Biasucci had a fine season in 1993 with a career-high 26 field goals. He was one of the most accurate kickers from 1987 to '89, hitting on 70 of 86 field goal attempts (81 percent) before slipping from 1990 to '92. Overall, he has a field goal accuracy mark of 70.4 percent (176 of 250).

The skinny: Biasucci's best years are behind him, but he could be a decent fantasy backup in '95.

MICHAEL HUSTED / BUCCANEERS

Year	XP	XPA	FG	FGA	Pts.
1993	27	27	16	22	75
1994	20	20	23	35	89
Distance	1–19	20–29	30–39	40–49	50+
1994	0/0	8/8	10/12	4/10	1/5

Comments: Husted was effective from short range in 1994, but he made just five of 15 field goal attempts from 40 yards and beyond. His field goal percentage of 65.7 percent was the second worst in the NFL. Husted did rank third in the NFC in field goals with 23, and he produced 14 touchbacks. He ranks sixth in team scoring history and he has four 50-yard field goals in two seasons. In 1993, his72.7 percent accuracy mark ranked only 11th in the NFC. His 57-yard field goal vs. the Raiders was a team record and one of the 15 longest in ever. But, playing for a woeful offense in Tampa Bay, Husted shouldn't be expected to be a high scorer anytime soon.

The skinny: Husted is a fantasy backup at best.

TONY ZENDEJAS / RAMS

Year	XP	XPA	FG	FGA	Pts.
1990	20	21	7	12	41
1991	25	26	17	17	76
1992	38	38	15	20	83
1993	23	25	16	23	71
1994	28	28	18	23	82
Distance	**1–19**	**20–29**	**30–39**	**40–49**	**50+**
1994	2/2	9/9	6/7	1/5	0/0

Comments: Zendejas had a good season on a bad team in '94. Hence, he had only 23 field goal attempts. He ranked fourth in the NFC in field goal percentage with a 78.3 percent accuracy mark. He did have a midseason string of 12 straight successful field goals. However, despite a reputation of being a good long-range kicker, Zendejas made only one of five kicks from beyond 40 yards last year. For his career, he is 17 of 23 from 50-yards-plus (11 straight at one point) and is the NFL's all-time percentage leader. Zendejas last scored over 100 points in 1989, when he had 115. In 1993, he was the lowest-scoring full-time kicker with just 71 points. In '91, Zendejas set an NFL record when he was good on all 17 of his field goal attempts. He had a streak of 23 straight field goals from 1990 to '92.

The skinny: Forget about drafting Zendejas this year.

SCOTT SISSON / JAGUARS

Year	XP	XPA	FG	FGA	Pts.
1993	15	15	14	26	57
1994	DNP				
Distance	**1–19**	**20–29**	**30–39**	**40–49**	**50+**
1994	—	—	—	—	—

Comments: Sisson has been given a chance by Jacksonville after being out of the NFL since the 1993 season. New England coach Bill Parcells benched Sisson with three weeks to go in 1993 after the rookie had missed 12 of his 26 field goal attempts. He was replaced by Matt Bahr, although Sisson continued to handle kickoffs.

The skinny: Sisson, who was a very good kicker in college, has a new lease on life with a new franchise.

DAVID TREADWELL / GIANTS

Year	XP	XPA	FG	FGA	Pts.
1990	34	36	25	34	109
1991	31	32	27	36	112
1992	28	28	20	24	88
1993	28	29	25	31	103
1994	22	23	11	17	55
Distance	**1–19**	**20–29**	**30–39**	**40–49**	**50+**
1994	1/1	5/5	4/7	1/4	0/0

Comments: Treadwell entered the '94 season as the third-best kicker in NFL history in field goal accuracy. But he was benched with three games to go after missing five of eight attempts and Brad Daluiso took his job. For his career, Treadwell has booted 135 of 175 field goal tries for 77.1 percent, the eighth-best mark in NFL history. He has scored more than 100 points in four of his six seasons. In 1993, Treadwell hit 80.6 percent of his 31 attempts for the second-highest percentage in Giants history, though it wasn't as good as the 83.3 percent (20 of 24) he had the year before in Denver. In 1991, his 27 field goals tied the Broncos record.

The skinny: Treadwell could end up starting somewhere else in '95.

ROOKIES

See Chapter 12, Rookie Report.

Other Kickers on Rosters

Cary Blanchard, Saints
Mike Cofer, Colts

KICKERS

Chapter 8
DEFENSES

Just as defense can win games in real football, it can also win games in fantasy football. That's why many fantasy leagues like to incorporate some form of defense into their game.

There are several commonly used methods for including defensive players in fantasy leagues.

The most common is to add an eighth "player" to each team in the form of a team defense (rather than individual defensive players). If an entire defense is drafted, any score by any member of that defense counts. Points are awarded every time a player on a team's defense scores a touchdown on a fumble return or an interception or when a player scores a safety (even a team safety, such as when an opposing punter steps out of the end zone). Most leagues also include touchdowns scored on blocked punts and field goals, as they are basically defensive scores, too.

Leagues can also draft special teams and award points for scores on punts and kickoff returns. Some leagues combine defensive scores *and* special-team scores.

Some leagues award points for other defensive categories, such as sacks and interceptions. A common scoring method is one point for a sack and two points for an interception (that is not returned for a score).

But fantasy leagues can also draft individual players. For example, every team can draft one defensive lineman, one linebacker and one defensive back (or more of each). The ways you can score points depend on your league and how detailed you want to get. But remember, as your league's scoring method gets more complicated, so does the work involved in determining the scores.

Believe it or not, there are some leagues that even count tackles. That's really getting complicated, perhaps overly complicated. The biggest problem with counting tackles is that they are unofficial statistics, and the quality of team statisticians ranges from conservative to liberal — for example, some teams' leading tacklers have 200 tackles, while other teams' top tacklers have only 100 or so. It's very subjective. Papers such as *USA Today* include tackles and assists in their game summaries, but team coaches change those figures drastically every Monday when they view the game film.

Also, if you draft individual players, it adds a lot of bookkeeping and score-tabulating chores for the commissioner.

So, if you want to include defense the easiest way, allow every team to draft a team defense and just count defensive scores — fumbles and interceptions returned for touchdowns, blocked kicks returned for touchdowns and safeties. This is the category that is most often pure luck. While you are looking to your quarterbacks, running backs and wide receivers for big scores, a defensive score is always a nice — and unexpected — bonus.

The average defensive team scored only about 15 points last season, which is the equivalent of only two and a half touchdowns per team. That's not much at all, but you will think six points is a lot when it happens to your team.

It's almost impossible to predict which defenses will score the most points in any given season. Perennially good defenses don't always score a lot of points on defense. Since defensive scores are most often a result of luck, you can never figure which teams will improve. For example, the Minnesota Vikings scored 42 points on defense in 1994 and 50 points in 1992. But in the year in between, 1993, they scored just 16 points. You just never know.

One thing you can count on is that defenses won't score as many points in 1995 as they did in 1992. That was the year of big defensive plays, when 47 interceptions were brought back for scores — six each by the Chiefs and Vikings. That was the most since 1984. Thirty-two fumbles were also returned for touchdowns, the most since 1983. The strategy has changed in pro football these days — once you get the ball, go for the end zone. But don't expect too many teams to score six times off interceptions in one season. Remember, luck is the biggest factor in defensive scores.

The Vikings returned seven turnovers for touchdowns last season, and four teams returned five of them for scores. But three teams didn't score a point off of a turnover, which is why it's such a crapshoot.

In 1994, 19 fumbles and 45 interceptions were returned for touchdowns. That's an average of just over two per team — not very many.

In drafting defenses, there are a lot of factors to take into consideration, such as which teams are most likely to make defensive scores (touchdowns on the returns of fumbles, interceptions or blocked kicks and safeties).

If your league drafts individual defensive players, you will want to know which players get the most sacks and interceptions.

Also in this chapter, because an important factor in determining which offensive players you will play each week is the defenses your players will

DEFENSES

face in real NFL games, some defensive statistics are included (rushing touchdowns and yards allowed, passing touchdowns and yards allowed, total points allowed, sacks and takeaways).

And, also in this chapter, special-teams scores from 1994 (kickoffs and punts returned for touchdowns) are detailed.

Draft Tips for Choosing Defenses

■ Don't spend too much time analyzing the teams to decide which defense you want to draft. Defensive scores are so rare that they really should be considered a bonus, rather than points that you should expect.

■ Don't waste a pick drafting a defense high in your draft; wait until the last few rounds. While a defensive score could mean the difference between winning and losing any given week, it's too chancy, and you are better off drafting players who have a better chance of scoring.

■ Draft a team with a strong defense. Those that force the most turnovers have the best chance of converting them into scores.

■ Look for opportunistic teams that convert turnovers into touchdowns, such as Minnesota, Philadelphia, Washington, San Francisco and New Orleans. Three teams that would be good picks to score more defensive points in 1995 than they did in '94 are Arizona, Houston and Kansas City.

1994 DEFENSIVE SCORES

	Team	Fum. /TD	Int. /TD	Blk. Kick /TD	Saf.	Pts.	3-Year Avg.
1.	Minnesota	3	4	0	0	42	36.0
2.	Washington	2	3	0	1	32	25.3
3.	Indianapolis	2	3	0	0	30	16.0
	L.A. Raiders	2	3	0	0	30	16.7
	San Francisco	1	4	0	0	30	22.0
6.	Detroit	1	2	0	1	20	18.7
	L.A. Rams	2	1	0	1	20	11.3
8.	Atlanta	1	2	0	0	18	10.0
	Dallas	0	3	0	0	18	16.7
	New Orleans	2	1	0	0	18	22.7
	N.Y. Jets	0	3	0	0	18	15.3
	Pittsburgh	1	2	0	0	18	16.0
	San Diego	0	3	0	0	18	12.0

14.	Philadelphia	0	2	0	1	14	24.7
	Seattle	0	2	0	1	14	16.0
16.	Cleveland	0	1	1	0	12	17.3
	New England	1	1	0	0	12	14.0
18.	Kansas City	0	1	0	2	10	27.3
19.	Arizona	0	1	0	1	8	16.7
	Buffalo	1	0	0	1	8	18.0
	Houston	0	1	0	1	8	24.0
22.	Green Bay	0	1	0	0	6	8.7
	Miami	0	1	0	0	6	10.0
24.	N.Y. Giants	0	0	0	2	4	6.0
25.	Cincinnati	0	0	0	1	2	14.0
26.	Chicago	0	0	0	0	0	10.7
	Denver	0	0	0	0	0	6.0
	Tampa Bay	0	0	0	0	0	12.0

TEAM DEFENSES

One of the hardest — but most enjoyable — aspects of fantasy football is trying to decide whom to start each week.

For example, should you start Barry Sanders against the tough Vikings run defense, or do you go with Lewis Tillman against the weak Buccaneers run defense? Or, at wide receiver, do you go with Fred Barnett against the excellent Cowboys defensive backs or John Taylor versus the woeful Falcons secondary?

The defensive charts that follow should help you decide. But, remember, they are from the 1994 season, and the performance of each team's defense can change drastically from year to year (especially in this era of free agency with so many players changing teams).

1994 RUSHING TOUCHDOWNS ALLOWED

	Team	Rushing TDs Allowed	Three-Year Average
1.	Arizona	7	11.0
	Pittsburgh	7	6.3
3.	Dallas	8	8.7
	Indianapolis	8	14.7

5.	Cleveland	9	7.7
	Green Bay	9	9.0
	Minnesota	9	11.3
8.	Buffalo	10	8.3
	Chicago	10	11.0
	New Orleans	10	8.3
11.	Kansas City	11	11.3
	L.A. Raiders	11	15.0
	New England	11	11.7
	N.Y. Giants	11	11.7
	Philadelphia	11	8.7
	San Diego	11	10.3
17.	Denver	12	9.3
	L.A. Rams	12	17.3
19.	Tampa Bay	13	14.3
20.	Miami	14	11.7
21.	Detroit	15	13.7
	Seattle	15	13.7
23.	Atlanta	16	16.7
	Cincinnati	16	15.3
	San Francisco	16	9.0
26.	Houston	17	10.7
	N.Y. Jets	17	13.0
28.	Washington	24	16.3

1994 RUSHING YARDS ALLOWED

	Team	Rushing Yards Allowed	Net Average Per Game
1.	Minnesota	1090	68.1
2.	San Francisco	1338	83.6
3.	Green Bay	1363	85.2
4.	Arizona	1370	85.6
5.	San Diego	1404	87.8
6.	Miami	1430	89.4
7.	Pittsburgh	1452	90.8
8.	Buffalo	1515	94.7
9.	L.A. Raiders	1543	96.4

10.	Dallas	1561	97.6
11.	Philadelphia	1616	101.0
12.	Indianapolis	1646	102.9
13.	Cleveland	1669	104.3
14.	Atlanta	1693	105.8
15.	N.Y. Giants	1728	108.0
16.	Kansas City	1734	108.4
17.	Denver	1752	109.5
18.	New Orleans	1758	109.9
19.	New England	1760	110.0
20.	L.A. Rams	1781	111.3
21.	N.Y. Jets	1809	113.1
22.	Detroit	1859	116.2
23.	Cincinnati	1906	119.1
24.	Chicago	1922	120.1
25.	Seattle	1952	122.0
26.	Tampa Bay	1964	122.8
27.	Washington	1975	123.4
28.	Houston	2120	132.5

1994 PASSING TOUCHDOWNS ALLOWED

	Team	Passing TDs Allowed	Three-Year Average
1.	Pittsburgh	12	14.3
2.	Cleveland	13	18.3
3.	San Francisco	15	19.3
	Seattle	15	14.0
5.	Chicago	16	16.0
	N.Y. Giants	16	17.0
7.	Houston	18	18.0
8.	Arizona	19	19.0
	Dallas	19	16.3
	N.Y. Jets	19	17.7
11.	Green Bay	20	17.3
	Philadelphia	20	20.7
	San Diego	20	18.0
14.	Detroit	21	20.0

DEFENSES

	New England	21	21.0
16.	Cincinnati	22	22.0
	Washington	22	20.3
18.	Kansas City	23	20.0
	L.A. Rams	23	19.3
	Miami	23	21.7
21.	Indianapolis	24	20.0
	L.A. Raiders	24	17.3
23.	Minnesota	25	16.0
	Tampa Bay	25	24.0
25.	Atlanta	26	25.7
	Buffalo	26	21.0
27.	Denver	28	23.3
	New Orleans	28	21.0

1994 PASSING YARDS ALLOWED

	Team	Net Passing Yards Allowed	Net Average Per Game
1.	Dallas	2752	172.0
2.	Houston	2795	174.7
3.	Pittsburgh	2874	179.6
4.	Arizona	3038	189.9
5.	Chicago	3087	192.9
6.	Philadelphia	3094	193.4
7.	Cleveland	3157	197.3
8.	N.Y. Giants	3222	201.4
9.	Cincinnati	3248	203.0
10.	Kansas City	3266	204.1
11.	Tampa Bay	3372	210.8
12.	L.A. Rams	3389	211.8
13.	Seattle	3397	212.3
14.	L.A. Raiders	3400	212.5
15.	Green Bay	3401	212.6
16.	New England	3447	215.4
17.	San Francisco	3501	218.8
18.	N.Y. Jets	3529	220.6
19.	Detroit	3546	221.6

20.	Washington	3634	227.1
21.	Minnesota	3652	228.3
22.	San Diego	3658	228.6
23.	Buffalo	3660	228.8
24.	Indianapolis	3679	229.9
25.	Miami	3794	237.1
26.	New Orleans	3811	238.2
27.	Atlanta	4136	258.5
28.	Denver	4155	259.7

1994 TOTAL POINTS ALLOWED

	Team	Total Points Allowed	Points Per Game	Three-Year Average
1.	Cleveland	204	12.8	16.4
2.	Pittsburgh	234	14.6	15.4
3.	Dallas	248	15.5	15.0
4.	Arizona	267	16.7	18.1
5.	Green Bay	287	17.9	18.0
6.	San Francisco	296	18.5	17.2
7.	Kansas City	298	18.6	17.8
8.	N.Y. Giants	305	19.1	18.3
9.	San Diego	306	19.1	17.4
10.	Chicago	307	19.2	18.7
11.	Philadelphia	308	19.3	18.1
12.	New England	312	19.5	20.0
13.	Minnesota	314	19.6	17.8
14.	Indianapolis	320	20.0	20.8
	N.Y. Jets	320	20.0	18.4
16.	Seattle	323	20.2	19.8
17.	L.A. Raiders	327	20.4	19.5
	Miami	327	20.4	20.0
19.	Detroit	342	21.4	20.1
20.	Tampa Bay	351	21.9	22.8
21.	Houston	352	22.0	17.7
22.	Buffalo	356	22.3	18.3
23.	L.A. Rams	365	22.8	23.2
24.	Atlanta	385	24.1	24.7
25.	Denver	396	24.8	21.0

DEFENSES

26.	Cincinnati	406	25.4	22.7
27.	New Orleans	407	25.4	19.8
28.	Washington	412	25.8	21.1

1994 SACKS

	Team	Sacks	Three-Year Average
1.	Pittsburgh	55	44.3
2.	Dallas	47	41.7
3.	San Diego	43	42.0
4.	Philadelphia	42	44.3
5.	Kansas City	39	41.3
	New England	39	31.0
7.	Cleveland	38	44.7
	L.A. Raiders	38	43.0
	San Francisco	38	41.0
10.	Green Bay	37	39.0
11.	Minnesota	36	44.0
	New Orleans	36	48.0
13.	Arizona	35	32.0
14.	Atlanta	32	30.0
15.	Cincinnati	31	32.7
	Houston	31	44.3
17.	Indianapolis	29	29.7
	Miami	29	31.3
	N.Y. Jets	29	32.3
	Seattle	29	37.7
21.	Chicago	28	39.0
	Washington	28	32.7
23.	Detroit	27	33.0
24.	L.A. Rams	26	30.7
	N.Y. Giants	26	30.7
26.	Buffalo	25	35.3
27.	Denver	23	39.7
28.	Tampa Bay	20	28.3

1994 TAKEAWAYS

	Team	Fumbles	Int.	Total	Three-Year Average
1.	New England	18	22	40	30.3
2.	Kansas City	26	12	38	38.3
	N.Y. Jets	21	17	38	38.0
4.	Arizona	13	23	36	30.0
5.	Philadelphia	14	21	35	35.7
	San Francisco	12	23	35	31.3
7.	Minnesota	16	18	34	36.7
8.	Atlanta	11	22	33	26.7
	Green Bay	12	21	33	33.3
10.	Miami	9	23	32	30.3
	N.Y. Giants	16	16	32	28.7
	San Diego	15	17	32	34.0
13.	Cleveland	13	18	31	28.7
	Dallas	9	22	31	30.0
	New Orleans	14	17	31	33.0
	Pittsburgh	14	17	31	37.3
17.	Seattle	11	19	30	33.0
18.	Buffalo	12	16	28	36.7
	Indianapolis	10	18	28	28.0
20.	Denver	14	12	26	29.3
	Houston	12	14	26	33.3
22.	L.A. Raiders	13	12	25	22.3
23.	Detroit	11	12	23	30.0
	Washington	6	17	23	29.3
25.	Chicago	10	12	22	27.3
26.	Tampa Bay	12	9	21	25.3
27.	L.A. Rams	6	14	20	24.3
28.	Cincinnati	8	10	18	25.7

1994 SPECIAL-TEAMS SCORES

Some leagues like to award points for touchdown returns of kickoffs and punts. Because of new rules last season that emphasized kick returns, 18 NFL teams scored touchdowns on returns, which was a record. A total of 32 touchdowns was scored (compared to only 11 in 1993 and 22 in 1992), which is an average of just more than one per team. That's not much, but it is a nice bonus if you include special-teams touchdowns in your scoring.

Here are those scores for the 1994 season:

	Team	Punt Ret/TD	Kickoff Ret/TD	Points	Three-Year Total
1.	Detroit	0	4	24	42
	San Diego	2	2	24	24
3.	Cleveland	2	1	18	42
4.	Dallas	1	1	12	36
	Green Bay	1	1	12	24
	Indianapolis	1	1	12	24
	New Orleans	0	2	12	30
	N.Y. Giants	2	0	12	24
	Washington	2	0	12	24
10.	Chicago	1	0	6	6
	Cincinnati	1	0	6	12
	Houston	1	0	6	6
	Kansas City	0	1	6	18
	L.A. Rams	1	0	6	18
	Philadelphia	0	1	6	12
	San Francisco	0	1	6	18
	Seattle	0	1	6	6
	Tampa Bay	1	0	6	6
19.	Arizona	0	0	0	6
	Atlanta	0	0	0	18
	Buffalo	0	0	0	6
	Denver	0	0	0	0
	L.A. Raiders	0	0	0	6
	Miami	0	0	0	12
	Minnesota	0	0	0	0
	New England	0	0	0	0
	N.Y. Jets	0	0	0	0
	Pittsburgh	0	0	0	6

Chapter 9
TEAM EVALUATIONS
ARIZONA CARDINALS

Who's New — Wide receivers Rob Moore and rookie Frank Sanders, and quarterback David Krieg.

Who's Gone — Quarterback Steve Beuerlein was drafted by Jacksonville in the expansion draft, wide receivers Gary Clark and Randal Hill signed with Miami, wide receiver Ricky Proehl was traded to Seattle, and running back Ron Moore was traded to the Jets.

Quarterbacks — Ageless David Krieg gives the Cardinals some savvy and is still a useful veteran while waiting for rookie Stoney Case to develop. Krieg proved last year in Detroit that he's not washed-up yet, as he threw 14 touchdown passes and only three interceptions in seven starts. The backups, Mike Buck, Jim McMahon and Jay Schroeder, aren't very good.

Running Backs — In his third season, Garrison Hearst will get every opportunity to become the featured back. Hearst did little until the final month of 1994, but Moore is now gone. Larry Centers is an excellent receiving back and third-down specialist. He caught 77 passes last season. Mark Higgs is a pretty good backup.

Wide Receivers — Moore will become the team's go-to man, and Sanders has a good shot at becoming the No. 2 wideout. Moore, a much-sought-after free agent in the offseason, had a career year last season with the Jets, making 78 catches (sixth best in the AFC) for 1,010 yards. Chuck Levy was moved from running back to wide receiver late last year. Bryan Reeves, Anthony Edwards and Patrick Robinson are backups.

Tight Ends — Coach Buddy Ryan was trying to swing a deal to get Keith Jackson. There's not a lot else on the roster (Chad Fann and Terry Samuels).

Kickers — Greg Davis booted 20 of 26 field goals and all 17 of his extra-point attempts last season. But he scored only 77 points because the team's offense was anemic. If the offense picks up, Davis may get the 100 points he scored in 1993.

Best Players to Draft — Running back Garrison Hearst and wide receiver Rob Moore.

ATLANTA FALCONS

Who's New — All-purpose player Eric Metcalf, who was obtained in a trade with Cleveland, and wide receiver J.J. Birden, who was signed as a free agent.

Who's Gone — Wide receiver Andre Rison, the top free agent in the 1995 market, signed with Cleveland in the offseason. Running back Erric Pegram left for Pittsburgh and kick returner Clarence Verdin signed with Tampa Bay.

Quarterbacks — Coming off a good season, Jeff George should return with renewed confidence in 1995. He completed 61.5 percent of his passes for 3,734 yards and 23 touchdowns in 1994. George no longer has Rison to throw to, but the Falcons still have a good group of receivers. His backups are capable veteran Bobby Hebert, who filled in well for George late in 1994, and a promising second-year prospect, Perry Klein, who played little in 1994.

Running Backs — Craig Hayward got his weight down and had an excellent comeback season in 1994, with 779 yards and seven touchdowns. There's not much else on the roster, as a good backup is sorely needed.

Wide Receivers — Terance Mathis took advantage of Andre Rison double-teams to post a dream season last year. He caught 111 passes for 1,342 yards and 11 touchdowns. Mathis is very good, but is he *that* good? Birden should fit very well in the run-and-shoot. Bert Emanuel is coming off a successful rookie season in which he caught 46 passes, and Ricky Sanders, who grabbed 67 passes a year ago, may have a year or two left. Trade acquisition Metcalf gives the Falcons one of the league's most dangerous players (he has been switched to slot receiver). He's also a premier punt returner. Metcalf scored seven touchdowns last year by rushing, receiving and punt returning.

Tight Ends — Harper LeBel and Mitch Lyons are the tight ends in an offense that rarely uses them. Forget about them in your draft.

Kicker — Norm Johnson had another outstanding season in 1994, hitting 21 of 25 field goals. He never missed from inside the 50-yard line last year and is the league's most accurate kicker since over the last two seasons. He has made 52 of his last 57 attempts in Atlanta, and is always good for 100 points.

Best Players to Draft — Quarterback Jeff George, running back Craig Heyward, wide receivers Terance Mathis and Eric Metcalf, and kicker Norm Johnson.

BUFFALO BILLS

Who's New — Running back Bobby Humphrey, who didn't play a down the last two years, was signed as a free agent.

Who's Gone — Tight end Pete Metzelaars, quarterback Frank Reich and wide receiver Don Beebe all left via free agency for Carolina. Nine-year veteran receiver Bill Brooks was cut.

Quarterbacks — Jim Kelly had an excellent season in 1994 to reverse a two-year slide, although Buffalo's deep passing game has been declining since 1992. Kelly was the third-leading passer in the AFC last year, completing 63.6 percent of his passes for 3,114 yards and 22 touchdown passes. But Kelly completed only two passes for more than 40 yards all year. Kelly will miss Metzelaars, Beebe and Brooks. Rookie Todd Collins will be groomed as Kelly's replacement, but don't look for him to play much this year.

Running Backs — Thurman Thomas had subpar numbers by his excellent standards in 1994, but he still rushed for 1,093 yards and finished fourth in the AFC with 1,442 combined yards. Thomas also caught 50 passes and scored nine touchdowns. After seven seasons, he may or may not have lost a step. Kenneth Davis, one of the league's top backup running backs for years, ran for 381 yards in 1994. Carwell Gardner scored four TDs, and Yonel Jourdain started to show something out of the backfield. The much-maligned Humphrey will get one final chance to clean up his act.

Wide Receivers — Andre Reed had an outstanding season in 1994, finishing second in the AFC in receptions with 90 and second in receiving yards with 1,303. Reed is still fearless going over the middle. With the departure of Brooks and Beebe, second-year man Bucky Brooks, Russell Copeland and rookie fourth-round draft pick Justin Armour will battle for the other receiving jobs. Brooks spent the 1994 season on the injured reserve list.

Tight Ends — Tony Cline, another rookie taken in the fourth round, will battle second-year man Lonnie Johnson for the starting job. The backup is A.J. Ofodile.

Kicker — Always-reliable Steve Christie booted 17 straight field goals in 1994. He made 24 of 28 field goal attempts and kicked all 38 of his extra-point tries to score 110 points — Christie's third straight year with 105 or more points.

Best Players to Draft — Quarterback Jim Kelly, running back Thurman Thomas, wide receiver Andre Reed and kicker Steve Christie.

TEAM EVALUATIONS

CAROLINA PANTHERS

Who's New — The entire roster is new — including quarterbacks Frank Reich, Kerry Collins and Jack Trudeau; wide receivers Don Beebe and Mark Carrier; tight ends Pete Metzelaars and Lawyer Tillman; and kicker John Kasay.

Quarterbacks — Former Bills quarterback Frank Reich, who has been considered to be among the best backups in the league, will probably start this season while first-round pick Collins gets his pro feet wet. Reich once rallied the Bills from a 35–3 third-quarter deficit to a shocking playoff victory over Houston. Collins brings great size and tremendous leadership qualities to Carolina. In time, he'll be the franchise quarterback. Jack Trudeau has passed for more than 10,000 yards in his nine-year career, but he is mostly a backup.

Running Backs — Because the Panthers traded down to draft Collins instead of Ki-Jana Carter, there isn't much talent at this position. Fullback Howard Griffith, a former Ram, may be the starter. He opened a lot of holes for Jerome Bettis but won't have anybody nearly that good running behind him now. Among the tailback candidates are former Colt Dewell Brewer, ex-Cowboy Derrick Lassic and former Bengal Eric Ball. Don't waste your time drafting any of them.

Wide Receivers — Mark Carrier gives the Panthers a legitimate No. 1 receiver. A former Pro Bowler, he entrenched himself into Cleveland coach Bill Belichick's doghouse last year and caught only 29 passes for 452 yards. All but five of those passes were good for first downs, and he scored five TDs. The year before, he had 43 receptions for 746 yards. The 6-foot-5 Steve Hawkins played sparingly in New England last year. Green caught 12 TD passes in 1991 and '92, but he has done little since. Other candidates for a starting job are former Ram Richard Buchanan, former Lion Larry Ryans and ex-Bronco Charles Swann.

Tight Ends — Pete Metzelaars, a 13-year veteran, is still among the league's top tight ends. He was signed as a free agent after catching 49 passes for 428 yards and five TDs last year for Buffalo. He has averaged five touchdowns a season over the last three years. Former Brown Lawyer Tillman is attempting a comeback after spending all of 1994 out of football.

Kicker — Strong-legged John Kasay converted 20 of 24 field goal attempts and 25 of 26 extra-point tries for Seattle in 1994. But will he get that many opportunities to kick for an expansion team?

Best Player to Draft — Tight end Pete Metzelaars.

CHICAGO BEARS

Who's New — Heisman Trophy winner Rashaan Salaam was drafted in the first round. Wide receiver Michael Timpson was signed as a free agent. Running backs Anthony Johnson and Darrell Thompson were signed to add depth.

Who's Gone — Wide receiver Tom Waddle signed with Cincinnati, kickoff returner Nate Lewis signed with Atlanta and tight end Marv Cook was cut.

Quarterbacks — Steve Walsh was 8–3 as a starter last year. His unspectacular but mistake-free play helped get the Bears into the playoffs. High-priced free-agent Erik Kramer played decent, but the team didn't play well with him at the helm. Kramer, who this year will get another chance to be the starter, completed 62.7 percent of his passes a year ago. Walsh completed 60.6 percent of his passes for 10 touchdowns and eight interceptions. Shane Matthews is the third-stringer.

Running Backs — Salaam will be handed the job as the Bears' every-down back. There are some question marks about his ability to run inside, and he gained many of his 2,055 yards last year outside on option pitches. Lewis Tillman, last year's starter, was adequate but averaged only 3.3 yards per carry despite seven touchdowns. Raymont Harris was Chicago's most productive rookie, with 464 rushing yards and 39 pass receptions. Robert Green is a productive third-down back. Green will battle Tim Worley, Johnson and Thompson for backup jobs.

Wide Receivers — Jeff Graham proved to be a bargain in a trade with Pittsburgh, catching a career-high 68 passes. Curtis Conway showed some signs of realizing his potential but was slowed by injuries. Timpson gives the Bears a legitimate deep threat. He caught 74 passes for 941 yards a year ago. Speedy rookie Jack Jackson could prove to be a fourth-round steal. He will step right in as a kick returner and backup slot receiver. Reserve Terry Obee spent the 1994 season on injured reserve.

Tight Ends — Chris Gedney struggled through a second straight injury-plagued season. He caught three touchdown passes before breaking a leg. Keith Jennings and Ryan Wetnight are solid backups.

Kickers — Kevin Butler had another rather inconsistent season in 1994, missing eight of his 29 field goal attempts. He does not boot kickoffs very deep, so rookie punter Todd Sauerbrun may handle them this season.

Best Players to Draft — Running back Rashaan Salaam and tight end Chris Gedney. It's up to you to decide which of the three receivers — Michael Timpson, Jeff Graham or Curtis Conway — will emerge.

CINCINNATI BENGALS

Who's New — Running backs Ki-Jana Carter, Eric Bieniemy and James Joseph and wide receiver Tom Waddle.

Who's Gone — Fullback Derrick Fenner signed with the Raiders, running back Eric Ball was picked by Carolina in the expansion draft, and running back Steve Broussard was waived.

Quarterbacks — Jeff Blake pumped life into the Bengals' offense when he took over the starting job for the final nine games of 1994. Blake, who threw four touchdown passes of 40 yards or longer, passed for 14 TD passes and nine interceptions. The team insists the job is open in 1995, but most people concede it to Blake. David Klingler has a 4–20 record in his first three seasons and appears to be only a backup. He completed just 56.7 percent of his 1994 attempts for six TDs and nine interceptions. Erik Wilhelm gets the third-string job.

Running Backs — Ki-Jana Carter, who was the highest-rated player in this year's draft, should resurrect the team's stagnant ground game that was led by Derrick Fenner's 468 yards last year. With such an explosive passing attack spreading defenses, Carter should post big numbers if he gets good blocking. Fenner could possibly be utilized as a goal-line back. James Joseph, Jeff Cothran and Harold Green, if he's retained, are the backups.

Wide Receivers — Carl Pickens has become one of the league's most dangerous deep threats, and Blake likes to go his way often. Pickens finished fifth in the AFC with 1,127 receiving yards and 10th in receiving last year. He led AFC receivers with 11 TD catches. Darnay Scott had an explosive rookie season, with an 18.8-yard average per catch and three TD catches of 40 or more yards. Sure-handed free-agent acquisition Waddle will replace Jeff Query as the third wideout. Veteran Tim McGee, who is nearing the end of his career, will fight rookie David Dunn for a roster spot.

Tight Ends — Tony McGee drops too many passes but possesses lots of talent. He caught 40 passes but found the end zone only once. The backup is ex-Cardinal Derek Ware.

Kicker — Doug Pelfrey is coming off an excellent season in which he kicked 28 of 33 field goal attempts and scored 108 points. Pelfrey kicked six of them in one game.

Best Players to Draft — Running back Ki-Jana Carter and wide receivers Carl Pickens and Darnay Scott. If the team improves and Blake proves last season was no fluke, he and kicker Doug Pelfrey could be good fantasy backups.

CLEVELAND BROWNS

Who's New — Wide receiver Andre Rison was the best free-agent catch of the offseason. Veteran running back Lorenzo White was another fine acquisition. Quarterback Eric Zeier was drafted in the third round.

Who's Gone — All-purpose running back Eric Metcalf was traded to the Falcons, and quarterback Mark Rypien is gone to the Rams.

Quarterback — Vinny Testaverde was far from spectacular in 1994 but didn't hurt his team, either, posting a 9–4 record as a starter. He completed 54.9 percent of his passes for 16 touchdowns and 18 interceptions. Zeier may be as close to being an NFL starter as any quarterback in the draft. He is not tall but possesses leadership qualities and will likely replace Testaverde in the next few years.

Running Backs — The acquisition of Lorenzo White gives the Browns a good every-down back. White regained his starting job in the midseason of 1994 for Houston, rushed for 757 yards and caught 21 passes. White's acquisition will reduce Leroy Hoard's playing time in 1995. Hoard scored nine TDs and rushed for almost 900 yards last year. He caught 45 passes and ranked seventh in the AFC in total yards from scrimmage. Tommy Vardell will attempt to come back from a torn knee ligament, which sidelined him for most of last season. Backup Earnest Byner may be on his last legs.

Wide Receivers — Rison makes the Browns a genuine Super Bowl contender, provided Testaverde can get the ball to him often — and that's a big *if*. Rison has averaged 80 catches and 10 touchdowns in each of his six seasons. He's unstoppable near the goal line but needs to control his volatile nature and confine his fireworks to the field. Veteran Michael Jackson is coming off a disappointing '94 season but should benefit from all of the attention directed toward Rison. Derrick Alexander turned in an excellent rookie season, with 48 catches and a 17.3-yard average.

Tight Ends — Belichick went ballistic when the Jets drafted Kyle Brady one pick ahead of the Browns in the first round. Walter Reeves is coming off last October's season-ending back surgery. Overachiever Brian Kinchen had a surprising season with 24 receptions.

Kicker — Matt Stover benefited from a much-improved team to post outstanding numbers in 1994. He missed just two of 28 field goal attempts and scored 110 points.

Best Players to Draft — Wide receiver Andre Rison and kicker Matt Stover. Look closely at the running backs in the preseason to see who gets the bulk of the carries.

DALLAS COWBOYS

Who's New — Running back Sherman Williams, tight end Kendall Watkins and wide receivers Eric Bjornson and Edward Hervey, were all rookie draft picks.

Who's Gone — Wide receiver Alvin Harper left to sign with Tampa Bay, Rodney Peete signed as a free agent with the Eagles and backup running back Derrick Lassic was lost to Carolina in the expansion draft.

Quarterbacks — Troy Aikman's contributions extend well beyond his mediocre production by fantasy football standards. He's a true team leader who repeatedly came back from vicious hits last season. Aikman completed nearly 65 percent of his aerials for 13 touchdowns and nearly 2,600 yards. The loss of Rodney Peete means Jason Garrett will likely be the backup in '95. Garrett was pressed into service on Thanksgiving Day due to injuries and delivered two TD passes against Green Bay.

Running Backs — The No. 1 player in fantasy football, Emmitt Smith keeps on producing phenomenal numbers. He led the NFL with 21 touchdowns in 1994 and rushed for 1,484 yards, despite being slowed by a hamstring injury. Smith also finished second on the team with 50 pass receptions. Fullback Daryl "Moose" Johnston is a great lead blocker who is capable of scoring a few TDs himself. Williams should step in as Smith's backup. He is a skillful runner with good hands.

Wide Receivers — Like Aikman, Michael Irvin is more valuable than his fantasy numbers suggest. He caught six TD passes last year — very close to his five-year average. Irvin caught 79 passes in '94 and ranked fifth in the NFC with 1,241 receiving yards. He's big, strong, and practically unstoppable one-on-one. With Harper gone, talented third-year man Kevin Williams has a golden opportunity to step into a starting role. Cory Fleming flashed promise in his rookie season and will get a long look.

Tight Ends — Jay Novacek, a big part of the Dallas offense, was re-signed in the offseason. He caught 47 passes for 475 yards and two scores last season and should produce a few TDs this year. Watkins might be moved from tight end to the offensive line. Otherwise, he will battle Scott Galbraith for the backup job.

Kicker — Chris Boniol emerged in the 1994 preseason to seal the job, then posted fine numbers in his rookie season. He booted 22 of 29 field goal attempts and made all 48 of his extra points.

Best Players to Draft — Quarterback Troy Aikman, running back Emmitt Smith, wide receiver Michael Irvin, tight end Jay Novacek and kicker Chris Boniol.

DENVER BRONCOS

Who's New — Running back Aaron Craver, wide receivers Vance Johnson (who un-retired) and Ed McCaffrey, tight end Frank Wainright and quarterback Bill Musgrave.

Who's Gone — Nobody at the skill positions.

Quarterbacks — Coming off a huge 1993 season by fantasy standards, John Elway was picked very early in most drafts last year. But the team struggled all year and Elway threw just 16 touchdown passes. He did finish second in the AFC in passer rating and completed 62.1 percent of his throws for 3,490 yards. With a great receiving corps, Elway's fantasy production should soar this year. His backups are Hugh Millen, Bill Musgrave and Will Furrer. The Broncos pray that none of them are pressed into service.

Running Backs — Leonard Russell led an anemic rushing attack with 620 yards last year, but he averaged only 3.3 yards per carry. Rod Bernstine's 1994 season was decimated by a severe knee injury in the fourth week. When healthy, he's a good NFL back. Either Bernstine or Russell should have a productive 1995 season. Glyn Milburn, who led the AFC's running backs with 77 receptions, is an excellent third-down back. Craver, the ex-Dolphin who was signed as a free agent, also has excellent hands. Backup Derrick Clark finished fourth on the team in rushing last year.

Wide Receivers — This is the Broncos' strongest position, which will only help Elway's production. Anthony Miller got into the team's offense late in the year and went wild with four 100-yard games in the final six weeks. Miller finished sixth in the conference in receiving yards with 1,107. Mike Pritchard started out 1994 on fire but suffered a lacerated kidney and missed most of the '94 season. He's an excellent possession receiver and should come back strong. McCaffrey is another good possession guy, and Derek Russell is a decent backup. Johnson, a former Bronco, was signed in the offseason after playing in San Diego last year.

Tight Ends — Shannon Sharpe is a premier tight end in the Kellen Winslow mold. He scored just four touchdowns last year but had 87 receptions and is capable of 10 TDs this year. Jerry Evans is the backup.

Kicker — Even in a year when the Broncos really struggled, Jason Elam finished third in the league among kickers with 119 points. He booted 30 of 37 field tries and had at least one field goal in 15 games.

Best Players to Draft — Quarterback John Elway, wide receiver Anthony Miller, tight end Shannon Sharpe and kicker Jason Elam.

TEAM EVALUATIONS

DETROIT LIONS

Who's New — Quarterbacks Don Majkowski and Donald Hollas, rookie tight end David Sloan and rookie wide receiver Kez McCorvey.

Who's Gone — Quarterback David Krieg signed with the Cardinals, running back Derrick Moore was traded to the 49ers and kick returner Mel Gray signed with Houston.

Quarterbacks — The Lions are still placing all of their eggs in one basket — carried by Scott Mitchell, who signed a huge contract before the 1994 season but really struggled. Mitchell broke his non-throwing hand in Game 9 and missed the rest of the year. He completed only 48.4 percent of his passes for 10 touchdowns and 11 interceptions in 246 attempts. The team's fate in '95 will largely rest on the shoulders of Mitchell, who has talent but not much experience. Don Majkowski, who started six games but didn't do much last year, will battle Don Hollas for the No. 2 job.

Running Backs — Lions coach Wayne Fontes might be the only man alive who can stop Barry Sanders. Fontes often replaces the superstar in goal-line situations, but the departure of Derrick Moore may result in many more touchdowns for Sanders in 1995 — unless backup Eric Lynch assumes that role. Sanders had an outstanding '94 season, leading the NFL with 1,883 yards and in yards per carry with a phenomenal 5.7 average. He scored eight touchdowns and will score a lot more this year if he stays on the field near the goal line.

Wide Receivers — Herman Moore catapulted himself into the group of elite receivers in the league last year by going over the top of defenders for 11 TD catches. He caught 72 passes for 1,173 yards. He is too tall and talented to be guarded man-to-man. Brett Perriman has been a good No. 2 receiver. He has good hands but at times drops too many passes. Perriman caught 56 passes for four TDs a year ago. Highly touted Johnnie Morton did almost nothing as a rookie but will be a much bigger part of the team's offense in '95. Anthony Carter and Aubrey Matthews are crafty veterans.

Tight Ends — Ron Hall is the veteran, Ty Hallock is the overachieving blue-collar worker and David Sloan is the developmental prospect. Hall was hobbled most of last season with a knee injury. Sloan played only two seasons of major college football but has the "upside potential" label.

Kicker — Jason Hanson had been regarded as one of the top young kickers until he had a poor 1994 season. He made only 18 of 27 field goal attempts but should bounce back.

Best Players to Draft: Quarterback Scott Mitchell, running back Barry Sanders, wide receiver Herman Moore and kicker Jason Hanson.

GREEN BAY PACKERS

Who's New — Tight end Keith Jackson (if he ever decides to report), wide receiver Mark Ingram, and three rookies — running back William Henderson, quarterback Jay Barker and wide receiver Antonio Freeman.

Who's Gone — Wide receiver Sterling Sharpe was cut due to a serious neck injury. Running back Reggie Cobb was picked by Jacksonville in the expansion draft. Tight ends Ed West and Reggie Johnson moved to Indianapolis and Philadelphia, respectively, and quarterback Mark Brunell was traded to the Jaguars.

Quarterbacks — Brett Favre is a top young gunslinger with a rocket arm and improving judgment. He completed 62.4 percent of his passes for 3,882 yards, 33 touchdowns and only 14 interceptions in 1994. Favre has greatly improved at spreading the wealth. He mainly throws underneath but has the arm to go deep. If he only had a deep threat. The backups are veterans Ty Detmer and T.J. Rubley, and Jay Barker, a rookie prospect.

Running Backs — The inability to land a top tailback in the offseason and the draft means Edgar Bennett has moved from fullback to tailback. Bennett has been a fantasy sleeper the past two seasons, with nine touchdowns last year and 10 the year before. He led all backs with 78 receptions last year, and he is a hard runner inside. The Packers might feature Bennett in some one-back sets. The fullbacks are promising second-year man Dorsey Levens and William Henderson, a third-round pick.

Wide Receivers —Mark Ingram, who was obtained from Miami in a trade, is a capable but just-above-average wideout. Robert Brooks is the team's biggest threat. He had just one touchdown in 38 previous games before scoring three times in Games 9 and 10 last year. Brooks caught 58 passes last season. Anthony Morgan, the team's third receiver last year, caught 28 passes and was a pleasant surprise. Charles Jordan has big-play potential but hasn't used it yet.

Tight Ends — Jackie Harris left the Packers before last season and veterans Ed West and Reggie Johnson bolted after the season. That leaves Mark Chmura, who is reliable but won't ever scare a defensive coordinator. Keith Jackson was obtained in a trade with Miami but hasn't decided whether or not he will report.

Kicker — Chris Jacke was somewhat inconsistent last year, when he missed two extra points and seven of his 26 field goal attempts. He's still one of the league's better kickers, though.

Best Players to Draft — Quarterback Brett Favre, running back Edgar Bennett and kicker Chris Jacke.

HOUSTON OILERS

Who's New — Quarterbacks Steve McNair and Chris Chandler, kick returner Mel Gray, and three rookies — wide receiver Chris Sanders, running back Rodney Thomas and tight end Michael Roan.

Who's Gone — Running back Lorenzo White signed with Cleveland as a free agent. Wide receiver Haywood Jeffires and running back Spencer Tillman were cut. Expect a veteran receiver or two to go before the 1995 season opener.

Quarterbacks — It may take a season or two before Steve McNair can put some air into the Oilers' passing game. He's a great prospect with no major-college experience, so he will go through a big adjustment period in the NFL. That means Cody Carlson will likely get the starting job again. Carlson had a nightmarish 1994 season, completing just 44.7 percent of his passes for one touchdown in five starts. That was before he missed 11 games due to knee and shoulder injuries. Chris Chandler will battle Bucky Richardson and journeyman Billy Joe Tolliver for the backup jobs.

Running Backs — The offseason departure of Lorenzo White means Gary Brown will get another chance to recapture his 1993 magic. Last year, the fumble-prone Brown gained 648 yards, averaged 3.8 yards per carry and lost his starting job to White. Rodney Thomas, a third-round pick from Texas A&M, has an excellent shot at becoming the No. 2 back. Thomas is a powerful, hard runner. Todd McNair will be used as a third-down back.

Wide Receivers — A changing of the guard may be in order for the receiving corps, which entered the offseason with veterans Ernest Givins and Webster Slaughter being pushed by a youth movement that includes speed-burning rookie Chris Sanders and 1994 third-round pick Malcolm Seabron. Gary Wellman, Travis Hannah and Reggie Brown are battling for roster spots. Slaughter and the departed Jeffires led the Oilers last season with 68 catches apiece, but the aging Givins caught only 36 balls.

Tight Ends — Pat Carter figures to become a much more prominent part of the Oilers' offense this season. He caught only 11 passes last year, when the run-and-shoot rendered the tight ends almost useless. Rookie fourth-round pick Michael Roan will battle for a backup job.

Kicker — Al Del Greco is among the NFL's more accurate kickers, but the team's free fall greatly reduced his production in 1994, when he scored just 66 points. Don't expect too many more points from him in '95.

Best Players to Draft — Running back Gary Brown and whichever receiver emerges as the No. 1 target.

INDIANAPOLIS COLTS

Who's New — Wide receiver Willie Anderson, quarterback Craig Erickson, tight ends Ed West and rookie Ken Dilger, placekicker Mike Cofer and rookie fullback Zack Crockett.

Who's Gone — Tight end Kerry Cash signed as a free agent with the Raiders, QB Don Majkowski left for the Lions and wide receiver Mark Jackson was waived.

Quarterbacks — The trade acquisition of Craig Erickson gives the Colts a legitimate starter. He has the arm that incumbent starter Jim Harbaugh lacks. Erickson ranked sixth in the NFC in passer rating last year, when he passed for 2,919 yards, 16 touchdown passes and just 10 interceptions. Harbaugh, who was benched twice last season, completed 61.9 percent of his passes but lacks the ability to go deep. Harbaugh is best suited for a backup role.

Running Backs — Start and end with Marshall Faulk, the 1994 Offensive Rookie of the Year and one of the best runners to enter the league in years. In 1994, his rookie season, Faulk finished third in the AFC in rushing with 1,282 yards and tied for the AFC lead in touchdowns with 12. Expect more of the same from Faulk, who posted four 100-yard games. Crockett was drafted to help open holes for Faulk, and veteran Roosevelt Potts is a decent fullback.

Wide Receivers — "Flipper" Anderson gives the Colts the deep threat they've so sorely lacked, and Erickson has the arm to get the ball downfield to him. Anderson, a free-agent acquisition, averaged 20.5 yards with his 45 pass receptions last season. He is a true game-breaker and could really open things up for Faulk. Sean Dawkins was another productive rookie in 1994, with 51 catches for 742 yards and five touchdowns. Veteran Floyd Turner had a fine comeback season, with 52 catches and six TDs.

Tight Ends — Ed West, a free-agent signee, is an excellent blocker with little speed but decent hands and a nose for the end zone. West caught 31 passes in Green Bay a year ago. Dilger, a big target, was drafted in the second round and will battle West for the starting job. Dilger could also become an H-back.

Kickers — Mike Cofer, who has never been Mr. Reliable, was signed because the team is not happy with Dean Biasucci, who missed one-third of his field goal attempts in 1994.

Best Players to Draft — Quarterback Craig Erickson, running back Marshall Faulk and wide receiver Willie Anderson.

JACKSONVILLE JAGUARS

Who's New — Take your pick on an expansion team, but quarterbacks Steve Beuerlein, Mark Brunell and Rob Johnson, running backs James Stewart and Reggie Cobb, wide receivers Desmond Howard and Kelvin Martin, tight end Derek Brown and kicker Scott Sisson are among the main fantasy players.

Quarterbacks — Steve Beuerlein will, in all probability, be the Opening Day starter. He started seven games in 1994, completing just 51 percent of his passes for five touchdowns and nine interceptions, then lost his starting job. But Beuerlein is a decent NFL quarterback when he doesn't have Cardinals coach Buddy Ryan breathing down his neck. He threw 18 TD passes in 1993 and should do a decent job while the Jaguars wait for Brunell, a third-year man, and rookie Rob Johnson to develop.

Running Backs — James Stewart will battle Reggie Cobb for the starting tailback job. Cobb says he can repeat his 1,000-yard season of 1992, but Stewart may not give him a chance. The 19th player chosen in the draft, Stewart might be the most powerful tailback in the Class of '95. He has what it takes to carry the ball 25 times in a game. Cobb is a decent runner who rushed for 579 yards last year but has always averaged less than four yards per carry. Former Packer Dexter McNabb is a decent fullback, but he won't gain much yardage.

Wide Receivers — In 1994, his third seasaon, Desmond Howard finally realized a portion of the potential that earned him the 1991 Heisman Trophy. He caught 48 passes for five touchdowns and will be given every opportunity to become the team's featured receiver. Kelvin Martin, who has caught 46 or more passes in five seasons, had 56 receptions last year in Seattle. Former Bronco Cedric Tillman caught 28 passes a year ago for Denver. Among the reserves are ex-Dolphin Mike Williams, former Cowboy Willie Jackson and ex-Steeler Charles Davenport.

Tight Ends — The Jaguars believe Derek Brown can be a significant part of their passing game. A first-round bust with the Giants, Brown played little and caught just 11 passes in three years. But he now has a new lease on life.

Kicker — Scott Sisson was the Patriots' kicker in 1993, but he made only 14 of 26 field goal attempts and was waived. He will get some competition in training camp.

Best Players to Draft — Quarterback Steve Beuerlein and running back James Stewart.

KANSAS CITY CHIEFS

Who's New — Wide receiver Victor Bailey was obtained in a trade from the Eagles, quarterback Rich Gannon returned to football and quarterback Steve Stenstrom and wide receiver Tamarick Vanover were drafted.

Who's Gone — QB Joe Montana retired, wide receiver J.J. Birden signed with Atlanta as a free agent, and two players were cut: tight end Jimmie Johnson and wide receiver Eric Martin.

Quarterbacks — A career backup to Joe Montana, Steve Bono will now try to replace a legend. Bono completed 56.4 percent of his 1994 pass attempts for four touchdowns and four interceptions. In his 10-year career, he has thrown 24 TD passes and just 15 interceptions. His backups are Rich Gannon, Matt Blundin and rookie Steve Stenstrom, whose college coach, Bill Walsh, taught Montana and Bono a thing or two in San Francisco.

Running Backs — Hall of Fame shoo-in Marcus Allen will eventually give way to talented young Greg Hill. Will this be the year, or will Allen be the team's leading rusher for the second straight season? Allen has 19 rushing TDs over the last two seasons and ranks fourth on the NFL career TD list with 120. But the chances are Hill will run the ball more than he did as a rookie in 1994, when he gained 574 yards in 141 attempts. Hill was the fifth-leading rookie ball carrier. Fullback Kimble Anders, who caught 67 passes last year, is a very productive third-down back.

Wide Receivers — Willie Davis, the only Chiefs wideout with some big-play ability, had 51 catches and five touchdowns in 1994. He has averaged 7.9 yards per catch since 1992, second in the NFL. With Birden gone, second-year player Lake Dawson will become the No. 2 receiver. He caught 37 passes as a rookie. Tamarick Vanover, a third-round pick this year, could help if he discovers the meaning of "work ethic." Chris Penn, another second-year player, has potential. Victory Bailey averaged 15.6 yards with his 20 receptions in '94.

Tight Ends — This is one of the Chiefs' strongest positions. Keith Cash was on his way to a fine 1994 season until suffering a season-ending sprained knee. He can get downfield for big plays. Derrick Walker replaced Cash and caught 36 passes. Tracy Greene is a fine third-stringer.

Kicker — Lin Elliott split the uprights on 25 of 30 field goal attempts last year and made all 30 of his extra-point attempts. He doesn't have an especially strong leg but did log his second straight 100-point season.

Best Players to Draft — Quarterback Steve Bono, running backs Marcus Allen and Greg Hill, and wide receiver Willie Davis. Keep a close eye on the running back position to determine the every-down player.

LOS ANGELES RAIDERS

Who's New — Running backs Napoleon Kaufman, Derrick Fenner and Joe Aska, tight end Kerry Cash and wide receiver Hassan Jones.

Who's Gone — Wide receiver Alexander Wright signed with the Rams as a free agent and injured running back Napoleon McCallum was cut.

Quarterbacks — Jeff Hostetler's 3,334 passing yards in 1994 was the second-highest season total in club history. His passer rating ranked sixth in the AFC, and he threw 20 touchdown passes and 16 interceptions. Hostetler struggled at times last year and had a much-celebrated sideline argument with fired coach Art Shell. Hostetler is still one of the most dangerous runners among NFL quarterbacks. His backup is 40-year-old Vince Evans and the untested Billy Joe Hobert.

Running Backs — The Raiders obviously weren't convinced Harvey Williams could repeat his good 1994 season, so they drafted Napoleon Kaufman in the first round. Kaufman is a hard worker with great speed but might not have the size to be an every-down back. Williams signed with the Raiders as a free agent in 1994 and rushed for 983 yards. His 1,374 combined yards ranked sixth in the AFC, and he caught 47 passes and scored seven touchdowns. Fenner led the Bengals in rushing with 468 yards last year, and he caught 36 passes. Aska, a third-round draft pick, has a great combination of size and speed and may have been one of the sleepers of the draft.

Wide Receivers — Tim Brown should be among the top receivers you consider drafting once Jerry Rice is gone. In 1994, Brown led the AFC in receiving yards with 1,309, ranked third in receptions with 89 and finished second among receivers in touchdowns with nine. The Raiders have lots of speed but not great hands at the other receiver position. Rocket Ismail caught 34 passes and is the Raiders' primary kickoff returner. James Jett had just 15 catches last year. When he fades back to pass, Hostetler almost always looks for Brown.

Tight Ends — Kerry Cash, a free-agent acquisition, was slowed by a foot injury last year and caught just 16 passes for 190 yards. He should rebound well, however, to approach his 1993 numbers (43 catches, 521 yards and three TDs). Andrew Glover was the team's most productive tight end last year with 33 catches.

Kicker — Jeff Jaeger posted decent numbers last season — 22 field goals in 28 attempts and 31 of 31 in extra-point tries.

Best Players to Draft — Quarterback Jeff Hostetler, wide receiver Tim Brown and kicker Jeff Jaeger.

MIAMI DOLPHINS

Who's New — Tight end Eric Green, wide receivers Randal Hill and Gary Clark and rookie tight end Pete Mitchell.

Who's Gone — Tight end Keith Jackson and wide receiver Mark Ingram were traded to the Packers, and running back Aaron Craver signed with the Broncos.

Quarterbacks — Nobody can stop Dan Marino's offense from piling up yardage and points; defenses can only hope to make Marino work hard to move the ball. In 1994, Marino started the season with a five-touchdown, 473-yard performance against the Patriots. He finished with 30 TD passes and 4,453 yards, and his passer rating led the AFC. Marino came back strong from a ruptured Achilles tendon that sidelined him most of 1993. Last year's backup, Bernie Kosar, might sign with another team, but will probably be back. And Dan McGwire was signed as a free agent.

Running Backs — A good preseason battle should ensue between Terry Kirby and his injury replacement last year, Bernie Parmalee. Kirby, who caught 75 passes in 1993, suffered a season-ending knee injury in Week 4 last year. Parmalee, one of the surprises in the league, took over and rushed for 868 yards and six touchdowns. Kirby's offseason rehabilitation appeared to be going well, better than that of the versatile Keith Byars, who is among the greatest pass-catching backs in league history. Irving Spikes displayed a few breakaway skills last year.

Wide Receivers — Irving Fryar has always been among the AFC's top receivers, and his numbers are flourishing with Marino throwing to him. In 1994, his second season in Miami, Fryar ranked third in the AFC with 1,270 receiving yards and ninth with 73 catches. He also scored seven TDs. Free-agent acquisitions Randal Hill and Gary Clark should also flourish in Miami. Hill caught 38 passes last year and will easily exceed that in '95. Clark is coming off a 50-catch season. O.J. McDuffie is a great third-down option who is gaining experience.

Tight Ends — Keith Jackson's hints about retiring prompted the Dolphins to sign Eric Green, who will greatly help the ground game. Green caught 46 passes for 618 yards and four touchdowns last year. Greg Baty and Pete Mitchell, a rookie fourth-round pick, are the backups.

Kicker — Pete Stoyanovich is among the most accurate kickers in the league. He made 24 of 31 field goal tries last year, a little subpar by his standards. He'll score between 110 and 135 points in '95.

Best Players to Draft — Quarterback Dan Marino, wide receiver Irving Fryar, tight end Eric Green and kicker Pete Stoyanovich.

TEAM EVALUATIONS

MINNESOTA VIKINGS

Who's New — Rookie quarterback Chad May, who may prove to be a fourth-round steal.

Who's Gone — Running back Terry Allen was cut but may be re-signed.

Quarterbacks — The Vikings hope to get a couple more years of solid play from Warren Moon while grooming Chad May as a possible replacement. Moon aired it out often (601 times) in 1994, completing 61.7 percent of his passes for 18 touchdowns and 19 interceptions. He ranks sixth on the NFL's all-time list with 37,949 passing yards. In 1994, his first season as a Viking, he led the NFC with 4,264 passing yards last year. But can he keep going strong at age 39?

Running Backs — Despite a talented quartet of Terry Allen, Amp Lee, Scottie Graham and Robert Smith, the Vikings ranked 20th in the NFL in rushing last year, and gained only 40 yards on 17 carries in a playoff loss to Chicago. If he's re-signed, Allen, who is coming off a 1,031-yard, eight-TD season, may share time more with Lee, who had just 104 rushing yards but caught 45 passes in 1994. Graham is a capable backup and Smith possesses breakaway speed.

Wide Receivers — Cris Carter caught more passes, 122, than any player in NFL history last year. He also scored seven TDs and ranked fourth in receiving yards with 1,256. The Vikings were glad to re-sign Jake Reed, keeping last year's most prolific NFL receiving duo intact. Reed hauled in 85 passes for 1,175 yards and four touchdowns. Qadry Ismail beat out rookie David Palmer for the No. 3 receiving job last season. Ismail, the team's best big-play threat, had six catches of over 30 yards. He's also an excellent kickoff returner. Palmer is the team's primary punt returner.

Tight Ends — Rookie Andrew Jordan proved to be a sixth-round steal. He caught 35 passes for 336 yards to lead the tight ends. Jordan took over for the injured Adrian Cooper in the final month. Cooper caught 32 passes for 363 yards. Expect a good preseason battle between these two for the starting job.

Kicker — Fuad Reveiz had a career year in 1994, tying for the NFC scoring lead with 132 points. He converted on 34 of 39 field-goal attempts and made all 30 extra-point tries.

Best Players to Draft — Quarterback Warren Moon, wide receiver Cris Carter and kicker Fuad Reveiz. Whomever is the top running back would be a good pick, too.

NEW ENGLAND PATRIOTS

Who's New — Running back Dave Meggett, who was signed as a free agent, and rookie running back Curtis Martin.

Who's Gone — Wide receiver Michael Timpson signed with the Bears and fullback Kevin Turner moved on to Philadelphia. Running back Marion Butts will probably be cut.

Quarterbacks — Drew Bledsoe led an offensive aerial assault that was very un–Bill Parcellian in 1994. The team scrapped its inept ground game — which is Parcells's bread and butter. Bledsoe set an NFL record with 691 pass attempts, and a league-record five players caught 50 or more passes. Bledsoe completed 57.9 percent of his passes for a league-high 4,555 yards, 25 touchdowns and 27 interceptions. While Bledsoe's efficiency should continue to improve, his fantasy production probably won't because Parcells will try to run the ball better and pass it less.

Running Backs — Marion Butts rushed for five touchdowns in the first four games, but the ground game bogged down. Despite the presence of the hard-running Butts and two good blocking fullbacks, the Patriots finished the season with an NFL-low 2.8-yard average per rush. Butts gained 703 yards and scored eight TDs, but he averaged only 2.9 yards per rush. The acquisition of Dave Meggett gives the Patriots a multidimensional threat and an outstanding punt returner. Leroy Thompson gained 312 yards in his first season with New England. Banger Sam Gash is the best fullback. With none of the top runners left on the board, the Patriots settled on Martin in the third round of the draft.

Wide Receivers — Vincent Brisby caught 58 passes for 904 yards and five TDs last year. With Timpson gone, expect Brisby, the team's top threat, to post bigger numbers. Also keep an eye on promising young Kevin Lee, who spent last season on injured reserve with a broken jaw. Ray Crittenden caught 28 passes a year ago. He's inconsistent but will get every opportunity to become a big part of the offense this year.

Tight Ends — Ben Coates set a team record with 96 pass receptions in 1994. He led the AFC in receptions and established himself as the top tight end in the NFL. Coates, who always seems to find the seams in a defense, scored four touchdowns in the first two games and finished with seven. Second-stringer John Burke is a plowhorse.

Kicker — The 39-year-old Matt Bahr had a great 16th season, with 103 points. He made 21 of 25 field goals and 40 of 41 extra-point attempts.

Best Players to Draft — Quarterback Drew Bledsoe, wide receiver Vincent Brisby, tight end Ben Coates and kicker Bahr.

NEW ORLEANS SAINTS

Who's New — Rookie fullback Ray Zellars, quarterback Timm Rosenbach and placekicker Cary Blanchard.

Who's Gone — Tight end Frank Wainright signed with Denver as a free agent, and quarterback Wade Wilson and fullback Brad Muster were cut (though Wilson could be brought back).

Quarterbacks — A change of scenery made all the difference for Jim Everett, who set single-season team records for attempts (540), completions (346), yards (3,855) and completion percentage (64.1 percent) in 1994. Everett threw 22 touchdown passes, one short of a Saints record. He has six 3,000-yard seasons in his career and should do it again in 1995 because the Saints have a very good receiving corps. Timm Rosenbach has been away from football for a year but will attempt to win the backup job.

Running Backs — There is a logjam of runners on the Saints, although second-year player Mario Bates may be the answer. Bates became the fourth straight rookie to lead the team in rushing. He gained 579 yards and six TDs last year, despite missing five games due to a broken jaw. Former No. 1 draft pick Vaughn Dunbar appears to be done. Derek Brown, who gained 489 yards last year, is a solid player. Lorenzo Neal will battle Ray Zellars, a second-round pick, for the starting fullback job. None of the Saints runners averaged four yards or better per carry last year.

Wide Receivers — The trio of Quinn Early, Michael Haynes and Torrance Small combined for 208 pass receptions and 14 touchdowns last season. Early finished sixth in the NFC in catches with 82, while Haynes finished 11th in the conference in receiving yards with 985. He's one of the game's best deep threats. Small, the third receiver, led the Saints with an average per catch of 14.7 yards. He had 20 receptions on third down and finished the season with a 200-yard, two-TD receiving day.

Tight Ends — The duo of Irv Smith and Wesley Walls combined for 79 catches last season. Smith scored three times and caught the most balls by a Saints tight end in nine years. Walls, who scored four TDs, was a free-agent steal.

Kickers — Morten Andersen ranked second in the NFC among kickers with 116 points. He did not have one of his usual outstanding seasons, however, because he missed 11 of his 39 field goal attempts. Cary Blanchard will provide competition in camp, but he won't win the job.

Best Players to Draft — Quarterback Jim Everett, running back Mario Bates and kicker Morten Andersen. Any one of the three top wideouts is capable of six or seven TDs.

NEW YORK GIANTS

Who's New — Two running backs: Herschel Walker, a free-agent pickup, and Tyrone Wheatley, a first-round pick.

Who's Gone — Running back David Meggett moved to New England and tight end Derek Brown was taken by Jacksonville in the expansion draft.

Quarterbacks — Dave Brown started 15 games in his first season as a regular. He completed 57.4 percent of his passes for 2,536 yards, 12 touchdowns and 16 interceptions. He started the 1994 season hot, then hit a midseason slump and was briefly benched . But, when he regained his job, he showed tremendous improvement over the final six games and has solidified himself as the starter. Brown led the Giants to comeback wins in three of the final four games. Kent Graham, who hasn't shown much in his brief opportunities, is again the backup.

Running Backs — Wheatley's arrival has made Rodney Hampton expendable. Last year, Hampton rushed for 1,075 yards, his fourth straight 1,000-yard season, to rank sixth in the NFL. But he averaged only 3.3 yards per carry, as the Giants' ground game bogged down. Wheatley has excellent size and speed and the explosive spark the team needs. Herschel Walker will likely fill Dave Meggett's role as the all-purpose back. Last year, Walker led the Eagles with eight TDs and 528 rushing yards. He ranked second in the league in kickoff return average, 27.7 yards, and he caught 50 passes.

Wide Receivers — Mike Sherrard is coming off a career year in which he caught 53 passes for 825 yards, a 15.6-yard average per catch, and he scored six touchdowns. Chris Calloway had a much-improved season with 43 catches and 666 yards. Big things are expected from Thomas Lewis, a first-round pick from a year ago. Lewis played primarily as a kickoff returner before suffering a season-ending knee injury in Game 9.

Tight Ends — The solid combination of Howard Cross and Aaron Pierce made former first-round bust Derek Brown expendable. Each scored four TDs last year, and they combined for 51 catches. Cross caught a career-high 31 passes.

Kicker — Brad Daluiso replaced David Treadwell as the Giants' field goal kicker in the final month of 1994. He had previously been used only for kickoffs, but he made all 11 of his field goal attempts last year and appears to have enough consistency to be the regular kicker.

Best Players to Draft — Running back Rodney Hampton and wide receiver Mike Sherrard.

NEW YORK JETS

Who's New — Tight end Kyle Brady, running backs Ronald Moore and Dexter Carter, quarterback Bubby Brister and wide receiver Tyrone Davis.

Who's Gone — Wide receiver Rob Moore was traded to Arizona, receiver Art Monk was cut, running back Anthony Johnson signed with the Bears and quarterback Jack Trudeau was taken by Carolina.

Quarterbacks — Boomer Esiason ranked eighth in AFC passer rating last season, when he completed 58 percent of his passes for 2,782 yards, 17 touchdowns and 13 interceptions. Esiason is still a good, steady veteran, but he will greatly miss the absence of Rob Moore this year. Bubby Brister was signed as a free agent. He is one of the best backups in the league.

Running Backs — Ronald Moore will battle versatile incumbent Johnny Johnson for the starting tailback job. Last year, Johnson rushed for 931 yards to rank sixth in the AFC, caught 42 passes for 303 yards and scored five TDs. Moore led the Cardinals in rushing yards with 780 yards and four TDs, but he is not as good as Johnson at receiving. Brad Baxter is still one of the top goal-line runners. He scored four times in '94. Reserve Adrian Murrell is an exciting young runner with a 4.7-yard rushing average in his first two seasons.

Wide Receivers — This is a real team weakness now that Rob Moore is gone. Promising second-year player Ryan Yarborough appears to be a lock to start, even though he caught only six passes last season. Tyrone Davis, a rookie drafted in the fourth round, has great size and averaged 20.9 yards per catch in college. Other receivers on the roster are speedy Orlando Parker and Stevie Anderson. Look for the Jets to acquire a veteran receiver before the 1995 season starts.

Tight Ends — Kyle Brady's surprising selection in the first round raises plenty of questions about plans for talented Johnny Mitchell, who ranked second on the Jets last season in receptions (58), yards (749) and TD catches (four). But Mitchell has not realized his vast potential and drops too many passes. Brady has great size and skills.

Kickers — Always steady and reliable, Nick Lowery had another excellent season last year but didn't get enough scoring attempts. He booted 20 of 23 field goal tries and 26 of 27 extra-point attempts.

Best Players to Draft — Quarterback Boomer Esiason and kicker Nick Lowery are the only sure bets, although the top two tight ends and running backs will be good picks.

PHILADELPHIA EAGLES

Who's New — Running backs Ricky Watters and Kevin Turner, quarterbacks Rodney Peete and Dave Barr, tight end Reggie Johnson and wide receivers Ron Lewis and Chris T. Jones.

Who's Gone — Running back Herschel Walker was waived and is now a Giant, wide receiver Victor Bailey was traded to the Chiefs, quarterback Bubby Brister signed with the Jets, and running back James Joseph signed with the Bengals.

Quarterbacks — Randall Cunningham no longer will be looking over his shoulder to see if Rich Kotite replaces him with Brister. Cunningham had a very average 1994 season, slumped late and was benched by Kotite for Week 15. But Ray Rhodes is the new head coach and he will leave the job to Cunningham, who completed just 54.1 percent of his passes last year for 3,229 yards, 16 touchdowns and 13 interceptions. Although he's still dangerous, Cunningham scrambles less than he once did. Dave Barr, a rookie, may someday replace Cunningham, but not this year.

Running Backs — The acquisition of Ricky Watters gives the Eagles the prime-time back they've lacked. He's at least as dangerous catching the ball as he is as a runner. Last season, Watters caught 66 passes for 719 yards and five TDs while with San Francisco. He rushed for 877 yards and six TDs in 239 attempts. Turner, a fullback, is a good blocker with great hands. He caught 52 passes last year in New England. Charlie Garner missed the first three games of 1994 due to a rib injury, then opened his pro career with two straight 100-yard games. After that, he was injured again and finished with 399 rushing yards.

Wide Receivers — Fred Barnett had a fine comeback season from a serious knee injury. He regained his status as the team's top receiver and showed no signs of having lost a step. He caught 78 passes for 1,127 yards and five TDs. Calvin Williams had another good season with 58 catches, although his TD total dropped down to three — all in the first two games. There's very little depth.

Tight Ends — Reggie Johnson, a free-agent acquisition, caught seven balls last year in Green Bay and 20 the year before in Denver. Maurice Johnson backed up Mark Bavaro last year and caught 21 passes for two touchdowns. Bavaro is probably going to retire.

Kicker — Eddie Murray did not kick a field goal longer than 42 yards last year, but he did not miss from inside that range.

Best Players to Draft — Quarterback Randall Cunningham, running back Ricky Watters and wide receivers Fred Barnett and Calvin Williams.

PITTSBURGH STEELERS

Who's New — Tight end Mark Bruener, quarterback Kordell Stewart and running back Erric Pegram.

Who's Gone — Tight end Eric Green and his attitude moved to Miami.

Quarterbacks — In 1994, Neil O'Donnell showed some ability to go deep when teams stacked the line to stop the run. He threw a league-low nine interceptions and did little to hurt the team. He finished as the AFC's seventh-ranked passer, with a 57.3 completion percentage, 2,443 yards and 13 touchdowns. O'Donnell missed two games due to hip and ankle injuries but completed 61 percent of his throws for eight TDs and just one interception in the final six games. Mike Tomczak is a decent backup. Kordell Stewart has enormous athletic ability and should eventually start, but not this year. He's a long-range project, and the team wants to win now.

Running Backs — The offseason acquisition of Erric Pegram allowed the Steelers to shop Barry Foster and his high salary. Pay attention to where Foster ends up, because he'll produce no matter where he goes (assuming he can stay healthy). Foster gained 851 yards and scored five times last season, despite missing five games due to injuries. Second-year bowling ball Bam Morris will take over as the starter. He gained 836 yards and led the team in TDs with seven a year ago. Pegram was benched in favor of Craig Hayward in Atlanta last season but gained 1,185 yards in 1993. John L. Williams is an outstanding receiving back who caught 51 passes in '94. He led the team's rushers with a 4.7-yard average per carry.

Wide Receivers — Last year's four-receiver rotation is probably a thing of the past. Charles Johnson, who led the receivers with 38 catches as a rookie in '94, will get every chance to be the main man. Johnson and Yancey Thigpen averaged 15.2 yards per catch. Thigpen had 36 catches and four TDs. Ernie Mills, Dwight Stone and Andre Hastings are the backups. Mills made the most of his 19 receptions last year, averaging 20.2 yards per catch.

Tight Ends — The loss of Eric Green will hurt both the passing game and ground game. He was a great in-line blocker. Mark Bruener, the second tight end taken in this year's draft, has good hands, size and blocking ability, but he won't dominate the way Green did.

Kicker — Gary Anderson made 24 of 29 field goal attempts and all 32 of his extra-point tries last year. He's steady.

Best Players to Draft — Running back Bam Morris and tight end Mark Bruener.

ST. LOUIS RAMS

Who's New — Wide receiver Alexander Wright was signed as a free agent, and the team drafted placekicker Steve McLaughlin and hybrid receiver Lovell Pickney.

Who's Gone — Wide receiver Willie Anderson signed with the Colts, quarterback Chris Chandler went to Houston and fullback Howard Griffith was taken by Carolina in the expansion draft.

Quarterbacks — Chris Miller has been erratic and injury-plagued but will again be the starter. Being reunited with his college coach, Rich Brooks, should help Miller's confidence. Last season, he completed 173 of 317 passes for 2,104 yards, 16 touchdowns and 14 interceptions. But Miller suffered three separate concussions and missed three games due to a pinched nerve in his throwing shoulder. With Chris Chandler gone, the backup job will be held by Tommy Maddox.

Running Backs — Jerome Bettis gained 1,025 yards in 1994, but he needed 319 carries to do it. His average per carry should be greatly improved from last year's 3.2-yard mark, because the team made rebuilding the offensive line an offseason priority. Bettis is hard to stop once he builds a head of steam, although he'll miss his blocking back, Howard Griffith. Johnny Bailey is an excellent third-down back. He caught 58 passes last season, and he's a fine punt and kickoff returner. Tim Lester and James Bostic will battle it out for the starting fullback job.

Wide Receivers — Alexander Wright was signed to fill the shoes of the departed Willie Anderson. Wright had a disappointing 1994 season, with just 16 catches as a Raider. He does have the speed to stretch a defense, but he can't hang on to the ball. The Rams have big plans for Isaac Bruce, a second-round pick from a year ago. Bruce should greatly improve on his 21-catch total of 1994. Veteran Jesse Hester caught 45 balls for 644 yards and three TDs last season. Todd Kinchen was a productive backup, with 23 catches and four scores.

Tight Ends — Troy Drayton didn't catch a pass in the first two games but eventually caught six TD passes to lead the team in touchdowns. He is one of the league's top tight ends, and Miller needs to go his way more often. Lovell Pickney, a fourth-round draft pick, has great size and speed.

Kickers — Tony Zendejas didn't have a bad '94 season, but the Rams drafted Steve McLaughlin, the best kicker in the draft, in the third round. Zendejas made 18 of 23 field goal attempts and all 28 extra-point tries.

Best Players to Draft — Running back Jerome Bettis and tight end Troy Drayton.

SAN DIEGO CHARGERS

Who's New — All rookies: running backs Terrell Fletcher and Aaron Hayden, and wide receivers Jimmy Oliver and Howard Payne.

Who's Gone — Running back Eric Bieniemy left for Cincinnati.

Quarterbacks — Nobody can question the toughness of Stan Humphries, who has been known to lead the Chargers to victory when he should have been in the hospital. Humphries is the leader of a big-play passing attack that included a 99-yard touchdown catch by Tony Martin last year. Humphries completed 264 of 453 passes for 3,209 yards, 17 TDs and 12 interceptions in 15 regular-season games. He rallied the Chargers in the AFC championship game with two second-half TD passes. His backup is the capable Gale Gilbert, who has played very little in nine NFL seasons but filled in well for the injured Humphries in two midseason 1994 games.

Running Backs — Means has developed into one of the game's premier ball carriers, and he should be strongly considered as the second or third running back in your fantasy draft. Means gained 1,350 yards and scored 12 TDs in 1994. He's a true pile driver and has better moves than one would expect from a big back. Means had six 100-yard games last year. Third-down specialist Ronnie Harmon tied for the team lead in pass receptions last year with 58. It's unclear how the Chargers will utilize Terrell Fletcher, who has many of the attributes of Eric Metcalf.

Wide Receivers — Mark Seay, a 49ers castaway, came out of virtually nowhere to tie for the team lead in receptions with 58. He scored six TDs — three in the first two games. Martin led the Chargers with seven TD catches, receiving yards with 885 and in average yards per catch, 17.7. Jefferson, who caught 43 passes for 627 yards and three TDs, was re-signed in the offseason. Oliver, a trackman with blazing speed, should only help the team's wide-open passing attack.

Tight Ends — Duane Young is a dominant blocker who helps the ground game. Young caught 17 passes last year, while Alfred Pupunu had 21 catches and two TDs. Shannon Mitchell had 11 receptions. None of the team's tight ends is a very good fantasy draft pick.

Kicker — John Carney proved that his 124-point season in 1993 was no fluke. Carney won the 1994 NFL scoring title with 135 points. He split the uprights on 34 of 38 field goal attempts and made all 33 of his extra-point boots. Carney converted on 18 straight field goals last year.

Best Players to Draft — Running back Natrone Means and kicker John Carney are franchise fantasy players.

SAN FRANCISCO 49ERS

Who's New — Rookie wide receiver J.J. Stokes and running back Derrick Moore, a trade acquisition.

Who's Gone — Free-agent running back Ricky Watters signed with the Eagles, running back Dexter Carter is now a Jet, wide receiver Ed McCaffrey and quarterback Bill Musgrave signed with Denver and running back Marc Logan was cut.

Quarterbacks — Yes, Steve Young can win the big one. Young erased any lingering doubts about his talents by leading the 49ers to a Super Bowl championship. Nobody came close to posting Young's numbers last season — an outstanding 112.8 passer rating, 70.3-percent completion accuracy, 35 TD passes and just 10 interceptions. Young rushed for 293 yards and seven TDs, making him even more valuable in fantasy football. Elvis Grbac did well in mop-up roles last year.

Running Backs — A potential team weakness due to Watters's departure. However, fullback William Floyd scored six TDs in the final 11 regular-season games of '94, then added five TDs in the playoffs. Expect a monster 1995 season from Floyd — 10 TDs at the least. Moore was obtained in a trade from the Lions, where he served as Barry Sanders's goal-line replacement. Derek Loville and Adam Walker have little experience.

Wide Receivers — Jerry Rice will soon own every major pass-receiving record, and he's still the No. 1 fantasy pick at his position. Rice scored 15 TDs last year (13 by air, two on runs) to rank third in the NFL behind Emmitt Smith and Sterling Sharpe. Rice caught a career-high 112 passes for 1,499 yards, so he hasn't slowed down at all in 10 seasons. John Taylor is still one of the best No. 2 receivers in the game — when healthy. He caught 41 passes for five TDs in 1994. The 49ers traded up in the first round of this year's draft to pick J.J. Stokes, who, at almost 6-foot-5, will quickly become a big part of the offense. Stokes has great hands.

Tight Ends — Brent Jones led all NFL tight ends with nine TDs last year. He has averaged just over four TDs over the past six seasons, so don't expect nine again this year. He is one of the best in the business, though.

Kicker — The 49ers' offense is so good, it usually puts the ball into the end zone rather than settling for field goals. As a result, Doug Brien booted 60 extra points but only 15 field goals in 20 attempts last year as a rookie. He scored 105 points and will at least match that in 1995.

Best Players to Draft — Quarterback Steve Young, running back William Floyd, wide receiver Jerry Rice, tight end Brent Jones and kicker Doug Brien.

SEATTLE SEAHAWKS

Who's New — Wide receivers Joey Galloway and Ricky Proehl, tight end Christian Fauria and quarterback John Friesz.

Who's Gone — Wide receiver Kelvin Martin was taken by Jacksonville in the expansion draft, quarterback Dan McGwire signed with the Dolphins, kicker John Kasay signed with Carolina and the Seahawks waived tight end Ferrell Edmunds and receiver Reggie Barrett.

Quarterbacks — Rick Mirer had a bit of a sophomore slump in 1994, completing just 51 percent of his passes. Mirer is smart enough not to force the ball; he threw only seven interceptions in 381 attempts, but he passed for only 11 touchdowns in 13 games. Mirer missed the final three games due to a broken thumb. Look for Mirer's numbers to improve in 1995. New coach Dennis Erickson plans to use more three-wide-receiver sets, and rookie Joey Galloway gives Mirer a legitimate deep threat. John Friesz has never been a good starter or a bad backup.

Running Backs — If Chris Warren played in a major TV market, he would be regarded as a superstar. Instead, he is underappreciated except in Seattle. Warren rushed for 1,545 yards last season to rank second in the NFL, and he posted a fine 4.6-yard average per carry. He ranked second in the league in combined yards with 1,868, and scored 11 TDs, third in the AFC. Tracy Johnson and Steve Smith are good lead blockers, and special-teams standout Mack Strong can play fullback and tailback.

Wide Receivers — Joey Galloway brings the big-play potential the Seahawks so sorely needed. The offense became predictable because Rick Mirer almost always threw short- and medium-range passes to Martin and Brian Blades. Galloway, the eighth player selected in the draft, has blazing speed. Blades ranked fifth in the AFC last year with 81 catches, a team record, and seventh in receiving yards with 1,086, but he has never been a big TD-maker and is not a good fantasy starter. Michael Bates and Terrance Warren are primarily kickoff returners.

Tight Ends — Christian Fauria's selection in the second round creates an interesting training-camp battle for the starting job. Incumbent Paul Green caught 30 passes last year, the most by a Seattle tight end in 10 years. Fauria has good hands and a great work ethic.

Kicker — Free agent Todd Peterson faces the job of filling free agent John Kasay's big shoes. Look for Seattle to bring in somebody else.

Best Players to Draft — Running back Chris Warren is the sure thing. Quarterback Rick Mirer is a decent fantasy backup, and wide receiver Joey Galloway could be worth a chance.

TAMPA BAY BUCCANEERS

Who's New — Wide receiver Alvin Harper was a big free-agent haul and Clarence Verdin was signed to return kicks.

Who's Gone — Quarterback Craig Erickson was traded to the Colts.

Quarterbacks — Trent Dilfer's performance will be a barometer for the team's success in 1995. The pieces seem to be in order for a much-improved team — if Dilfer comes through in his second season. Last year, a contract holdout cut Dilfer's preseason short and he struggled in his five regular-season appearances. He completed only 38 of 82 passes for 433 yards, one touchdown and six interceptions. He clearly wasn't ready for prime time last year. But, by trading Erickson in the offseason, the team signaled that it thinks Dilfer is ready now. Backups Casey Weldon and Peter Tom Willis aren't the answer.

Running Backs — In Errict Rhett, the Buccaneers have one of the game's top young ball carriers. Rhett didn't even start the first eight games of 1994, his rookie season, but he gained 1,011 yards to rank sixth in the NFC and scored seven TDs. Rhett gained 707 yards in the final seven games, an indication of what's to come in '95. Fullback Anthony McDowell, Rhett's main blocking back, caught 29 passes last year. Vince Workman is a reliable backup with excellent hands.

Wide Receivers — Alvin Harper led the NFL with an incredible 24.9-yard average per catch last season. He made the most of just 33 pass receptions by rolling up 821 yards and eight TDs. Harper is a perfect complement to a solid group of possession receivers. Lawrence Dawsey missed the first six games of 1994 due to a serious 1993 knee injury, and he still led the Bucs in receiving with 46 receptions for 673 yards. Courtney Hawkins had 37 receptions and five TDs, and Charles Wilson had a very surprising 21-yard average with his 31 pass receptions. He also scored six TDs. Horace Copeland is a capable backup.

Tight Ends — Jackie Harris was off to a good start in his first season with Tampa Bay, then suffered a shoulder injury that sidelined him for the final seven games. Harris led the team in receiving with 26 receptions up to that point. Harper's acquisition should help open up the middle for Harris. Tyji Armstrong caught 22 passes in 1994 but is better at blocking.

Kickers — Michael Husted was accurate from within 40 yards but made only five of 15 field goals from beyond 40 yards. He made just 23 of 35 field goal tries but may well exceed last season's 89-point total.

Best Players to Draft — Running back Errict Rhett, wide receiver Alvin Harper and tight end Jackie Harris.

WASHINGTON REDSKINS

Who's New — Wide receiver Michael Westbrook, fullback Marc Logan and running back Larry Jones.

Who's Gone — Wide receiver Desmond Howard went to Jacksonville in the expansion draft, tight end Ethan Horton was cut and quarterback John Friesz was signed by Seattle.

Quarterbacks — Rookie first-round draft pick Heath Shuler got off to a terrible NFL start but showed much improvement in the final month of 1994. In his first six games (four starts), Shuler completed only 40.7 percent of his passes for four touchdowns and nine interceptions. In the final four games, he completed 51.3 percent of his attempts for six TDs and just three interceptions. Shuler is the team's quarterback of the future — and the future is now. Gus Frerotte is now the No. 2 man. In his NFL debut in 1994, he completed 17 of 32 tosses for 226 yards and two TDs.

Running Backs — This could be a free-for-all position in training camp, with Reggie Brooks trying to fend off Ricky Ervins and Brian Mitchell for the starting tailback job. Brooks, who was coming off a 1,000-yard 1993 season but gained just 297 yards in 100 attempts last year, suffered a rib injury and was later benched. Ervins lost the job to Brooks in 1993 but regained it last year and rushed for a team-high 650 yards. Mitchell, who had 311 rushing yards in 1994, led the league in punt returns with a 14.1-yard average. He's also a fine kickoff returner. Larry Jones, a rookie, and Marc Logan, a waiver pickup from the 49ers, are fullbacks.

Wide Receivers — Joey Westbrook, the fourth player picked in this year's draft, has great size and hands. He can overpower defenders for the ball and block well. Henry Ellard was a great free-agent acquisition in 1994. He finished second in the NFL with 1,397 receiving yards. He caught 74 passes for six TDs. He's in his 13th season but obviously isn't slowing down. Tydus Winans caught 19 balls last year and has big-play potential.

Tight Ends — Ethan Horton's departure clears the way for James Jenkins, who produced four TDs on just eight pass receptions last year. Jamie Asher, a fifth-rounder, has a golden opportunity to make the team.

Kicker — Chip Lohmiller's fortunes seem to mirror that of the team. He had his second straight subpar year, with 20 field goals in 28 attempts. He averaged 125 points in his first five seasons, when the Redskins were an NFL power.

Best Players to Draft — There are no sure bets but lots of chancy ones, such as quarterback Heath Shuler, running back Reggie Brooks, wide receiver Michael Westbrook and kicker Chip Lohmiller.

Chapter 10

PICKING THE PLAYERS

Steve Young or Emmitt Smith? Do you want 35 touchdown passes and seven TD runs from a quarterback or 21 touchdown runs from a running back? You could make a case for either of these two superstars as the No. 1 pick in fantasy football in 1995. In leagues that award three points for each touchdown pass (as is usually the case), the decision is tough. In leagues that award six points per TD pass, there is no choice — take Young.

While Young, Smith and wide receiver Jerry Rice are clearly the top picks at their respective positions, tight end is not quite so obvious, and trying to pick the No. 1 kicker is a bit of a crapshoot.

Here's a look at the five positions, with the rankings made on the basis of a combined scoring system.

Quarterbacks — After Young, Dan Marino is the best pick because he's always good for 25 or more TD passes. John Elway, Brett Favre and Drew Bledsoe are all capable of throwing 30 TD passes, but Marino is a better choice. Elway might produce the outstanding fantasy numbers that so many people predicted last year. After the top five, there are several solid quarterbacks who would make good fantasy football starters. Among them are Jeff George, Warren Moon, Jim Kelly, Randall Cunningham and Jeff Hostetler. Troy Aikman is an excellent NFL quarterback, but he is not a great fantasy player. Players such as Jim Everett, Vinny Testaverde, Craig Erickson and Rick Mirer should post decent numbers. And there are the question marks — players who could reward you with a career year or finish the season on the bench and break your heart. They include Erik Kramer, Jeff Blake, Heath Shuler, Scott Mitchell and Trent Dilfer.

Running Backs — Among the biggest question marks this year is Barry Sanders, who scored only seven TDs last year because he came out during goal-line situations. Fantasy players who had him last year were frustrated time and time again, as Sanders would break a long run but get hauled down inside the five-yard line. Then somebody else would score the points. Now, with Derrick Moore gone, Sanders is likely to get more chances to score. Marshall Faulk and Natrone Means are virtual locks to gain well over 1,000 yards and double-digit TDs this season. Ricky Watters is gone from San Francisco, so fullback William Floyd is likely to have a great year. But after those six players, nobody is a sure bet to finish among the league leaders in scores. Chris Warren, Thurman Thomas, Errict Rhett, Bam Morris and Edgar Bennett should post pretty good numbers. Rodney Hampton is a question mark because the Giants drafted Tyrone Wheatley. And Jerome Bettis scored only three TDs last year. After them, a large group of players could produce well for a fantasy team.

Wide Receivers — There is a lot of depth at this position, with 12 to 14 players quite capable of eight to 10 TD receptions. Last year, 19 players had 1,000 receiving yards; the year before, only nine players hit the 1,000-yard mark. Five wide receivers had 10 or more TD catches last year, compared with just four in '93. After Rice, six or seven players are all worthy choices as the No. 2 receiver, and it could be any one of them. Andre Rison is a bit of a question mark, because he'll have Vinny Testaverde throwing to him. Tim Brown, Herman Moore and Carl Pickens are excellent No. 1 wideouts for a fantasy team. And Cris Carter and Terance Mathis are coming off spectacular seasons. If you get one of these eight players, you're in pretty good shape. After them, players such as Michael Irvin, Andre Reed, Irving Fryar, Fred Barnett, Alvin Harper and Michael Haynes would make an excellent second receiver for your team.

Tight Ends — Ben Coates has emerged as the best tight end in the NFL, but that doesn't necessarily mean he will lead tight ends in touchdown passes. Shannon Sharpe and Eric Green are also capable of eight or more touchdowns. If this trio is off your draft board, wait until the middle rounds instead of using a high draft pick for your top tight end (if Keith Jackson decides to keep playing, he'd make an excellent pick). A couple of other rookies, such as the Jets' Kyle Brady and Pittsburgh's Mark Bruener, could have good years.

Kickers — After three straight excellent seasons, John Carney deserves the distinction of being the No. 1 fantasy kicker. In reality, though, any one of about six or seven kickers could lead the league in scoring in 1995. Pete Stoyanovich, Fuad Reveiz, Doug Brien, Jason Elam and Morten Andersen will all probably score 110 or more points. Don't waste a high draft pick on a kicker; in the seventh or eighth round, there will still be kickers on the board who will score 100 or more points — that's guaranteed. It's never a bad idea to pick all of your other starters before drafting a kicker. Several kickers should rebound from subpar 1994 seasons. Among them are Jason Hanson and Chris Jacke.

Overall — Wide receiver appears to be the strongest position, while running back might be a little thin in terms of fantasy poduction. Only about six or seven running backs are locks, while the wide receiver position goes almost twice that deep. You should strongly consider taking a running back with one of your first two picks. There is a dropoff after the top five quarterbacks, although several more are almost a sure bet to throw 20 TD passes. There are plenty of possibilities for a backup quarterback, so don't pick your second one too early. Instead, load up on runners and receivers.

Quarterbacks

1. Steve Young, 49ers
2. Dan Marino, Dolphins
3. John Elway, Broncos
4. Brett Favre, Packers
5. Drew Bledsoe, Patriots
6. Jeff George, Falcons
7. Jeff Hostetler, Raiders
8. Warren Moon, Vikings
9. Randall Cunningham, Eagles
10. Jim Kelly, Bills
11. Jim Everett, Saints
12. Troy Aikman, Cowboys
13. Vinny Testaverde, Browns
14. Stan Humphries, Chargers
15. Craig Erickson, Colts
16. Erik Kramer, Bears
17. Rick Mirer, Seahawks
18. Scott Mitchell, Lions
19. Jeff Blake, Bengals
20. Chris Miller, Rams
21. Dave Brown, Giants
22. Steve Bono, Chiefs
23. Heath Shuler, Redskins
24. Neil O'Donnell, Steelers
25. Trent Dilfer, Buccaneers
26. Boomer Esiason, Jets
27. Dave Krieg, Cardinals
28. Steve Beuerlein, Jaguars
29. Frank Reich, Panthers
30. Chris Chandler, Oilers

Running Backs

1. Emmitt Smith, Cowboys
2. Barry Sanders, Lions
3. Natrone Means, Chargers
4. Marshall Faulk, Colts
5. Chris Warren, Seahawks
6. Ricky Watters, Eagles
7. William Floyd, 49ers
8. Bam Morris, Steelers
9. Thurman Thomas, Bills
10. Ki-Jana Carter, Bengals
11. Jerome Bettis, Rams
12. Errict Rhett, Buccaneers
13. Edgar Bennett, Packers
14. Rodney Hampton, Giants
15. Lorenzo White, Browns
16. Garrison Hearst, Cardinals
17. Barry Foster, Panthers
18. Ronald Moore, Jets
19. Marcus Allen, Chiefs
20. Gary Brown, Oilers
21. Rashaan Salaam, Bears
22. Terry Kirby, Dolphins
23. Marion Butts, Patriots
24. Craig Heyward, Falcons
25. Mario Bates, Saints
26. Amp Lee, Vikings
27. Rod Bernstine, Broncos
28. Leroy Hoard, Browns
29. Herschel Walker, Giants
30. Terry Allen, cut by Vikings
31. Reggie Brooks, Redskins
32. Dave Meggett, Patriots
33. Harvey Williams, Raiders
34. Greg Hill, Chiefs
35. Napoleon Kaufman, Raiders
36. Leonard Russell, Broncos
37. James Stewart, Jaguars
38. Keith Byars, Dolphins
39. Brad Baxter, Jets
40. Tyrone Wheatley, Giants
41. Robert Smith, Vikings
42. Johnny Johnson, Jets
43. Larry Centers, Cardinals
44. Derrick Moore, 49ers
45. Bernie Parmalee, Dolphins
46. Derek Brown, Saints
47. Kevin Turner, Eagles
48. Raymont Harris, Bears
49. Ricky Ervins, Redskins
50. John L. Williams, Steelers

PICKING THE PLAYERS

Wide Receivers

1. Jerry Rice, 49ers
2. Andre Rison, Browns
3. Tim Brown, Raiders
4. Herman Moore, Lions
5. Carl Pickens, Bengals
6. Anthony Miller, Broncos
7. Michael Irvin, Cowboys
8. Cris Carter, Vikings
9. Terance Mathis, Falcons
10. Irving Fryar, Dolphins
11. Andre Reed, Bills
12. Fred Barnett, Eagles
13. Alvin Harper, Buccaneers
14. Jake Reed, Vikings
15. Willie Anderson, Colts
16. Michael Haynes, Saints
17. Vincent Brisby, Patriots
18. Rob Moore, Cardinals
19. Henry Ellard, Redskins
20. Willie Davis, Chiefs
21. Calvin Williams, Eagles
22. Mike Pritchard, Broncos
23. Gary Clark, Dolphins
24. Robert Brooks, Packers
25. Mike Sherrard, Giants
26. Michael Westbrook, Redskins
27. John Taylor, 49ers
28. Darnay Scott, Bengals
29. Michael Timpson, Bears
30. Tony Martin, Chargers
31. Kevin Williams, Cowboys
32. Charles Johnson, Steelers
33. Joey Galloway, Seahawks
34. Derrick Alexander, Browns
35. Quinn Early, Saints
36. Lawrence Dawsey, Buccaneers
37. Randal Hill, Dolphins
38. Mark Ingram, Packers
39. Sean Dawkins, Colts
40. Isaac Bruce, Rams
41. J.J. Birden, Falcons
42. J.J. Stokes, 49ers
43. Jeff Graham, Bears
44. Brian Blades, Seahawks
45. Michael Jackson, Browns
46. Qadry Ismail, Vikings
47. Torrance Small, Saints
48. Eric Metcalf, Falcons
49. Ray Crittenden, Patriots
50. Mark Seay, Chargers

Tight Ends

1. Ben Coates, Patriots
2. Shannon Sharpe, Broncos
3. Eric Green, Dolphins
4. Brent Jones, 49ers
5. Keith Jackson, Packers (if he plays)
6. Troy Drayton, Rams
7. Jay Novacek, Cowboys
8. Jackie Harris, Buccaneers
9. Johnny Mitchell, Jets
10. Chris Gedney, Bears
11. Irv Smith, Saints
12. Pete Metzelaars, Panthers
13. Kyle Brady, Jets
14. Howard Cross, Giants
15. Keith Cash, Chiefs
16. Mark Bruener, Steelers
17. Kerry Cash, Raiders
18. Adrian Cooper, Vikings
19. Tony McGee, Bengals
20. Lonnie Johnson, Bills
21. Walter Reeves, Browns
22. Mark Chmura, Packers
23. Derek Brown, Jaguars
24. Ed West, Colts
25. Ron Hall, Lions
26. Paul Green, Seahawks
27. James Jenkins, Redskins
28. Pat Carter, Oilers
29. Alfred Pupunu, Chargers
30. Reggie Johnson, Eagles

Kickers

1. John Carney, Chargers
2. Pete Stoyanovich, Dolphins
3. Jason Elam, Broncos
4. Fuad Reveiz, Vikings
5. Doug Brien, 49ers
6. Morten Andersen, Saints
7. Chris Boniol, Cowboys
8. Matt Bahr, Patriots
9. Steve Christie, Bills
10. Gary Anderson, Steelers
11. Matt Stover, Browns
12. Norm Johnson, Falcons
13. Chris Jacke, Packers
14. Jeff Jaeger, Raiders
15. Jason Hanson, Lions
16. Doug Pelfrey, Bengals
17. Lin Elliott, Chiefs
18. Michael Husted, Buccaneers
19. Eddie Murray, Eagles
20. Kevin Butler, Bears
21. Brad Daluiso, Giants
22. Nick Lowery, Jets
23. Todd Peterson, Seahawks
24. Chip Lohmiller, Redskins
25. Dean Biasucci, Colts
26. Tony Zendejas, Rams
27. Greg Davis, Cardinals
28. Steve McLaughlin, Oilers
29. John Kasay, Panthers
30. Scott Sisson, Jaguars

Defenses

1. Minnesota Vikings
2. Arizona Cardinals
3. San Francisco 49ers
4. Dallas Cowboys
5. Cleveland Browns
6. Washington Redskins
7. Philadelphia Eagles
8. Los Angeles Raiders
9. Kansas City Chiefs
10. Pittsburgh Steelers

Sleepers

1. Robert Smith, RB, Vikings
2. Kevin Lee, WR, Patriots
3. Robert Brooks, WR, Packers
4. Tony McGee, TE, Bengals
5. Malcom Seabron, WR, Oilers
6. Torrance Small, WR, Saints
7. Kevin Williams, WR, Cowboys
8. Ryan Yarborough, WR, Jets
9. Isaac Bruce, WR, Rams
10. Derek Brown, TE, Jaguars

Possible Busts

1. Keith Jackson, TE, Packers
2. Scott Mitchell, QB, Lions
3. Jeff Blake, QB, Bengals
4. Cody Carlson, QB, Oilers
5. Erik Kramer, QB, Bears
6. Pete Metzelaars, TE, Panthers
7. Andre Rison, WR, Browns
8. Harvey Williams, RB, Raiders
9. Johnny Mitchell, TE, Jets
10. Rodney Hampton, RB, Giants

Top 100 Picks

1. Steve Young, QB, 49ers
2. Emmitt Smith, RB, Cowboys
3. Jerry Rice, WR, 49ers
4. Barry Sanders, RB, Lions
5. Natrone Means, RB, Chargers
6. Marshall Faulk, RB, Colts
7. Dan Marino, QB, Dolphins
8. Chris Warren, RB, Seahawks
9. Andre Rison, WR, Browns
10. Tim Brown, WR, Raiders
11. John Elway, QB, Broncos
12. Herman Moore, WR, Lions
13. Carl Pickens, WR, Bengals
14. Ricky Watters, RB, Eagles
15. Brett Favre, QB, Packers
16. William Floyd, RB, 49ers
17. Anthony Miller, WR, Broncos
18. Drew Bledsoe, QB, Patriots
19. Michael Irvin, WR, Cowboys
20. Bam Morris, RB, Steelers
21. Thurman Thomas, RB, Bills
22. Ben Coates, TE, Patriots
23. Ki-Jana Carter, RB, Bengals
24. Jeff George, QB, Falcons
25. Cris Carter, WR, Vikings
26. Jeff Hostetler, QB, Raiders
27. Terance Mathis, WR, Falcons
28. Irving Fryar, WR, Dolphins
29. Warren Moon, QB, Vikings
30. Shannon Sharpe, TE, Broncos
31. Randall Cunningham, QB, Eagles
32. Eric Green, TE, Dolphins
33. Jerome Bettis, RB, Rams
34. Jim Kelly, QB, Bills
35. Andre Reed, WR, Bills
36. Errict Rhett, RB, Buccaneers
37. Edgar Bennett, RB, Packers
38. Fred Barnett, WR, Eagles
39. Alvin Harper, WR, Buccaneers
40. Rodney Hampton, RB, Giants
41. John Carney, K, Chargers
42. Pete Stoyanovich, K, Dolphins
43. Lorenzo White, RB, Browns
44. Garrison Hearst, RB, Cardinals
45. Barry Foster, RB, Panthers
46. Brent Jones, TE, 49ers
47. Jake Reed, WR, Vikings
48. Ronald Moore, RB, Jets
49. Marcus Allen, RB, Chiefs
50. Jim Everett, QB, Saints
51. Jason Elam, K, Broncos
52. Keith Jackson, TE, Packers
53. Gary Brown, RB, Oilers
54. Rashaan Salaam, RB, Bears
55. Willie Anderson, WR, Colts
56. Michael Haynes, WR, Saints
57. Vincent Brisby, WR, Patriots
58. Troy Aikman, QB, Cowboys
59. Terry Kirby, RB, Dolphins
60. Marion Butts, RB, Patriots
61. Fuad Reveiz, K, Vikings
62. Craig Heyward, RB, Falcons
63. Rob Moore, WR, Cardinals
64. Henry Ellard, WR, Redskins
65. Mario Bates, RB, Saints
66. Amp Lee, RB, Vikings
67. Rod Bernstine, RB, Broncos
68. Troy Drayton, TE, Rams
69. Jay Novacek, TE, Cowboys
70. Doug Brien, K, 49ers
71. Willie Davis, WR, Chiefs
72. Calvin Williams, WR, Eagles
73. Mike Pritchard, WR, Broncos
74. Jackie Harris, TE, Buccaneers
75. Morten Andersen, K, Saints
76. Johnny Mitchell, TE, Jets
77. Gary Clark, WR, Dolphins
78. Robert Brooks, WR, Packers
79. Mike Sherrard, WR, Giants
80. Herschel Walker, RB, Giants
81. Vinny Testaverde, QB, Browns
82. Chris Boniol, K, Cowboys
83. Matt Bahr, K, Patriots
84. Stan Humphries, QB, Chargers
85. Michael Westbrook, WR, Redskins
86. John Taylor, WR, 49ers
87. Darnay Scott, WR, Bengals
88. Steve Christie, K, Bills
89. Gary Anderson, K, Steelers
90. Michael Timpson, WR, Bears
91. Tony Martin, WR, Chargers
92. Terry Allen, RB, cut by Vikings
93. Reggie Brooks, RB, Redskins
94. Kevin Williams, WR, Cowboys
95. Charles Johnson, WR, Steelers
96. Joey Galloway, WR, Seahawks
97. Dave Meggett, RB, Patriots
98. Harvey Williams, RB, Raiders
99. Craig Erickson, QB, Colts
100. Derrick Alexander, WR, Browns

Chapter 11
OFFSEASON UPDATE
THE INJURY REPORT

Fantasy football players should not rely strictly on last year's statistics when drafting their team. A lot of NFL players suffered injuries in 1994 that either lowered their statistics considerably or hampered them enough to the point where they didn't have typical seasons.

Here's a look at the players who were injured last season, as well as a report on their recovery as of mid-May.

Quarterbacks

CODY CARLSON, Oilers — In his first year as Houston's starter, Carlson suffered two shoulder injuries. Then he injured his left knee, finally undergoing arthroscopic surgery on December 7. However, he is on schedule in his rehab.

TRENT DILFER, Buccaneers — Dilfer sprained his ankle playing pickup basketball on Christmas, but the injury was not serious and he will be Tampa Bay's starter this season.

JOHN ELWAY, Broncos — Elway underwent arthroscopic surgery on February 24 and was healing in the spring. It was not serious.

BRETT FAVRE, Packers — Favre had offseason surgery to repair a hernia and check on his intestines (which were seriously injured when he was in college). He's okay.

JEFF GEORGE, Falcons — George suffered a broken left pinky finger in Game 15 last year but has recovered fully.

DON HOLLAS, Lions — Hollas suffered a separated shoulder last October while with Cincinnati but has recovered well. He was signed by Detroit as a free agent.

STAN HUMPHRIES, Chargers — Humphries spent some time in the hospital after undergoing elbow surgery after the Super Bowl. He did some limited throwing during the April minicamp and will be ready to go this year.

JIM KELLY, Bills — Kelly stretched ligaments in his left knee in the 14th game of 1994 and missed the final two games. He should be okay, but since he's 35, his rehab bears some watching. His doctor, however, says

Kelly has better knees than John Elway.

DAVID KLINGLER, Bengals — On January 3, Klingler underwent arthroscopic surgery on his throwing elbow, and his recovery should be complete. The injury was suffered in a preseason game, but the pain got worse as the season progressed (and he finally lost his starting job).

ERIK KRAMER, Bears — Kramer underwent successful surgery on his right shoulder during the offseason. He will battle Steve Walsh for the team's starting job.

CHRIS MILLER, Rams — True to form, Miller suffered all kinds of injuries in 1994 — an abdominal muscle pull, damaged rib cartilage, a slight shoulder separation and several concussions. Though he should be healthy heading into '95, he has always been injury-prone and he is the one quarterback most likely to get injured again.

RICK MIRER, Seahawks — For the second straight season, Mirer ended the year injured. Last year he fractured a thumb on his right throwing hand and missed the final two games. He has recovered well.

SCOTT MITCHELL, Lions — Mitchell suffered a broken right (non-throwing) hand in the ninth game of 1994 and missed the rest of the season. His rehab has gone well.

WARREN MOON, Vikings — Moon missed the final regular-season game with a sprained knee but returned for the team's playoff loss, although he wasn't 100 percent. He has recovered fully.

Running Backs

DONNELL BENNETT, Chiefs — Bennett missed the last game of 1994 with a knee injury. He's okay.

REGGIE BROOKS, Redskins — Brooks sprained a knee April 29 during a practice but should be fine by the start of training camp. He had hamstring and rib injuries in 1994.

KEITH BYARS, Dolphins — On November 6 of last season, Byars suffered cartilage and ligament damage in his right knee. His rehab was going slowly during the offseason and it is questionable whether or not he will be 100 percent by the end of the preseason.

BOB CHRISTIAN, Panthers — Christian spent the final three weeks of 1994 on injured reserve with a knee injury while with Chicago. He recovered quickly and was selected by Carolina in the expansion draft.

BARRY FOSTER, Steelers — Knee and back injuries sidelined Foster for several games in 1994. He has recovered, but he was being shopped to other teams during the offseason and will most likely play elsewhere in '95.

CHARLIE GARNER, Eagles — Garner underwent surgery last December 19 to repair a ruptured patella tendon in his left knee. His rehab bears some watching.

CLEVELAND GARY, Rams — Gary missed the final six games of 1994 with a hamstring injury. He's now healthy.

LeSHON JOHNSON, Packers — Johnson tore his left knee ligament in a playoff game against Detroit last season. His recovery will continue into the 1995 season.

VICTOR JONES, Chiefs — In his first game with Kansas City after playing most of the season with Pittsburgh, Jones suffered an Achilles injury and missed the final four games. He should be fine for '95.

TERRY KIRBY, Dolphins — Kirby got off to a good start in 1995 before tearing the anterior cruciate ligament in his right knee. He missed the rest of the season, but the Dolphins expect him to be ready for the start of training camp.

DERRICK LASSIC, Panthers — Lassic missed all of 1994 with a torn quadriceps. The Cowboys thought he would be able to come back, but they finally gave up and placed him on injured reserve on December 5. He's close to 100 percent and was to be ready for the start of the July training camp. He went all-out for the first time at the May mini-camp.

DAVE MEGGETT, Patriots — Meggett has a bothersome bone spur on his right ankle, but the Patriots don't seem very concerned, as they paid him $9.1 million on a five-year contract as a free agent.

BAM MORRIS, Steelers — Late-season ankle and finger injuries sidelined Morris somewhat, but he has recovered well and will be Pittsburgh's featured back in 1995.

ROOSEVELT POTTS, Colts — Potts had his knee scoped during the offseason, rather than undergoing major surgery, as was initially feared. He will be 100 percent.

LEONARD RUSSELL, Broncos — Russell underwent surgery last December 14 to repair a ruptured disk in his neck and has recovered completely.

EMMITT SMITH, Cowboys — Smith missed last year's final regular-season game and was slowed in the playoffs. He will be 100 percent heading into the 1995 season.

LAMAR SMITH, Redskins — Smith was the driver of the car that paralyzed teammate Mike Frier last season. In that accident, Smith suffered a back injury. He missed the final few weeks of the season but will be fine.

TOMMY VARDELL, Browns — In last season's fifth game,

Vardell tore a tendon and a ligament in his left knee and was sidelined for the rest of the year. He had immediate surgery, then underwent a second surgery in February to bring his joint up to football toughness. Thus, he faces an uncertain future, and the Browns didn't seem to be counting on him very much as the offseason progressed.

Wide Receivers

MELVIN BONNER, Broncos — A second-year pro, Bonner missed all of 1994 with a leg injury. He'll be back, but his chances of making the team are not good.

BUCKY BROOKS, Bills — Brooks was placed on injured reserve before Game 11 of last season. He had injured his knee three weeks earlier. He'll be fine and will contend for a starting job this year.

ISAAC BRUCE, Rams — A pretty good rookie in 1994, Bruce was out the final three weeks of the season because of a knee injury. He has completely recovered and will start in 1995.

RICHARD BUCHANAN, Panthers — Although he missed the last two months of the 1994 season with a hamstring injury, Buchanan had recovered enough to be chosen by Carolina in the expansion draft.

ANTHONY EDWARDS, Cardinals — Edwards missed the entire 1994 season with a knee injury. He's fine, but he's not a starter.

COURTNEY HAWKINS, Buccaneers — Hawkins suffered a sprained medial collateral ligament in Game 14 of last year and missed the final two games. He will be fine heading into training camp.

HAYWOOD JEFFIRES, Oilers — A free agent who had not yet signed with a new team, Jeffires had offseason knee surgery but was expected to be 100 percent.

VANCE JOHNSON, Broncos — After not playing in 1994, Johnson re-signed with Denver. He missed the end of the 1993 season with a broken ankle but has recovered fully.

KEVIN LEE, Patriots — Lee missed his entire rookie season because of a broken jaw. He's now healthy.

THOMAS LEWIS, Giants — A knee injury put Lewis on injured reserve for the end of his rookie season in 1994. He is healthy.

TERRY OBEE, Bears — Obee missed all of 1994 with a broken leg suffered during the preseason. He will be close to 100 percent, but the Bears didn't have him in their 1995 plans.

MIKE PRITCHARD, Broncos — Pritchard missed most of the 1994 season with a lacerated kidney. The team originally hoped he would return for the December playoff run, but he was finally placed on injured reserve in November. His recovery went well.

STERLING SHARPE, Packers — Sharpe will sit out the 1995 season but hopes to return in 1996. He suffered a serious neck injury in the final regular-season game of 1994 and underwent risky surgery to fuse two vertebrae together. He was then cut by Green Bay, who couldn't keep him on injured reserve all of '95 and continue to pay his salary. He'll probably never play again.

STEVE TASKER, Bills — Tasker broke an arm in Game 15 of last season but has recovered.

JOHN TAYLOR, 49ers — Don't be surprised if Taylor is cut by the 49ers, who are worried about an arthritic condition in Taylor's right knee. He underwent arthroscopic surgery at midseason and was to undergo major surgery in the offseason. But that second surgery was canceled and he was told to just rest his knee. In other words, he is not 100 percent.

Tight Ends

MARK BAVARO, Eagles — Bavaro is expected to retire. He missed much of the second half of the 1994 season with a foot injury.

FERRELL EDMUNDS, cut by Seahawks — Edmunds was most likely going to sign with another team, but two bulging disks in his back have some teams worried.

CHRIS GEDNEY, Bears — Although injury-prone, the talented Gedney should be healthy in 1995. He underwent left foot surgery during the offseason but will be 100 percent when training camp rolls around.

RON HALL, Lions — Hall underwent arthroscopic surgery after the sixth game of 1994. He is healthy.

JACKIE HARRIS, Buccaneers — Harris injured a shoulder last November 6, underwent surgery and was placed on injured reserve two weeks later after the team figured he would not be able to return quick enough. He figures big in the team's plans for 1995.

ANDREW JORDAN, Vikings — A rookie surprise in 1994, Cooper was forced onto injured reserve for the final three weeks of the regular season with a shoulder injury. He is healthy again.

DEEMS MAY, Chargers — May spent the final eight weeks of 1994 on injured reserve (not including three weeks on the inactive list), as well as the playoffs and the Super Bowl, with a foot injury. He is 100 percent.

A.J. OFODILE, Bills — Ofodile spent 1994 on the physically unable to perform list with a knee injury. He is okay.

WALTER REEVES, Browns — Reeves had surgery on his lower back on October 10 and was placed on injured reserve, missing the remainder of the season. He will have recovered completely by the start of training camp.

SHANNON SHARPE, Broncos — Two bad ankles kept Sharpe out of last season's Pro Bowl, but he is fine now.

FRANK WAINRIGHT, Broncos — While with New Orleans in 1994, Wainright missed the final three weeks with a knee injury. He has recovered and was signed by Denver as a free agent.

WESLEY WALLS, Saints — Walls played with torn ligaments in his left shoulder joint much of last season. He should be 100 percent heading into training camp.

ROSTER CHANGES

Like it or not, free agency is now a fact of life in pro football. It was also a very prominent factor in the writing of this book, because players were changing teams practically every day when this book went to press in mid-May. The free-agency period ran to July 15, so there will undoubtedly be many changes that could not be included in this book.

However, not very many big-name stars changed teams as free agents in 1995. In fact, no top quarterback and only one star running back switched teams through free agency. Several very good wide receivers did go to new teams, however. From a fantasy football standpoint, the best players who changed teams were: quarterbacks Dave Krieg (from Detroit to Arizona) and Frank Reich (from Buffalo to Carolina); running backs Ricky Watters (from San Francisco to Philadelphia) and Derrick Fenner (from Cincinnati to the Raiders); wide receivers Andre Rison (from Atlanta to Cleveland), Alvin Harper (from Dallas to Tampa Bay) and Willie Anderson (from the Rams to Indianapolis); tight ends Eric Green (from Pittsburgh to Miami) and Pete Metzelaars (from Buffalo to Carolina); and kicker John Kasay (from Seattle to Carolina).

Here's a list of the skill-position players who changed teams through free agency:

Arizona Cardinals — **Signed:** QB Dave Krieg. **Lost:** WR Gary Clark, WR Randal Hill.

Atlanta Falcons — **Signed:** WR J.J. Birden, WR Nate Lewis, WR Eric Metcalf, WR Clarence Verdin. **Lost:** RB Erric Pegram, WR Andre Rison.

Buffalo Bills — **Signed:** None. **Lost:** WR Don Beebe, TE Pete

Metzelaars, QB Frank Reich.

Carolina Panthers — **Signed:** RB Randy Baldwin, WR Don Beebe, K John Kasay, TE Pete Metzelaars, QB Frank Reich, RB Vernon Turner.

Chicago Bears — **Signed:** RB Anthony Johnson, RB Darrell Thompson, WR Michael Timpson. **Lost:** WR Nate Lewis, WR Tom Waddle.

Cincinnati Bengals — **Signed:** RB Eric Bieniemy, RB James Joseph, WR Tom Waddle. **Lost:** RB Derrick Fenner, QB Don Hollas.

Cleveland Browns — **Signed:** WR Andre Rison, RB Lorenzo White. **Lost:** RB Randy Baldwin, TE Thomas McLemore, RB Eric Metcalf, QB Mark Rypien.

Dallas Cowboys — **Signed:** None. **Lost:** WR Alvin Harper, QB Rodney Peete.

Denver Broncos — **Signed:** RB Aaron Craver, WR Ed McCaffrey, QB Bill Musgrave, TE Frank Wainright. **Lost:** None.

Detroit Lions — **Signed:** QB Don Hollas, QB Don Majkowski. **Lost:** RB Mel Gray, QB Dave Krieg.

Green Bay Packers — **Signed:** RB Pat Chaffey. **Lost:** TE Reggie Johnson, RB Darrell Thompson, TE Ed West.

Houston Oilers — **Signed:** QB Chris Chandler, RB Mel Gray. **Lost:** RB Lorenzo White.

Indianapolis Colts — **Signed:** WR Willie Anderson, TE Thomas McLemore. **Lost:** TE Kerry Cash, QB Don Majkowski, RB Ed Toner.

Jacksonville Jaguars — **Signed:** WR Mike Williams.

Kansas City Chiefs — **Signed:** None. **Lost:** WR J.J. Birden.

Los Angeles Raiders — **Signed:** TE Kerry Cash, RB Derrick Fenner. **Lost:** WR Alexander Wright.

Miami Dolphins — **Signed:** WR Gary Clark, TE Eric Green, WR Randal Hill, QB Dan McGwire. **Lost:** RB Aaron Craver, RB Cleveland Gary, WR Mike Williams.

Minnesota Vikings — **Signed:** None. **Lost:** None.

New England Patriots — **Signed:** RB Dave Meggett. **Lost:** WR Michael Timpson, RB Kevin Turner.

New Orleans Saints — **Signed:** None. **Lost:** TE Frank Wainright.

New York Giants — **Signed:** None. **Lost:** RB Dave Meggett.

New York Jets — **Signed:** QB Bubby Brister, RB Dexter Carter. **Lost:** RB Anthony Johnson.

Philadelphia Eagles — **Signed:** TE Reggie Johnson, QB Rodney Peete, RB Kevin Turner, RB Ricky Watters, TE Ed West. **Lost:** QB Bubby Brister, RB James Joseph.

Pittsburgh Steelers — **Signed:** RB Erric Pegram, RB Ed Toner.

Lost: TE Eric Green.

St. Louis Rams — **Signed:** RB Cleveland Gary, QB Mark Rypien, WR Alexander Wright. **Lost:** WR Willie Anderson, QB Chris Chandler.

San Diego Chargers — **Signed:** None. **Lost:** RB Eric Bieniemy.

San Francisco 49ers — **Signed:** None. **Lost:** RB Dexter Carter, WR Ed McCaffrey, QB Bill Musgrave, RB Ricky Watters.

Seattle Seahawks — **Signed:** QB John Friesz. **Lost:** RB Pat Chaffey, K John Kasay, QB Dan McGwire.

Tampa Bay Buccaneers — **Signed:** WR Alvin Harper. **Lost:** WR Clarence Verdin.

Washington Redskins — **Signed:** None. **Lost:** QB John Friesz.

FREE AGENTS RE-SIGNED

The following players could have changed teams during the offseason but decided to re-sign with the teams they played for in 1994:

Player	Position	Team
Bobby Hebert	Quarterback	Atlanta
Brad Johnson	Quarterback	Minnesota
Jamie Martin	Quarterback	St. Louis
Rick Strom	Quarterback	Buffalo
Steve Walsh	Quarterback	Chicago
Johnny Bailey	Running Back	St. Louis
Brad Baxter	Running Back	N.Y. Jets
Corey Croom	Running Back	New England
Chuck Evans	Running Back	Minnesota
Scottie Graham	Running Back	Minnesota
Mark Higgs	Running Back	Arizona
Derek Loville (a)	Running Back	San Francisco
Eric Lynch	Running Back	Detroit
Brian Mitchell	Running Back	Washington
Bernie Parmalee	Running Back	Miami
Cedric Smith	Running Back	Washington
Harvey Williams	Running Back	L.A. Raiders
Tim Worley	Running Back	Chicago
Frank Wycheck	Running Back	Washington
Jeff Campbell	Wide Receiver	Denver
Cris Carter	Wide Receiver	Minnesota

Jessie Hester (b)	Wide Receiver	St. Louis
Haywood Jeffires	Wide Receiver	Houston
Michael Irvin	Wide Receiver	Dallas
Tim McGee	Wide Receiver	Cincinnati
Greg McMurtry	Wide Receiver	Chicago
Scott Miller	Wide Receiver	Miami
Carl Pickens (c)	Wide Receiver	Cincinnati
Jake Reed	Wide Receiver	Minnesota
Torrance Small (d)	Wide Receiver	New Orleans
Rico Smith	Wide Receiver	Cleveland
Jeff Sydner	Wide Receiver	Philadelphia
Lamar Thomas	Wide Receiver	Tampa Bay
Charles Wilson	Wide Receiver	Tampa Bay
Fred Baxter	Tight End	N.Y. Jets
Kirk Botkin	Tight End	New Orleans
Jerry Evans	Tight End	Denver
Keith Jennings	Tight End	Chicago
Trey Junkin	Tight End	L.A. Raiders
Harper LeBel	Tight End	Atlanta
Jay Novacek	Tight End	Dallas
Aaron Pierce	Tight End	N.Y. Giants
Derrick Walker (e)	Tight End	Kansas City
Ronnie Williams	Tight End	Miami
Matt Bahr	Kicker	New England
Brad Daluiso	Kicker	N.Y. Giants

(a) — matched offer made by Denver; (b) — matched offer made by Seattle; (c) — matched offer made by Arizona; (d) — matched offer made by Seattle; (e) — matched offer made by Washington.

TRADES

There were again quite a few big offseason trades involving skill-position players between the end of the 1994 season and mid-May. Many of these will have big impacts on their teams in 1995. Here's a list of those trades.

Player	1994 Team	1995 Team
QB Mark Brunell	Green Bay	Jacksonville

QB Craig Erickson	Tampa Bay	Indianapolis
RB Derrick Moore	Detroit	San Francisco
RB Ronald Moore	Arizona	N.Y. Jets
RB Eric Metcalf	Cleveland	Atlanta
WR Victor Bailey	Philadelphia	Kansas City
WR Mark Ingram	Miami	Green Bay
WR Rob Moore	N.Y. Jets	Arizona
WR Ricky Proehl	Arizona	Seattle
TE Keith Jackson	Miami	Green Bay

CUTS

The following veteran skill-position players were cut during the offseason:

Player	Position	Team
Cary Conklin	Quarterback	Philadelphia
Todd Philcox	Quarterback	Miami
Wade Wilson	Quarterback	New Orleans
Terry Allen	Running Back	Minnesota
Steve Broussard	Running Back	Cincinnati
Marc Logan	Running Back	San Francisco
Napoleon McCallum	Running Back	L.A. Raiders
Spencer Tillman	Running Back	Houston
Herschel Walker	Running Back	Philadelphia
Johnnie Barnes	Wide Receiver	San Diego
Bill Brooks	Wide Receiver	Buffalo
Mark Jackson	Wide Receiver	Indianapolis
Haywood Jeffires	Wide Receiver	Houston
Eric Martin	Wide Receiver	Kansas City
Art Monk	Wide Receiver	N.Y. Jets
Sterling Sharpe	Wide Receiver	Green Bay
Marv Cook	Tight End	Chicago
Ferrell Edmunds	Tight End	Seattle
Ethan Horton	Tight End	Washington
Jimmie Johnson	Tight End	Kansas City

ROSTER ADDITIONS

Here is a list of players who signed contracts during the offseason. Many of them were cut by other teams during the offseason and therefore appear in the previous list.

Player	Last team	1995 Team
QB Mike Buck	New Orleans	Arizona
QB Bob Gagliano	Atlanta (1993)	San Francisco
QB Rich Gannon	Washington (1993)	Kansas City
QB Jeff Graham	Seattle (1993)	L.A. Raiders
QB Trent Green	San Diego (1993)	Washington
QB Todd Philcox	Cleveland	Miami (cut)
QB Todd Philcox	Miami	Tampa Bay
QB Timm Rosenbach	Phoenix (1992)	New Orleans
QB T.J. Rubley	L.A. Rams (1993)	Green Bay
QB Peter Tom Willis	Chicago (1993)	Tampa Bay
RB Bobby Joe Edmunds	L.A. Raiders (1989)	Tampa Bay
RB Brian Henesey	Arizona	Philadelphia
RB Bobby Humphrey	Miami (1992)	Buffalo
RB John Ivlow	San Francisco	Denver
RB Marc Logan	San Francisco	Washington
RB Ostell Miles	Cincinnati	Denver
RB Ernie Thompson	Kansas City (1993)	Washington
RB Herschel Walker	Philadelphia	N.Y. Giants
WR Johnnie Barnes	San Diego	Pittsburgh
WR Wesley Carroll	Cincinnati (1993)	Kansas City
WR Harrison Houston	Atlanta	Kansas City
WR Vance Johnson	Denver (1993)	Denver
WR Hassan Jones	Kansas City (1993)	L.A. Raiders
WR Sean LaChappelle	L.A. Rams	Kansas City
WR Damon Mays	Houston (1992)	Pittsburgh
WR Pat Newman	Cleveland	Washington
WR Jimmy Smith	Philadelphia	Jacksonville
WR Milt Stegall	Cincinnati (1993)	Green Bay
TE Rob Coons	Miami	Buffalo
TE Craig Thompson	Cincinnati	Pittsburgh
K Mike Cofer	San Francisco (1993)	Indianapolis
K Cary Blanchard	N.Y. Jets (1993)	New Orleans
K Todd Peterson	Arizona	Seattle

OFFSEASON UPDATE

EXPANSION DRAFT

The Carolina Panthers and Jacksonville Jaguars conducted their expansion drafts in February, selecting more than 30 players each off the rosters of the 28 current teams. Carolina drafted 35 players, most of them with low salaries, while Jacksonville went after more big-name veterans. Here are the skill-position players that were drafted by the two teams:

CAROLINA PANTHERS

Player	Position	1994 Team
Doug Pederson	Quarterback	Miami
Jack Trudeau	Quarterback	N.Y. Jets
Eric Ball	Running Back	Cincinnati
Dewell Brewer	Running Back	Indianapolis
Bob Christian	Running Back	Chicago
Howard Griffith	Running Back	L.A. Rams
Derrick Lassic	Running Back	Dallas
Brian O'Neal	Running Back	Philadelphia
Richard Buchanan	Wide Receiver	L.A. Rams
Mark Carrier	Wide Receiver	Cleveland
Eric Guliford	Wide Receiver	Minnesota
Steve Hawkins	Wide Receiver	New England
David Mims	Wide Receiver	Atlanta
Larry Ryans	Wide Receiver	Detroit
Charles Swann	Wide Receiver	Denver
Kurt Haws	Tight End	Washington
Vince Marrow	Tight End	Buffalo

JACKSONVILLE JAGUARS

Player	Position	1994 Team
Steve Beuerlein	Quarterback	Arizona
Reggie Cobb	Running Back	Green Bay
Mazio Royster	Running Back	Tampa Bay
Marcus Wilson	Running Back	Green Bay
Charles Davenport	Wide Receiver	Pittsburgh
Desmond Howard	Wide Receiver	Washington
Willie Jackson	Wide Receiver	Dallas
Kelvin Martin	Wide Receiver	Seattle
Cedric Tillman	Wide Receiver	Denver
Derek Brown	Tight End	N.Y. Giants

Chapter 12

ROOKIE REPORT

The 1995 draft was the best in several years. Quite a few impact players should begin making almost immediate contributions, and most teams utilized the draft to build depth. There was good talent in the draft at running back, quarterback and tight end, but the crop of wide receivers appears to be relatively weak. So was kicker.

Quarterback is one position at which rookies usually make the smallest contribution — at least right away. Not one rookie quarterback made a significant impact in 1994, although two of them — Heath Shuler and Trent Dilfer — will be given starting opportunities this season.

This year's draft may produce a pair of starters in Steve McNair and Kerry Collins, and quite a few other rookies should surface in the coming years. But with free agency changing the game, teams are much less likely to spend a few years developing young quarterback prospects only to see them move on elsewhere. Hence, this year's draft produced some mighty disappointed quarterbacks who had expected to be taken in the first two rounds but were picked in the fourth and fifth rounds. Only two quarterbacks were drafted in each of the first three rounds, but four of them were drafted in Round 4 and three more were selected in the fifth round.

It looks as if four rookie running backs — Ki-Jana Carter, James Stewart, Rashaan Salaam and Napolean Kaufman — will start this season. And the Giants might move Rodney Hampton in a trade and fill his big shoes with exciting rookie Tyrone Wheatley. The Packers drafted fullback William Henderson in the third round and hope to use him as the blocking back for versatile Edgar Bennett, who has made the move from fullback to tailback.

Carter, considered the premier player in the entire draft, gives the Bengals a dangerous offense — if their offensive line can do a decent job of blocking. Carter should complement speed-burning wide receivers Carl Pickens and Darnay Scott perfectly to provide an explosive offense. In other words, the Bengals have a pretty good offense for a change.

At wide receiver, only two or three rookies are likely to make a significant contribution right away. Michael Westbrook will start in Washington, and Joey Galloway gives the Seahawks the big-play threat they so sorely needed. Several others, such as Frank Sanders in Arizona, Chris Sanders in Houston and Green Bay's Antonio Freeman, will battle for

ROOKIE REPORT

starting jobs. San Francisco did a typical 49ers move, trading up to pick J.J. Stokes in the first round. He'll be groomed to fill the shoes of Jerry Rice and John Taylor. Stokes should contribute more and more as the season progresses.

Five tight ends were drafted in the first two rounds, and several of them could make an immediate impact. Kyle Brady will likely start from day one for the Jets, and Mark Bruener should start in Pittsburgh, as well. Christian Fauria (Seattle), Ken Dilger (Colts) and David Sloan (Lions) might win starting jobs.

Only two placekickers were drafted. They are Steve McLaughlin, who will try to take the job away from Tony Zendejas in St. Louis, and Cole Ford, who is unlikely to beat Gary Anderson out of a job in Pittsburgh (unless Anderson holds out or is traded).

Rookies in this chapter are evaluated and ranked according to the impact they might make this season, based on their expected playing time.

QUARTERBACKS

STEVE McNAIR, Oilers — The biggest question mark surrounding McNair is not his ability but his lack of high-level experience. He racked up astronomical numbers at Alcorn State (14,496 passing yards and 119 touchdown passes) and was a legitimate Heisman Trophy candidate. He's built like a linebacker, has a cannon arm and can make incredible plays. McNair also can scramble with the best of them (he rushed for 2,327 yards in college) and he can pass with touch or zip. In fact, McNair's potential is almost unlimited, but he will need quite a bit of refining.

KERRY COLLINS, Panthers — Carolina traded away the first pick in the draft in order to move down four spots and pick Collins, whom they regard as the franchise quarterback they can build the team around. Collins has great size and excellent leadership intangibles. He has a good arm and can put good touch on his passes. He does have a somewhat slow delivery; however, he lacks mobility and he needs some work on his mechanics. After driving a team with Rolls Royce talent surrounding him at Penn State, Collins must lead an expansion club that is building from the ground up.

STONEY CASE, Cardinals — Regarded as an overachiever, Case was surprisingly drafted in the third round, ahead of several higher-rated prospects. He is smart, tough and competitive, and Cardinals coach Buddy Ryan likes those intangibles. Case had an excellent senior season, completing 233 of 409 passes for 3,117 yards and 22 touchdowns, and he ran for 12 more scores at New Mexico. He is slender, lacks a strong arm and is not very accurate. But on a team with only one quality quality — the well-traveled David Krieg — Case could become the starter rather quickly.

ERIC ZEIER, Browns — Zeier lacks the size of Cleveland's starting quarterback, Vinny Testaverde, but he possesses all of the intangibles of the NFL's top passers — toughness, leadership, poise and presence. He passed for 11,143 yards and 67 TDs in four seasons in the tough SEC. However, Zeier is barely over six feet tall, not very mobile and he lacks great arm strength. But he is a supreme overachiever.

KORDELL STEWART, Steelers — The extremely athletic Stewart could provide some intriguing competition for Neil O'Donnell at some point down the road. A second-round project, Stewart ran the option in college. He has exceptional speed and quickness and a strong arm. But he's a streaky passer, has a low release and has had trouble finding secondary receivers. Stewart has lots to learn before he'll be ready, but he has NFL ability.

TODD COLLINS, Bills — Collins really came on during his final two collegiate seasons, and he completed 65 percent of his passes the past three years. He has excellent size and intelligence, and he can read coverages. But he is not very mobile. He will be groomed to replace the aging Jim Kelly, but he won't play right away.

ROB JOHNSON, Jaguars — The Jaguars were thrilled to see Johnson still on the board after the first day of the draft, so they grabbed him with the first pick in the fourth round. Johnson has deadly accuracy from short and medium range. He completed 67 percent of his passes the past two seasons. He had a terrific junior year, completing 308 of 449 attempts for 3,630 yards and 29 TDs in 1993. His numbers dropped somewhat during an injury-plagued senior season. Johnson has thrown just 12 interceptions in his last 725 attempts. He'll be groomed as Jacksonville's quarterback of the future.

CHAD MAY, Vikings — May was considered to be a late-first-round or second-round pick, but he plummeted all the way down to the fourth round. He may be Minnesota's next quarterback, but the Vikings hope to get another year or two out of Warren Moon. May is adept at reading defenses and calling audibles. He has a very strong arm and can avoid a pass rush. He isn't very tall and is streaky and erratic. But he is a tough, cocky prospect.

DAVE BARR, Eagles — Barr will compete with Rodney Peete for the backup job behind Randall Cunningham. He finished second in the nation in passing efficiency as a junior but broke his collarbone as a senior. Barr performed very well in the East-West Shrine Game, completing 12 straight passes at one point. He has good size and moves well in the pocket.

JOHN WALSH, Bengals — Walsh no doubt regrets entering the draft a year early, as he wasn't selected until the seventh round. He had a very productive college career and ran a pro-style offense at Brigham Young. Walsh has excellent arm strength, timing and touch. But he lacks strength and athleticism, and is streaky.

RUNNING BACKS

KI-JANA CARTER, Bengals — Carter has the skills to become a great NFL runner. A combination of size, speed, quickness, acceleration and explosiveness made him the top player in the 1995 draft. He can explode through a hole and cut back against the grain. Carter rushed for 1,539 yards last year and 1,026 yards in 1993. He is a good receiver but has not shown much blocking ability. Carter was redshirted as a freshman because he was coming off minor knee surgery, and he has not been very durable. If he stays healthy, Carter could carry the Bengals.

RASHAAN SALAAM, Bears — Almost immediately after picking Salaam, Bears coach Dave Wannstedt said the rookie would start at tailback. The 1994 Heisman Trophy winner, Salaam is a hard runner with very good size. He has better acceleration than speed, and he is a good goal-line runner, makes tacklers miss and can catch well. Salaam led the nation in rushing, scoring and all-purpose running in 1994, rushing for 2,055 yards and 24 touchdowns on 298 attempts. He runs upright, however, and he gained many yards outside on option pitches.

JAMES STEWART, Jaguars — Jacksonville traded up in the draft to pick Stewart and will most likely be the team's starter over Reggie Cobb. One of the best big backs in the draft, Stewart is a big, strong power runner who runs with authority. He can also catch the ball well. But he is not a great breakaway threat and will fumble at times. He started as a freshman and senior, but he played behind Charlie Garner his sophomore and junior years.

TYRONE WHEATLEY, Giants — An interesting draft pick by the Giants, who already had Rodney Hampton and Herschel Walker. Wheatley gives the Giants an explosive, big and powerful back who can run, catch and return kicks. Wheatley can make tacklers miss or take them on, and he and can find the cutback lane. He missed time his final two years due to a separated shoulder, but he still ran for 1,000 yards three straight seasons.

NAPOLEON KAUFMAN, Raiders — At the least, Kaufman will be a situational back and kick returner, but he may win the starting job from Harvey Williams. Kaufman has great speed and is a big-play threat. He is very well-built for his small size, and has run vision and cutback moves. A very productive college player, Kaufman rushed for 4,041 yards in four seasons. He struggles to catch the ball at times and is not big enough to be an effective blocker, but he could become the ideal third-down back.

CURTIS MARTIN, Patriots — Bill Parcells was unable to land one of the five premier backs in the draft, so he settled on Martin in the third round.

Martin has good running skills, quickness and balance. He runs hard and catches the ball well. A severely sprained ankle sidelined Martin for all but two games at Pittsburgh his senior season. He rushed for 1,075 yards as a junior. He has average size, but he has not played an entire season injury-free.

WILLIAM HENDERSON, Packers — The Packers liked Henderson's blocking skills so much that they drafted him in the third round ahead of Florida State's Zack Crockett. Henderson was not highly rated in the draft but will battle Dorsey Levens for the starting fullback job. He gained only 251 yards as a senior at North Carolina but has good hands.

RAY ZELLARS, Saints — Zellars will compete for a starting fullback job on a team loaded with running backs. He is a well-built, powerful, hard runner with good blocking skills. Zellars became a team leader his senior season, when he rushed for 466 yards. However, he is not very big for a fullback and his pass-catching skills are suspect.

ZACK CROCKETT, Colts — Crockett backed up William Floyd in 1992 and was redshirted the next season, but he emerged as a senior. He has excellent size and power and is an effective goal-line runner. Crockett can also catch well and is a willing blocker, but he is not very elusive. He will battle Roosevelt Potts for the job as Marshall Faulk's lead blocker.

RODNEY THOMAS, Oilers — With the departure of Lorenzo White, Thomas will battle for the starting job but will probably back up Gary Brown. He shared playing time in the Texas A&M backfield the past three seasons, gaining more than 800 yards each year. He is a well-built, hard runner, but he lacks elusiveness and is not a top blocker.

JOE ASKA, Raiders — Considered one of the sleepers of the 1995 draft, Aska has a rare combination of sprinter's speed and a fullback's size. He played at Division II Central State (Okla.), where he rushed for 1,629 yards and 15 touchdowns as a senior. But he almost never had to block or catch passes. He may be a great long-term prospect.

SHERMAN WILLIAMS, Cowboys — Williams was drafted in the second round to back up Emmitt Smith. He seems to run better and better as a game goes on. He is an agile, elusive runner with quick acceleration. Williams rushed for 1,341 yards as a senior and had a tremendous Citrus Bowl, with 166 rushing yards and eight catches for 155 yards. He is small, however, and he needs to work on his blocking.

TERRELL FLETCHER, Chargers — Fletcher appears to be a tailor-made third-down back, but the Chargers already have Ronnie Harmon. Thus, Fletcher may be hard-pressed for playing time, though he could return kicks. Fletcher is quick, shifty and elusive and has game-breaking speed. He is a good receiver, but he has had problems fumbling the ball. He is small and doesn't block very well.

LARRY JONES, Redskins — Jones never played full-time at Miami (Fla.), where he was redshirted for a year after undergoing reconstructive knee surgery. He runs with power at times and can catch, but he is an inconsistent blocker with little speed.

WIDE RECEIVERS

MICHAEL WESTBROOK, Redskins — The biggest, strongest, most gifted receiver in the draft, Westbrook has all of the tools to make an instant impact. He has great size and large, strong hands. A martial-arts expert, Westbrook can overpower jamming cornerbacks and outfight them for the ball. He is a tremendous blocker with good speed. In 1992, his most productive receiving year, Westbrook caught 76 passes for 1,060 yards. But it was his game-winning catch of a "Hail Mary" pass against Michigan last year that gained him notoriety. If Westbrook can shake his very cocky attitude and work to improve, he'll be a great one. He'll start immediately.

JOEY GALLOWAY, Seahawks — Galloway will team with Rick Mirer to provide the game-breaking big-play capability the Seahawks eed. Among the fastest players in the draft, Galloway is a top-notch athlete with tremendous speed, quickness and acceleration. He is well-built, has good hands and can turn little plays into big ones. But he is not very big and is not a polished route-runner. Galloway returned from 1992 knee surgery to catch 45 passes for 927 yards in 1993. He'll start opposite Brian Blades.

J.J. STOKES, 49ers — The 49ers always seem to draft the player they want, and they moved up in the draft to take Stokes. He will learn the ropes from the best receiver to ever play the game, Jerry Rice. Stokes has outstanding size, great hands and long arms. Although not a speed-burner, he runs faster in pads than his so-so 40-yard dash time. In 1993, he finished seventh in the Heisman balloting after catching 82 passes for 1,181 yards and 17 TDs. An injured quadriceps sidelined Stokes for much of the '94 season.

TYRONE DAVIS, Jets — A fourth-round pick, Davis may earn a starting job on a Jets team seriously thin at wide receiver. Davis has great size and can run after the catch. He averaged 20.9 yards per catch during his collegiate career. In 1994, he caught 38 passes for 691 yards and 10 TDs. Davis is not as strong as his size might suggests and he drops easy passes.

FRANK SANDERS, Cardinals — Sanders improved his production each season at Auburn, catching 58 passes for 910 yards and seven touchdowns as a senior. He is well-built and uses his size well to shield off defenders and sky for the ball. Sanders can muscle defenders a little like Dallas's Michael Irvin, and he wants the ball in the clutch. But he drops too many passes. He'll compete for Arizona's No. 3 receiving job.

CHRIS SANDERS, Oilers — Sanders should be at the forefront of a youth movement on a team aging at receiver. Often overshadowed by Joey Galloway in college, Sanders has exceptional speed (he's a track All-American). He came on in '94 with 35 catches for 533 yards and eight TDs. He has great jumping ability and decent hands, but he lacks experience.

ANTONIO FREEMAN, Packers — The Packers wanted a good possession receiver and hope they found one in Freeman, who holds Virginia Tech records for career receptions (121) and touchdown catches (22). Freeman is a very good punt returner who can turn a screen pass into a big play. He is sneaky-quick and has good instincts, but he is not very fast and may be a little afraid to make a catch over the middle.

JACK JACKSON, Bears — Once regarded as the fourth-best receiver in the draft, Jackson fell into the fourth round and could possibly become one of the steals of the draft. He has blazing speed, exceptional athletic ability and acceleration and very good hands. He is very small but can catch the ball away from his frame and protect it well. Jackson caught 26 TD passes the past two seasons at Florida.

CHRIS T. JONES, Eagles — Although very inconsistent, Jones may be talented enough to earn a job as the Eagles' No. 3 or 4 receiver this year. He is a very big target who can make catches in a crowd and can get deep at times, but he lacks great quickness. Jones needs to catch more with his hands.

JIMMY OLIVER, Chargers — A three-time track All-American, Oliver was more productive running the 100-meter dash than running pass routes at Texas Christian. He caught 23 passes for 547 yards as a senior. He showed his tremendous potential in the regular-season finale, catching seven passes for 206 yards and two TDs. Oliver has legitimate home-run speed and a mean streak for blocking. But he lacks experience. He is an intriguing developmental prospect.

ROELL PRESTON, Falcons — Preston has the speed and burst to contribute in Atlanta's run-and-shoot offense. His stock rose in this year's Blue-Gray All-Star Game. But he tends to be moody and self-centered and he runs undisciplined routes.

TAMARICK VANOVER, Chiefs — Vanover entered the draft after a bad rookie season in the Canadian Football League. He has excellent talent and good size, and is a good runner after making the catch. But he is often overweight, lacks concentration and has a poor work ethic.

KEZ McCORVEY, Lions — Although not very fast or well-built, McCorvey has good moves and fine hands. He knows how to get open in a zone, and he caught 59 passes for 870 yards as a senior. McCorvey performs better in a football game than at a scouting combine.

TIGHT ENDS

KYLE BRADY, Jets — Perhaps the surprise pick of the draft, Brady was taken by the Jets with the ninth pick in the first round, one slot ahead of Cleveland, which had coveted him. The Jets already have immensely talented Johnny Mitchell, but Brady was just too talented to pass up. The top tight end prospect in the draft, Brady is a huge target who creates mismatches with his size and yet has mobility. He catches the ball well and finishes his blocks. Brady caught 27 passes for 365 yards last year. He is not a great runner, but he has the ability to become a great pro player. Brady will play right away.

MARK BRUENER, Steelers — Eric Green was lost to free agency, and Bruener was the best tight end on the board when the Steelers drafted in the first round. He has good size, knows how to sustain his blocks and reads coverages well. Bruener has good hands and can adjust to poorly thrown passes. He caught 85 passes the last three seasons. He lacks deep speed and running ability but could be a perfect fit for a blue-collar town like Pittsburgh.

CHRISTIAN FAURIA, Seahawks — Fauria might battle Paul Green for Seattle's starting job or he may become the team's H-back. He lacks great size but he's an overachiever who rarely drops a pass. Fauria is a tenacious, if not overpowering, blocker. He lacks good speed but plays better than he looks. Fauria caught 35 passes for 356 yards last season.

KEN DILGER, Colts — Dilger has an excellent chance to become the Colts' starting tight end soon, as free-agent acquisition Ed West is approaching the end of his career. Dilger caught 41 passes for 547 yards and five touchdowns as a senior. He moves well for a big tight end. He is a finesse blocker, not an overpowering one. Dilger can play tight end or H-back.

LOVELL PICKNEY, Rams — Pickney is a "tweener," meaning he has the size of a tight end and the speed of a wideout. He has soft hands and can overpower defenders for the ball. But he is undisciplined and self-centered (he was suspended three times in 1994).

KICKERS

STEVE McLAUGHLIN, Rams — McLaughlin may be the only pro prospect in this year's crop of placekickers. He has enough range to challenge Rams incumbent Tony Zendejas, who is not noted for his range. McLaughlin can boom deep kickoffs. In 1994, he made all 26 of his extra-point attempts and 23 of 29 field goals, including three of five from 50-plus yards. However, he was erratic before his senior year.

Chapter 13

STATISTICS
1994 QUARTERBACKS

Player	Team	GP/GS	PASSING						RUSHING	
			ATT	CMP	YDS	TD	INT	RTG	YDS	TD
Steve Young	S.F.	16/16	461	324	3969	35	10	112.8	293	7
Brett Favre	G.B.	16/16	582	363	3882	33	14	90.7	202	2
Dan Marino	Mia.	16/16	615	385	4453	30	17	89.2	−6	1
John Elway	Den.	14/14	494	307	3490	16	10	85.7	235	4
Jim Everett	N.O.	16/16	540	346	3855	22	18	84.9	35	0
Troy Aikman	Dall.	14/14	524	233	2676	13	12	84.9	62	1
Jim Kelly	Buff.	14/14	448	285	3114	22	17	84.6	77	1
Joe Montana	K.C.	14/14	493	299	3283	16	9	83.6	17	0
Jeff George	Atl.	16/16	524	322	3734	23	18	83.3	66	0
Craig Erickson	T.B.	15/15	399	225	2919	16	10	82.5	68	1
Stan Humphries	S.D.	15/15	453	264	3209	17	12	81.6	19	0
Jeff Hostetler	Raid.	16/16	455	263	3334	20	16	80.8	159	2
Warren Moon	Minn.	15/15	601	371	4264	18	19	79.9	55	0
Neil O'Donnell	Pitt.	14/14	370	212	2443	13	9	78.9	80	1
Steve Walsh	Chi.	12/11	343	208	2078	10	8	77.9	4	1
Boomer Esiason	NYJ	14/14	440	255	2782	17	13	77.3	59	0
Jeff Blake	Cin.	10/9	306	156	2154	14	8	76.9	204	1
Randall Cunningham	Phil.	14/14	490	265	3229	16	13	74.4	288	3
Drew Bledsoe	N.E.	16/16	691	400	4555	25	27	73.6	40	0
Chris Miller	Rams	13/10	317	173	2104	16	14	73.6	100	0
Dave Brown	NYG	15/15	350	201	2536	12	16	72.5	196	2
Vinny Testaverde	Clev.	14/13	376	207	2575	16	18	70.7	37	2
Rick Mirer	Sea.	13/3	381	195	2151	11	7	70.2	153	0
Jay Schroeder	Ariz.	9/8	238	133	1510	4	7	68.4	59	0
David Klingler	Cin.	10/7	231	131	1327	6	9	65.7	85	0
Billy Joe Tolliver	Hou.	10/7	240	121	1287	6	7	62.6	37	2
Scott Mitchell	Det.	9/9	246	119	1456	10	11	62.0	24	1
Steve Beuerlein	Ariz.	9/7	255	130	1545	5	9	61.6	39	1
Heath Shuler	Wash.	11/8	265	120	1658	10	12	59.6	103	0
Non-qualifiers										
Dave Krieg	Det.	14/7	212	131	1629	14	3	101.7	35	0
Jim Harbaugh	Ind.	12/9	202	125	1440	9	6	85.8	223	0
Bucky Richardson	Hou.	7/4	181	94	1202	6	6	70.3	217	1
John Friesz	Wash.	16/4	180	105	1266	10	9	77.7	1	0
Chris Chandler	Rams	12/6	176	108	1352	7	2	93.8	61	1
Erik Kramer	Chi.	6/5	158	99	1129	8	8	79.9	−2	0
Don Majkowski	Ind.	9/6	152	84	1010	6	7	69.8	34	3
Cody Carson	Hou.	5/5	132	59	727	1	4	52.2	17	0
Hugh Millen	Den.	5/2	131	81	893	2	3	77.6	57	0
Mark Rypien	Clev.	6/3	128	59	694	4	3	63.7	4	0
Steve Bono	K.C.	7/2	117	66	796	4	4	74.6	−1	0
Dan McGwire	Sea.	7/3	105	51	578	1	2	60.7	−6	0
Bobby Hebert	Atl.	8/0	103	52	610	2	6	51.0	43	0

Gus Frerotte	Wash.	4/4	100	46	600	5	5	61.3	1	0
Frank Reich	Buff.	16/2	93	56	568	1	4	63.4	0	0
Mike Tomzcak	Pitt.	6/2	93	54	804	4	0	100.8	22	0
Jack Trudeau	NYJ	5/2	91	50	496	1	4	55.9	30	0
Trent Dilfer	T.B.	5/2	82	38	433	1	6	36.3	27	0
Bubby Brister	Phil.	7/2	76	51	507	2	1	89.1	7	0
Gale Gilbert	S.D.	15/1	67	41	410	3	1	87.3	-3	0
Rodney Peete	Dall.	7/1	56	33	470	4	1	102.5	-2	0
Kent Graham	NYG	13/1	53	24	295	3	2	66.2	11	0
Elvis Grbac	S.F.	11/0	50	35	393	2	1	98.2	1	0
Jim McMahon	Ariz.	2/1	43	23	219	1	3	46.6	32	0
Brad Johnson	Minn.	4/0	37	22	150	0	0	68.5	-2	0
Sean Salisbury	Minn.	1/1	34	16	156	0	1	48.2	2	0
Vince Evans	Raid.	9/0	33	18	222	2	0	95.8	25	0
Jason Garrett	Dall.	2/1	31	16	315	2	1	95.5	-2	0
Wade Wilson	N.O.	4/0	28	20	172	0	0	87.2	15	0
Mark Brunell	G.B.	2/0	27	12	95	0	0	53.8	7	1
Browning Nagle	Ind.	1/1	21	8	69	0	1	27.7	12	0
Tommy Maddox	Rams	5/0	19	10	141	0	2	37.3	1	0
Bernie Kosar	Mia.	2/0	12	7	80	1	1	71.5	17	0
Stan Gelbaugh	Sea.	1/0	11	7	80	1	0	115.7	10	0
Casey Weldon	T.B.	2/0	9	7	63	0	0	95.8	0	0
Glenn Foley	NYJ	1/0	8	5	45	0	1	38.0	0	0
Scott Zolak	N.E.	16/0	8	5	28	0	0	68.8	-1	0
Matt Blundin	K.C.	1/0	5	1	13	0	1	0.0	0	0
Donald Hollas	Cin.	2/0	2	0	0	0	1	0.0	0	0
Perry Klein	Atl.	2/0	1	0	0	0	0	39.6	0	0

1994 RUNNING BACKS

Player	Team	GP/GS	RUSHING			RECEIVING		
			ATT	YDS	TD	REC	YDS	TD
Barry Sanders	Det.	16/16	331	1883	7	44	283	1
Chris Warren	Sea.	16/15	333	1545	9	41	323	2
Emmitt Smith	Dall.	15/15	368	1484	21	50	341	1
Natrone Means	S.D.	16/16	343	1350	12	39	235	0
Marshall Faulk	Ind.	16/16	314	1282	11	52	522	1
Thurman Thomas	Buff.	15/15	287	1093	7	50	349	2
Rodney Hampton	NYG	14/13	327	1075	6	14	103	0
Terry Allen	Minn.	16/16	255	1031	8	17	148	0
Jerome Bettis	Rams	16/16	319	1025	3	31	293	1
Errict Rhett	T.B.	16/8	284	1011	7	22	119	0
Harvey Williams	Raid.	16/10	282	983	4	47	391	3
Johnny Johnson	NYJ	16/14	240	931	3	42	303	2
Lewis Tillman	Chi.	16/15	275	899	7	27	222	0
Leroy Hoard	Clev.	16/12	209	890	5	45	445	4
Ricky Watters	S.F.	16/16	239	877	6	66	719	5
Bernie Parmalee	Mia.	15/10	216	868	6	34	249	1
Barry Foster	Pitt.	13/10	216	851	5	20	124	0
Bam Morris	Pitt.	15/6	198	836	7	22	204	0
Ronald Moore	Ariz.	16/16	232	780	4	8	52	1
Craig Heyward	Atl.	16/11	183	779	7	32	335	1
Lorenzo White	Hou.	15/8	191	757	3	21	188	1
Marcus Allen	K.C.	15/13	189	709	7	42	349	0
Marion Butts	N.E.	16/15	243	703	8	9	54	0
Ricky Ervins	Wash.	16/10	185	650	3	51	293	1
Gary Brown	Hou.	12/8	169	648	4	18	194	1
Edgar Bennett	G.B.	16/15	178	623	5	78	546	4
Leonard Russell	Den.	14/13	190	620	9	38	227	0
Mario Bates	N.O.	11/7	151	579	6	8	62	0
Reggie Cobb	G.B.	16/13	153	579	3	35	299	1
Greg Hill	K.C.	16/1	141	574	1	16	92	0
Herschel Walker	Phil.	16/14	113	528	5	50	500	2
Derek Brown	N.O.	16/9	146	489	3	44	428	1
Derrick Fenner	Cin.	16/13	141	468	1	36	276	1
Raymont Harris	Chi.	16/11	123	464	1	39	236	0
Steve Broussard	Cin.	13/3	94	403	2	34	218	0
Charlie Garner	Phil.	10/8	109	399	3	8	74	0
Kenneth Davis	Buff.	16/1	91	381	2	18	82	0
Erric Pegram	Atl.	13/5	103	358	1	16	99	0
Larry Centers	Ariz.	16/5	115	336	5	77	647	2
Roosevelt Potts	Ind.	16/15	77	336	1	26	251	1
Eric Metcalf	Clev.	16/8	93	329	2	47	436	3
Vaughn Hebron	Phil.	16/2	82	325	2	18	137	0
John L. Williams	Pitt.	15/12	68	317	1	51	378	2
Irving Spikes	Mia.	12/1	70	312	2	4	16	0
Leroy Thompson	N.E.	16/1	102	312	2	65	465	5
Brian Mitchell	Wash.	16/7	78	311	0	26	236	1
William Floyd	S.F.	16/11	87	305	6	19	145	0
David Meggett	NYG	16/3	91	298	4	32	293	0
Reggie Brooks	Wash.	13/5	100	297	2	13	68	0
Eric Bieniemy	S.D.	16/0	73	295	0	5	48	0
Vince Workman	T.B.	15/8	79	291	0	11	82	0
Terry Kirby	Mia.	4/4	60	233	2	14	154	0

STATISTICS

Kimble Anders	K.C.	16/13	62	231	2	67	525	1
Harold Green	Cin.	14/11	76	223	1	27	267	1
Ernest Byner	Clev.	16/1	75	219	2	11	102	0
Richie Anderson	NYJ	13/5	43	207	1	25	212	1
Scottie Graham	Minn.	16/0	64	207	2	1	1	0
James Joseph	Phil.	14/5	60	203	1	43	344	2
Glyn Milburn	Den.	16/3	58	201	1	77	549	3
Mark Higgs	Mia.-Ariz.	11/1	62	195	0			
Lincoln Coleman	Dall.	11/0	64	180	1	8	46	0
Donnell Bennett	K.C.	15/0	46	178	2	7	53	0
Brad Baxter	NYJ	15/9	60	170	4	10	40	0
Garrison Hearst	Ariz.	8/0	37	169	1	6	49	0
Derrick Clark	Den.	16/4	56	168	3	9	47	0
Adrian Murrell	NYJ	10/1	33	160	0	7	7?	0
Marc Logan	S.F.	10/5	33	143	1	16	9?	1
Carwell Gardner	Buff.	16/7	41	135	4	11	89	0
Daryl Johnston	Dall.	16/16	40	138	2	44	325	2
Blair Thomas	N.E.-Dall.	6/1	43	137	2	4	16	0
Robert Green	Chi.	15/0	25	122	0	24	199	2
Tom Rathman	Raid.	16/16	28	118	0	26	194	0
Mack Strong	Sea.	8/1	27	114	2	3	3	0
Kevin Turner	N.E.	16/9	36	111	1	52	471	2
Robert Smith	Minn.	14/0	31	106	1	15	105	0
Amp Lee	Minn.	13/9	29	104	0	45	368	2
LeShon Johnson	G.B.	12/0	26	99	0	13	168	0
Derek Loville	S.F.	14/0	31	99	0	2	26	0
Tyrone Montgomery	Raid.	6/6	36	97	0	8	126	1
Jon Vaughn	Sea.-K.C.	12/0	27	96	1	1	5	0
Ronnie Harmon	S.D.	16/0	25	94	1	58	615	1
Calvin Jones	Raid.	7/0	22	93	0	2	6	0
Rod Bernstine	Den.	3/3	17	91	0	9	70	0
Lorenzo Neal	N.O.	16/7	30	90	1	2	9	0
Sam Gash	N.E.	13/6	30	86	0	9	61	0
Jeff Cothran	Cin.	14/4	26	85	0	4	24	1
Ronald Humphrey	Ind.	15/0	18	85	0	3	19	0
Reggie Rivers	Den.	16/1	43	83	2	20	136	0
Steve Smith	Sea.	16/0	26	80	2	11	142	1
Lamont Warren	Ind.	11/0	18	80	0	3	47	0
Randy Baldwin	Clev.	16/0	23	78	0	3	15	0
Keith Byars	Mia.	9/9	19	64	2	49	418	5
Rodney Culver	S.D.	3/0	8	63	0			
Anthony McDowell	T.B.	14/11	21	58	0	29	193	1
Yonel Jourdain	Buff.	9/0	17	56	0	10	56	0
Adam Walker	S.F.	8/0	13	54	1			
Derrick Moore	Det.	16/0	27	52	4	1	10	0
Gary Downs	NYG	14/0	15	51	0	2	15	0
Fred McAfee	Ariz-Pitt.	13/0	18	51	2	1	4	0
Cedric Smith	Wash.	14/8	10	48	0	15	118	1
Tommy Vardell	Clev.	5/5	15	48	0	16	137	1
Kenyon Rasheed	NYG	16/7	17	44	0	10	97	0
Tracy Johnson	Sea.	16/10	12	44	2	10	91	0
Aaron Craver	Mia.	8/0	6	43	0	24	237	0
Derrick Ned	N.O.	16/1	11	36	0	13	86	0
Johnny Bailey	Rams	14/0	11	35	1	58	516	0
Dexter Carter	S.F.	16/0	8	34	0	7	99	0
David Lang	Rams	13/0	6	34	0	8	60	0

STATISTICS

Name	Team							
Howard Griffith	Rams	16/10	9	30	0	16	113	1
Bob Christian	Chi.	12/0	7	29	0	2	30	0
Merril Hoge	Chi.	5/5	6	24	0	13	79	0
Chuck Evans	Minn.	14/0	6	20	0	1	2	0
Tim Worley	Chi.	5/0	9	17	1	1	8	0
James Saxon	Mia.	16/7	8	16	0	27	151	0
Dorsey Levens	G.B.	14/0	5	15	0	1	9	0
Chuck Levy	Ariz.	11/0	3	15	0	4	35	0
Anthony Johnson	NYJ	15/0	5	12	0	5	31	0
Spencer Tilman	Hou.	16/0	2	12	0			
Cleveland Gary	Mia	2/0	7	11	0	2	19	0
Ed Toner	Ind.	9/0	1	11	0			
Tim Lester	Rams	14/4	7	14	0	1	1	0
Vernon Turner	T.B.	12/1	4	13	0			
Vaughn Dunbar	N.O.	8/0	3	9	0			
Mazio Royster	T.B.	14/1	9	7	0	7	36	0
Beno Bryant	Sea.	2/0	1	6	0			
Tyrone Hughes	N.O.	15/5	2	6	0			
Napoleon McCallum	Raid.	1/0	3	5	1			
Tommie Agee	Dall.	15/0	5	4	0	1	2	0
Steve Avery	Pitt.	14/1	2	4	0	1	2	0
Nate Turner	Buff.	13/0	2	4	0	1	26	1
Keith Elias	NYG	2/0	2	4	0			
Steve Hendrickson	S.D.	16/0	1	3	0			
Brad Muster	N.O.	7/1	1	3	1	10	88	0
Kevin Smith	Raid.	3/0	1	2	0	1	8	0
Eric Ball	Cin.	16/0	2	0	0	1	4	0
Ron Dickerson	K.C.	9/0	1	0	0	2	11	0
Rudy Harris	T.B.	8/0	2	0	0	2	11	0
Eric Lynch	Det.	12/3	1	0	0	2	18	0
Jamal Anderson	Atl.	3/0	2	−1	0			
Lamar Smith	Sea.	2/0	2	−1	0			
Robert Wilson	Dall.-Mia.	4/0	1	−1	0			
Darrell Thompson	G.B.	8/0	2	−2	0			
Wes Bender	Raid.	9/0	0	0	0	2	14	0

STATISTICS

1994 WIDE RECEIVERS

Player	Team	GP/GS	RECEIVING REC	RECEIVING YDS	RECEIVING TD	RUSHING ATT	RUSHING YDS	RUSHING TD
Cris Carter	Minn.	16/16	122	1256	7			
Jerry Rice	S.F.	16/16	112	1499	13	7	93	2
Terance Mathis	Atl.	16/16	111	1342	11			
Sterling Sharpe	G.B.	16/16	94	1119	18	3	15	0
Andre Reed	Buff.	16/16	90	1303	8	10	87	0
Tim Brown	Raid.	16/16	89	1309	9			
Jake Reed	Minn.	16/15	85	1175	4			
Quinn Early	N.O.	16/13	82	894	4	2	10	0
Andre Rison	Atl.	15/14	81	1088	8			
Brian Blades	Sea.	16/16	81	1086	4	2	32	0
Michael Irvin	Dall.	16/16	79	1241	6			
Fred Barnett	Phil.	16/16	78	1127	5			
Rob Moore	NYJ	16/16	78	1010	6	1	-3	0
Michael Haynes	N.O.	16/16	77	985	5	4	43	0
Henry Ellard	Wash.	16/16	74	1397	6	1	-5	0
Michael Timpson	N.E.	15/14	74	941	3	2	14	0
Irving Fryar	Mia.	16/16	73	1270	7			
Herman Moore	Det.	16/16	72	1173	11			
Carl Pickens	Cin.	15/15	71	1127	11			
Jeff Graham	Chi.	16/15	68	944	4			
Webster Slaughter	Hou.	16/12	68	846	2			
Haywood Jeffires	Hou.	16/16	68	783	6			
Ricky Sanders	Atl.	14/12	67	599	1			
Anthony Miller	Den.	16/15	60	1107	5	1	3	0
Vincent Brisby	N.E.	14/11	58	904	5			
Calvin Williams	Phil.	16/14	58	813	3	2	11	0
Robert Brooks	G.B.	16/16	58	648	4	1	0	0
Mark Seay	S.D.	16/14	58	645	6			
Brett Perriman	Det.	16/14	56	761	4	9	86	0
Kelvin Martin	Sea.	16/15	56	681	1			
Mike Sherrard	NYG	16/14	53	825	6	1	-10	0
Floyd Turner	Ind.	16/16	52	593	6	3	-3	0
Willie Davis	K.C.	14/13	51	822	5			
Sean Dawkins	Ind.	16/16	51	742	5			
Ricky Phoehl	Ariz.	16/16	51	651	5			
Tony Martin	S.D.	16/1	50	885	7	2	-9	0
Gary Clark	Ariz.	15/2	50	771	1			
Torrance Small	N.O.	16/0	49	719	5			
Derrick Alexander	Clev.	14/12	48	828	2	4	38	0
J.J. Birden	K.C.	13/13	48	637	4			
Willie Anderson	Rams	16/16	46	945	5	1	11	0
Darnay Scott	Cin.	16/12	46	866	5	10	106	0
Lawrence Dawsey	T.B.	10/5	46	673	1			
Bert Emanuel	Atl.	16/16	46	649	4	2	4	0
Art Monk	NYJ	16/15	46	581	3			
Qadry Ismail	Minn.	16/3	45	696	5			
Jessie Hester	Rams	16/15	45	644	3	2	28	0
Mark Ingram	Mia.	15/13	44	506	6			
Chris Calloway	NYG	16/14	43	666	2	8	77	0
Shawn Jefferson	S.D.	16/16	43	627	3	3	40	0
Bill Brooks	Buff.	16/9	42	482	2			
John Taylor	S.F.	15/15	41	531	5	2	-2	0

Desmond Howard	Wash.	16/15	40	727	5	1	4	0
Don Beebe	Buff.	13/11	40	527	4	2	11	0
Curtis Conway	Chi.	13/12	39	546	2	6	31	0
Charles Johnson	Pitt.	16/9	38	577	3	4	−1	0
Randal Hill	Ariz.	14/14	38	544	0			
Lake Dawson	K.C.	12/6	37	537	2	3	24	0
O.J. McDuffie	Mia.	15/13	37	488	3	5	32	0
Courtney Hawkins	T.B.	13/12	37	438	5			
Yancey Thigpen	Pitt.	15/6	36	546	4			
Ernest Givins	Hou.	16/16	36	521	1	1	−5	0
Raghib Ismail	Raid.	16/0	34	513	5	4	31	0
Alvin Harper	Dall.	16/14	33	821	8			
Charles Wilson	T.B.	14/7	31	652	6	2	15	0
Mark Carrier	Clev.	16/6	29	452	5	1	14	0
Aubrey Matthews	Det.	14/3	29	359	3			
Cedric Tilman	Den.	16/4	28	455	1			
Ray Crittenden	N.E.	16/2	28	397	3			
Anthony Morgan	G.B.	16/0	28	397	4			
Derek Russell	Den.	12/12	25	342	1	1	6	0
Tom Waddle	Chi.	9/1	25	244	1			
Todd Kinchen	Rams	13/0	23	352	3	1	44	1
Eric Martin	K.C.	10/1	21	307	1			
Michael Jackson	Clev.	9/7	21	304	2			
Nate Singleton	S.D.	16/1	21	294	2			
Isaac Bruce	Rams	12/0	21	272	3	1	2	0
Russell Copeland	Buff.	15/4	21	255	1	1	−7	0
Victor Bailey	Phila.	16/0	20	311	1			
Pat Coleman	Hou.	10/2	20	298	1	1	2	0
Andre Hasting	Pitt.	16/8	20	281	2			
Ernie Mills	Pitt.	15/6	19	384	1	3	18	0
Tydus Winans	Wash.	15/0	19	344	2	1	5	0
Mike Pritchard	Den.	3/0	19	271	1			
Horace Copeland	T.B.	16/2	17	308	0			
Alexander Wright	Raid.	16/15	16	294	2			
Arthur Marshall	NYG	16/0	16	219	0	2	8	0
James Jett	Raid.	16/1	15	253	0			
Mike Williams	Mia.	15/0	15	221	0			
Bryan Reeves	Ariz.	14/0	14	202	1	1	−1	0
Kevin Williams	Dall.	15/2	13	181	0	6	20	0
Tim McGee	Cin.	14/1	13	175	1	1	−18	0
Ed McCaffrey	S.F.	16/0	11	131	2			
Keenan McCardell	Clev.	13/3	10	182	0			
Gary Wellman	Hou.	8/0	10	112	0	1	3	0
Willie Green	T.B.	5/0	9	150	0			
Leonard Harris	Atl.	8/2	9	113	0			
Steve Anderson	NYJ	10/0	9	90	0			
Greg McMurtry	Chi.	9/4	8	112	1			
Anthony Carter	Det.	4/1	8	97	3			
Mark Jackson	NYG-Ind.	14/0	8	97	1			
Ron Lewis	G.B.	6/1	7	108	0			
Lamar Thomas	T.B.	11/0	7	94	0			
Dwight Stone	Pitt.	15/1	7	81	0	2	7	0
Danan Hughes	K.C.	16/0	7	80	0			
Scott Miller	Mia.	9/0	6	94	1			
David Palmer	Minn.	13/1	6	90	0			
Ryan Yarborough	NYJ	13/0	6	42	1			
Michael Bates	Sea.	15/0	5	112	1	2	−4	0

STATISTICS

Player	Team							
David Palmer	Minn.	13/1	5	82	0	1	1	0
Richard Buchanan	Rams	3/0	5	60	0			
Daryl Hobbs	Raid.	10/0	5	52	0			
Jeff Query	Cin.	10/4	5	44	0			
Robb Thomas	Sea.	16/1	4	70	0			
Thomas Lewis	NYG	9/0	4	46	0			
Reggie Brown	Hou.	4/0	4	34	0			
Terry Mickens	G.B.	12/0	4	31	0			
Chris Brantley	Rams	15/0	4	29	0			
Johnnie Morton	Det.	14/0	3	39	1			
Greg Primus	Chi.	3/1	3	25	0			
Travis Hannah	Hou.	9/0	3	24	0			
Chris Penn	K.C.	8/0	3	24	0			
David Mims	Atl.	2/2	3	14	0			
Olanda Truitt	Wash.	9/0	2	89	1			
Rico Smith	Clev.	5/4	2	61	0			
Darryl Spencer	Atl.	8/0	2	51	0			
Damon Thomas	Buff.	3/0	2	31	0			
Aaron Bailey	Ind.	13/0	2	30	0			
Steve Hawkins	N.E.	7/0	2	22	0			
Tony Kimbrough	Den.	12/0	2	20	0			
Shannon Baker	Ind.	4/0	2	15	0			
Nate Lewis	Chi.	13/0	2	13	1			
Jermaine Ross	Rams	4/0	1	36	1			
Jeff Campbell	Den.	16/1	1	22	1	2	6	0
Derrell Mitchell	N.O.	14/0	1	13	0			
Ronnie Harris	N.E.-Sea.	2/0	1	11	0			
Jeff Sydner	Phil.	16/0	1	10	0			
Leslie Shepard	Wash.	3/0	1	8	0			
Orlando Parker	NYJ	2/0	1	7	0			
Johnnie Barnes	S.D.	11/0	1	6	0			
Patrick Robinson	Ariz.	15/0	1	5	0			
Terrence Warren	Sea.	14/0	0	0	0	3	15	0
Charles Jordan	G.B.	10/0	0	0	0	1	5	0

1994 TIGHT ENDS

Player	Team	GP/GS	RECEIVING			RUSHING		
			REC	YDS	TD	ATT	YDS	TD
Ben Coates	N.E.	16/16	96	1174	7	1	0	0
Shannon Sharpe	Den.	15/13	87	1010	4			
Keith Jackson	Mia.	16/16	59	673	7			
Johnny Mitchell	NYJ	16/14	58	749	4			
Brent Jones	S.F.	15/15	49	670	9			
Pete Metzelaars	Buff.	16/16	49	428	5			
Jay Novacek	Dall.	16/14	47	475	2			
Eric Green	Pitt.	15/14	46	618	4			
Irv Smith	N.O.	16/16	41	330	3			
Tony McGee	Cin.	16/16	40	492	1			
Wesley Walls	N.O.	15/7	38	406	4			
Derrick Walker	K.C.	15/11	36	382	2			
Andrew Jordan	Minn.	16/12	35	336	0			
Kevin Glover	Raid.	16/16	33	371	2			
Adrian Cooper	Minn.	12/11	32	363	0			
Troy Drayton	Rams.	16/16	32	276	6	1	4	0
Ed West	G.B.	14/12	31	377	2			
Howard Cross	NYG	16/16	31	364	4			
Paul Green	Sea.	16/11	30	208	1			
Jackie Harris	T.B.	9/9	26	337	3			
Brian Kinchen	Clev.	16/11	24	232	1			
Tyji Armstrong	T.B.	16/9	22	265	1	1	−1	0
Alfred Pupunu	S.D.	13/10	21	214	2			
Marv Cook	Chi.	16/8	21	212	1			
Maurice Johnson	Phil.	16/10	21	204	2			
Aaron Pierce	NYG	16/11	20	214	4			
James Thornton	NYJ	15/5	20	171	0			
Keith Cash	K.C.	6/5	19	192	2			
Duane Young	S.D.	14/14	17	217	1			
Mark Bavaro	Phil.	12/11	17	215	3			
Derek Ware	Ariz.-Cin.	15/12	17	171	1			
Rodney Holman	Det.	15/7	17	163	0			
Kerry Cash	Ind.	16/16	16	190	1			
Ethan Horton	Wash.	16/15	15	157	3			
Mark Chmura	G.B.	14/4	14	165	0			
Chris Gedney	Chi.	7/7	13	157	3			
Ted Popson	S.F.	16/1	13	141	0			
Jerry Evans	Den.	16/11	13	127	2			
Chad Fann	Ariz.	16/9	12	96	0			
Shannon Mitchell	S.D.	16/6	11	105	0			
Ryan Wetnight	Chi.	11/0	11	104	1			
Keith Jennings	Chi.	9/1	11	75	3			
Pat Carter	Hou.	16/13	11	74	1			
Troy Sadowski	Cin.	15/1	11	54	0			
Ron Hall	Det.	13/10	10	106	0			
John Burke	N.E.	16/6	9	86	0			
Terry Samuels	Ariz.	16/6	8	57	0	1	1	0
James Jenkins	Wash.	16/3	8	32	4			
Reggie Johnson	G.B.	9/2	7	79	0			
Ty Hallock	Det.	15/10	7	75	0			
Mitch Lyons	Atl.	7/2	7	54	0			
Ferrell Edmunds	Sea.	7/7	7	43	0			
Tracy Greene	K.C.	7/2	6	69	1			
Walter Reeves	Clev.	5/5	6	61	1			
Jonathan Hayes	Pitt.	16/6	5	50	1			

STATISTICS

Vince Marrow	Buff.	10/0	5	44	0				
Jeff Wilner	G.B.	11/1	5	31	0				
Dave Moore	T.B.	15/5	4	57	0				
Scott Galbraith	Dall.	16/2	4	31	0				
Lonnie Johnson	Buff.	10/1	3	42	0				
Jamie Williams	Raid.	16/0	3	25	0				
Steve Jordan	Minn.	4/1	3	23	0				
Frank Hartley	Clev.	10/5	3	13	1				
Fred Baxter	NYJ	11/1	3	11	1				
Ronnie Williams	Mia.	14/0	2	26	0				
Deems May	S.D.	5/2	2	22	0				
Carlester Crumpler	Sea	9/4	2	19	0				
Greg Baty	Mia.	16/0	2	11	0				
Brett Carolan	S.F.	4/0	2	10	0				
Jimmie Johnson	K.C.	7/1	2	7	0				
Brent Novoselsky	Minn.	12/0	2	7	0				
Kevin Smith	Raid.	3/0	1	8	0	1	2	0	
Charles Arbuckle	Ind.	7/1	1	7	0				
Carlos Etheredge	Ind.	9/0	1	6	0				
Brian Kozlowski	NYG	16/2	1	5	0				
John Henry Mills	Hou.	16/1	1	4	0				
Craig Keith	Pitt.	16/1	1	2	0				
Trey Junkin	Sea.	16/0	1	1	1				

1994 KICKERS

Player	Team	GP	XP	XPA	FG	FGA	PCT	PTS
John Carney	S.D.	16	33	33	34	38	89.5	135
Fuad Reveiz	Minn.	16	30	30	34	39	87.2	132
Jason Elam	Den.	16	29	29	30	37	81.1	119
Matt Bahr	N.E.	16	36	36	27	34	79.4	117
Morten Anderson	N.O.	16	32	32	28	39	71.8	116
Chris Boniol	Dall.	16	48	48	22	29	75.9	114
Steve Christie	Buff.	16	38	38	24	28	85.7	110
Matt Stover	Clev.	16	32	32	26	28	92.9	110
Doug Pelfrey	Cin.	16	24	25	28	33	84.8	108
Pete Stoyanovich	Mia.	16	35	35	24	31	77.4	107
Doug Brien	S.F.	16	60	62	15	20	75.0	105
Lin Elliott	K.C.	16	30	30	25	30	83.3	105
Gary Anderson	Pitt.	16	32	32	24	29	82.8	104
Chris Jacke	G.B.	16	41	43	19	26	73.1	98
Jeff Jaeger	Raiders	16	31	31	22	28	78.6	97
Eddie Murray	Phil.	16	33	33	21	25	84.0	96
Norm Johnson	Atl.	16	32	32	21	25	84.0	95
Jason Hanson	Det.	16	39	40	18	27	66.7	93
Chip Lohmiller	Wash.	16	30	32	20	28	71.4	90
Michael Husted	T.B.	16	20	20	23	35	65.7	89
Kevin Butler	Chi.	16	24	24	21	29	72.4	87
Nick Lowery	NYJ	16	26	27	20	23	87.0	86
Dean Biasucci	Ind.	16	37	37	16	24	66.7	85
John Kasey	Sea.	16	25	26	20	24	83.3	85
Tony Zendejas	Rams	16	28	28	18	23	78.3	82
Greg Davis	Ariz.	14	17	17	20	26	76.9	77
Al Del Greco	Hou.	16	18	18	16	20	81.1	66
David Treadwell	NYG	13	22	23	11	17	64.7	55
Brad Daluiso	NYG	16	5	5	11	11	100.0	38
Todd Peterson	Ariz.	2	4	4	2	4	50.0	10
Pat O'Neil	N.E.	16	0	0	0	1	0.0	0

STATISTICS

APPENDIX

1995 NFL SCHEDULE

WEEK 1
SUNDAY, SEPT. 3

Cincinnati at Indianapolis	1:00
Cleveland at New England	1:00
Houston at Jacksonville	1:00
Carolina at Atlanta	1:00
San Francisco at New Orleans	12:00
Tampa Bay at Philadelphia	1:00
St. Louis at Green Bay	12:00
Detroit at Pittsburgh	1:00
N.Y. Jets at Miami	4:00
San Diego at Los Angeles	1:00
Kansas City at Seattle	1:00
Arizona at Washington	4:00
Minnesota at Chicago	3:00
Buffalo at Denver	6:00

MONDAY, SEPT. 4

Dallas at N.Y. Giants	9:00

WEEK 2
SUNDAY, SEPT. 10

Miami at New England	1:00
Los Angeles at Washington	1:00
Pittsburgh at Houston	12:00
New Orleans at St. Louis	12:00
Detroit at Minnesota	12:00
Carolina at Buffalo	1:00
N.Y. Giants at Kansas City	12:00
Tampa Bay at Cleveland	1:00
Denver at Dallas	3:00
Indianapolis at N.Y. Jets	4:00
Seattle at San Diego	1:00
Jacksonville at Cincinnati	4:00
Atlanta at San Francisco	1:00
Philadelphia at Arizona	5:00

MONDAY, SEPT. 11

Green Bay at Chicago	8:00

WEEK 3
SUNDAY, SEPT. 17

San Diego at Philadelphia	1:00
Indianapolis at Buffalo	1:00
Los Angeles at Kansas City	12:00
Cleveland at Houston	12:00
St. Louis at Carolina	1:00
Atlanta at New Orleans	12:00
Arizona at Detroit	1:00
N.Y. Giants at Green Bay	12:00
New England at San Francisco	1:00
Cincinnati at Seattle	1:00
Jacksonville at N.Y. Jets	4:00
Washington at Denver	2:00
Chicago at Tampa Bay	4:00
Dallas at Minnesota	7:00

MONDAY, SEPT. 18

Pittsburgh at Miami	9:00

WEEK 4
SUNDAY, SEPT. 24

Chicago at St. Louis	12:00
New Orleans at N.Y. Giants	1:00
Washington at Tampa Bay	1:00
Minnesota at Pittsburgh	1:00
N.Y. Jets at Atlanta	4:00
Denver at San Diego	1:00
Houston at Cincinnati	4:00
Kansas City at Cleveland	4:00
Arizona at Dallas	3:00
Philadelphia at Los Angeles	1:00
Green Bay at Jacksonville	8:00

MONDAY, SEPT. 25

San Francisco at Detroit	9:00

(Open Date: Buffalo, Carolina, Indianapolis, Miami, New England, Seattle)

WEEK 5
SUNDAY, OCT. 1

New England at Atlanta	1:00
Miami at Cincinnati	1:00
Tampa Bay at Carolina	1:00
Philadelphia at New Orleans	12:00
Dallas at Washington	1:00
St. Louis at Indianapolis	12:00
Kansas City at Arizona	1:00
Jacksonville at Houston	3:00
Denver at Seattle	1:00
San Diego at Pittsburgh	4:00
N.Y. Giants at San Francisco	1:00
Los Angeles at N.Y. Jets	8:00

MONDAY, OCT. 2

Buffalo at Cleveland	9:00

(Open Date: Chicago, Detroit, Green Bay, Minnesota)

WEEK 6
SUNDAY, OCT. 8

Cincinnati at Tampa Bay	1:00
N.Y. Jets at Buffalo	1:00
Pittsburgh at Jacksonville	1:00
Green Bay at Dallas	12:00
Washington at Philadelphia	1:00
Carolina at Chicago	12:00
Houston at Minnesota	12:00
Cleveland at Detroit	4:00
Indianapolis at Miami	4:00
Seattle at Los Angeles	1:00
Arizona at N.Y. Giants	4:00
Denver at New England	8:00

MONDAY, OCT. 9

San Diego at Kansas City	9:00

(Open Date: Atlanta, New Orleans, St. Louis, San Francisco)

WEEK 7

THURSDAY, OCT. 12

Atlanta at St. Louis	7:00

SUNDAY, OCT. 15

Seattle at Buffalo	1:00
New England at Kansas City	12:00
Philadelphia at N.Y. Giants	1:00
Detroit at Green Bay	12:00
Minnesota at Tampa Bay	1:00
San Francisco at Indianapolis	12:00
Chicago at Jacksonville	1:00
Miami at New Orleans	3:00
N.Y. Jets at Carolina	4:00
Washington at Arizona	3:00
Dallas at San Diego	1:00

MONDAY, OCT. 16

Los Angeles at Denver	7:00

WEEK 8

THURSDAY, OCT. 19

Cincinnati at Pittsburgh	8:00

SUNDAY, OCT. 22

Houston at Chicago	12:00
Miami at N.Y. Jets	1:00
Jacksonville at Cleveland	1:00
New Orleans at Carolina	1:00
Detroit at Washington	1:00
Minnesota at Green Bay	12:00
Atlanta at Tampa Bay	1:00
Kansas City at Denver	2:00
Indianapolis at Los Angeles	1:00
San Diego at Seattle	1:00
San Francisco at St. Louis	3:00

MONDAY, OCT. 23

Buffalo at New England	9:00

(Open Date: Arizona, Dallas, N.Y. Giants, Philadelphia)

WEEK 9

SUNDAY, OCT. 29

Jacksonville at Pittsburgh	1:00
N.Y. Jets at Indianapolis	12:00
Cleveland at Cincinnati	1:00
Dallas at Atlanta	1:00
St. Louis at Philadelphia	1:00
Green Bay at Detroit	1:00
Carolina at New England	1:00
Buffalo at Miami	4:00
Seattle at Arizona	1:00
New Orleans at San Francisco	1:00
Tampa Bay at Houston	3:00
N.Y. Giants at Washington	8:00

MONDAY, OCT. 30

Chicago at Minnesota	8:00

(Open Date: Denver, Kansas City, Los Angeles, San Diego)

WEEK 10

SUNDAY, NOV. 5

Buffalo at Indianapolis	12:00
New England at N.Y. Jets	1:00
Houston at Cleveland	1:00
Detroit at Atlanta	1:00
St. Louis at New Orleans	12:00
Green Bay at Minnesota	12:00
Washington at Kansas City	12:00
Pittsburgh at Chicago	3:00
Los Angeles at Cincinnati	4:00
Carolina at San Francisco	1:00
Arizona at Denver	2:00
N.Y. Giants at Seattle	1:00
Miami at San Diego	5:00

MONDAY, NOV. 6

Philadelphia at Dallas	8:00

(Open Date: Jacksonville, Tampa Bay)

WEEK 11

SUNDAY, NOV. 12

Indianapolis at New Orleans	12:00
Los Angeles at N.Y. Giants	1:00
Atlanta at Buffalo	1:00
New England at Miami	1:00
Cincinnati at Houston	12:00
Seattle at Jacksonville	1:00
Carolina at St. Louis	12:00
Tampa Bay at Detroit	1:00
Chicago at Green Bay	12:00
Kansas City at San Diego	1:00
San Francisco at Dallas	3:00
Minnesota at Arizona	1:00
Denver at Philadelphia	8:00

MONDAY, NOV. 13

Cleveland at Pittsburgh	9:00

(Open Date: N.Y. Jets, Washington)

WEEK 12

SUNDAY, NOV. 19

Seattle at Washington	1:00
Jacksonville at Tampa Bay	1:00
Indianapolis at New England	1:00
Pittsburgh at Cincinnati	1:00
St. Louis at Atlanta	1:00
Arizona at Carolina	1:00
N.Y. Giants at Philadelphia	1:00
Detroit at Chicago	12:00
Green Bay at Cleveland	1:00
San Diego at Denver	2:00
Buffalo at N.Y. Jets	4:00
Dallas at Los Angeles	1:00
New Orleans at Minnesota	3:00
Houston at Kansas City	7:00

MONDAY, NOV. 20

San Francisco at Miami	9:00

WEEK 13

THURSDAY, NOV. 23

Minnesota at Detroit	12:30
Kansas City at Dallas	3:00

SUNDAY, NOV. 26

Miami at Indianapolis	1:00
New England at Buffalo	1:00
Cincinnati at Jacksonville	1:00
Chicago at N.Y. Giants	1:00
Philadelphia at Washington	1:00
Tampa Bay at Green Bay	12:00
Denver at Houston	3:00
N.Y. Jets at Seattle	1:00
Pittsburgh at Cleveland	4:00
St. Louis at San Francisco	1:00
Atlanta at Arizona	1:00
Carolina at New Orleans	7:00

MONDAY, NOV. 27

Los Angeles at San Diego	6:00

WEEK 14

THURSDAY, NOV. 30

N.Y. Giants at Arizona	5:00

SUNDAY, DEC. 3

Indianapolis at Carolina	1:00
Cincinnati at Green Bay	12:00
Houston at Pittsburgh	1:00
Atlanta at Miami	1:00
New Orleans at New England	1:00
St. Louis at N.Y. Jets	1:00
Tampa Bay at Minnesota	12:00
Jacksonville at Denver	2:00
Kansas City at Los Angeles	1:00
Cleveland at San Diego	1:00
Washington at Dallas	3:00
Philadelphia at Seattle	1:00
Buffalo at San Francisco	5:00

MONDAY, DEC. 4

Chicago at Detroit	9:00

WEEK 15

SATURDAY, DEC. 9

Cleveland at Minnesota	11:30
Arizona at San Diego	1:00

SUNDAY, DEC. 10

Buffalo at St. Louis	12:00
N.Y. Jets at New England	1:00
Indianapolis at Jacksonville	1:00
New Orleans at Atlanta	1:00
San Francisco at Carolina	1:00
Dallas at Philadelphia	1:00
Chicago at Cincinnati	1:00
Detroit at Houston	12:00
Seattle at Denver	2:00
Pittsburgh at Los Angeles	1:00
Washington at N.Y. Giants	4:00
Green Bay at Tampa Bay	8:00

MONDAY, DEC. 11

Kansas City at Miami	9:00

WEEK 16

SATURDAY, DEC. 16

New England at Pittsburgh	12:30
Green Bay at New Orleans	3:00

SUNDAY, DEC. 17

Jacksonville at Detroit	1:00
Miami at Buffalo	1:00
Cincinnati at Cleveland	1:00
New York Jets at Houston	12:00
Atlanta at Carolina	1:00
Arizona at Philadelphia	1:00
Tampa Bay at Chicago	12:00
Washington at St. Louis	12:00
Denver at Kansas City	3:00
San Diego at Indianapolis	4:00
N.Y. Giants at Dallas	3:00
Los Angeles at Seattle	5:00

MONDAY, DEC. 18

Minnesota at San Francisco	5:00

WEEK 17

SATURDAY, DEC. 23

San Diego at N.Y. Giants	12:30
Detroit at Tampa Bay	4:00
New England at Indianapolis	8:00

SUNDAY, DEC. 24

Pittsburgh at Green Bay	12:00
Houston at Buffalo	1:00
Seattle at Kansas City	12:00
Cleveland at Jacksonville	1:00
San Francisco at Atlanta	1:00
Philadelphia at Chicago	12:00
New Orleans at N.Y. Jets	1:00
Minnesota at Cincinnati	1:00
Carolina at Washington	4:00
Denver at Los Angeles	1:00
Miami at St. Louis	3:00

MONDAY, DEC. 25

Dallas at Arizona	6:00

POSTSEASON

SATURDAY, DEC. 30
AFC and NFC wild-card games
SUNDAY, DEC. 31
AFC and NFC wild cards
SATURDAY, JAN. 6
AFC and NFC divisional playoffs
SUNDAY, JAN. 7
AFC and NFC divisional playoffs
SUNDAY, JAN. 14
AFC and NFC championship games
SUNDAY, JAN. 28
Super Bowl XXX at Tempe, Ariz.
SUNDAY, FEB. 4
Pro Bowl at Honolulu

APPENDIX

FANTASY FOOTBALL SCHEDULES

Six-Team League

Team #	1	2	3	4	5	6
Week #						
1	2	1	4	3	6	5
2	3	6	1	5	4	2
3	4	5	6	1	2	3
4	5	3	2	6	1	4
5	6	4	5	2	3	1
6	2	1	4	3	6	5
7	3	6	1	5	4	2
8	4	5	6	1	2	3
9	5	3	2	6	1	4
10	6	4	5	2	3	1
11	2	1	4	3	6	5
12	3	6	1	5	4	2
13	4	5	6	1	2	3
14	5	3	2	6	1	4
15	6	4	5	2	3	1
16	Playoffs					
17	Championship Game					

Eight-Team League

Team #	1	2	3	4	5	6	7	8
Week #								
1	2	1	4	3	6	5	8	7
2	3	4	1	2	8	7	6	5
3	4	8	6	1	7	3	5	2
4	5	6	8	7	1	2	4	3
5	6	5	7	8	2	1	3	4
6	7	3	2	5	4	8	1	6
7	8	7	5	6	3	4	2	1
8	2	1	4	3	6	5	8	7
9	3	4	1	2	8	7	6	5
10	4	8	6	1	7	3	5	2
11	5	6	8	7	1	2	4	3
12	6	5	7	8	2	1	3	4
13	7	3	2	5	4	8	1	6
14	8	7	5	6	3	4	2	1
15	Playoffs							
16	Championship Game							
17	(Season over)							

10-Team League

Team #	1	2	3	4	5	6	7	8	9	10
Week #										
1	2	1	4	3	10	7	6	9	8	5
2	4	5	8	1	2	9	10	3	6	7
3	6	3	2	5	4	1	8	7	10	9
4	9	10	6	7	8	3	4	5	1	2
5	2	1	5	9	3	7	6	10	4	8
6	5	7	4	3	1	10	2	9	8	6
7	10	6	7	8	9	2	3	4	5	1
8	4	3	2	1	10	9	8	7	6	5
9	3	5	1	9	2	8	10	6	4	7
10	5	4	8	2	1	10	9	3	7	6
11	8	9	10	6	7	4	5	1	2	3
12	7	8	9	10	6	5	1	2	3	4
13	3	7	1	5	4	8	2	6	10	9
14	6	4	5	2	3	1	9	10	7	8
15	10	6	7	8	9	2	3	4	5	1
16	Playoffs									
17	Championship Game									

12-Team League

Team #	1	2	3	4	5	6	7	8	9	10	11	12
Week #												
1	2	1	4	3	6	5	8	7	10	9	12	11
2	3	4	1	2	7	8	5	6	11	12	9	10
3	4	3	2	1	8	7	6	5	12	11	10	9
4	5	6	11	12	1	2	9	10	7	8	3	4
5	6	7	9	10	11	1	2	12	3	4	5	8
6	12	11	8	6	9	4	10	3	5	7	2	1
7	11	10	6	5	4	3	12	9	8	2	1	7
8	7	8	12	9	10	11	1	2	4	5	6	3
9	8	9	7	11	12	10	3	1	2	6	4	5
10	10	12	5	7	3	9	4	11	6	1	8	2
11	9	5	10	8	2	12	11	4	1	3	7	6
12	2	1	4	3	6	5	8	7	10	9	12	11
13	3	4	1	2	7	8	5	6	11	12	9	10
14	4	3	2	1	8	7	6	5	12	11	10	9
15	Playoffs											
16	Championship Game											
17	(Season over)											

APPENDIX

INDEX

INDEX

INDEX

ABOUT THE AUTHOR

Jody Korch is the sports editor of the *Marinette Eagle-Star*, a daily newspaper in northeast Wisconsin, which is in the process of merging with its sister newspaper in Menominee, Michigan. Korch has received eight awards from the Wisconsin and Illinois Press Associations for sportswriting, sports page design, newswriting and feature writing.

A lifelong National Football League junkie, Korch is single and lives in Marinette, Wisconsin.

He is the brother of Rick Korch, who was the author of the first four editions of this book. Rick Korch now works for the Jacksonville Jaguars.

SUGGESTIONS

Anyone wishing to write to the author with comments or suggestions for next year's edition of this book, please do so. Write to:

Jody Korch
P.O. Box 1254
Marinette, WI 54143

See next page for FREE Draft Day Update offer!

Get a FREE Draft Day Update prepared by Jody Korch, author of *The Fantasy Football Guide 1995*! Included are:

- ★ 1995 Final Draft Rankings
- ★ Team-by-Team Depth Charts
- ★ Training Camp News
- ★ Injury Update
- ★ Sleepers and Busts
- ★ 1995 Rookie Report
- ★ Last-Minute Draft Strategy

To get your Draft Day Update, remove and send this page together with a self-addressed, stamped #10 envelope (a business letter–size envelope) and proof of purchase, such as a cash register receipt or bar code clipped from the back cover, to:

Draft Day Update
Contemporary Books, Dept. GB
Two Prudential Plaza, Suite 1200
180 North Stetson Avenue
Chicago, IL 60601-6790

Your letter must be postmarked no later than August 14, 1995. Your Draft Day Update will be mailed from Chicago via the U.S. Postal Service on August 21, 1995 (or whenever your valid request is received, whichever is later), in time for your Fantasy Draft. We cannot be responsible for lost or misdirected mail.